The
EVOLUTION
of
PROGRESS

The
EVOLUTION
of
PROGRESS

The End of Economic Growth
and the Beginning of
Human Transformation

C. OWEN PAEPKE

Random House   New York

Library of Congress Cataloging-in-Publication Data
Paepke, C. Owen.
The evolution of progress : the end of economic growth and the
beginning of human transformation / C. Owen Paepke.
p.   cm.
Includes bibliographical references and index.
ISBN 0-679-41582-3
1. Technological forecasting.   I. Title.
2. Progress
HB3730.P247   1993
338.9—dc20   92-22123

It is one of the bitter anxieties of the thinker to feel in the darkness progress asleep, without being able to waken it.

—VICTOR HUGO

In the past we have had a light which flickered, in the present we have a light which flames, and in the future there will be a light which shines over all the land and sea.

—WINSTON CHURCHILL

PREFACE

Like most people, I have always been vaguely aware of progress: *aware*, because progress has been one of the few enduring verities throughout the industrial era, and *vaguely* for the same reason. Each generation lives better than its parents', and better than even the wealthiest members of its grandparents'. This progress has defied a dozen or more Malthusians (including a few before Malthus), who have proven that the scarcity of some precious resource (firewood, food, whale oil, iron, or clean air, for example) would stop and quite possibly reverse the process within a few decades. But progress is an elusive target; it dodges shortages faster than it creates them. This resilience has produced a complacency about the prospects for continued progress, reflected in the pervasive assumption that rapid economic growth is the norm, and any departure from it the result of policy errors or malevolent scheming by the villain du jour.

I first began to question these familiar assumptions during the 1988 Presidential campaign. Some little-noticed feature articles reported that productivity and wages had been essentially flat in the United States since 1973. Economic policy blunders, no matter how egregious, could hardly have produced a pause that has continued nearly twice as long as the Depression. Exploring further, I learned that the same trends had spread throughout the developed world during the 1980s, which precluded any uniquely American explanation. My research relentlessly pushed me toward an unwelcome conclusion: the sources of material progress have finally and irreversibly dried up. The pause is, in reality, a full stop.

But another and very different kind of progress is beginning to emerge. Past progress has transformed the conditions of human life, while leaving its essential attributes untouched. People have remained the same while changing everything around them. Fundamental advances in genetic engineering, the neurosciences, longevity research, and artificial intelligence promise the ability to change not just how we live, but who we are, beginning within the lifetimes of today's children. Controversy and opposition may slightly alter the course of these developments, but it will not stay them.

I was surprised in 1988 that no one had published either of these conclusions. I am even more surprised in 1992. They seem so glaring once the facts are assembled. My best explanation is that the sheer breadth of progress defeats the efforts of specialists to understand it. Explaining the world within the accepted framework of their specialties is the raison d'être of experts. Modern economic theory starts from an equilibrium model, and equilibrium is the antithesis of progress. Economists therefore treat the sources of progress as external and unpredictable events, like the weather. Historians do not regard mere material progress as the meat of history; it does not start wars, change governments, or initiate political movements often enough to suit them. Scientists and engineers regard their discoveries and inventions as ends in themselves, blithely equating scientific and practical significance. The canons of each discipline impose a straitjacket on its practitioners and virtually compel a hypertrophic elaboration of increasingly sterile premises. Only an amateur, who can search with a floodlight rather than a laser beam, has any hope of discovering phenomena that spread across a vast intellectual, historical, and factual terrain. Seminal works of Marshall McLuhan, Jane Jacobs, and Rachel Carson were conspicuous demonstrations of the strength of a generalist's perspective. The narrow and deep credentials that now dominate the intellectual landscape are a serious if not fatal impediment to any understanding of progress.

For whatever reason, neither of these conclusions has appeared in print. Both the end of material progress and the emerging ability to sculpt human traits and abilities are watershed events. They will affect every item on the public agenda that they do not set outright. Their appearance on that agenda is long overdue.

. . .

A few notes on the approach of this book may assist (or forewarn) the reader. Part I of the book is concerned with the history, causes, and inherent limitations of material progress. The illustrations and analysis are therefore drawn from the productive and relatively affluent economic strata within the developed nations. I recognize, of course, that these comprise a relatively small percentage of the world's people. For reasons suggested in Chapter 7, progress (or the lack of it) at the top of the heap profoundly affects everyone below. Otherwise, distributional questions are outside the scope of this work.

The focus on material progress also minimizes discussion of aesthetic, artistic, religious, and other social and cultural developments. This is not intended to suggest that the rest of life is a mere appendage to production and consumption. It is, however, worth observing that the greatest progress in these less tangible realms has been firmly footed on a foundation of material prosperity. In the words of Trevor Williams, a leading historian of technology, "Civilization has many facets, but how man lives depends very much on what he can make."

The scope of this work forces some compromises between thoroughness and readability. Part I describes only the milestones of progress, not the journeys between. The concern is with progress in multiples or orders of magnitude, rather than in fractions. The economic analysis snubs some of the niceties in order to preserve the framework uncluttered. Part II's brief treatments of advances on some scientific frontiers cannot do justice to the ferment and excitement in those fields. This is not an apology: the picture is only sketched in places, but the sketches are accurate. Genuine conflicts between substance and presentation have been resolved in favor of the former. The footnotes set out sources ranging from the popular to the scholarly for those who want to experience the full flavor of any of these topics.

Finally, I will presume to suggest how the critical reader should approach this book. I began this work four years ago not (as too often seems the case) with an agenda but with questions. A wealth of overlapping and reinforcing facts drove me to one answer that I did not expect or want and another that I find hopeful and inspiring. Readers are not asked to (indeed, are asked not to) accept my conclusions (or my preferences) on faith but to form their own. The facts are here; find some other interpretation for them, if you can.

Acknowledgments

The author wishes to thank the following for their assistance:

Heidi Ewart, Carol Ray, and Geri Crane, for their clerical help;

Charlene Trainor and Brad Frese, for tracking down obscure government documents;

Mead Data Central, for the use of its extensive database of periodicals and journals;

Judith Appelbaum, for navigating this work through the shoals of the publishing process; and

Jon Karp, to whom the reader also owes a debt of gratitude, for enabling an amateur to transform an idea into a book.

This book is dedicated to the thousands of authors I have known through their writings, and to the woman who unwittingly made this effort possible.

CONTENTS

INTRODUCTION

This book is about the end and the beginning of progress. The end of one kind of progress, material progress, lies at the heart of the many puzzling changes that are contributing to a growing undercurrent of surliness and despair. The new kind of progress, which makes human traits and abilities the subject rather than just the source of change, will dominate the agenda of the next century, perhaps even the next decade. But these watershed events have somehow escaped notice. The purpose of this book is to bare them for public examination.

Material progress is a comparative newcomer on the historical scene. Economic historian Joel Mokyr concluded *The Lever of Riches*, his recent survey of economic growth and technological advance from antiquity to 1914, by observing that "we are living in an exception. . . . Our age is unique: only in the last two centuries has Western society succeeded in raising the standard of living of the bulk of the population beyond the minimum of subsistence." From the beginning of the Roman Empire until the eighteenth century, a period of almost two millennia, the conditions of life scarcely improved. Napoleon's subjects ate food, wore clothes, and lived in houses that were about the same as those of Caesar. The sick still received more sympathy than cures. Manure remained the state-of-the-art fertilizer. Horses were the fastest form of transportation, and of communication, since information traveled as freight. Water and windmills supplied energy in a few areas. Elsewhere, it was extracted, bit by painful bit, from draft animals and men. The ancient Roman could easily have adapted to the work, the technology, and the life-styles in eighteenth-century France. The present, by contrast, would seem like a scene from Mount Olympus.

With the beginning of the Industrial Revolution, material progress quickly began to make up for lost time. It has virtually defined the era. Nations wax and wane; creeds and philosophies gain and lose favor; political and social structures evolve; but progress itself continues. Despite the wars, natural disasters, political detours, economic dislocations, and other temporary setbacks that dominate the history texts, every generation has surpassed its predecessor, even in nations in relative decline. Famine, never more than two bad harvests away before the nineteenth century, has been buried by mountains of surplus food in every advanced economy, with even India occasionally exporting grain. The typical supermarket daily offers a wider selection than people of just a few generations past ate in a lifetime. Houses with running water, refrigerators, more bedrooms than people, and other commonplace miracles have replaced dirt-floored hovels shared by three or more generations. Improved health care has stretched life expectancies from less than fifty years in 1900 to more than seventy today. Before railroads, people rarely left their home counties. Many thousands now cross continents and oceans each day. In 1900, not one student in ten earned a high school diploma, the presumptive minimum for entry into the workplace since World War II. Telecommunication makes knowledge of events, still the dearest of commodities through the early nineteenth century, available worldwide, instantly, at little or no cost. Progress has been the only true status quo of the modern era.

This progress has transformed daily life not once, but repeatedly. The much-pitied industrial worker of late-Victorian England had already progressed far beyond the nobleman of the preceding century in many of the material aspects of life. The nineteenth-century robber baron could only envy the diet, mobility, medical care, and general comforts and amenities available to the average American worker of the 1950s. The present middle-class American, so often portrayed as a victim of the 1980s, lives better than even the wealthiest plutocrat of the 1920s. These long-term improvements owe little to the clamor for reform and everything to the expanded output that progress has routinely delivered. The productivity and technology of the nineteenth century deliver only nineteenth-century squalor, whenever and wherever they occur and however humanely their output is divided.

Two centuries of material progress in many nations with sharply differing governments and cultures through countless economic cycles have etched an improving standard of living in the public's mind as one of the few eternal verities. Rising incomes, larger houses, and more and better things, all obtained with less effort, are the normal state of affairs, the baseline against which an economy's actual performance is judged.

That complacency is unwarranted. The current era of progress is over. It will not return.

Prophecies like this one tend to evoke an immediate and profound skepticism. Past progress occurred in defiance of the many prophets who proved that it could not happen. Maximilien de Béthune, Duc de Sully, may claim the dubious distinction of being the first: in 1638, he opined that living standards would fall because of an irreversibly worsening scarcity of firewood. Thomas Malthus honed this pessimism to a science with his *Essay on the Principle of Population*. Malthus argued that the natural fecundity of the species would quickly transform any excess food supply into a larger population, leaving society always at the edge of famine. Population would tend to grow geometrically (1, 2, 4, 8), while food output would, at best, grow linearly (1, 2, 3, 4), an equation that only starvation would balance. (In the event, of course, precisely the opposite occurred. The output of food and almost everything else expanded geometrically, while rising affluence restrained the birthrate.) More recently, the Club of Rome sought to endow the same thesis with mathematical certitude by using computer models encompassing a range of natural resources and environmental constraints to prove that continued economic growth assured global catastrophe. The oil shock and gas lines even gave gloom some fleeting political prominence in the 1970s, when an earlier incarnation of Jerry Brown tried to ride an "era of limits" theme into the White House. The common element of such prophecies is a threatened shortage of one or more resources, with food, energy, clean air, and minerals among the common candidates.

Intervening events have refuted all such predictions. The fatal flaw has always been the same: progress not only creates shortages, it also provides the means to negate or circumvent them. Technology expands the planet's ability to provide for human needs at a dizzying pace. Natural resources steadily become less, not more, important. Until recently, communication required either copper or the electromagnetic spectrum, both finite resources. With fiber optics, sand replaces copper, and one California beach would supply enough to carry all the messages of the planet for centuries to come. A pound of plutonium provides more energy than a forest of trees. Hybrid seeds triple the amount of grain that each acre of land produces. Even in such grubby areas as metallic ores and fossil fuels, recoverable reserves now satisfy projected usage for longer than they did a generation ago. In practical terms, the planet's resources have become not scarcer, but more plentiful. During the same period, and despite the impression conveyed by activists and the media, environmental quality has generally improved in the developed nations. Resource limitations have never caused more than fleeting inconvenience in the past, nor will they do so in the future.

But limits of a very different kind have virtually halted material progress in the leading economies. Living standards in the United States have barely budged since 1973. People react like heirs deprived of their birthright and begin looking for the culprit. Japan seems to be the leading suspect. Polls identify it as the principal threat to the United States. A supposedly free-market president mouths imprecations over its refusal to buy cars that Americans have shunned in droves and that suffer from the minor additional shortcoming of having their steering wheels on the wrong side. *Rising Sun* topped the best-seller lists not for its undeniable virtues as a mystery, but for its Geraldo-like exposé of Japan's plan to dominate the world. But the facts strike a discordant note in this chorus. Japan's bubble economy has popped, its banks are tottering, its multinationals' profits have nearly vanished, and a tide of retrenchment is in full flood. To the Japanese, of course, the villains are on this side of the Pacific.

There are no villains, here or there. Material progress began when four forces coincided in late-eighteenth-century England. Their continuing presence, alternating in leading and supporting roles, explains its persistence during the intervening two hundred years. Progress in its accustomed form will not survive their passing.

1. **GROWTH OF KNOWLEDGE.** Technology was, both
figuratively and literally, the motive force behind the Industrial Revolution. Watt's engine and Crompton's "mule" started the overthrow
of traditional handicraft production. Iron began to supplant wood in
machinery, heavy construction, and transportation as large coal-fired
blast furnaces made the metal available in quantity. Germany and the
United States followed England's lead, pioneering in nitrogen fertilizers, internal combustion engines, automobiles and airplanes, electric
power systems, the telegraph and telephone, assembly lines, synthetic
materials, and antibiotics. Improved communications and transportation assured the spread and permanence of these advances. The gains
in every field have been immense. Technology has been the proverbial
free lunch, delivering more and better for less.

But technology, however ingenious, must obey physical laws, and
those laws limit the tangible benefits to be realized from further
advances. Consider transportation. Crossing the United States in a
Conestoga required considerable grit, some luck, and six months. It
now occupies a few hours spent sitting in an easy chair. The next
century could shave another hour or two from the transit time, but
that improvement would be negligible compared to what technology
has already accomplished. Satellites and fiber optics communicate
information in all forms worldwide at the speed of light, an absolute
physical limit. Energy flows freely from fossil, hydroelectric, and
nuclear sources. Contrary to the common perception, it has become
not scarce and expensive but abundant and cheap. Vaccines and
antibiotics have nearly eliminated the threat from contagious disease
in the developed world, allowing all but a small minority to live full
life spans. Labor-saving mechanization and rising yields have reduced
the number of farmers, once a majority of the population, to negligible levels. Manufacturing productivity increases—more than tenfold
in this century alone—are doing the same for blue-collar labor. In
these and other fields, future progress will be confined to ever smaller
increments between the state of the art and the limits of the possible.

2. **FREE MARKETS.** Commercial freedom provided the incentives and the framework for progress. The prosperity of the Italian
city-states and Holland suggested an alternative to the slavery and
feudalism that gripped most of Europe through the sixteenth and
into the seventeenth century. The tiny middle class began to grow

and to encroach upon the powers and privileges of the hereditary nobility. England's tradition of private property rights, dating back to the Magna Carta, accelerated its progress toward free markets. By the eighteenth century, myriad personal freedoms, originally exceptions carved out of despotic and arbitrary rule, had coalesced to produce the twin concepts of limited government and the rule of law. People came to regard travel, exchange, and voluntary employment as matters of right, not privilege. They could work, spend, and invest by their own lights. Freight moved with little regulation, money circulated freely, and entrepreneurs defied and defeated the restrictive sanctions of trade guilds. By 1776, Adam Smith had observed enough of the emerging commercial freedom to become its original theoretician, philosopher, and chronicler. Born even a century earlier, he would have had little to chronicle.

In the intervening two centuries, free markets spread across most of the world. Their superiority in promoting progress has become too obvious to require discussion. Eastern Europeans and others who have not yet tasted their fruits have become their most zealous and committed advocates. But the very completeness of capitalism's triumph shows that the freeing of markets has already made its major contribution. The restrictions that remain in the developed economies are more irritants than serious impediments. The gains remaining to be realized from this source will necessarily be minor compared to those enjoyed in the past.

3. MARKET EXPANSION. Advances in transportation technology widened markets, the third source of progress in the modern era. A few miles surrounding a village once defined the limits of the accessible marketplace. Food rarely traveled more than ten miles from the farm, cloth no more than forty miles from the loom. When longer haulage could not be avoided, it often cost more than the goods themselves. People were scarcely more mobile than freight, with employment prospects effectively restricted to the dimensions of a county. Seasonal market and hiring fairs provided only sporadic commercial intercourse between otherwise isolated regions. Virtual self-sufficiency remained the norm through the eighteenth century.

Canals, railroads, and improvements in shipping broke this multimillennial tyranny of distance, opening the way for large-scale industry as businesses expanded to serve customers over a wider area. Rapid communications made control of these farther-flung enterprises possible. The pace of change quickened as innovators were able to deploy advances over larger markets. The overseas explorations of the sixteenth and seventeenth centuries brought even foreign lands into the market. England led in all these developments. Textile mills in Manchester turned raw cotton from the American South into clothing for much of the Western world, while Russian royalty dined on Wedgwood china. The rest of the world soon learned and followed. Regions and nations began to specialize in their fields of comparative advantage. The United States was a particular beneficiary because of its continental expanse. Iowans no longer had to raise cattle or Texans grow corn. Coal from the Appalachians and iron ore from the Mesabi became steel in Pittsburgh. The resulting efficiencies have been incalculable.

But market expansion has reached an obvious and absolute limit. All the advanced nations are integrated into a single worldwide economy. Americans drive European cars burning Arabian oil on roads paved with Mexican cement. Pakistani-born engineers design chips for American companies to fabricate in Singapore and sell to Japan. Japanese automakers build factories in the United States, following the trail of foreign direct investment blazed by England and the United States. Political impediments continue to restrict international trade in some highly visible products, but the restrictions have less long-term impact than is commonly hoped or feared. With worldwide markets already the norm, any further gains from this source will be inconsequential compared to those of the past.

4. ACCUMULATION OF CAPITAL. Stable financial institutions and joint-stock companies began the process of concentrating capital for commercial purposes in late-eighteenth-century England. Before that time, only the state, through its ability to tax, could collect funds widely enough to support large projects. This produced military might and some impressive public works, but no comparable undertakings in the private sector. The few merchant houses that accumulated sizable wealth devoted it to trading, not production. As a result, most private enterprise was based on the use of relatively abundant labor, not scarce capital. But labor without sufficient capital produces little surplus, perpetuating the capital shortage while leaving workers on the edge of subsistence.

Private investment combined with labor-saving technology to break this vicious cycle. Gross capital investment nearly doubled in a single generation. It flowed into pottery and textile production, roads and canals, and manufactories of all kinds. This capital lifted incomes above subsistence, further increasing private saving and producing an accumulating, self-generating surplus that enabled the economy to expand further. This virtuous cycle has continued (almost) to the present, producing the vast aggregation of factories, machinery, transportation equipment, health care facilities, public infrastructure, and communication networks that characterize every advanced economy.

Everyday observation suggests the importance of this accumulation. Orange juice costs more than gasoline, even though growing an orange tree is much simpler than drilling for oil and refining it. The explanation lies in the disparate use of capital: orange growers employ many workers and little capital, while oil wells, refineries, and pipelines are vast concentrations of capital that require little labor. This is not an isolated example: filet mignon costs more per pound than a Hyundai, and theater tickets cost more than a dozen videotape rentals. The principal difference in each instance is the use of capital to achieve efficient mass production.

But capital expansion is reaching effective limits in the developed world. Capital is the accumulated saving of prior generations. Rising incomes have always added to capital by enhancing the *ability* to save. At some point, however, they also diminish the *incentive* to do so. Hardship, not ease, is the mother of frugality. Households with enough assets and earnings to satisfy their wants, and an expectation that those earnings will continue, lack the motivation to accumulate more capital in order to expand their incomes further. Material progress pushes an ever increasing percentage of households into this group. These are, of course, the very households that have the greatest ability and historical propensity to save. Government programs and private insurance and pension plans reinforce this income effect by cushioning against many of the risks that formerly motivated rainy-day savings. (The same factors play havoc with the work ethic, as the stubbornly high unemployment rate throughout the long economic expansion of the 1980s demonstrates.)

These limits are not absolute, but their impact is already evident. Savings rates in the United States declined sharply in the 1970s and through most of the 1980s, despite lower marginal tax rates and higher real interest rates that should have encouraged more savings. In the 1980s, this trend spread to *every* developed nation, including the saving machine that is Japan.

The forces of progress are spent. Without them, living standards are stagnating. President Carter's much-derided "malaise" was a harbinger of this shift. The return to economic vitality that began in 1983, while temporarily masking the transition, was largely a reshuffling of resources. Millions of immigrants and women entered the work force, accounting for most of the resurgence. The rising number of families with two wage earners barely maintained household incomes, and only at the expense of parental child care and involvement in schools, housekeeping, volunteer work, and other services not measured by the economic statistics. Immigration provided the United States with some of its best workers, while depriving other nations of the same workers. Expanding the work force in this way raises measured output, just as a return to sixty-hour work weeks or child labor would, but only on a one-time, irreproducible basis. Untapped reservoirs of labor like nonworking wives of the 1950s and 1960s no longer exist.

The growth of the 1980s, welcome as it was, did not mark a sustainable return to progress. Productivity in the United States has been virtually unchanged since 1973. Output has increased not because of improved *efficiency* of labor or capital, but because of increased *amounts* of capital and, particularly, labor. This contributes little to the standard of living. Indeed, average weekly earnings in constant dollars have actually fallen slightly since 1973. These trends are utterly without precedent since these statistics have been compiled. Not even the Depression produced such a prolonged loss of economic momentum.

This measurable decline is both a symptom and a cause of an immeasurable but significant change in attitude. Americans are becoming less interested in progressing (i.e., producing more and better at lower cost) than in perpetuating the status quo or securing a larger slice of the existing pie. Businesses increasingly seek competitive advantage through legislation and litigation rather than investment and innovation: paid Senate lobbyists rose from a few hundred in 1960 to over 33,000 in 1990, and the number of attorneys nearly doubled in the 1980s alone. The EPA, FDA, and various other federal agencies pursue an objective of zero risk with little regard for the costs they impose on society. The explosion of the *Challenger*, after twenty-four consecutive successful shuttle flights, grounded all manned space missions by the United States for more than two years. The delay barely evoked comment; it was simple prudence, a matter of course given the tragedy. But contrast the early history of aviation, when thirty-one of the first forty pilots hired by the Post Office died in crashes within six years, with no suspension of service. Playing it safe has replaced the pioneering, enterprising, and risk-taking spirit traditionally associated with America.

The economic trends, having persisted through two decades, cannot be dismissed as transitory or cyclical phenomena or as statistical flukes. The sharply differing domestic policies of the Ford, Carter, Reagan, and Bush administrations virtually foreclose attempts to assign the blame to any particular political agenda. Indeed, international data preclude any uniquely American explanation. Every member nation of the Organization for Economic Cooperation and Development (OECD), including Japan, experienced declines in productivity gains in the 1980s compared to the 1970s, a fact conveniently omitted from lamentations over the supposed loss of U.S. competitiveness. No satisfactory explanation has been advanced. Experts, blinkered by their intense specialization, lack the multidisciplinary perspective needed to grasp these trends. Even with better understanding, the standard political and economic nostrums would scarcely alter the present direction. Policies designed to regain past glory only succeed in further sapping the forces of long-term progress: stimulating consumer demand discourages capital accumulation; trade measures disintegrate the world market. The current decline of material progress cannot be reversed.

Some social critics and environmental activists will initially rejoice at this news. Events will disappoint them. They identify progress with smog, traffic jams, and crass materialism, emphasizing the discomforts and dislocations inherent in all change to belittle the practical benefits and question even the idea of progress. The common thread in such criticisms is an intense sensitivity to the costs of economic growth coupled with a virtual disregard of its value. Progress cossets these critics, providing a life-style that enables them to take such a lofty, detached, and contemptuous attitude toward the mere means of existence. But the reality of slow growth will prove less pleasing than the prospect. The end of progress will create a zero-sum game, sharply narrowing the range of society's options. The preferences of privileged elites will not long hold sway when those preferences entail real sacrifice: loggers deprived of their livelihoods will reassert their priority over owls, and drivers with static incomes will refuse to spend more for cleaner vehicles. Grab and hold could become a prevalent attitude. The future will not conform to the "small is beautiful" world that some critics may envision.

The end of material progress will thus produce few winners. But as one form of progress ends, another begins that may more than compensate for the stagnation in living standards. Beginning early in the next century, people will enjoy vastly expanded intelligence and other abilities, finally escaping the natural limitations under which the species has labored since it first appeared.

Such predictions, commonly encountered only in the realm of science fiction, also provoke a skeptical response borne of long experience. Two centuries of otherwise pervasive progress have left intrinsic human traits and abilities almost untouched. Machines add strength and speed, houses and clothing provide warmth and protection, telephones extend the range of communication, civilization cushions and enriches life, but the species itself remains unchanged. Even medicine, the most intimate of technologies, merely strives to restore the body to its natural condition, not to change that condition. But current research establishes the feasibility of improving on innate human characteristics.

One such improvement will be to lengthen the life span. Scientists can "evolve" longer-lived animal strains in the laboratory by killing the offspring of all short-lived parents in each generation. They have also stretched the life spans of dozens of species 50 percent or more by restricting their food intake. These animals do not linger on in decrepit old age; they actually age less quickly. Underfed rats, for example, play, mate, resist disease, and learn new mazes long after their fully fed siblings have lapsed into rodent senescence. Tests on spider monkeys are now under way, and the preliminary results appear promising. The physiological and genetic findings from this research will allow direct intervention in the human aging process within a generation. Even children born during the next few years may reasonably expect to live decades longer than their parents.

This may be the least of the changes they will experience. The Human Genome Project is mapping and sequencing human chromosomes. That monumental compilation will begin a process leading to discovery of the genetic sources of exceptional mental abilities and other favorable traits. The DNA of acknowledged geniuses, both living and dead, will supply researchers with desired patterns. Genetic engineering techniques developed for research and conventional medical purposes promise the ability to select and ultimately to substitute and modify genes with precision at the finest level of detail. Genetic libraries for (re)producing desired and even superhuman traits on demand will follow automatically from these technologies.

Advances in neuroscience may provide an alternative route to extraordinary abilities. New tools are enabling researchers to identify some biological indicators of intelligence. For example, smart brains use less energy and conduct nerve signals faster and more uniformly than average brains. These correlations may prove to be effects rather than causes, but they open the prospect of medical treatments to enhance ability. Meanwhile, neurobiologists are painstakingly teasing out the details of brain cell function and the intricate networks that the cells form. Scientists have learned to culture brain cells using a newly discovered class of neurochemicals (nerve growth factors). Direct administration of such chemicals and nerve cell implants have enhanced learning and memory in monkeys and in human patients suffering from degenerative conditions of the brain. From an anatomical perspective, new radiological techniques and microscopic electrodes are providing detailed maps of brain activity and circuitry. Theories of memory formation and other higher mental functions are being actively investigated, although a synthesis remains elusive. As understanding of the processes grows, the ability to enhance them is likely to follow.

Biology is not the only option for exceeding natural human abilities. Chips with a million transistors and switching times measured in billionths of a second have vastly increased the power of computers. But they remain dependent and servile tools, precisely following detailed instructions provided by people to perform tasks assigned by people. Recent hardware, software, and design advances promise the ability to simulate ever larger realms of intelligence. The next chess champion of the world will be a computer. An experimental neural network system creates its own "rules" of English pronunciation simply from hearing a list of words spoken, while neural nets diagnose heart attacks better than trained emergency room physicians. The Microelectronics and Computer Consortium is now more than midway through its CYC project, which should allow computers to read and understand natural language and to add to their information bases with little or no human assistance. Ever-larger-scale semiconductor integration, optical computing, refinement of expert system designs, and other more familiar kinds of progress continue apace. Each of these developments will slightly enhance performance in some traditional computing tasks. Together, they promise something much more important—systems that will be capable of self-improvement, leading ineluctably to useful machine intelligence in diverse fields.

All this research is far more advanced than is widely appreciated. Machines will be unquestioned leaders in some fields within a generation. Children born in this decade may be receiving treatments to augment their intelligence by middle age. Their children will almost certainly be genetically or biologically engineered for improved brain function. This process will continue and accelerate in future generations, as enhanced minds and intelligent machines shun the well-worked and decreasingly fertile fields of material progress in favor of the fresh challenge of improving human abilities.

These developments will predictably generate opposition, which, just as predictably, the advancing tide will sweep away. The prevention of disease and other uncontroversial objectives will justify the basic research. After it is completed, the resulting knowledge will not be prohibitively expensive or difficult to use. The demand will be irresistible. Consider, for example, the current spending on cosmetics, clothing, and health clubs, which deliver just the *appearance* of youth. The appeal of real youth and longer life will be infinitely greater. An effective ban on any of these technologies is utterly fanciful, as the widespread illegal use of steroids by athletes convincingly demonstrates. Their known availability will trigger a cascade.

xxx Even assuming that most parents would prefer a world without genetic or biological enhancement, few would knowingly disadvantage their own children in order to exercise that preference. Any country even considering the possibility of outlawing these technologies would quickly be discouraged by the near certainty that other countries would press ahead. The instability of such a situation is evident. The existence of the knowledge will create a technological imperative, assuring its widespread use. Those nations (and individuals) that embrace this future will fare better than those that attempt to renounce it.

Both the end of material progress and the transformation of human abilities are thus inevitable. Public awareness and political leadership would ease what promises to be a difficult passage. Despite occasional Luddite opposition, ordinary material progress has become a comfortable form of change for most people. Indeed, it provides hope to those unhappy with their immediate circumstances and minimizes class tension and other economic, social, and political frictions. The erosion of that bulwark against despair threatens a rise in factionalism. And the ability to remake and surpass the species will be anything but a soothing prospect to many people; the Frankenstein myth has been a recurrent plot among mankind's worst nightmares.

The current terms of public discourse provide scant grounds for optimism. Like generals always fighting the last war, politicians are planning for a future that is past. The immediate objective is to return to "normal" economic growth, which the United States has not experienced in twenty years and which is, in reality, forever lost. Any speculation about the longer-term potential of technology resembles a scene out of *Star Trek*, where sleek machines do wondrous things, many of which conveniently defy physical law, but the people have not changed. Even the token android is little more than a human with enhanced data storage and retrieval.

The real future will be a mirror image of that picture. The machines will surely differ from those of the present, but what they do, and how well they do it, will not have changed nearly to the same extent as in recent centuries. The people, on the other hand, will be so vastly improved as to defeat current understanding and probably imagination as well. Indeed, even using the word "people" to denote these beings is an anachronism. Within a century or two, genetic engineering will likely have changed our descendants so greatly as to prevent them from mating with humans in their present form, making them biologically a separate species.

The ancient Chinese had a curse: "May you live in interesting times." This cusp in the evolution of progress makes for very interesting times. Recognizing what these trends portend will not cause the problems to vanish. But it is the only option worth contemplating.

Part I

The
END
of
PROGRESS

Material progress has largely defined the industrial era. Its impact on daily life has dwarfed that of any war, revolution, election, depression, or political or social movement in history, an importance belied by historians' relative neglect of the topic. "In high school, we are taught to view [history] as not much more than a succession of dynasties, laws, and wars, all given some 'political' interpretation."[1] As a result, reasonably studious adolescents can identify obscure presidents, Civil War generals, and the occasional senator or cabinet head. But a roll call of the giants of material progress (e.g., Joseph Aspdin, Justus von Liebig, Joseph Lister, I. K. Brunel, Alfred Marshall, Lee de Forest, Lawrence Fleming, Samuel Insull, Frank Whittle, Wallace Carothers, John von Neumann, and Robert Noyce) would send even *Jeopardy* champions scrambling for their Britannicas.

The rising tide of specialization accounts for much of this neglect. Whether from necessity or choice, few of the academics, writers, and others paid to analyze and interpret events will stray far from the narrow domains where their credentials establish their authority and assure their views some deference.[2] But the specialist's field of view is simply too restricted to encompass the sources of material progress, or its prospects for the future. This discussion will therefore analyze past material progress from several diverse perspectives,[3] attempting to distill the few ingredients that account for its sudden appearance in eighteenth-century England and its subsequent spread around the globe and through every aspect of life.

4   That analysis arrives at a bittersweet conclusion. The victory of material progress is nearly complete; it has already accomplished most of what it can in the United States and other advanced nations.[4] In some areas of technology, performance has approached limits that no amount of further ingenuity will circumvent. In others, the state of the art, although still far from any absolute limit, already satisfies any foreseeable human need. Some signal triumphs of past progress—a vastly expanded knowledge base, integrated world markets, great accumulations of capital, and widespread prosperity in the developed world—undermine any opportunity for that progress to continue. This combination of extrinsic and intrinsic limits has already slowed the rate of progress, and the effects are steadily widening and becoming more severe. Living standards have reached a plateau of indefinite duration. Progress in the future will lie in a very different realm.

NOTES

1. Reuven Brenner, *History—The Human Gamble,* Ch. 6, p. 198, Univ. of Chicago Press, 1983.
2. "It seems to be thought a violation of academic propriety, and evidence of shallowness, to venture from the field of specialization listed in the faculty directory." Edward Seidensticker, *This Country, Japan,* p. ix, Kodansha, 1984.
3. This multidisciplinary approach naturally forces some severely condensed treatments of topics long reserved to highly credentialed specialists, not all of whom suffer day-trippers lightly. "Insofar as I refer to general ideas, I shall be devoured by the scholarly eagles, and . . . insofar as I refer to particular details, I shall be eaten alive by the scholarly sharks." Irving Kristol, *Reflections of a Neoconservative: Looking Back, Looking Ahead,* p. 95, Basic Books, 1983. The sources in the notes may partially atone for the author's many sins of omission.
4. This book is mostly concerned with the productive sectors of the developed nations. Chapter 7 briefly discusses the prospects of developing nations and the roles of inequality in world and national economies. Otherwise, distributional questions are ignored.

Chapter One

THE PRELUDE TO PROGRESS

Before the Industrial Revolution began, nothing from history suggested any general tendency toward improvement; life continued with no discernible change for centuries together. Since that time, scarcely a decade has passed without important and irreversible changes for the better. The transition from stagnation to progress occurred around the end of the eighteenth century. But a few crucial developments during the preceding centuries laid the foundation.

THE LONG STAGNATION

A man trudges along a rutted track. He is carrying a few utensils he traded for in a village now five miles behind him. No money changed hands; indeed, his simple dealings rarely require any money. He wears most of the clothes he owns. They are plain, worn, grimy, and scratchy. His feet are bare. He stinks, although no one from his time would notice. He passes a wagon drawn by an ox, which has covered less than twenty miles in the course of a long day.

His house is made from mud brick and thatching. A floor of rough planking over the beaten earth makes it better than some of his neighbors'. It has one door and no windows. It is bare except for a crude table and a few chairs. Sacks of straw serve for bedding. The fireplace supplies heat, light, and the only place to cook. The air is damp, fetid, and smoky. Water is drawn from a well just one hundred yards away. The house measures twenty by twenty-five feet. He shares it with his wife, three children (two others having died in infancy), and a pig.

Supper this night will be some coarse-grained bread, a welcome change from the usual gruel. The occasional one-pot stew represents high cuisine. He has rarely tasted sugar, pepper, or tea. Tomorrow, as on most days, he will work the land of his master, using a few rough wooden tools. His ten-year-old son will join him.

He cannot read. He will not learn of events occurring a few hundred miles away for weeks, if ever. Nor would they be of much interest; his concerns run no farther than the nearest town. He lives near his birthplace and has rarely ventured outside his home county, never having owned a horse. He has nothing that comes from beyond a hundred miles.

He has survived several famines and epidemics during his lifetime. This luck will not hold forever. He has little chance of reaching fifty. Disease will likely be the immediate cause of death, but no one will summon a doctor, and the best physicians of the day could not offer a cure anyway. If, perchance, he were to reach old age, he would continue working; a period of retirement is exclusively a modern expectation. Between his birth and his death, life will have changed little more than the dirt under his feet.

Is this man a seventeenth-century Frenchman, or an Italian from 100 B.C.?

The answer, of course, could be either. And his life would have been fairly typical of either time and place. Until the eighteenth century, most of the world "remained one vast peasantry, where between 80 percent and 90 percent of people lived from the land and nothing else."[1] Serfdom was not finally abolished in the Scottish coal mines and salt pits until 1775, in France until 1789, or in Germany until the 1830s.[2] What would now be regarded as a subhuman existence was the accepted lot of mankind for many centuries.

Daily life wore this deep rut because the world's production processes and even its fund of practical knowledge had stagnated. Rudimentary crop rotation and manuring remained the state of the agricultural art. Through unremitting toil, a peasant farmer fed his own family and perhaps half of another. Unavoidably, most of the

8 population worked the soil. Horses, oxen, pack mules, and wheeled carts defined the limits of transportation technology. The cost of forage and drivers over any distance greater than a few miles often exceeded the value of the goods carried. Wood continued as the almost exclusive fuel for heating, cooking, and metalworking, while water wheels (where the topography permitted), draft animals, and people themselves were the only meaningful sources of mechanical energy. The works of Galen, a Roman physician of the second century, remained the unchallenged source of medical knowledge for nearly fifteen hundred years.[3] Unfortunately, the Galenic conception of disease as an imbalance among the body's four cardinal "humors"—blood, phlegm, black bile, and yellow bile—made bleeding and purging the most widely prescribed treatments. In short, seventeenth-century life would have seemed quite familiar to the ancients.[4]

This never-ending sameness naturally influenced thinkers' views of the past and expectations for the future. The idea of progress, the belief in irreversible and inevitable change for the better, rarely held sway before the seventeenth century.[5] The popular myths of the ancient Greeks painted the past as a golden age of heroes and gods, proud forebears of what must have seemed, in comparison, a sadly diminished race. Ancient philosophers generally described history as a series of cycles, in which each civilization would bloom, then wither, to be replaced by another at substantially the same level of achievement. The dominant Christian doctrine of the Middle Ages viewed all earthly experience as a miserable interlude between the original fall from grace and the inevitable apocalypse. Even Renaissance thought, enthralled by classical learning, held out little prospect that past accomplishments could or would be continually surpassed.[6]

Toward the end of this long night, signs of the dawn began to appear. These initially had little impact on production processes or daily life. Their significance was not widely appreciated. In retrospect, however, they were both harbingers and indispensable precursors of an age of material progress.

OVERSEAS EXPLORATION

Europe was a backward area in most respects during the Middle Ages. Byzantium, an open trading center even in the eleventh century, dazzled the crusaders with its brilliance and market-generated wealth. The Arabs were far more advanced than Europeans in mathematics and chemistry, particularly pharmacology. China invented paper, movable print, and gunpowder more than a millennium before the West. Even with due allowance for differing cultures, Europe did not begin to rival the East in artistic or aesthetic attainments until the Renaissance: the first (surviving) novel was published in Japan early in the eleventh century, six hundred years before the appearance of *Don Quixote*. For several centuries before 1500, only a few primitive, tribal lands clearly trailed Europe in development, a remarkable decline in standing from the commanding heights achieved by ancient Rome.

But Europe excelled in one respect that soon helped to negate its many disadvantages—ocean voyaging.[7] Prince Henry the Navigator and his successors relentlessly pushed Portuguese mariners ever farther south along the coast of Africa (whence they returned with cargoes of gold, ivory, and spices). By the end of the fifteenth century, Bartolomeu Dias and Vasco da Gama had rounded the Cape and established a permanent trading presence in India and the spice islands. Columbus blundered into the Americas, starting a series of explorations and settlements too well known to need recounting here. Portuguese and later Dutch voyagers began charting sea routes to the East Indies, China, and Japan early in the next century.

The results of these explorations were profound, but not immediately apparent. The danger, uncertainty, and high cost of ocean voyages during the sixteenth century essentially restricted trade to small cargoes that could earn large profits, mostly precious metals, spices, tea, silk, and other exotic goods to be sold as luxury items in Europe. Some areas, including North America and the South Pacific, were too wild and undeveloped to offer much of value. Meaningful markets for most goods were local, and certainly did not stretch across oceans through the seventeenth century. Domestic production and consumption continued to dwarf imports. The expanding world thus remained peripheral to European life.

But the seeds of later progress had taken root. The early voyagers clung to the coasts rather than striking out across the open ocean not, as is often supposed, from any fear of monsters or falling off the edge of the earth. Without visual points of reference (i.e., *land*marks), they were simply lost. Dead reckoning was the best means of knowing

10   their position. The magnetic compass (in common use by the sixteenth century) told them their headings with tolerable accuracy. But
the only method for determining speed was to play out a line astern
and time the passing of equally spaced knots with an hourglass (hence
the "knot" as a measure of speed). This was notoriously unreliable.
When Magellan, the greatest of all the sixteenth-century explorers,
reached the Philippines, he had miscalculated his position by 3,400
miles.[8] One island often appeared two or more times under different
names on the same map because different discoverers had reported it
in locations separated by many hundreds of miles. Navigators routinely missed their destinations altogether, including targets as large
as New Zealand. Any voyage that landed *somewhere* and returned had
to be counted a success by its captain and crew (if not its sponsors).

But this risky game of blindman's buff gradually accumulated a
priceless treasure: maps, charts, and all-important rutters (detailed
notes of pilots from previous voyages) that recorded depths, currents,
prevailing winds, and other crucial clues to guide future pilots. Trade
routes became established. Passages became more predictable and
faster. Technology finally eliminated much of the complicated guess-
work by providing navigators the means for locating a ship's position
on the globe. The angle of the sun above the southern horizon at
noon told them their latitude, but only precise timekeeping would
allow them to determine longitude: for each hour of "delay" in the
sunrise compared to the home port, the ship had moved 15 degrees
west (one time zone in modern parlance). Pendulum clocks, the most
accurate timepieces of the fifteenth and sixteenth centuries, were
hardly suited to shipboard conditions. In 1714, the British Parliament
offered a munificent £20,000 prize for a reliable means of determining longitude, indicating its importance to the seafaring nations. That
prize provided the needed incentive: spring-driven chronometers accurate to within a minute per month appeared within a few decades.
Meanwhile, shipbuilders strengthened hulls and generally improved
seaworthiness for the long crossings.[9] Such advances gradually eliminated the element of adventure from open ocean voyaging.

While that element remained, overseas trade offered fabulous
profits, which made successful merchants into capitalists-in-waiting.
The wages of native labor set the cost of supply in one market; the
demand of the wealthy for luxury items set the price in the other.

Cargoes of spices, for example, sometimes fetched twenty times as much in Northern Europe as they cost in the East Indies. The merchants pocketed the difference.[10] Initially, these profits went into additional expeditions and ostentatious display. But increasing competition and the merchants' rising wealth made the risks of trade less attractive, and they began "backward integrating" into production.[11] They thus financed or became some of the first industrialists.

In many initially backward lands, the early explorations began a development process that later led to more meaningful trade. Timber and cotton from North America, sugar from the Caribbean islands, and guano and base metals from South America replaced gold and silver as the chief exports of the Americas. In other instances, the reverse process occurred. Rising trade overcame the efforts to ban importation of inexpensive, high-quality printed calicoes from India, forcing the mechanization that ultimately established England's world dominance in textiles. As the industrial era dawned, the access to overseas markets was to become one of the dynamos of progress.

THE KNOWLEDGE REVOLUTION

Foreign lands were not the only *terra incognita* explored during the sixteenth and seventeenth centuries.

The leading scientific authority of sixteenth-century Europe had died nearly two thousand years before. Aristotle's writings stretched across every field of knowledge, a reach that, not surprisingly, exceeded his grasp. As a philosopher, he was prone to elaborate deductions from *a priori* assumptions when, as often happened, unaided observation failed him. (Aristotle ruled out controlled experimentation as "unnatural.") Greek civilization waned before other thinkers could amend his work, and the Romans cared little for abstract knowledge, which left Aristotle the classical authority for the Renaissance to discover and worship. Science thus entered Western civilization as a branch of philosophy—static, with little empirical basis, few useful theories, and no method for advancement.

The decisive break from this tradition came in astronomy. For Aristotle, explaining the motion of the stars was rather simple: spheres and circles are perfect figures, so the stars must be located on crystal

12 spheres and trace a circle around the earth. The second-century
astronomer Ptolemy elaborated this geocentric view into a wonder-
fully complex system of epicycles, deferents, and equants to explain
the apparent motion of the planets in the sky. It all worked, after a
fashion, and the combined authority of Aristotle and Ptolemy kept it
unchallenged until the Polish astronomer Copernicus published his
heliocentric theory in 1543.

Like every revolution, this one had to contend with powerful
entrenched forces.[12] Protestant leaders, including Luther and Calvin,
swiftly denounced Copernicus, relying on the plain language of the
Bible to declare that the earth must be the unmoving center of the
universe. The heliocentric theory nevertheless rapidly gained favor
among astronomers because of its elegant resolution of growing
problems in the Ptolemaic system. The Catholic Church kept aloof
for a while, presumably because of Copernicus's impeccable Catholic
credentials. (He had been encouraged to publish by cardinals and
bishops and had dedicated his book to the Pope. Even so, Copernicus
apparently feared the wrath of the Church: he delayed publication of
his work for over twenty years, finally authorizing its release only on
his deathbed.) By 1616, the Church had consigned Copernicus's
work to the Index Librorum Prohibitorum (where it stayed until
1835!) and condemned any belief in the movement of the earth as
heresy.

Galileo became the lightning rod in this storm.[13] His observations
with the newly invented telescope persuaded him that Copernicus (as
amended in 1609 by Johannes Kepler's publication of the laws of
planetary motion) was right. His 1632 publication *Dialogue on the
Two Chief Systems of the World,* although technically an exposition of
both Ptolemaic and Copernican theories, left little doubt about where
the truth lay. Galileo was by then internationally famous and on
excellent terms with several princes of the Church. If he assumed this
would immunize him from serious reprisals, he was mistaken. The
Inquisition summoned him from Florence, rejecting pleas based on
his ill health, advanced age, and failing eyesight, and compelled him
to testify under threat of torture. The Pope's verdict forced him into
public abjuration of his heresy, followed by solitary confinement that
continued almost until his death.

The Inquisition's treatment of Galileo was not quixotic or aberrational, as the modern reader would like to assume, but part of a calculated and comprehensive effort to maintain the Church's pretensions outside the moral sphere. Toward that end, the Church removed the arbitration of theological matters (which, as defined by the Church, encompassed almost everything) from the community of scholars and assigned it to the clerical administrators of the Inquisition.[14] This effort to suppress progress succeeded to a far greater extent than is commonly appreciated. Astronomers throughout Europe privately accepted heliocentricity, but none dared state his views publicly from 1633, when Galileo recanted, until 1686, when Fontenelle published his *Conversation on the Plurality of Worlds.* Ultimately, "the conservative forces failed to stop the great scientific achievements of the seventeenth century, but not for lack of trying."[15]

This battle over the soul of science was just part of a larger struggle. At the same time, the Church fought to maintain its monopoly over the printed word. It had originally earned this monopoly by the most praiseworthy and exemplary efforts. After the fall of Rome, Benedictine monks, working in cold and ill-lighted scriptoria, took over the work of the Greek scribes. They kept many of the ancient writings alive across the generations by dint of endless recopying, producing richly decorated manuscripts on parchment or vellum (cleaned and stretched animal skins), stitched together at the side or top.[16] The expense of producing one of these manuscripts goes far toward explaining the lack of literacy during the period. Copying one short volume could occupy a monk for a month and consume the skins of twenty sheep for the parchment. Paper entered Europe (from China by way of Byzantium) beginning in the twelfth century, but it was not widely used. Parchment's greater durability lessened the frequency of recopying, which was an even greater expense than the sheepskins. With one book costing as much as two cows, reading matter was decidedly a luxury item.[17] The monks literally chained books to the tables of their libraries to prevent theft.

The magnitude of this "publication" effort severely restricted the supply of information. Reaching even a limited audience with a new work meant paying scribes for months, an expense only those with wealth or wealthy patrons could consider. Fewer manuscripts were published in all of history before 1500 than now appear in print in any

14 single year. Even this tiny intellectual inheritance was insecure. Fire, water, rats, insects, vandalism, and other everyday perils could easily destroy the few dozen existing copies of a work in the course of a single generation. Even brief neglect of a work by the scribes (either inadvertently or at the direction of the abbots) often meant its permanent disappearance. Some writers of antiquity vanished without a trace. With few writings in existence, and those largely inaccessible, common people had little incentive to learn to read, much less write. The result was a pervasive and self-perpetuating ignorance.

Johannes Gutenberg cut this Gordian knot with a series of inventions between about 1435 and 1455. His principal contribution was not the printing press, as is commonly thought, but movable metal type. Using his skill as a goldsmith, he cast type "sticks" of uniform height in a mold with a die in its base indented to form the shape of a letter. These he wedged into a frame, which he placed into a screw press similar to those then used in winemaking and inked with an oil-based ink that he had also developed. Typesetting a work required about the same time as copying it by hand. But each copy printed after the first consumed hours rather than months. By the early sixteenth century, print runs of one or two thousand copies were common, the output of a lifetime for a scribe. Keeping the presses and the typesets busy meant publishing a steady flow of new works. Some of these were classics, producing the Renaissance revival of Roman and Greek learning that had lain dormant in the Western world for nearly a thousand years. But this intellectual archaeology was only the beginning. Modern manuscripts, news sheets, and political and religious pamphlets began to pour from the presses in unprecedented volume.

This sudden release from the responsibility for preserving the world's knowledge did not produce the rejoicing that it should have in Rome. The Church had exploited its virtual monopoly over learning and literacy to shape the prevailing views of cosmology, nature, economic relations, and other areas now considered well within the secular sphere. When the printing press destroyed the natural barriers to information flow, the Church erected artificial ones. Pope Pius IV revived the long-dormant Index in 1559, just as the flow of new works began to assume respectable proportions. Backed by the threats of excommunication and the Inquisition, the Index remained a formidable deterrent to new ideas through the seventeenth century.

The Church was, of course, not the only institution with a vested interest in the status quo. Secular authorities were equally uncomfortable with the widening criticism made possible by inexpensive printing, and several rulers responded with stringent censorship.

The futility of such efforts is clear with hindsight. Presses adequate to the needs of pamphleteers quickly became too cheap to be suppressed effectively. England's break with Rome accelerated the process there; the machinery of censorship had essentially dissolved by the 1640s.[18] Some rulers began to respond to criticism not with suppression but with paid propagandists. By the eighteenth century, even critical and heretical views could usually find an outlet in print throughout Western Europe and North America. Literacy expanded with the volume and practical interest of reading materials. Learning joined religion and the arts as an outlet for creative impulses among the gentry. The prospect of improving life through an understanding of nature and history increasingly turned intellectuals away from the spiritual, the metaphysical, and the speculative and toward the temporal and the positive. Encyclopedists in France and England began their efforts to catalog and memorialize all existing knowledge. The coming era of progress was predicated on this ability to accumulate and apply information.

The resistance to science met a similar end. The Church had achieved its immediate objectives with the persecution of Galileo, but its willingness to deny an increasingly obvious truth and to use draconian methods to force others to do the same ultimately served to diminish its secular authority. Although the battle would be fought again, most notably over Darwinism, quotation from the scriptures could no longer intimidate scientists into silence, and popular opinion increasingly accepted science as the ultimate authority on the workings of nature.

England led in this process, aided again by its break from Rome. Isaac Newton, born appropriately enough in the year of Galileo's death, triumphantly completed his work, integrating Galileo's mechanics into generalized laws of motion and force and explaining Kepler's third law through a universal law of gravitation.[19] He decisively dethroned and nearly banished Aristotle from the realm of science. To state and formalize his major discoveries, he invented differential and integral calculus (with Leibniz). He was feted, knighted, and celebrated in verse. The sweep and elegant simplicity

16 of his theories caught the imagination of the English gentry. Even untutored amateurs became active, adding their trickles to growing freshets of knowledge through papers and manuscripts published at private expense.[20] With Newton, the power of the scientific method to explain seeming mysteries of nature in a precise and useful way became undeniable. Much of his work survived into the twentieth century without material modification. Newton thus marked the end of the revolutionary period and the beginning of the sustained scientific progress that has continued to the present.

The growth of science translated more or less directly into material progress. The ability to understand and predict the workings of nature implied the potential mastery of those workings for human ends. Francis Bacon had charted the course much earlier with his insistence that scientists cooperate and contribute "to the endowment and benefit of man's life."[21] Dozens of scientific societies sprang up, particularly in England, most of them dedicated not only to investigating some field, but also to turning the results to practical advantage. Ability and interest were the only entrance requirements; the gentry listened attentively to talks by ironmongers.[22] Their published proceedings found an avid readership among some leading early industrialists. Josiah Wedgwood, James Watt, and others joined these societies, corresponded actively with leaders in the relevant fields, and applied scientific methods of hypothesis and experimentation to improve their designs and methods.[23] By the late eighteenth century, science was transforming the means of production.[24]

Less tangibly but no less importantly, scientific discoveries enthroned the idea of progress. The pace of progress, although still slow by current standards, at least became perceptible to contemporary observers. During a few decades in the mid-seventeenth century, Robert Hooke described the elastic behavior of solids, Robert Boyle quantified the relationship between pressure and volume in a gas, and William Harvey proved that blood circulates. The printing press cemented each advance into a rising edifice of knowledge. This concrete and irreversible erosion of ignorance belied any conception of history as cyclical or declining. The educated laity exhibited a growing faith that the future would always surpass the present, taking science as their touchstone.[25] Condorcet, Auguste Comte, and others built positive theories of social progress from a foundation of scientific progress. Continuous material improvement began to appear as a legitimate and attainable goal of policy.

INVENTING THE MARKET

Working for money and using that money to buy goods and services hardly seems a radical innovation. Indeed, from the modern perspective, it is not easy to imagine an economy functioning any other way. But the market became the predominant mechanism for satisfying material needs only during the last few centuries. Without this economic revolution, the Industrial Revolution could never have begun.

Tradition and command, rather than voluntary exchange, were the organizing principles for the economy through most of history.[26] Slavery was one obvious manifestation. Slave labor on a massive scale supplied the productive foundation of almost all ancient societies. Feudalism altered that foundation only slightly. "Ancient customs" and the whim of the manorial lord minutely governed the serfs' lives.[27] Their labor was tied to the land. Their output was divided between their own tables and the manor house. Their occasional involvement with the outside world—some local haulage or wood-cutting or exchanging a few eggs or some vegetables for a pot or a knife—was decidedly ancillary to the daily problem of sustaining life.

The seigneur transacted little more business in the market than his serfs. Manorial estates were primarily social and political, not economic, entities. The lord received his rents in kind, not in cash, using the grain from the peasants to feed blacksmiths and the like and hoarding the occasional surplus against famine or siege. The land was his to control but not to sell. He was as closely tied to that land and to the way of life it dictated as the peasantry. Land and labor were viewed not as transferable factors of production, but as two strands in a web of reciprocal obligations, inextricable and indissoluble.

Artisans and merchants, although outside of this web, shared much of the same outlook. Guilds that traced their origins to the Roman Empire minutely regulated the conduct of their members through rules and customs. Royal charters granted the guilds effective monopolies and quasi-governmental powers. They fixed the terms of service and wages of journeymen and apprentices (whose station in society

18 differed little from that of the peasants), as well as the terms of sale. Luring a customer from another guild member was forbidden. Innovation without the (highly unlikely) consent of the guild was considered an act of disloyalty. Fabrics made with false (i.e., unauthorized) dyes or having too many or too few threads per inch could be confiscated; their makers could be pilloried for repeat offenses. French guilds punished the selling of imported calicoes by a term in the galleys, breaking on the wheel, and even death. The modern objectives of output and profit remained decidedly secondary to preserving a stable and well-defined way of life, at almost any cost. Perpetuation, not progress, was the objective. The inherent disorderliness of a free market was out of synch with the times.

Religion's hostility to the emerging world extended to the market economy as well. The Church discouraged Christians from becoming merchants and preached the moral superiority of poverty. Acquisitiveness was an urge to be restrained. Aquinas discoursed at length on the concept of the "just price," which, for example, condemned a seller for charging more in response to a shortage and a buyer for paying less because of a surplus. Such doctrines fought the most fundamental economic incentives and effectively precluded a self-adjusting market. Usury, broadly defined to include almost any lending of money at interest, was a *mortal* sin, not a rule designed to encourage the transfer of capital to productive uses. According to the bookkeeping of the Church, most forms of financial gain represented losses on the ledger of the soul, a decidedly unequal bargain given the widespread preoccupation with the afterlife and the dominant role of religion in political and social life.

These conditions relegated the market to a minor role in human affairs. Military, political, and religious positions offered far better prospects than economic activity for wealth and social advancement, and talent and energy predictably followed this pattern of rewards.

All these conditions had begun to change by the seventeenth century, particularly in England. In contrast to the Continent, most English peasants were "free" by 1500. They discharged their continuing obligations mostly through periodic payments of money. This forced the lords into the labor market to have their lands tended, and the peasants into some form of market activity to raise the needed stipend. At about the same time, the rising price of wool expanded the need for pasturage. This demand produced the first wave of enclosures (c. 1470–c. 1530), especially in the southern counties. Tens of thousands of dispossessed subsistence farmers formed a wage-seeking proletariat. The transition was brutal, but it started a much-needed divorce between labor and land.[28]

The power of the guilds eroded under the pressures of rising imports and new production methods. In 1503, Parliament deprived the guilds of their law-making and enforcement authority. Many narrow guilds merged to become a few broad ones, blurring the lines between different crafts and widening the scope of effective competition. The influence of the guilds did not vanish overnight: as late as 1598, the hosiers persuaded the Privy Council to outlaw the newly invented stocking frame as a threat to their livelihood. But the gradual replacement of craft work by mechanized industry produced much the same effect as enclosure in the realm of agriculture. Masters evolved into employers, and apprentices into mobile wage labor, employed on terms set by the market.

The curtailment of religion's reach also contributed to the rise of the market. Where the Church had generally denigrated earthly concerns, the leading Protestant sects promoted the virtues of diligence and thrift, which, together, unavoidably produce saving and capital improvements. England naturally benefited most from this difference in attitude, but the Reformation forced some relaxation throughout Europe. Although usury continued to be condemned, for example, Catholic doctrine redefined it as the charging of *excessive* interest, a limit that proved to be highly elastic. Capitalists escaped the bounds of religion much as scientists and writers had, and with similar results.

Telescoping several centuries of change into a few pages makes the transition to a market-based economy seem more sudden and complete than it actually was. Tradition and command continued to play important roles. By Adam Smith's time, however, most households procured the means of existence principally by buying and selling goods and services for money. Success in commerce increasingly became a source of wealth and position. A combination of necessity, opportunity, and social acceptability channeled "the uniform, constant, and uninterrupted effort of every man to better his condition" into market activities, releasing the forces that have driven the progress of the modern era.

NOTES

1. Fernand Braudel, *The Structures of Everyday Life*, p. 53, Harper & Row, 1981.

2. Robert Heilbroner, *The Making of Economic Society*, Ch. 3, p. 69, Prentice-Hall, 6th ed., 1980; Paul Mantoux, *The Industrial Revolution in the Eighteenth Century*, Part 1, Ch. 1, p. 74, Harper & Row, 1962.

3. Daniel Boorstin, *The Discoverers*, Chs. 44–47, Random House, 1983, describes the long influence and ultimate erosion of Galen's doctrines.

4. See, e.g., Baumol, Blackman & Wolff, *Productivity and American Leadership: The Long View*, Ch. 2, MIT Press, 1989.

5. J.B. Bury, *The Idea of Progress: An Inquiry into Its Origin and Growth*, Macmillan, 2d ed., 1932, describes the slow emergence and ultimate dominance of the idea of progress. Also see Sidney Pollard, *The Idea of Progress: History and Society*, Chs. 1 and 2, C.A. Watts, 1968; and Christopher Lasch, *The True and Only Heaven: Progress and Its Critics*, Ch. 1, W.W. Norton, 1991.

6. See Bury, *Idea of Progress*, Ch. 3, p. 66; and Pollard, *Idea of Progress*, Ch. 1, p. 8.

7. Boorstin, *Discoverers*, Chs. 21–23 and 34, describes the early voyages and their effects.

8. Trevor Williams, *The Triumph of Invention*, Ch. 11, p. 111, Macdonald, 1987.

9. Williams, *Triumph of Invention*, Ch. 11, and Boorstin, *Discoverers*, Chs. 21 and 29, describe the advances in navigation and shipbuilding.

10. On merchants' profits from the early overseas trade in luxuries, see Fernand Braudel, *The Wheels of Commerce*, Ch. 4, especially pp. 403–8, Harper & Row, 1982.

11. Carlo Cipolla, *Before the Industrial Revolution: European Society and Economy, 1000–1700*, Ch. 9, p. 239, W.W. Norton, 2d ed., 1980. Braudel, *Wheels of Commerce*, Ch. 3, pp. 297–349 and 372–73, and Mantoux, *Industrial Revolution in the Eighteenth Century*, Part I, Ch. 1, pp. 62 and 90, describe the merchants' almost accidental drift into manufacturing during the seventeenth and eighteenth centuries.

12. For descriptions of the religious opposition to Copernicanism, see Thomas Kuhn, *The Copernican Revolution*, Ch. 6, Vintage Books, 1959; and Garraty & Gay (eds.), *Columbia History of the World*, Ch. 61, Harper & Row, 1972.

13. Boorstin, *Discoverers,* Chs. 40 and 41, describes Galileo's support of heliocentricity and subsequent trial by the Inquisition.

14. Margaret Jacob, *The Cultural Meaning of the Scientific Revolution,* Ch. 1, p. 15, Knopf, 1988.

15. Joel Mokyr, *The Lever of Riches,* Ch. 11, p. 298, Oxford Univ. Press, 1990.

16. Boorstin, *Discoverers,* Ch. 1, describes the Benedictines' preservation of classical works through the Middle Ages.

17. Cipolla, *Before the Industrial Revolution,* Ch. 6, p. 178.

18. Jacob, *Cultural Meaning of the Scientific Revolution,* Ch. 3, p. 76.

19. Charles Singer, *A Short History of Scientific Ideas to 1900,* Ch. 7, Oxford Univ. Press, 1959, and Garraty & Gay (eds.), *The Columbia History of the World,* Ch. 59, describe the scientific revolution in the seventeenth century.

20. This amateur enthusiasm for the sciences continued into the Victorian era. "The natural sciences in all their branches—rocks, fossils, birds, beasts, fish, and flowers—were a national hobby." G.M. Young, *Portrait of an Age: Victorian England,* Sec. XI, p. 85, Oxford Univ. Press, 1977 ed. To similar effect are Paul Johnson, *The Birth of the Modern: World Society 1815–1830,* Ch. 7, p. 543, HarperCollins, 1991; and T.W. Heyck, *The Transformation of Intellectual Life in Victorian England,* Ch. 3, p. 52, St. Martin's Press, 1982.

21. Jacob, *Cultural Meaning of the Scientific Revolution,* Ch. 1, p. 31.

22. Johnson, *Birth of the Modern,* Ch. 7, p. 544.

23. Musson & Robinson, *Science and Technology in the Industrial Revolution,* Manchester Univ. Press, 1969. Mantoux, *Industrial Revolution in the Eighteenth Century,* Part 3, Ch. 2, describes the Lunar Society (so called because it met when the moon was full in order to provide adequate light for travel), whose members included Sir Joseph Banks (president of the Royal Society), the astronomer William Herschel, the chemist Joseph Priestley, and the naturalist Erasmus Darwin, as well as Watt, Matthew Boulton, and occasionally Wedgwood.

24. Jacob, *Cultural Meaning of the Scientific Revolution,* Ch. 7, pp. 237–45.

25. Jacob, *Cultural Meaning of the Scientific Revolution,* Ch. 4, p. 105.

26. Pre-market economics are described in Heilbroner, *Making of Economic Society,* Ch. 2, and William Ashley, *An Introduction to English Economic History and Theory,* Chs. 1–3, Longmans, Green, 1919. Karl Polanyi, *The Great Transformation,* Chs. 3–5, Beacon Press, 1944, describes the great social dislocations brought by the transition to a market-based economy.

27. In return for their labor and obedience, serfs received protection against marauders and a dole of grain during famine. Christopher Lasch has suggested that "the compensatory security of clearly defined social status, reciprocal obligations, and the reassuring knowledge that the future would closely resemble the past" may have been adequate recompense for the peasants' miserable life-styles. *True and Only Heaven,* Ch. 3, p. 114. Only analytical detachment from the realities of life and a profound distrust of modern society could explain such a suggestion. The worst victims of progress identified by Professor Lasch—industrial and clerical workers unsettled and alienated by the modern pace of change and the loss of a

22   sense of community—have shown little inclination to exchange their "meaning-less" but remunerative jobs and wide-ranging life-styles for the grinding poverty and oxlike existence of their peasant predecessors.

28. On the role of the first enclosure movement in the birth of the market, see Heilbroner, *Making of Economic Society,* Ch. 3, pp. 59–61, Karl Marx, *Capital,* Part 8, Ch. 27, 1867; and Polanyi, *Great Transformation,* Ch. 3.

Chapter Two

PARAGONS OF PROGRESS

A market economy, the rise of science, the retreat of religion from secular affairs, and long-distance trading were just precursors, with little immediate impact on daily life. Meaningful progress began with a rush in late-eighteenth-century England. Japan achieved a similar takeoff in the late nineteenth century, as did South Korea another hundred years later. These sudden flowerings, each of them springing from less than promising soil, reveal the forces that have produced and sustained material progress during the last 250 years.

THE MORE THAN INDUSTRIAL REVOLUTION

Adam Smith, who was a perceptive social observer as well as one of the giants of economics, managed to live through the early decades of the Industrial Revolution without noticing it. His paradigm of industry was a pin-making workshop, with neither significant capital equipment nor technology. In eighteenth-century France, the Physiocrats continued to maintain that manufacturing could not possibly be a productive sector in the economy. Indeed, not one of the classical economists of the eighteenth and early nineteenth centuries recognized or understood the Industrial Revolution even as it occurred around them.[1] The politicians of the day were no more discerning. "Lord North [prime minister from 1770 to 1782] went

24 to his grave without knowing he had presided over an Industrial Revolution."[2]

Overlooking one of the seminal events of world history would seem like a serious black mark on the résumés of these intellectual and political leaders. But today's highly paid observers, with two more centuries of learning at their command, would fare no better. Look back at the economic and social trends of eighteenth-century England through the standard-issue lens of the nightly news correspondent.

The family farm, the very heart of the economy, was in crisis. The gentry had begun a second wave of enclosures, joining the contiguous parcels of small freeholders under single ownership and eliminating common lands and pasturing rights.[3] Parliament passed thousands of private enclosure acts during the 1700s, encompassing a total of three million acres.[4] These enclosures made British farms enormous by European standards.[5] Owners of the large estates collected rents from the tenant farmers, who became the agricultural entrepreneurs.[6] Perhaps forty to fifty thousand small farms disappeared in the process. Some of the dispossessed yeomen began to work the land for wages, but most simply lost their livelihoods, because this newly rationalized structure produced a specialized and more intensive farming that needed less labor to produce the same amounts of grain and meat. Indeed, reducing the number of workers was a principal, if rarely acknowledged, purpose of the gentry. The trend in rural landownership was thus clearly at the expense of the poor. It was tailor-made for fifteen hundred words or a ten-minute news feature on the plight of farming families, complete with interviews of able-bodied peasants trying to find work and not so subtle overtones of class warfare.

The long-term prospects were no better. Jethro Tull's seed drill and the improved all-iron plow were harbingers of the mechanization that would further reduce employment for farm laborers. Robert Bakewell started systematic breeding programs that more than doubled the size of cattle and sheep during the eighteenth century, good news for gentlemen farmers and for the privileged few who regularly dined on meat, but bad for the many yeomen trying to keep bread on the table by raising a few head of the scrawny native stock. Worst of all, as the Americas developed, the prospect of cheap imported grain and other food became increasingly obvious. The crowded and

heavily worked land of England could not hope to compete with the
endless virgin expanses of the New World. Rising commercial interests, brandishing the arguments of Adam Smith, urged relaxation or
repeal of the Corn Law tariffs, the only protection against this grave
threat to rural livelihoods. The combination of labor-saving agricultural machinery and declining food prices would spawn rick burning
and rural riots by 1830.

The news from industry was at least equally bleak. Woolen production had long been a stable source of employment for many thousands of yeoman households and artisans alike. Housewives
supplemented farm incomes with spinning. The weavers' guilds,
combined with the intense conservatism of the labor force, effectively
discouraged any disruption in the traditional modes of producing
cloth. India, with its locally grown cotton and endless supply of cheap
labor, made some inroads in the English market with its light printed
calicoes, but the continued employment of hand spinners and weavers would have looked fully secure early in the eighteenth century. "A
wave of gadgets" needed only a few decades to transform this comfortable arrangement beyond recognition.[7] Intricate machinery and
mechanical energy substituted for nimble fingers and strong arms,
decreasing the labor required for weaving tenfold and for spinning an
astonishing hundredfold.[8] Meanwhile, across the Atlantic, Eli Whitney's cotton gin was substantially eliminating the labor needed to
clean the raw cotton.

Thus, at each link in the chain of production, new technology
threatened people's livelihoods. The resulting privations would have
provided plenty of promising material for human-interest stories.
While a few industrialists became immensely wealthy by the standards
of the time, many unemployed artisans had to rely on the meager dole
provided by the Poor Law.[9] Woolen producers and workers, more
established and influential than the nascent cotton industry, were
better able to resist change in traditional production methods, but the
low price competition of cotton exacted a toll. Some home spinners
and hand weavers hung on for decades, but suffered steady declines
in income as mechanization progressively narrowed the margin between the cost of raw materials and the price of finished goods. Hand
spinners' earnings declined by half or more between 1764 and
1780.[10] Child labor was a natural outgrowth of the inability of many

26 workers to earn a living wage. Workers struck back at their mechanical tormentors in 1779. Mobs numbering in the hundreds and perhaps thousands attacked the mills, smashing and burning the hated machines.

Governmental policy was anything but supportive of workers' grievances. Parliament decreed the death penalty for destroying any building containing machinery. Troops were dispatched without hesitation to suppress workers' riots. Petitions to curtail mechanization evoked little sympathy and less action. "[B]etween 1750 and 1850 the British political system unflinchingly supported the winners over the losers on . . . matters of technological progress. . . . "[11] The spin that any modern journalist (or opposition politician) would place on these facts is obvious beyond the necessity of discussion: the government had chosen to sacrifice the tangible and immediate interests of yeomen and artisans, the largest working segments of the population and the blood and sinew of the society, for the benefit of a few rich landowners and upstart factory owners, all in pursuit of the theoretical and speculative benefits of mechanization and free trade. The occasional violence of the Luddites would be quickly dismissed as pardonable excess provoked by the government's deplorable failure to protect them from the rigors of the market and assure them a decent living.

Anyone with an "England first" agenda would have ascribed some of the economic difficulties to the seeming preoccupation with foreign and military affairs. Continued British meddling in the West Indies precipitated the Anglo-Spanish War in 1739, which soon merged into the larger War of the Austrian Succession, which continued until 1748. The Seven Years' War with France (1756–63) arose largely out of colonial tensions and conflicts. Victory brought added territory in North America and hegemony in India, but also massive debts. The American Revolution (1775–83) added more debt, plus the humiliation of defeat by its erstwhile colonists and the French and the loss of most of the North American gains. By comparison, the American experience during the late twentieth century has been positively quiescent. Even during the brief intervals of peace, Britain's foreign holdings seemed a decidedly mixed blessing. The British East India Company, which exercised sovereign authority in India, suffered periodic financial crises, and the meager taxes collected from North America never repaid the cost of garrison troops.

A sharp shift in spending patterns would have provided additional cause for concern. People began to save a significantly larger portion of their incomes after 1760. Thousands of individuals who might otherwise have consumed their earnings invested a portion instead, hoping to profit from the opportunities created by the new technologies. Any observer with a smattering of Keynesian economics would confidently have predicted that the loss of consumer spending would produce a shortfall in aggregate demand, resulting in slower growth or recession. But the government, understandably (and blissfully) ignorant of the teachings of this future lord of the realm, actually promoted institutions that reinforced this shift. The emergence of deposit banking provided a smooth conduit between private saving and investment. The government began to charter limited-liability joint-stock companies, which served as vehicles for securing equity capital from strangers.

Judged by the familiar criteria of the evening news, eighteenth-century England was thus in a sorry state: its principal economic sectors in disarray, with unemployment high and wages falling; an apparently widening gulf between rich and poor; its work force sullen and occasionally belligerent; government policies indifferent if not hostile to the people's interests; distracted by war and foreign entanglements; its consumers refusing to spend. In a modern democracy, the pack would be in full cry, and the government's prospects for remaining in office would be bleak.

Critics could draw further support by invidious comparisons of England to its chief rival. France in 1750 wore all the indicia of power and prosperity.[12] Both its population and its share of world manufacturing output were more than double those of England. Its peasants and freeholders maintained their small plots with just the normal interference from the seigneurs. The government did not encourage destabilizing changes in domestic production, offering no patent protection until 1791. French guilds assured continuity and stability in the principal crafts, retaining the power to ban innovations outright into the eighteenth century.[13] Needless to say, invention offered bleak prospects for either fame or fortune.[14] The government supported the guilds in suppressing cheap imports, with the stated purpose of assuring French self-sufficiency. France's military ability to protect itself could hardly be questioned in light of Napoleon's many triumphs just a few decades in the future. England could only envy

28   France, with its continental expanse, its natural resources, its culture, the wealth and power of its nobility, and, most of all, its stability.

Hindsight, of course, sees a different picture. In just two generations, England dominated the world both commercially and militarily, while France was falling behind Germany and even the United States. The factors that had so roiled England in the eighteenth century were the forces of progress that established its ascendancy in the nineteenth.

1. TECHNOLOGY.   The ability of the French guilds to suppress labor-saving innovation kept Britain's technology lead in spinning and weaving unchallenged for decades, assuring its sustained dominance in textiles. British cotton cloth output rose from forty million yards in 1785 to more than two billion yards in 1850, a fiftyfold increase in two generations.[15] The cotton textile industry, which accounted for less than 0.5 percent of British national income in the 1760s, rose to more than 4 percent by 1802 and more than 7 percent by 1812.[16] Manchester became an international commercial center almost overnight, catapulted from obscurity by the burgeoning mills. English textiles spread around the world, as India's natural advantages proved no match for England's superior technology. The price of cotton cloth fell by 85 percent between 1780 and 1850.[17] Falling prices initially eroded profit margins, bringing hard times to the nascent industrial sector. Continuing declines, however, made manufactured cloth affordable for ordinary people who had always simply done without, effecting a minor revolution in life-styles.[18] Employment in textiles regained and then surpassed its prior levels, and labor unrest subsided.

British iron-making followed a parallel course over roughly the same period.[19] At the beginning of the eighteenth century, England was a net importer of iron, despite ample reserves of iron ore and coal. Charcoal had always been used to smelt iron, and the prospect of deforestation loomed.[20] Abraham Darby in about 1709 learned how to smelt iron by first coking coal to remove impurities and improve its heating value, techniques later perfected by his son of the same name. Henry Cort completed this chain of invention in 1784 with his puddling and rolling process for converting pig iron into high-quality malleable iron. The results were immediate, with iron production nearly tripling between 1788 and 1806. The ironmaster John Wilkinson quickly adapted this newly abundant material to novel applications, including iron bridges, iron-plated ships, cast-iron pipe for the Parisian water system, and precision-bored cylinders for Watt's steam engine. England soon excelled the world in iron-making and iron machinery.

The other key innovation of the Industrial Revolution was the steam engine. Thomas Newcomen, an English engineer, invented the first engine of any commercial use in 1712, but it converted only about 1 percent of the heat energy expended into work. James Watt introduced the crucial design improvements beginning in 1769. By separating the condenser from the working cylinder, so that the cylinder remained hot throughout the cycle, and introducing live steam alternately to opposite sides of the piston, Watt roughly quadrupled the efficiency of Newcomen's engine.[21] Before his patent expired in 1800, Watt and his partner, Matthew Boulton, had sold about five hundred engines. The combined output of these engines may not have exceeded ten thousand horsepower, but it was energy on demand, available where and when needed. Smelters and ironworks could be located near their raw materials, rather than on a suitable stream. Miners could mine, rather than constantly pumping water out of the shafts. Mill owners began to supplement water power with steam to eliminate bottlenecks in processing. Without steam power, it could scarcely have been an *industrial* revolution.

2. MARKET EXPANSION.   Through the first half of the eighteenth century, most English roads remained almost impassable.[22] Teams of horses and oxen dragged carts through the mud at no more than a few miles per hour. Prices in London differed significantly from those in Cambridge, only about sixty miles away, because of the high cost of transport. Grain rarely traveled more than ten miles from the field, or cloth more than forty miles from the loom.[23]

The eighteenth-century response was a series of relatively low-tech public improvements. Parliament passed hundreds of acts providing for the establishment and maintenance of turnpikes, which formed a fairly dense web by 1775. A flurry of canal building followed, supported by prominent industrialists (including Wedgwood and Boulton) who recognized their need to tap larger markets. Before it ended

30   early in the nineteenth century, over two thousand miles of canals had
been constructed and an approximately equal length of river courses
had been made navigable. These reduced the cost of moving bulk
goods along their routes by as much as two thirds[24] and made much
of the interior cheaply accessible to ocean shipping.

But it was the railroad that comprehensively stretched people's
horizons beyond the confines of their villages. Rail transportation in
the eighteenth century consisted of horses hauling ore carts on
wooden rails at the mines. Watt's engines were tried, but they were
low-pressure engines that generated too little power for their weight
to be useful for locomotive applications. After Watt's patent expired
in 1800, Richard Trevithick of Cornwall quickly succeeded in building engines that worked at pressures of up to ten atmospheres. But
Trevithick's rudimentary locomotives still cracked the wooden rails,
and iron was too expensive for large-scale use. James Neilson
removed this bottleneck in 1828 with his introduction of the hot-air
blast in iron-making. Neilson used flue gas to preheat the air entering
the furnace, tripling the quantity of iron produced per ton of coal and
permitting the use of lower-grade ores.[25] The resulting savings made
iron available in tons rather than pounds.

These innovations combined to produce the railroad. In October
1829, as the first commercial rail line was nearing completion between Liverpool and Manchester, the proprietors held the famous
Rainhill trial to select the locomotives that would operate on it,
offering a prize of £500 to the winner. George Stephenson, who
engineered and built the new line, joined with his son Robert to
design and build the *Rocket*. It employed a high-pressure engine that
vented steam through the chimney to improve the draft in the boiler.
The *Rocket* prevailed over four other entrants (one of which was
disqualified when it was found to contain a horse), achieving a top
speed of more than thirty miles per hour on its victory run. Spectators
feared that the rush of air had killed the engine driver. No previous
form of transportation could hope to compete in speed or capacity.[26]

The primacy of the Liverpool-to-Manchester line was no accident.
It carried raw cotton shipped from the American South to the vora-
cious mills in Manchester, and returned to Liverpool with textile
goods for a national and world market. The low cost and high
capacity of rail transport made this extended supply and distribution

pattern feasible. Less constrained by geography, railroads soon formed a denser transportation network than canals. By 1850, Great Britain had 6,620 miles of rail, more than one quarter of the world total.[27] The cost savings alone from the use of railroads have been estimated at 5 percent of the United Kingdom's national income by 1865.[28] Railroads also added speed, extending the markets for even perishable goods to hundreds of miles. These transportation improvements had essentially integrated England into a single market by midcentury.

The rising scale of industrial production virtually demanded that foreign markets be tapped as well, as the output of even the earliest textile mills vastly exceeded local demand.[29] Cotton textile exports rose twentyfold from 1780 to 1802.[30] From 1819 to 1841, England exported half of its total output of cotton textiles.[31]

This overseas trade required more reliable and cheaper ocean shipping. Improving knowledge of prevailing winds and currents shortened passage times, and incremental design improvements allowed smaller crews to sail larger ships, improving productivity.[32] Total export tonnage more than doubled between 1774 and 1800.[33] Larger volumes contributed to a continuing decline in freight rates through the first half of the century,[34] which produced a sharp rise in the share of exports destined for North America, Asia, and other distant markets.[35] England accelerated these developments by steadily reducing tariffs beginning in 1824. International trade was born, and England was its midwife.

Larger markets produced an ever finer division of labor, just as Adam Smith had said that they would.[36] Josiah Wedgwood pioneered industrial specialization in his Etruria pottery works. Instead of having master craftsmen complete individual pieces, Wedgwood divided the work among ordinary laborers, each of whom performed just one task. This saved the time previously wasted in changing tasks and allowed each worker to perfect a narrow range of skills. These methods produced both the lowest cost and the highest quality, which enabled Wedgwood to overcome the still very substantial costs of transportation. By 1800, Wedgwood's dishes had spread throughout Europe and the Americas,[37] and his fine china graced the tables of both French and Russian nobility.

Specialization also accelerated advances in technology.[38] The black-

32 smith, a fairly typical preindustrial artisan, confronted dozens of different tasks each day, and naturally performed each in the accepted way using some general purpose tools. Puzzling out separate new approaches or equipment for making horseshoes, wheel rims, plow blades, spikes, and nails would have dwarfed the resulting efficiencies. Only specialists have the knowledge, the focus, and the interest needed to resolve the problems and eliminate the bottlenecks they meet repeatedly in their work. Adam Smith evidently considered this the primary source of innovation as of the late eighteenth century.

> Men are much more likely to discover easier and readier methods of attaining any object when the whole attention of their minds is directed towards that single object than when it is dissipated among a great variety of things. . . . A great part of the machines made use of in those manufactures in which labour is most subdivided, were originally the inventions of common workmen, who, being each of them employed in some very simple operation, naturally turned their thoughts towards finding out easier and readier methods of performing it.[39]

The furious pace of innovation in the highly specialized textile industry amply confirmed Smith's observation. But this specialization, in turn, depended on the size of the accessible market.

3. CAPITAL ACCUMULATION. Would-be industrialists needed more than ingenuity and markets. The canals, roads, railways, mines, and factories were sizable investments for the time.

"It was the growth of savings, and of a readiness to put these at the disposal of industry, that made it possible for Britain to reap the harvest of her ingenuity."[40] Gross capital investment in Great Britain rose from 8 percent of gross national product per annum in the 1760s to 14 percent by the 1790s, where it thereafter remained.[41] Both the size and the timing of this shift are significant. An 8 percent investment rate barely replaces productive capital as it wears out and supplies new workers with the same inadequate equipment. The higher rate of investment raised the standard of living while starting an accumulating, self-generating surplus (reflected by declining interest rates through most of the period) that enabled the economy to

expand further. The occurrence of this increase *before* the large output gains from industrialization establishes that it was initially a cause
and not an effect of those gains.

The use of capital also shifted. Agriculture had long consumed
most investment, accounting for three quarters of total British capital
in 1760. The rapid rise of transportation and industry lowered agriculture's share to little more than one third by 1860.[42] Within the
commercial sector, merchants had traditionally kept capital tied up in
inventories and trading goods. As late as 1760, such circulating
capital outweighed the total capital fixed in productive investments.
By 1860, with the intervening rise of industry, transportation, and
mining, the amount of fixed capital was triple that of circulating
capital.[43]

France, despite its many apparent advantages, lacked these three
forces of progress. While the descendants of Francis Bacon and Isaac
Newton experimented and blundered their way forward, those of
Descartes insisted on rationality and perfect order. Not surprisingly,
France shunned or but slowly assimilated the new technologies that
regularly bubbled out of England. The French failed even to develop
the potential of steam power, the foundation of all later industrial
methods; they reluctantly imported a few engines from England,
along with the engineers and technicians to operate them. The persistence of feudalism under the *ancien régime* precluded the development of capitalist agriculture. The land "reforms" of the French
Revolution merely substituted an inefficient pattern of small holdings.
With its intensely rationalistic tradition, France distrusted the inherent untidiness of the free market and unplanned change.[44] Ministers
of the Crown minutely controlled the activities of the early joint-stock
trading companies. This tradition persisted after the Revolution, as
the French government took an active role in owning or otherwise
attempting to control developing industries that threatened the status
quo.[45] The nimble and highly motivated entrepreneurs of England
easily outdistanced the French bureaucrats. Internal tariffs and heavy
regulation of domestic transportation impeded formation of a national market, in sharp contrast to England, which was the largest
unregulated and untaxed market area in Europe.[46] High tariffs and,
later, the strategically motivated Continental System (combined, of
course, with the loss of its North American and Indian colonies)

34 limited France's foreign commerce and distorted incentives. Rigid mercantilism prohibited circulation of specie, preventing efficient employment of capital in new enterprises. In England, by contrast, money circulated freely.

The long-term results more than compensated England for its earlier hardships. By 1850, England had firmly established its economic superiority. Its share of world manufacturing output was more than double that of France, its national output per capita more than 50 percent higher,[47] with most of the gain concentrated in the textile, iron, and transportation sectors,[48] precisely those most influenced by innovation, investment, and market expansion. England had nearly seven times as much steam power as France by 1840, and produced nearly ten times as much coal in 1850.[49] England's gains drastically altered the political and military balance with its multicentury rival as well, making England the dominant world power and ushering in Pax Britannica.

Even more durable and significant was the improvement in living standards. The prices of manufactured goods and fuel declined in the decades following the Napoleonic wars,[50] while money wages generally rose. The threat of famine receded. Real incomes doubled between 1810 and 1850, and consumption of consumer goods rose rapidly.[51] Average people could afford shoes and changes of clothing. They began to enjoy a standard of living that comfortably exceeded subsistence for the first time in history.

> The Industrial Revolution . . . was more than an expansion of commerce, more than a series of changes in the technology of certain industries, more even than an acceleration of general economic growth. It was a revolution in men's access to the means of life, in control of their ecological environment, in their capacity to escape from the tyranny and niggardliness of nature.[52]

The era of progress had begun.

MEIJI JAPAN

That progress arrived in Japan in 1853 in the unwelcome form of Commodore Perry's black ships.

Their arrival ended centuries of Japanese isolation. Decades of civil war culminated in 1600 with the apocalyptic Battle of Sekigahara,[53] an incredibly sanguinary Japanese version of Gettysburg. Ieyasu, the victor, declared himself shogun (supreme military ruler) and founded the Tokugawa dynasty, which reigned without interruption for 260 years. Local government was the responsibility of daimyos (feudal lords), who owed their allegiance to the shogun and in turn commanded the obedience of samurai retainers. The Tokugawa shogunate engaged in no foreign adventures and suffered little domestic unrest, in sharp contrast to Europe, the Americas, and China during the same period. The crossed swords of the samurai soon became ceremonial as peace prevailed and civil disorder almost vanished. The arts, culture, and scholarship became the principal preoccupations of privileged classes. The remarkable productivity of rice-paddy-based agriculture prevented the food shortages that regularly plagued Europe.[54] The housing, clothing, and hygiene of the common people almost certainly excelled those prevailing in seventeenth-century Europe. The society was well ordered and tranquil. It "would have looked to an observer like a marvelous machine which promises to run automatically forever."[55] Japanese arrogance toward the early Portuguese and Dutch explorers thus had some objective foundation.

By 1854, however, a nation that had not even existed when the Tokugawa dynasty began could bring Japan to heel without firing a shot. Japan's many initial advantages counted for little against its lack of the essential ingredients of progress.

Production methods had stagnated for more than two hundred years. Craft guilds, authorized and empowered by the shogun, strictly regulated the activities of artisans. They forbade most forms of competition. Changes in methods of operation required mutual agreement, which predictably prevented any advances that would threaten even backward members.

A policy of strict isolation from the outside world precluded the importation of new technology. A rebellion by the Christian daimyos in 1637 had provoked the shogun into excluding all disruptive foreign influences. He banished the Portuguese and in 1640 proceeded to execute en masse a large Portuguese legation attempting to reestablish relations, inviting the Portuguese to do the same to any Japanese who ventured onto foreign soil.[56] It was an effective deterrent to unauthorized contact in either direction. He confined trade

36 with the Dutch to the tiny island of Deshima. Some trade continued with China, both directly and through the quasi-independent Ryukyu islands (present-day Okinawa), but the Chinese shunned innovation at least as completely as Japan. A series of edicts prohibited the building of ships in excess of seventy-five tons and forbade any Japanese vessel or subject from going abroad, on pain of death. As late as the 1820s, solemn decrees commanded local inhabitants to arrest or kill any foreigners landing on Japanese soil and condemned Western learning as wicked and useless.[57]

Even domestic trade was hobbled. The daimyos restricted the movement of valuable commodities and issued their own currency notes, effectively confining the marketplace to the boundaries of their domains. Inadequate roads, internal tariffs, and legal impediments (including the need in some instances for a passport issued by an official of the shogunate) limited communication between fiefs.

No group in this carefully structured society had both the ability and the motivation to accumulate and invest capital. The shogunate carefully kept the daimyos from becoming too wealthy by a combination of levies and required public works.[58] The samurai code of bushido taught contempt for commerce and the virtues of a Spartan life. Artisans were generally prohibited from expanding their operations beyond household size. Merchants accounted for only about 5 to 6 percent of the population, and many of them were little more than peddlers. A few amassed some wealth through wholesale trade, but guild restrictions and the merchants' lowly social status (officially below peasants and just above the *burakumin,* Japan's untouchables) discouraged them from exposing that wealth by committing it to long-term projects.

A closed and fragmented market without new technology or capital does not progress. Japan in the early nineteenth century had changed very little in two centuries.[59] It remained a feudal, subsistence economy, with no commercial or industrial enterprises of any significance, its isolation from a rapidly changing world becoming steadily less splendid.

The arrival of Commodore Perry's steam-powered warships in 1853 shattered this stagnant tranquillity.[60] The shogun's representatives temporized, but neither polite diplomacy nor haughty rejection deflected Perry from his mission. He returned the following year with ten ships, the largest peacetime American fleet assembled to that date. With Perry obviously able to enforce his demands, the shogun capitulated and signed a treaty establishing an American consulate. This was followed in 1858 by a commercial treaty. European trading nations promptly secured similar treaties. The prediction of Townsend Harris, first U.S. consul-general to Japan, would prove a masterpiece of both prophecy and understatement: "The resources of Japan, when developed by the action of free trade, would show a vast amount of exchangeable values."[61]

The undeniable superiority of Western technology (and specifically military technology) discredited the long-standing policy of isolation. The shogun promptly rescinded his ban on the construction of oceangoing ships and founded various institutes of foreign studies. Periodicals featuring translations from Western journals began to appear. The shogun and several prominent samurai families sent young men to Europe and the United States for education in engineering.

It was too little and too late to save the etiolated and sclerotic Tokugawa shogunate. In 1864, a joint British and French squadron bombarded Shimonoseki in retaliation for an attack on foreign shipping, reducing the "impregnable" walls of the Choshu forts to rubble in a matter of hours. This action convincingly demonstrated the shogun's impotence in resisting foreign powers, an intolerable condition for a military ruler of any nation and particularly of Japan. Formerly subservient daimyos became restive and agitation began for restoration of effective power to the Emperor. This occurred in 1867 with the shogun's resignation.

The pace of change quickened during the Meiji Restoration, as the society veered sharply and with typically Japanese cohesion from feudalism to a market-based economy.[62] In 1869, the major daimyos voluntarily surrendered their lands to the Emperor, who finally abolished feudalism in 1871. The transferability of land encouraged the aggregation of holdings, increasing agricultural efficiency. Education, once the exclusive privilege of the samurai, was extended to all classes, with modern curricula and teaching methods imported from the West and state subsidies providing the classrooms and teachers. Primary school attendance rose from less than 30 percent in 1873 to more than 90 percent in 1902.[63] The Emperor founded universities on the

38 Western model. The Land Tax Reform of 1873 shifted assets to the modern economic sector, effectively pensioning the prominent daimyos and forcing their samurai retainers into the productive sector (where some of them founded firms that evolved into the powerful *zaibatsu* of the present).[64] Finally, in 1890, a new constitution established a representative assembly, although the Emperor remained the center of power.

Considerable domestic upheaval accompanied these changes, as the succession of three governments within a generation suggests. The replacement of feudalism by capitalist agriculture initially squeezed the peasants severely.[65] Some Tokugawa adherents resisted the restoration, even marching on Kyoto (the imperial city) before being defeated. Prominent officials of the government fell to assassins, and attacks on foreigners brought reprisals and forced the payment of reparations.[66] Stripping the samurai of their hereditary privileges provoked one insurrection of respectable proportions, the Satsuma Rebellion of 1877. Into this period, Japan also managed to compress two wars, with China (1894–95) and Russia (1904–5).

One-sided treaties, foreign interference, excessive military spending, domestic insurrection, and wars against larger neighbors are not ingredients in the World Bank's recommended formula for economic development. But these distractions counted for little against the forces of progress.

The Emperor had vowed that "knowledge shall be sought from all over the world," and the West brought a store of new technologies to be assimilated and exploited. "As a latecomer to industrialization Japan could use what the world had already learned. She could start with the most modern machines available without the burden of obsolete machinery that still carried capital obligations; she could start without unnecessary capital expenditures to cover the developmental process; she could use the latest managerial techniques. . . ."[67] The government spent its precious foreign exchange not on consumer goods, but on Western technical experts and education at Western universities.

Economies of scale required a national market. The government abolished internal tariffs and improved roads long accustomed to horses and palanquins to carry wheeled vehicles. Western engineers built the first railroad in 1872 and the first telegraph line in 1886. By 1907, the country had 3,276 miles of railways and nearly 100,000

miles of telegraph wires, including a submarine cable to Formosa.
The nation had unified itself economically in the course of one
generation.

Japan also reversed its prior seclusion from world markets with a
vengeance. Foreign trade required shipping: total tonnage of merchant steamships increased from 26,000 tons in 1873 to 1.5 million
tons by 1913, giving Japan the world's fifth-largest merchant fleet.[68]
Treaties with the Western powers limited import duties to a nominal
5 percent.[69] Though bitterly resented by the Japanese, these limits
forced the new industries to emulate Western competitors. In textiles,
for example, "predatory" American and European suppliers ravaged
Japanese producers during the early Meiji years.[70] The Japanese
fought back using Western technology, with imports of spinning
machinery rising fortyfold between 1887 and 1897.[71] Equipment
manufacturers helped their new customers, and the Japanese Cotton
Manufacturers' Association distributed a journal discussing the best
production practices. The results were immediate, with textile manufacturing output rising from ¥34 million in 1875 to ¥622 million in
1910, a seventeenfold increase.[72] Japan not only ceased importing
textiles, but substantially supplanted the United States as mainland
Asia's second source of cotton cloth. Manufactured exports increased
from ¥8 million in 1875 to ¥418 million in 1910, constituting nearly
80 percent of total exports by that date.[73] Overall, Japanese exports
grew at an average annual rate of 8.4 percent between 1880 and
1913, more than twice the rate of increase managed by the United
States.[74]

Both foreign and domestic capital fueled this progress. Western
firms invested heavily in the early railroads and mines and in the new
Japanese government's first bond issues. Anxious over possible foreign domination, the government sought to encourage saving and
investment. The incidence of taxation fell almost entirely on land and
consumption. With cheap labor and advanced technology, the nascent textile industry generated hefty profits for reinvestment. Overall, gross capital formation has been estimated at 10 percent of total
output during the early Meiji period, rising to 17 percent between
1886 and 1913.[75] Stock exchanges arose beginning in 1878 to funnel
this capital into private investment.

Together, these forces were irresistible. By 1896, there were nearly

40 five thousand commercial and industrial companies, including some sizable joint-stock companies, up from essentially none in 1853. Productivity increased sharply, particularly in the modern sectors. Total manufacturing output rose ninefold between 1870 and 1913.[76] Gross national product per capita rose 2.4 percent per year (adjusted for inflation) between 1890 and 1910, faster than the growth rate of the United States and more than twice that of the United Kingdom during the same period.[77] Japan had telescoped four generations of progress into as many decades.

The contrast to China during the same period is instructive.[78] Similarly closed to anything of barbarian (i.e., foreign) origin for centuries, China was similarly opened, by the Opium War of 1840 and the joint British-French march on Peking in 1860, a bloodier version of Commodore Perry's show of force in Japan. The results, however, were entirely different.[79] The Manchu dowager Empress, Yehonala Tzu Hsi, pursued an unrelenting policy of resistance (overt when possible, covert when not) to all forms of Western influence, whether political, cultural, or commercial, up to and including her tacit support for the Boxer Rebellion in 1900.[80] The peasants remained subservient and uneducated. Commercial enterprise depended upon, and was closely linked to, the pervasive Manchu bureaucracy. Officially protected monopolies were common.[81] The bureaucracy responded to Western contact by retreating into Confucian obscurantism and inertia. The government was forced to tolerate but certainly did not encourage foreign commerce, which remained largely restricted to major coastal and river ports. Shunning the foreign devils, China deprived itself of Western technology, trade, and capital, condemning its society to continuing stagnation and backwardness.

Despite its superior resources, China rapidly fell behind Japan. Its vast deposits of coal and iron ore did not prevent it from becoming a net importer of iron and steel. Attempts to establish a rail network repeatedly failed. By 1910, only three thousand miles of railway were constructed, less mileage than in Japan, despite China's more than twenty times greater expanse. Exports, roughly four times those of Japan as late as 1875, amounted to only about a third of Japan's by 1908. China remained a subsistence peasant-farming-based economy.

The Sino-Japanese War of 1894, although still early in Japan's

emergence, provided tangible proof of its rapid economic development. Despite China's seemingly overwhelming numerical and spatial
advantages, Japan's economic resources, particularly its superior navy
and commercial shipping, produced faster mobilization and better
logistical support, resulting in a series of rapid and decisive victories
with minimal casualties. Economic progress had accomplished for
Japan what centuries of martial discipline never could. China's humiliation by its traditional East Asian rival, combined with the Western
response to the Boxer Rebellion, began to bring China into the
modern world, a process that further internal turmoil promptly interrupted.

SOUTH KOREA

Almost exactly one hundred years later, another backward and isolated Asian nation proved that the formula still works.

Korea's chance at economic prosperity was long delayed by a
history of isolation, foreign interference, and internal discord. Having
narrowly warded off a Japanese invasion in 1592, and forced to pay
tribute to China for centuries, Korea became known as the Hermit
Kingdom for its assiduous avoidance of foreign contact. Japan was
the first to broach this isolation with a trade treaty in 1876, an
opening that the Western powers soon followed. Modernization
began. But a coup against the hereditary king in 1884 brought both
Chinese and Japanese involvement, and Korea became a pawn in the
struggle for East Asian supremacy. The Sino-Japanese War was, in
fact, precipitated by the intervention of both powers in response to
Korea's Tonghak Revolt in 1894. The Treaty of Shimonoseki (1895)
recognized Japanese hegemony in Korea. Japan's peace treaty with
Russia, its only other rival, further consolidated its position, leading
to the assumption of suzerainty over Korea in 1905. The Korean
emperor finally ceded complete sovereignty to Japan in 1910.

Japan's stewardship was harsh. Japan managed the Korean economy primarily for its own benefit, obtaining the rice, minerals, and
other raw materials needed to support its industrialization in return
for cotton textiles and other manufactured goods.[82] Japanese owned
the industrial capital introduced into Korea and retained control of its

42 investment through substantially all the managerial and technical positions. Koreans, deprived of most political, social, and commercial freedoms, directed their energies toward throwing off Japan's rule, not toward emulating the advanced economies of the West.

World War II ended Korea's colonial status, but at the cost of dividing the country into opposing areas of occupation, an Asian Berlin, writ large, with the North possessing most of the natural resources. The North's attempt at unification by force killed 1.3 million South Koreans, destroyed much of the industrial and housing base, and burdened the already overcrowded South with five million refugees. Korea was left backward, divided, and desolate, poorer than the Sudan, its people living on coarse rice and barley, utterly dependent on American charity for even this meager existence, with the armed hostility of the North requiring a military budget that regularly exceeded 5 percent of its output. Contemporary observers considered its case hopeless, wondering openly whether the game had been worth the candle. Even with hindsight, "the problems facing [South Korea's] leaders after the Korean War—a devastated infrastructure, huge military budgets and almost total dependence on loans from overseas—were no less daunting than those of the Japanese following the Second World War."[83]

One scant generation later, an ostensibly serious candidate for the presidency of the richest nation on earth could urge sanctions and protection against the economic threat posed by South Korea.

An infusion of foreign technology was crucial.[84] New hybrid strains of rice, mechanization, and synthetic fertilizers and pesticides enabled Korea to feed itself while freeing workers for industry. Inexpensive labor attracted direct investment from the United States and Japan, bringing access to advanced manufacturing technologies and allowing South Korea to leapfrog a century of development. As in Meiji Japan, European textile machinery manufacturers provided modern equipment, which, along with some Japanese technical assistance, allowed South Korea to progress quickly to higher-value-added synthetic-blend fabrics. The World Bank considered steelmaking "premature" in South Korea, but the Pohang Iron and Steel Co. (POSCO) adopted Japanese technology wholesale and sent hundreds of employees overseas for training, quickly becoming one of the most efficient integrated steel producers in the world. Hyundai followed the "apprentice" approach, assembling vehicles for Ford before launching its own models built under technology licenses from Japan. Korea's electronics industry did the same, beginning as a cheap assembler for American and Japanese concerns, and quickly integrating forward into brand-name consumer electronics and backward into semiconductors, growing from $138 million in sales in 1971 to $3.8 billion by 1981. Hyundai Heavy Industries started with complete European dockyard and ship designs and soon became the world's largest shipbuilder. Nuclear power figured prominently in the drive for electrification, which reduced the need for imported oil. None of this would have been possible without openness to new technology.[85]

Or without foreign markets. The tiny Korean market would support few industries on a competitive scale. Korea regularly exported the majority of its electronics and ships and much of its textile, cement, and steel output. In all, exports rose from negligible levels in 1961 to more than a third of GNP by the late 1980s, an average growth rate of more than 30 percent per year, twice that of Japan. Despite the inevitable (and sometimes justified) complaints of foreign competitors and their political supporters, Korea was itself anything but a closed market. Indeed, an endemic trade *deficit* troubled both Koreans and international economists through much of this period.

Korea needed a vast expansion of both physical and human capital to sustain this growth. Foreign loans and investment were crucial to initiate the process, after which domestic savings rose to supply the need, as the following table indicates.[86]

2.1 SOUTH KOREAN CAPITAL FORMATION, 1960–1980
(IN PERCENT OF GNP)

	Foreign Transfers	Gross Domestic Savings
1961–65	7.2	5.3
1966–70	3.9	13.7
1971–75	1.4	19.5
1976–80	0.9	25.4

44   A revamped and expanded educational system provided the skilled
and literate workers that the developing economy needed.[87] Primary
education was universal by the mid-1960s. Secondary enrollments
rose from 35 percent in 1965 to 87 percent in 1988, and higher
education enrollments from 6 percent to 37 percent during the same
period,[88] with heavy emphasis on vocational and technical training. In
all, the average number of years of formal schooling more than
doubled.[89] By training, culture, or luck, the labor force was conspicuously diligent and motivated. A belated political liberalization began
in the mid-1980s, defusing tensions and quelling agitation.

Even the bare statistics suggest the extent of the transformation.[90] Per capita gross domestic product in constant 1980 prices
rose from $564 in 1950 to $4,143 in 1987, moving Korea from
abject poverty into the upper middle class of nations.[91] Food intake,
housing, automobile and telephone ownership per capita, and every
other measure of consumption reflect this rise.[92] Literacy increased
from less than half of the population after World War II to 80
percent in the mid-1960s and 92 percent by the late 1980s. Life
expectancy, fifty-three years in the late 1950s, rose to seventy years
by 1989. A century of progress had been compressed into a single
generation.

The natural comparison is to North Korea, with its identical history
and superior natural resources. Under communist rule, North Korea
socialized substantially all production and closed itself off from world
markets; most of its meager trade was with the Soviet Union and
Eastern Europe. This insularity prevented the North from acquiring
the technology and know-how that the South exploited so effectively.
Without capitalism, capital remained scarce. Inflated official figures
placed per capita gross national product at $910 in 1988, one fourth
the level of South Korea. As of 1983, North Korea was estimated to
have twenty automobiles and one telephone receiver per two thousand people (compared to fifty-eight automobiles and four hundred
telephones in the South). Communicable diseases remain prevalent.
The country is mired in centrally planned poverty. Its recent overtures
to the South, after decades of overt and often violent hostility, are
striking admissions of failure.

.   .   .

These examples are not unique. The United States and Germany, for example, enjoyed sustained bursts of innovation, market expansion, and investment during the late nineteenth century, and quickly surpassed England as a result. These few forces assure progress, and their absence equally assures stagnation, almost without regard to other considerations. This is a less encouraging conclusion than it may initially sound, because those forces are irretrievably spent.

NOTES

1. Douglass North, *Structure and Change in Economic History*, Ch. 12, p. 160, W.W. Norton, 1981. To similar effect is Donald McCloskey, "The Industrial Revolution 1780–1860: A Survey," Ch. 2, at p. 53, in Joel Mokyr (ed.), *The Economics of the Industrial Revolution*, Rowman & Littlefield, 1985.

2. Paul Johnson, *The Birth of the Modern: World Society 1815–1830*, Ch. 7, p. 571, HarperCollins, 1991.

3. Paul Mantoux, *The Industrial Revolution in the Eighteenth Century*, Part I, Ch. 3, Harper & Row, 1962, describes the eighteenth-century enclosure movement.

4. *Encyclopaedia Britannica*, 11th ed., Vol. 6, pp. 782–83, 1910.

5. Johnson, *Birth of the Modern*, Ch. 5, p. 375.

6. See Fernand Braudel, *The Wheels of Commerce*, pp. 280–82, Harper & Row, 1983.

7. T.S. Ashton, *The Industrial Revolution 1760–1830*, Ch. 3, Oxford Univ. Press, 1968 cd. Mantoux, *Industrial Revolution in the Eighteenth Century*, Part 2, Chs. 1 and 2, provides a succinct treatment of the early inventions in textile manufacturing.

8. Samuel Crompton's mule reduced the time needed to spin one hundred pounds of cotton thread to three hundred man-hours, compared to fifty thousand hours for an Indian hand spinner. Joel Mokyr, *The Lever of Riches*, Ch. 5, pp. 98–99, Oxford Univ. Press, 1990.

9. Robert Heilbroner, *The Making of Economic Society*, Ch. 4, p. 80, Prentice-Hall, 1980; Johnson, *Birth of the Modern*, Ch. 7, p. 544.

10. Mantoux, *Industrial Revolution in the Eighteenth Century*, Part 3, Ch. 3, p. 404.

11. Mokyr, *Lever of Riches*, Ch. 10, p. 256.

12. On France's dominant position in the middle of the eighteenth century, see Paul Kennedy, *The Rise and Fall of the Great Powers*, pp. 73–177, Random House, 1987.

13. Mokyr, *Lever of Riches*, Ch. 10, p. 258.

14. Mokyr, *Lever of Riches*, Ch. 10, p. 253.

15. Fernand Braudel, *Perspective of the World*, Ch. 6, p. 573, Harper & Row, 1984.

16. Deane & Habakkuk, "The Take-off in Britain," reprinted in W.W. Rostow

(ed.), *The Economics of Take-off into Sustained Growth,* Ch. 4, pp. 69–70, Macmil- **47**
lan, 1963.

17. Mokyr, *Lever of Riches,* Ch. 5, p. 111.

18. "The sound of six sous seemed to act as a trigger. Millions of buyers, poor
people, who had never bought [textiles] before, began to stir. . . . [T]he result was
a . . . revolution in cleanliness and the suddenly improved appearance of the poor
home: people had bed linen, body linen, linen for the table and the window: it was
now possessed by whole classes who had never had any since the world began."
Braudel, *Wheels of Commerce,* Ch. 2, p. 183, quoting Jules Michelet. This was an
early illustration of the life-transforming potential of technology.

19. Mantoux, *Industrial Revolution in the Eighteenth Century,* Part 2, Ch. 3, and
Charles Hyde, *Technological Change in the British Iron Industry 1700–1870,* Part
1, Princeton Univ. Press, 1977, describe eighteenth-century developments in iron-
making.

20. Fernand Braudel, *Structures of Everyday Life,* Ch. 5, pp. 362–67, Harper &
Row, 1981, estimates that Europe consumed 200 million tons of firewood and
charcoal in 1789. In order to conserve wood, blast furnaces and ironworks commonly operated only one year in two or three.

21. Mokyr, *Lever of Riches,* Ch. 5, p. 85.

22. Mantoux, *Industrial Revolution in the Eighteenth Century,* Part 1, Ch. 2, p.
113.

23. Braudel, *Wheels of Commerce,* Ch. 1, p. 43.

24. See McCloskey, "The Industrial Revolution 1780–1860: A Survey," Ch. 2, at
p. 64, in Mokyr (ed.), *Economics of the Industrial Revolution;* Hawke & Higgins,
"Transport and Social Overhead Capital," Ch. 12, at p. 234, in Floud & McClos-
key (eds.), *The Economic History of Britain Since 1700,* Vol. 1; *1700–1860,*
Cambridge Univ. Press, 1981 (hereafter *Economic History of Britain*); and Braudel,
Perspective of the World, Ch. 6, p. 583.

25. Hyde, *Technological Change in the British Iron Industry,* Part 2, Ch. 9, and
Mokyr, *Lever of Riches,* Ch. 5, p. 95, describe Neilson's hot blast process and its
effect on British iron-making.

26. The *Rocket* was, of course, no more than a hint of the locomotive potential
of steam. Within a year, Peter Cooper in the United States had built the *Tom
Thumb,* with triple the traction power of the *Rocket.*

27. W.W. Rostow, *The World Economy: History and Prospect,* Table III-21, p.
152, Univ. of Texas Press, 1978.

28. G.R. Hawke & J.P.P. Higgins, "Transport and Social Overhead Capital," Ch.
12, pp. 242–44, in *Economic History of Britain.*

29. See Rosenberg & Ezell, *How the West Grew Rich: The Economic Transformation of the Industrial World,* Ch. 5, pp. 163–65, Basic Books, 1986, arguing that
nineteenth-century manufacturing technology so increased output that expanded
markets became essential.

30. W.W. Rostow, *The Stages of Economic Growth,* p. 54, Cambridge Univ. Press,
2d ed., 1971.

31. Supplying the mills also expanded trade: Britain imported three million pounds

48   of raw cotton in 1750, sixty million pounds in 1802. Mantoux, *Industrial Revolution in the Eighteenth Century,* Part 2, Ch. 2, p. 252.

32. See McCloskey, "The Industrial Revolution 1780–1860: A Survey," Table 2.2 and accompanying text, in Mokyr (ed.), *Economics of the Industrial Revolution,* estimating the productivity gain in shipping at 2.3 percent per year.

33. Mantoux, *Industrial Revolution in the Eighteenth Century,* Part 1, Ch. 2, pp. 100–2, charts total export tonnage and value from 1700 to 1800.

34. Mokyr, *Lever of Riches,* Ch. 6, p. 129.

35. Deane & Habakkuk, "The Take-off in Britain," Ch. 4, p. 79, in Rostow (ed.), *Economics of Take-off into Sustained Growth.*

36. *Wealth of Nations,* Book 1, Chs. 1–3.

37. Mantoux, *Industrial Revolution in the Eighteenth Century,* Part 3, Ch. 2. Wedgwood, a member of the Royal Society, also pioneered in the chemistry of clays and glazes and the manufacture of earthenware drain and water pipes.

38. "Invention . . . rarely thrives in a community of simple peasants or unskilled manual labourers: only when division of labour has developed, so that men devote themselves to a single product or process, does it come to harvest." Ashton, *Industrial Revolution,* Ch. 1, p. 12.

39. *Wealth of Nations,* Book 1, Ch. 1.

40. Ashton, *Industrial Revolution,* Ch. 4, p. 66.

41. C.H. Feinstein, "Capital Accumulation and the Industrial Revolution," Ch. 7, Table 7.2, in *Economic History of Britain.* The rate of investment before the 1760s was likely even lower.

42. Feinstein, "Capital Accumulation and the Industrial Revolution," Ch. 7, Table 7.1, in *Economic History of Britain.* Additions to capital stock by sector from 1761 to 1860 are tabulated in Table 7.3.

43. Joel Mokyr, "The Industrial Revolution and the New Economic History," Ch. 1, p. 34, in Mokyr (ed.), *Economics of the Industrial Revolution.* "The transmutation of mercantile into fixed capital was an important cause (as well as a result) of the expansion of manufacture." Ashton, *Industrial Revolution,* Ch. 4, p. 69.

44. See Friedrich Hayek, *The Constitution of Liberty,* Ch. 4, Univ. of Chicago Press, 1960, and Edmund Burke, *Reflections on the Revolution in France,* pp. 99–100, Liberal Arts Press, 1955.

45. See, for example, John Chamberlain, *The Roots of Capitalism,* p. 38, Liberty Press, 1959, regarding French regulation of textiles.

46. See Braudel, *Wheels of Commerce,* pp. 354, 360–61, for a comparison of transport in France and England in the eighteenth century. Removal of internal trade barriers in England began as early as the end of the thirteenth century. See Braudel, *Perspective of the World,* p. 289.

47. Kennedy, *Rise and Fall of Great Powers,* pp. 149, 171.

48. McCloskey, "The Industrial Revolution 1780–1860: A Survey," in Mokyr (ed.), *Economics of the Industrial Revolution,* Ch. 2, Table 2.2. Feinstein, "Capital Accumulation and the Industrial Revolution," in *Economic History of Britain,* Ch. 7,

Tables 7.5–7.7 and accompanying text, attributes most of the gain in productivity to **49** innovation, economies of scale, and improvement in the quality of workers.

49. Carlo Cipolla, *The Economic History of World Population*, Ch. 2, Table 3, Barnes & Noble, 7th ed., 1978; Michel Beaud, *A History of Capitalism 1500–1980*, p. 86, Macmillan, 1984.

50. Rostow, *World Economy*, Ch. 12, p. 130.

51. Lindert & Williamson, "English Workers' Living Standards During the Industrial Revolution: A New Look," in Mokyr (ed.), *Economics of the Industrial Revolution*, Ch. 9, Table 9.5 and Fig. 9.1. To similar effect is R.M. Hartwell, *The Industrial Revolution and Economic Growth*, Ch. 13, Methuen, 1971.

52. Harold Perkin, *The Origins of Modern English Society, 1780–1880*, p. 3, Univ. of Toronto Press, 1969. To similar effect is Johnson, *Birth of the Modern*, Ch. 10, p. 794.

53. James Clavell, *Shogun*, Atheneum, 1975, is a fictionalized account of the events leading up to the Battle of Sekigahara. Aside from changing the names of the principals and some very un-Japanese romantic embroidery, the plot sticks closely to the historical record, including the improbable involvement of Will Adams, a shipwrecked English pilot (the Blackthorne character in the novel), as a counselor to Ieyasu (Toranaga).

54. Rice paddies in the eighteenth century produced roughly five times as many calories per acre as wheat fields. Braudel, *Structures of Everyday Life*, Ch. 2, pp. 147–51.

55. Sumiya & Taira (eds.), *An Outline of Japanese Economic History 1603–1940*, Ch. 1, pp. 22–23, Univ. of Tokyo Press, 1979.

56. *Encyclopaedia Britannica*, 11th ed., Vol. 15, p. 235, 1910.

57. Johnson, *Birth of the Modern*, Ch. 10, pp. 802–3.

58. Sumiya & Taira (eds.), *Outline of Japanese Economic History*, Ch. 5, pp. 93–94.

59. Foreign powers began to knock loudly at Japan's closed door early in the 1800s, which motivated some efforts to change, most notably the Tenpo Reform in 1830. So long as these efforts continued to be predicated on a closed feudal society, they produced little progress.

60. See Peter Booth Wiley, *Yankees in the Land of the Gods: Commodore Perry and the Opening of Japan*, Viking Penguin, 1990, for a description of Perry's mission from both American and Japanese perspectives.

61. Harris is quoted in Klein & Ohkawa (eds.), *Economic Growth: The Japanese Experience Since the Meiji Era*, Ch. 6, p. 162, Richard D. Irwin, 1968.

62. Meiji, meaning "enlightened rule," was the name taken by the emperor upon his accession. On the emergence of the modern Japanese economy generally, see William Lockwood, *The Economic Development of Japan: Growth and Structural Change 1868–1938*, Princeton Univ. Press, 1954.

63. Sumiya & Taira (eds.), *Outline of Japanese Economic History*, Ch. 12, p. 227.

64. Sumiya & Taira (eds.), *Outline of Japanese Economic History*, Ch. 14, pp. 254, 259, 262–63.

50 65. Angus Maddison, *Economic Growth in Japan and the USSR*, Ch. 2, p. 11, W.W. Norton, 1969.

66. Stephen Turnbull, *The Book of the Samurai*, Chs. 10 and 11, Gallery Books, 1982, describes some of the tumult associated with the passing of the Tokugawa era.

67. Marion Levy, "Contrasting Factors in the Modernization of China and Japan," Ch. 17, p. 529, in Simon Kuznets (ed.), *Economic Growth: Brazil, India, Japan*, Duke Univ. Press, 1955. Japan was, in this regard, a paradigm of the underdeveloped nation positioned to use advances developed at substantial cost in more advanced economies. See the discussion below and in Chapters 3 and 7.

68. Maddison, *Economic Growth in Japan and the USSR*, Table 7, p. 29.

69. Import duties permitted under the treaties rose to 15.65 percent in 1899. Japan regained complete tariff autonomy only in 1911.

70. Maddison, *Economic Growth in Japan and the USSR*, Ch. 2, pp. 24–25.

71. Shigeto Tsuru, "The Take-off in Japan, 1868–1900," Ch. 8, p. 139, in W.W. Rostow (ed.), *Economics of Take-off into Sustained Growth*.

72. Yuichi Shionoya, "Patterns of Industrial Development," Table 3A-1, in Klein & Ohkawa (eds.), *Economic Growth: The Japanese Experience Since the Meiji Era*. Ironworks and steel foundries followed a similar pattern, with total output of metals rising thirty-six-fold over the same period. Adjusting the figures for inflation would roughly halve the overall increase.

73. Shionoya, "Patterns of Industrial Development," Table 3A-4, in Klein & Ohkawa (eds.), *Economic Growth: The Japanese Experience Since the Meiji Era*.

74. Maddison, *Economic Growth in Japan and the USSR*, Ch. 2, p. 29.

75. Raymond Goldsmith, *The Financial Development of India, Japan, and the United States*, Ch. 3, pp. 25–26, Yale Univ. Press, 1983. The early Meiji data are not considered reliable. See also Edwin Reubens, "Foreign Capital and Domestic Development in Japan," Ch. 6, pp. 181–82, 198, in Kuznets (ed.), *Economic Growth: Brazil, India, Japan*, and Maddison, *Economic Growth in Japan and the USSR*, Ch. 2, p. 33.

76. Maddison, *Economic Growth in Japan and the USSR*, Table F-1, p. 164. Shionoya, "Patterns of Industrial Development," Table 3A-1, in Klein & Ohkawa (eds.), *Economic Growth: The Japanese Experience Since the Meiji Era*, estimates a thirteenfold increase, not adjusted for inflation, between 1875 and 1910.

77. Rostow, *World Economy*, pp. 388, 418. To similar effect is Simon Kuznets, "Trends in Level and Structure of Consumption," in Klein & Ohkawa (eds.), *Economic Growth: The Japanese Experience Since the Meiji Era*, Ch. 7, Table 7-1 (showing indexed gross domestic product per capita from 1879).

78. Milton Friedman, *Free to Choose*, pp. 31, 53–54, Harcourt Brace, 1979, compares Meiji Japan to India after independence from Britain to reach similar conclusions. China after the Taiping Rebellion was selected for this comparison because of the many parallels in time and circumstances.

79. The cause of China's sharply differing response to outwardly similar events is, of course, a matter of speculation. Braudel, *Wheels of Commerce*, pp. 131, 136, and

585–94, suggests that the pervasive Manchu bureaucracy stultified development of preindustrial markets, with lasting repercussions. See also Levy, "Contrasting Factors in the Modernization of China and Japan," Ch. 17, in Kuznets (ed.), *Economic Growth: Brazil, India, Japan,* arguing that differences in the importance of the family and the status of merchants contributed significantly to the differing responses.

80. Yehonala rose from being an imperial concubine to become, through some high daring, the regent upon the emperor's death, the last absolute queen in history. Pearl Buck's *Imperial Woman,* 1956, is a romanticized version of her life. For a less flattering fictional portrait of the young Yehonala, as well as the events surrounding the British-French march on Peking, see George MacDonald Fraser, *Flashman and the Dragon,* Collins Harvill, 1985.

81. Rostow, *World Economy,* p. 528. By contrast, Restoration Japan depended primarily on private enterprise, privatizing inefficient state-owned enterprises and not interfering with the textile industry, its principal early source of exports. Rostow, p. 417.

82. Byung-Nak Song, *The Rise of the Korean Economy,* Ch. 3, p. 44, Oxford Univ. Press, 1990.

83. Kotkin & Kishimoto, *The Third Century: America's Resurgence in the Asian Era,* Ch. 2, p. 48, Ballantine Books, 1988. Herman Kahn, *World Economic Development: 1979 and Beyond,* Ch. 6, Westview Press, 1979, describes a number of the factors that contributed to the South Korean economic takeoff.

84. Alice Amsden, *Asia's Next Giant: South Korea and Late Industrialization,* Chs. 10–12, Oxford Univ. Press, 1989, discusses foreign technology transfers in several industries.

85. "Not enough credit has been given to the outside world. It was the progress in many other countries which provided the tremendous backlog of products and know-how that could be tapped. . . . The primary springboard for leapfrogging was access to more advanced technologies." Jon Woronoff, *Korea's Economy: Man-Made Miracle,* pp. 184–85, Pace Int'l Research, 1983.

86. The data in Table 2.1 are from Yusuf & Peters, *Savings Behavior and Its Implications for Domestic Resource Mobilization: The Case of the Republic of Korea,* Table 1, World Bank Staff Working Papers No. 628, 1984. All figures have been rounded. Foreign Transfers include direct investment, loans, and development aid. To similar effect is Angus Maddison, *The World Economy in the Twentieth Century,* Table 6.7, p. 76, OECD, 1989.

87. Amsden, *Asia's Next Giant,* Ch. 9, provides data on the rising education levels of the South Korean work force from 1946 through 1983.

88. World Bank, *World Development Report 1991,* Table 29, pp. 260–61, Oxford Univ. Press, 1991.

89. Maddison, *World Economy in the Twentieth Century,* Table C-12.

90. Unless otherwise indicated, current Korean data are from World Bank, *World Development Report 1991,* or *Britannica World Data Annual 1991.*

52   91. Maddison, *World Economy in the Twentieth Century*, Table 1.3, p. 19 (conversion from won to dollar based on purchasing power parity).

92. The *Economist*, 14–20 July 1990, p. 19, estimates South Korean food intake at 2,900 calories per day, telephone and television ownership at two hundred per thousand population, and passenger car ownership at twenty-nine per thousand population.

Chapter Three

THE DWINDLING FORCES
OF PROGRESS

Elections do more than pick legislators and presidents. They also serve to educate the public. The 1992 election was no exception. It proved to anyone who was still in doubt that neither party has any grasp of the dominant long-term trends gripping the American (and world) economy.

Not that the candidates ignored economic issues. Their speeches, debates, and position papers were full of diagnoses and prescriptions. Taxes are too high (on capital gains), or too low (on the rich). Spending is too low to rebuild the cities or pull the economy out of recession, or too high to narrow the deficit. There is too much or too little regulation. Foreigners (read Asians) are selling too much and charging too little, or they are not buying enough. Food is too expensive (for the single parent) or too cheap (for the farmer). The economy is recovering nicely, or the recovery is a statistical mirage. American manufacturers have lost their competitiveness, or they are sacrificing their workers on the altar of profits. Consumers are spending too little, or they have too much debt. And so on. The point is not that the positions are conflicting and sometimes incoherent, which is to be expected, but that they are almost irrelevant.

The political time horizon is simply too short to encompass much that matters. Candidates and commentators limit their discussions to conditions that can change or be changed before the next election. This means moving the economy closer to its short-term capacity

54   limits, with consumers spending, people working, factories humming, businesses investing, etc. The gap between actual and potential production depends on the business cycle, interest rates, budget and trade deficits, inflation, consumer confidence, and other short-term factors. Politicians can influence these factors, however imperfectly, by pulling the right fiscal, monetary, regulatory, and foreign policy levers.

Real progress, on the other hand, stretches the boundaries of productive capacity. The factors that govern such progress have little in common with those that govern economic cycles; indeed, the rate of progress may suffer from policies that produce short-term prosperity and vice versa.[1] A progress platform could promise years of sacrifice for important interest groups, with the uncertain benefits spread among the public at large over a span of decades. Few candidates seem eager to stake out that territory. Most economists follow the politicians in neglecting the long term,[2] in part because the forces of progress are alien to the standard economic models and cannot be manipulated with economists' familiar tools.[3] Keynesian demand management, supply-side tax cuts, easy monetary policy, public works projects, and the like may stimulate output under the right circumstances, but the sustained rise in productive capacity over the last 250 years owes nothing to them.[4] Despite the attention lavished on such short-term policies, their role in deciding an economy's output of goods and services pales in comparison to that of long-term progress: a jet airplane does not need full throttle to outdistance a Conestoga.

Material progress is, in any event, passing from the realm of politics into that of history. Three forces—innovation, market expansion, and capital accumulation—produced and sustained it, and they are spent. Any effort to understand the long-term trends must begin with an analysis of these forces and the limitations they are confronting.

INVENTING WEALTH

The free market virtually forces competitors to innovate.[5] Consider the beleaguered owner of a widget factory. The price his widgets fetch in the marketplace barely covers his labor, raw material, and capital costs. Other widget makers, who incur about the same costs and whose widgets are comparable, undercut him when he tries to charge more. The need to end this "cutthroat" price competition has been floated more than once, but the effort falls apart almost before it starts, and he rightly suspects that the Justice Department would have taken a dim view if such an attempt had ever succeeded.[6] He strives to eliminate waste and raise quality, but so do his competitors, with about equal success. All too rarely, demand creeps ahead of supply, buyers cannot squeeze him so hard, and he is able to pad his margins. Such respites are always brief. Some competitor, either foreign or domestic, adds capacity, and margins fall again. The profit on the books at the end of the year is little more than the owner could earn by selling the factory and investing the proceeds in securities. It seems a poor reward for all the effort, risk, and sacrifice.

His research and development department delivers one of two solutions:

(1) It has discovered an improved widget-making process that increases production using the same amounts of labor and material. No one else has caught on yet, so the market price stays the same. By barely shaving his price, the owner can sell the entire increased output. The cost reduction is pure profit.[7]

(2) It has enhanced the widget with a new feature that adds nothing to the cost of manufacture. A patent blocks competitors from copying the feature immediately. The customers complain and chafe, but most ultimately agree to pay more to obtain the added feature. The higher price drops straight to the bottom line.

For once, the owner has some breathing space.

It will not last. His profit arises from the loss of equilibrium in the market.[8] He sells more units, his competitors less. His higher profitability allows him to expand capacity, win the close bids, or extend his distribution to build market share. To survive, his competitors must respond in kind.[9] This creates a Wonderland existence, with every firm innovating as fast as it can just to maintain its place. When enough competitors match the original innovation, equilibrium is restored. Either (1) the price falls to the new lower cost of production, or (2) the new feature becomes standard on widgets selling at the old price. In either case, profits return to their unsatisfactory pre-innovation levels, and the cycle starts anew.

56   This cycle of competitive innovation (which the Appendix presents graphically) has produced the regular product improvements or cost reductions in steel, automobiles, telephone service, pharmaceuticals, consumer electronics, computers,[10] and myriad other goods and services in the market, accounting in the process for much of the progress of the industrial era.[11]

But it has come at a price. The advanced economies had to invest an ever rising share of their expanding national incomes in research and development to maintain the pace of innovation. Total research and development spending in the United States rose from 0.1 percent of the gross national product in 1920, to 0.7 percent in 1940, to an average of 2.8 percent during the 1960s.[12] Scientists and engineers were doubling in number every eleven years, an exponential rise that would have consumed the entire work force within a few decades.[13] This trend obviously could not continue, and it has not done so. Research and development spending declined to less than 2.3 percent of gross national product in the 1970s, before partially rebounding to nearly 2.6 percent in the 1980s.[14] Much of the spending increase in the 1980s was in defense-related research, not all of which contributes to market production. Flat or declining investment in innovation may in part reflect the slower growth of the economy or a dearth of research projects that show real commercial promise. But this symptom also becomes a cause of slowing progress by strangling innovation at the source.[15]

This plateau in spending coincides uncomfortably with an ongoing and irreversible rise in the cost of conducting scientific research.[16] Scientific discovery depends on research tools to gather and analyze data. The available technology is rarely adequate to the task, as the subsisting theory by definition already explains the preexisting observations. Only new technology that yields new observations can establish the superiority of a new theory.[17] The required tools necessarily become more costly as the subject of inquiry becomes more distant from the powers of unaided human observation. Many of the tourists visiting Edison's laboratory at Greenfield Village can readily understand (and could, if they wished, afford to buy or have made) the equipment he used. As recently as 1952, Watson and Crick divined the molecular structure of DNA using Tinkertoy-like models, X-ray photographs, and scientific knowledge that a talented undergraduate could have mastered in a week.[18]

But scientists have already made the easy (or, more precisely, cheap) conquests; nature has reserved her remaining favors for the very well heeled. Even the ordinary tools of current scientific research—mass spectrometers, scanning-tunneling microscopes, supercomputers, radio telescopes—represent major investments. The equipment needed for the most advanced research is frequently beyond the understanding even of its users and beyond the budget of all but governments and large institutions. "To carry out a scientific experiment in the new era literally takes 'an act of Congress.' "[19] The Hubble Space Telescope, launched at a cost of $1.5 billion, requires 290 technicians for its monitoring and control. The expense of extracting deeper secrets from subatomic particles is staggering: the superconducting supercollider is projected to cost $8 billion to construct. Other branches of science are not immune from this trend. Many research protocols in biology and medicine now require detailed lifetime or multigenerational studies of tens of thousands of laboratory animals or test subjects. The tension between flat or slowly rising total spending and the exponentially increasing cost of conducting research unavoidably slows the pace of discovery, a trend that bodes ill for continuing material progress.

Many discoveries that do occur are becoming ever farther removed from, and conspicuously useless in serving, human needs.[20] A nineteenth-century writer on technology could fairly observe that "discoveries in science, however remote from the interests of every-day life they may at first appear, ultimately confer unforeseen and incalculable benefits on mankind."[21] Such a statement would now seem naive or ill-informed. Two of the signal scientific advances of the twentieth century, the special and general theories of relativity, have had only a negligible impact on daily life seventy years after their announcement.[22] Physicists create and annihilate particles and antiparticles using ever larger accelerators in a race to detect the last few remaining quarks, leptons, and force carriers in the "standard model."[23] Once every few million collisions, some interesting particle is produced and survives for a period measured in trillionths of a trillionth of a second, an existence so fleeting that it is not so much an observation as an inference teased out of reams of computer data. The energy levels required are far higher than those in the center of the sun. Many of these particles are believed to have existed independently for only a fraction of a second following the Big Bang. In the

58   words of one respected particle physicist, "it is hard to escape the view that this process is reaching its natural end."[24] This is the purest of science; no possible utility is claimed for the discoveries sought.

Particle physicists have plenty of company in plumbing the depths of esoterica. Mathematical physicists want to know whether space is quantized at dimensions of 10^{-32} centimeter, about one trillionth of the diameter of a proton.[25] The great astronomical discoveries of the last few decades (quasars, pulsars, etc.) are at distances of millions or billions of light-years. The distribution of galaxies in space became the subject of intense research as a result of recent discoveries of dense concentrations (walls) and voids (bubbles) of galaxies in the universe, measuring tens or hundreds of millions of light-years across.[26] Among the scheduled tasks of the Hubble Space Telescope are the more accurate measurement of the distances to other galaxies and of the rate of expansion of the universe. Research like this may shed light on the prognosis for the universe in 100 billion years. Most high-level work in mathematics has ceased to be of any interest to scientists in even the most mathematically oriented specialties.[27] Journals in the United States alone publish on the order of one million scientific and technical papers per year, most of them obviously intended to be read only by other researchers in the field and cited in still more papers.[28] Government-sponsored research into irrelevant topics has become standard fare for Congressional speechmaking when an appearance of thriftiness is needed.

Scientists do not spend their lives in such work out of any fetish for the obscure or desire to waste public money. On the contrary, questions with at least some possible human significance have always headed the agendas of scientists and those who pay them. But most of those questions have already been answered adequately, and hordes of researchers pursue the remainder. Scientific research occurs at the frontiers. From quantum electrodynamics at one end of the spectrum to general relativity at the other, physicists have pushed those frontiers to distances both smaller and larger and velocities and energies greater than those of any possible practical concern.[29] They have all but given up looking for anything new within the realm of normal experience. "[W]e should not expect any real surprises in future investigations of physical phenomena on the ordinary human scale. . . . [O]ur understanding of phenomena on this scale is accurate enough that any new discoveries will also fit easily into the picture we have."[30] Astronomers have already answered all the questions of any terrestrial moment. Mathematicians from ancient Greece through Newton, Leibniz, Fourier, and others provided the mathematical tools necessary to formalize and represent discoveries in the physical sciences. Understanding is less complete, and certainly less precise, in other sciences, but the same principle applies. Nature is invariant. As scientists exhaust its more familiar regions, they must migrate to its hinterlands in search of something new to discover. The uselessness in any material sense of much current research is a tribute to the breadth of the successes already achieved. Science has largely mastered and therefore outgrown its merely human tasks.

Prophets of the limitless bounty of science are fond of citing past predictions that the era of scientific progress had ended, predictions that were, of course, followed by major breakthroughs. The most oft-quoted statement is probably that of A. A. Michelson in 1894: "The more important fundamental laws and facts of physical science have all been discovered and these are now so firmly established that the possibility of their ever being supplanted in consequence of new discoveries is exceedingly remote. . . . '[F]uture discoveries must be looked for in the sixth place of decimals,' "[31] The twentieth century soon made that statement laughable. (Michelson's statement was odd even without the benefit of hindsight, as nineteenth century physics had no explanation for such basic phenomena as the solidity of matter. A physicist of Michelson's caliber surely knew that the science of the day was, at a minimum, seriously incomplete.) Michelson's prediction may, of course, have been premature rather than wrong; even the boy who cried wolf was eventually correct.[32] But the argument here rests on a much more modest proposition: that the discoveries with the greatest bearing on daily life, and specifically on economic man, have already been made, and those that remain will require ever larger investments of resources to uncover.

Which could evoke another facile response: some of today's science may just be wrong, as much science of the past was. But every new scientific theory, no matter how revolutionary, must conform to the preexisting theory within its realm of validity, that is, where the theory itself conforms to the facts. Quantum mechanics and special relativity upset Newtonian mechanics, but Newton's equations remain an

60 excellent approximation for, and continue to be used to describe, the portion of nature that he was able to observe. A new theory thus differs from the old one only at the boundaries, not within the realm that had already been adequately explained, which, in this case, is the realm that affects people's lives.[33]

The diminishing practical returns available from research may, in turn, discourage the expenditures that would be needed to extract what potential remains.[34] To those not part of the process, only tangible benefits justify society's continuing investment in science.[35] This may be too pinched a view. Discovering the secrets of nature, including those that lack any practical application, is surely a praiseworthy undertaking, and no less deserving of support than many others that the public subsidizes.[36] But the declining harvest of useful advances inevitably produces questions about the wisdom of the ongoing investment.[37] The general lack of interest in the space program suggests that science for its own sake faces growing skepticism. Flagging public support for research only compounds the increasing difficulty and scarcity of significant new discoveries.

These trends bode ill for the prospect of unabated material progress. The deceleration of science and technology must produce a corresponding slowdown in the appearance of science-initiated products and services.[38] Historically, these have included many of the major gains in the ability to satisfy human needs and wants. They are as close to a free lunch as the dismal science permits. Without dividends from innovation, only more effort and sacrifice would improve living standards. A trend toward more effort and sacrifice has not been evident in recent years, nor is such a development likely, for reasons discussed below and in Chapter 6. The story of economic progress with a shrinking contribution from new technology will be *Hamlet* without the Prince.

TRADE WINDS

The least appreciated source of material progress has been market expansion. Technology and capital have vanquished distance, bringing buyers and sellers together across continents and oceans. In one crucial respect, foreign trade is the same as buying groceries at the local supermarket: both parties benefit from the transaction. The United States is richer, not poorer, for having inexpensive and high-quality goods on offer from foreign sellers. "Fair trade," the accepted euphemism for protectionism, means paying more for less, which is not a promising formula for material gain. But even if rational self-interest triumphs over the latest spate of economic masochism, most of the progress available from this source has already been extracted. Market expansion has nearly arrived at its logical end—worldwide market integration.

THE SHRINKING WORLD. With mid-nineteenth century England increasingly unified and accessible by road, canal, and railroad, the focus shifted to foreign markets.

Open-ocean sailing depended on the vagaries of the weather and was sharply curtailed in stormy winter months. Atlantic crossings required three weeks eastbound and six weeks westbound through the first half of the nineteenth century. Freight charges remained high. Longer voyages required faster vessels, which American shipbuilders supplied in the form of the clippers.[39] Their long and narrow V-shaped keels and sharp bows allowed them to slice through the water with minimal resistance. With sails fully set, they carried up to twelve thousand square yards of canvas (an area greater than two football fields). This design brought speed, but at a price. The clippers' narrow hulls provided limited room for cargo, and crews of fifty or more were needed to set the vast expanses of sail. The result was freight charges of $50 or more per ton to the Far East, effectively limiting cargoes to high-value goods.

Steam and iron were again the answer. Steamers were squat and ungainly next to the majestic clippers. But what they lacked in style they made up in practicality. Their high-pressure compound steam engines turned screw propellers to push them through fair weather and foul, enabling them to complete twice as many transatlantic crossings per year as sailing ships. Their iron hulls made them not only more durable, but also larger and stronger.[40] By the late 1800s, the standard British tramp steamers carried five times the cargo of the largest clippers with only a slightly larger crew.[41] As a result, ocean freight rates declined an average of 1.5 percent per year during the second half of the nineteenth century.[42] By 1900, steamers repre-

62 sented more than 90 percent of the carrying capacity of the world's merchant shipping.[43]

The telegraph promoted the efficient use of this expanding capacity.[44] Merchants had always chosen their cargoes and destinations based on stale information, then placed a trusted agent on board each ship to negotiate the sale and to purchase a cargo for the return voyage. Some achieved wealth, others bankruptcy, but the process hardly assured that goods would move from areas of surplus to areas of scarcity. In 1866, however, the first transatlantic telegraph cable was laid. Within a few decades, traders could track market conditions worldwide, reducing the risk of shifts in supply or demand that often occurred during extended round trips. The ships themselves could be operated more efficiently, with sales and return cargoes arranged in advance to minimize unproductive time in port.

These trends continued through the twentieth century. Freight has moved ever faster and at ever lower cost with new transportation technologies, notably including diesel power for ships, trucking to supplement railroads, and airplanes for perishable and other time-critical merchandise. Radio communications track shipments instantaneously, worldwide.

Innovation has also expanded trade by literally shrinking the mix of goods.[45] Less than one hundred pounds of optical fiber has the same message-carrying capacity as a ton of copper cable. Plastic composites are much lighter than steel of equal strength. The most technologically advanced goods are commonly the smallest and lightest for their value. One hundred tons of cement, an automobile, two personal computers, a few hundred doses of some advanced antibiotics, or a dozen state-of-the-art microprocessors have comparable retail values, but they obviously do not cost the same amount to ship.

In all, world trade has increased about a hundredfold since 1850.[46] This rate of growth significantly outpaced that of either gross output or world industrial production.[47] In 1989, the merchandise exports of the United States totaled $364 billion, those of Japan $275 billion, and those of the European Community nations combined approximately $1.25 trillion, out of a world total of more than $4 trillion.

COMPARATIVE ADVANTAGE. Growing markets spur progress in diverse ways that are widely misunderstood. Consider a five-

hundred-acre farm in Iowa and a two-thousand-acre ranch in Texas.
The Iowa farmer can grow one hundred bushels of corn or raise five
head of cattle on each acre. The Texas rancher can grow only twenty
bushels of corn or raise two head of cattle per acre on his drier and
less fertile land. Initially, each divides his land equally between corn
and cattle to serve local markets. Then a rail line connects Iowa and
Texas. The farmer converts his land to corn, the rancher converts his
to grazing. The results are tabulated below:

3.1 GAIN FROM TRADE

	Iowa Before	Iowa After	Texas Before	Texas After	Total Before	Total After
Corn	25,000	50,000	20,000	0	45,000	50,000
Cattle	1,250	0	2,000	4,000	3,250	4,000

Five thousand more bushels of corn and 750 more head of cattle have
materialized from the same land. This trade dividend is the result of
comparative advantage. Each region concentrates on its most productive enterprise, and the welfare of both rises.

David Ricardo fully explicated the advantages of trade early in the
nineteenth century, but they still elude the comprehension of politicians and pundits everywhere. The dominant concern in Congress
and on the nightly news is that the Japanese (or Koreans, Mexicans,
etc.) might charge Americans too little for their cars (textiles, steel,
etc.). "Too cheap to buy" is an oxymoron. It conjures up visions of
a masochistic car buyer demanding that the dealer raise the price.
Making the seller Japanese and the buyer American does nothing to
change this picture. Paying less for something is cause for a minor
celebration, not high-level political and diplomatic posturing, who-
ever the seller is.

Neither does Japan's perverse refusal to buy American cars with
their steering wheels on the wrong side go far toward justifying the
popular perception. Texans buys Iowa's corn without insisting on
selling it Texas corn in return. Iowans buy beef instead, just as the
Japanese buy American pharmaceuticals, airplanes, and software.
Japan is America's second-largest export customer, after Canada.
The Japanese obviously have a comparative advantage in producing
automobiles; no sinister plot is required to explain their failure to

64 import many Chryslers, which Americans have not exactly flocked to in recent years.[49]

SPECIALIZATION. Comparative advantage represents only the direct gain from expanding markets. Larger markets permitted a finer division of labor than Wedgwood or Smith could ever have imagined. The key nineteenth-century advance was the use of interchangeable parts, pioneered by Marc Brunel, a French émigré engineer working in England. The British Navy was plagued by a shortage of wooden pulley blocks. Each ship of the line required nearly a thousand to set its sails, roughly the annual output of a skilled artisan. Brunel used early steam-powered machine tools to produce interchangeable component parts for easy assembly into the final product. He was able to produce over one hundred thousand blocks per year using ten unskilled workers, compared to the 110 craftsmen required with prior methods.[50] Eli Whitney made the same advance almost simultaneously in the United States. He contracted with the government to supply ten thousand muskets, an astronomical number by the standards of the time. To fulfill the contract, Whitney modeled each part of the weapon, then hired ordinary workmen to machine parts precisely duplicating each model. He demonstrated the success of his approach in 1801 by selecting parts randomly from piles and assembling and firing four muskets.

America seized on Whitney's approach and rode it to industrial dominance. High-speed machine tools with tungsten-alloy cutting edges allowed machinists to maintain tolerances measured in millionths of an inch,[51] more than a thousand times more precise than those achieved by Whitney. This precision combined with minute division of labor to permit inexpensive mass production of machinery too complex for any craftsman of an earlier generation to have attempted. Henry Leland (stealing a page from Whitney) demonstrated the potential to an incredulous British audience in 1908 by disassembling three Cadillacs, mixing the parts, rebuilding three vehicles, and driving them away.[52]

This shift from individual craft work to mass production required profound changes in the human component of manufacturing. Frederick Taylor became the most famous (or notorious) exponent of "scientific management."[53] An eccentric, abstemious, and difficult man from an affluent Philadelphia Quaker background, he eschewed a comfortable legal career in favor of the grittiest blue-collar work-places. He developed a secular religion of production with one com-mandment: Thou shalt not waste. He scorned the workers for goldbricking, then turned the same contempt on management for failing to reward increased output adequately. Both sides reciprocated his feelings: the workers denounced his time-and-motion studies as mere pretexts for sweating them, and more than one employer fired him for his outspoken insistence on higher pay for performance. But his methods worked. He consistently preached the need to subdivide work into its component parts, with each worker assigned to perform just one task constantly.[54] The ultimate objective was to have each worker be as perfectly integrated into production and to function as automatically as the tools and machinery.

Henry Ford nearly achieved this objective with the assembly line, the apotheosis of these trends and a tangible testament to the effi-ciencies of specialization.[55] Ford built the early Model Ts in the traditional manner, with each worker performing a variety of tasks on one chassis, then moving to the next. Workers spent most of their time moving themselves, their tools, and parts and in switching tasks. Ford and his general manager, Charles Sorenson, resolved the assem-bly process into a sequence of small steps, each step requiring roughly the same amount of time and needing the same tool. Each worker remained in one position and performed a few simple tasks as a chain drive pulled assemblies past him and parts were supplied to him. The results are tabulated below.[56]

3.2 ASSEMBLY LINE PRODUCTIVITY GAINS

	Worker Minutes to Assemble		Percentage
	1913	1914	Reduction
Engine	594	226	62
Magneto	20	5	75
Axle	150	27	83
Vehicle from Components	750	93	88

Within three years, the assembly line reduced the total number of man-hours required to assemble an automobile by 80 percent.[57]

66   Capital underwent much the same transformation as labor, with specialized industrial machinery increasingly supplanting the journeyman's few hand tools, grain combines replacing scythes, and synthetic fertilizer factories eliminating one of the principal reasons for keeping livestock.

Market expansion drove or at least accommodated all of these changes. Even Brunel's hundred thousand pulley blocks or Whitney's ten thousand muskets required access to a fairly broad market. Without cheap bulk transportation, manuring and crop rotation enjoyed a decisive cost advantage over synthetic fertilizer. The economies of assembly line and processing facilities stem from uninterrupted high volume throughput, which may exceed local, regional, or even national demand.[58] After Rockefeller formed the Standard Oil Trust, for example, three refineries produced one quarter of the world's kerosene, at a small fraction of the previous cost. Similar economies of scale now permeate the manufacturing sector. In plastic resins and other petrochemicals, an individual production complex often accounts for more than a tenth of the total national output. The great productivity of such facilities depends on access to national or even world markets.

Larger markets fostered research and development by similar mechanisms. The spectacular successes of Edison and other independent inventors and the increasing role of science in invention led General Electric, Du Pont, and other large companies to create product development departments staffed by scientists and engineers recruited from academic research.[59] The ability to concentrate on the tasks of product and process development without being distracted by the daily demands of production and to stay abreast of changes in pertinent fields confers the same advantages as specialization in any other activity. The concentration of research and development in the largest firms was not coincidental.[60] Larger manufacturers spread the cost (or, conversely, reap the benefits) of development across a larger sales base. Recent consolidation in the automotive industry illustrates these economies of scale. American Motors, Lotus, Jaguar, and Saab were acquired in part because they had too few models to support development efforts at a level adequate to keep their products abreast of the rapidly changing state of the art in automotive design. Out of the dozens of companies that have built airplanes, only Boeing,

Airbus, and perhaps McDonnell Douglas can still afford to develop new commercial jets. These industries are unusual, and perhaps unique, in the breadth and expense of the development efforts required to remain competitive. But in any industry, firms must reach a critical mass to sustain the needed investment in innovation.

As the market expands, more research becomes economically feasible. Discovering new knowledge consumes trained researchers, laboratories, and other real resources. But the cost of using the resulting knowledge is negligible, while the return varies directly with the number of potential customers. Matthew Boulton captured the point quite succinctly in a letter written to James Watt at the beginning of their partnership: "It is not worth my while to manufacture [the steam engine] for three counties only; but I find it very well worth my while to make it for the whole world."[61] The incremental benefit from expanded use of an innovation due to market growth is thus pure gain.[62]

That gain is potentially unlimited. Consider the original cost of such inventions as the telephone, the jet engine, xerographic copying, integrated circuits, and laser beams. The effective social rates of return on these investments would surely be measured in billions of percent per year, far larger than on any investment in physical capital. Much of this gain is attributable to the distribution of these devices throughout all advanced economies of the world. Confining any of these inventions to a single country, as frequently occurred before communication and transportation technology shrank the world so drastically, would have severely curtailed the benefits realized from it.

Market expansion also accelerates innovation by enlarging the pool of potential innovators. When two nations become part of a single market, the people in both begin to benefit from advances occurring in either. Thus, American consumers now enjoy vastly improved automobiles and consumer electronics because of Japanese innovations. And the firms in each nation must either quickly imitate the advances of foreign competitors or innovate to offset those advances. Those that fail to respond adequately shrink or die, leaving only the most innovative and efficient in the market. Recent developments in the United States provide tangible evidence of this process. Japanese competition finally caught the attention of the bloated steel and automotive industries, forcing them to adopt new production tech-

68 nologies and product enhancements to remain in the market. These were among the few sectors of the American economy that registered appreciable productivity gains during the 1970s and 1980s.[63] Expanding markets thus discourage complacency among domestic firms.

Major advances in technology are particularly effective at producing a sort of involuntary international collaboration to maximize the resulting benefits. Advances have value only if people learn of them. History is littered with examples of breakthrough discoveries and technologies lying dormant or confined to a single narrow area for extended periods.[64] Wider markets and high-speed communications virtually foreclose that possibility. The announcement of high-temperature superconductors, for example, produced a blizzard of facsimile transmissions among interested scientists, who could not wait even a few weeks for journals to publish the papers. The same process occurs at the more pedestrian level of product development. European and American firms pioneered in magnetic tape recording, but only JVC's refinements transformed the technology into an economically viable home videocassette recorder.

The accelerated introduction of knowledge into production confirms the importance of this dynamic.[65] The average period between an original scientific discovery and its incorporation in a commercial product or process declined from thirty-seven years at the end of the nineteenth century to fourteen years in the two decades following World War II, while the succeeding lag between the first appearance of a new product and peak production of the product declined from thirty-four years before 1920 to eight years between 1939 and 1959. Compressing the period between scientific discovery and maximum commercial exploitation from about seventy years to about twenty greatly accelerated the pace of progress.

In addition, an invention may have applications in other product markets, thus generating positive "externalities."[66] A rupture-resistant helicopter fuel system, for example, may be readily adaptable to make automobiles safer. Advances like these percolate among industries with little delay, which helps to explain why society routinely benefits much more from successful inventions than their inventors do.[67] Recognition of such possibilities is at least partly a matter of chance. Disseminating an initial advance to a wider audience thus increases the pace of product introduction and the likelihood that someone will apply it usefully in a different context. By all these mechanisms, "[l]arger markets induce more research and faster growth."[68]

THE WORLD MARKET. As of this writing, much of the world seems intent on reversing these gains. The Uruguay Round is foundering on European farmers' insistence that taxpayers and consumers maintain them in their accustomed life-styles and American negotiators' asserted unwillingness to accept half a loaf. The French government, apparently unacquainted with any economist since Colbert, protects its national champions and tries to forge the European Community into an insular trading bloc. In the United States, two ostensibly free-trade administrations have bludgeoned allies into "voluntary" export restraints, violated the General Agreement on Tariffs and Trade (GATT) by imposing selective antidumping tariffs, and acquiesced in Congressional pandering to powerful domestic lobbies, all at the expense of both American consumers and more efficient producers in poorer nations. Japan maintains policies and practices that entrench domestic suppliers and effectively exclude foreign competition from important sectors, bristling at any hint of foreign interference with the sovereign right to allow its people to be overcharged for almost everything. Rising protectionist sentiment throughout the developed world does not augur well for further economic integration.[69]

But even a complete reversal of the protectionist tide would add little to material progress, simply because integration is already so nearly complete. Prior GATT rounds have lowered the average tariff on industrial products from about 40 percent to 4.7 percent.[70] A world market already sets the price structure for most commodities, industrial products, and consumer durables.[71]

This integration has not been limited to merchandise. Offshore production facilities can sometimes replace exports of goods, as Japanese automakers have recently shown in the United States. The United States, Japan, West Germany, Britain, and France together invested more than $100 billion in other countries in 1988, up tenfold since 1970. Worldwide, accumulated foreign capital investments now total more than $1.5 trillion.[72] Capital thus appears to be losing its national identity.[73]

Trade in services has grown even more rapidly than in goods over

70   the last few decades. Transportation, financial, insurance, engineering, construction, and accounting services are increasingly offered on a global basis, and a similar trend is unfolding in some fields of law. Worldwide, exports of services exceed $600 billion, with the United States accounting for nearly 15 percent of the total.

Money moves around the globe faster than goods, capital, and services combined. Worldwide foreign exchange transactions in major money centers now exceed $35 trillion annually, and annual turnover among world financial institutions on the London Eurodollar market is even larger.[74] Such international money flows rapidly adjust the values of each currency to that of the dollar, the deutsche mark, or the yen, creating, if all too imperfectly, world currency integration.

The existence of a single world technology base is apparent from everyday observation. Automobiles, airplanes, appliances, consumer electronics, machine tools, computers, buildings, and communications equipment and medical equipment, to name only a few examples, incorporate essentially the same technology wherever produced. Leading scientific and technical journals circulate worldwide. The repeated successes of Japan and developing Asian nations in bringing technologies originated elsewhere to commercial fruition reflect the transparency of national boundaries to science and engineering.

In short, most goods, services, and factors of production already trade on a worldwide basis. The multicentury expansion of markets is essentially complete. As a result, the potential further gains pale in comparison to those of the past. The Office of the U.S. Trade Representative, which is hardly prone to understating the potential gains from trade, estimates that a successful conclusion of the Uruguay Round could raise U.S. GNP by 3 percent in the year 2000, which, even if true, would hardly transform the economy. The similarly disposed OECD predicts that a new GATT agreement would add $195 billion in world income, truly a pittance in a world economy measured in tens of trillions of dollars.[75] This source of progress has dried up.

THE (EXCESS) WEALTH OF NATIONS

CAPITALIST TOOLS. Few would question the importance of physical capital in fostering progress and prosperity. Tools and equipment make labor more productive, which raises wages. The same year Ford introduced the assembly line, he began paying his workers $5 per day, an astonishing 90 percent increase that other manufacturers soon had to match. With the more than fourfold gain in productivity from the assembly line, effective labor costs still dropped sharply. This link between capitalization and wage rates is pervasive. The capital-intensive manufacturing sector pays more than the thinly capitalized service and retail sectors. A farm worker using tractors and grain combines earns more than one with horses and scythes. The wage rates in developed economies, with their wealth of productive capital, are uniformly higher than in backward and developing economies, where sweat too often substitutes for power and hands are the principal tools.

Higher wages make still more savings and investment possible. They also create an economic environment that is conducive to innovation. Advances in manufacturing technique commonly pay for themselves by saving labor. Saving expensive labor provides a stronger justification than saving cheap labor. The concentration of new technology in wealthy countries is thus not coincidental.[76] Over the course of generations, this self-reinforcing cycle has produced the vast aggregation of factories, agricultural and industrial machinery, transportation and communication equipment, and commercial buildings that mark the advanced economies.

But softer and less conspicuous forms of capital are often not even recognized as such.[77] Supermarket chains provide a vastly more cost-effective means of distributing food to people than the thousands of small, independent groceries that prevailed little more than a generation ago. The knowledge of how to organize and operate supermarkets is thus part of the inherited social capital, even though no one discovered it in any meaningful sense, no one now owns it, and it is not included in any accounting of a nation's wealth. The same could be said of most of the institutions and organizations of a modern economy. They evolve out of decades or even centuries of experience.

72 Competitors imitate the efficient forms, while the inefficient ones disappear.

At an individual level, skills, knowledge, and adaptability affect productivity greatly. An automotive engineer adds more value than an assembly-line worker, who in turn contributes more than a janitor. A trained and experienced mechanic, secretary, or machinist can be several times more productive than a novice. Specific skills and training rest on a foundation of inculcated attitudes and ethics.

> The most important inheritance of all—the thing that decisively advantages middle class children—is the cultural bequest from their parents. That parental transfer of language, of values, and of psychological well-being sets the stage for all the formal learning and achievements of later years.[78]

The same point applies internationally. Irving Kristol's observation that "if India or Peru were inhabited by Swiss and Dutchmen, they would be fairly prosperous countries, not poor ones,"[79] makes up in insight what it lacks in diplomacy.

Such intangible forms of capital are not inherently exclusive, unlike physical capital. Two people cannot simultaneously use a tool, fly an airplane, or grow a crop in a field. If the market is functioning efficiently, the use to which the physical capital is put will be the most valuable, but the excluded alternatives may nevertheless represent substantial opportunities forgone. Knowledge, on the other hand, can be used by all simultaneously.[80] Manufacturers throughout the world emulated the assembly line within a decade of its first appearance at Ford. Thus, knowledge is available not only for its most valuable use, but also for all its lesser uses. This characteristic allows intangible capital to accumulate very rapidly. If one person teaches a skill to another, human capital increases because both can then use the knowledge. A book, an article, or a class may pass skills or knowledge to many others simultaneously.

Also unlike physical capital, intangible capital often increases the productivity even of those who do not possess it. Efficient forms and institutional arrangements may exist without any living person actually knowing why they are preferable to the alternatives. Standard methods preserve prior discoveries and advances. A driver buys a car for $10,000, and at no extra cost receives two centuries of advances in thermodynamics, mechanical engineering, petroleum refining, metallurgy, and electronics, none of which the driver needs to comprehend. Workers often understand little of the operation of their tools and equipment. "[T]he knowledge which any individual mind consciously manipulates is only a small part of the knowledge which at any one time contributes to the success of his action."[81]

Intangible capital cannot be quantified in any useful way,[82] but its importance would be almost impossible to overstate. A concentration of human capital in a nation almost guarantees a level of prosperity over the long term, regardless of other factors. Postwar Japan provides a dramatic illustration of this assertion. A nation of many islands, virtually without natural resources, isolated and feudal until the middle of the nineteenth century, its physical capital stock and most of one male generation destroyed by the War, it has become the second-largest economy on the planet. Its prosperity stems from a hardworking, disciplined, intelligent, motivated, and educated populace, accumulating and applying advanced technology, functioning in a (mostly) free and intensely competitive market. The German example is only slightly less striking. "It seems . . . utterly obvious that the technological knowledge possessed by its people played a bigger role in Germany's post–World War II recovery than did the devastated and rundown plant which survived the war."[83]

Conversely, a paucity of intangible capital virtually assures impoverishment over any but the shortest term. Mexico is a prominent recent example. The discovery of huge oil and gas reserves in Tabasco and Chiapas at the height of OPEC's power seemingly assured Mexico's emergence from underdevelopment and poverty. Mineral wealth, however, did not alleviate widespread illiteracy, inefficiencies and constrictions in the economic structure, corruption in government, or the flight of the most industrious citizens to the United States. After brief and uneven affluence, largely (and, in retrospect, unwisely) financed by Western banks mesmerized by the promise of oil wealth, Mexico relapsed into economic torpor, its per capita gross national product comparable to those of Malaysia and Uruguay, its debts in default and widely assumed to be unpayable. Only after the value of the petroleum reserves had declined sharply and President Salinas

74 shifted the policymaking focus to the intangibles did Mexico begin to regain economic respectability.

THE VEHICLE OF PROGRESS. Capital accumulation and innovation tend to move in tandem. Profit is, after all, the objective of most investments in innovation; progress is merely the happy by-product, an instance of Smith's invisible hand at work. The gains are most apparent from the occasional breakthrough invention—xerography, instant photography, the birth-control pill, the hand-held calculator—which may carry a business for decades. But, as noted above, even ordinary business profits depend heavily on routine little process and product innovations. In the aggregate, such profits are the second leading source of capital accumulation (after personal savings). Innovation attracts whatever capital it cannot create. Emerging industries and technologies need capital to expand and are able to pay a premium for it from their enhanced profits. Firms producing obsolete or declining products, by contrast, have excess capacity and earn subnormal profits. Capital thus automatically flows from static or declining industries to more innovative sectors.

Physical capital also serves as the principal conduit for introducing new technology into the production function.[84] In steelmaking, for example, the basic oxygen process had been fully developed by the mid-1950s. Implementing it, however, required huge sums to erect new facilities. (Indeed, the reluctance of American producers to scrap their fully functional open hearth furnaces enabled Japan to gain a decisive advantage in efficiency.) Automobiles needed roads and service stations. X-rays became diagnostic tools only by way of X-ray machines. Even the integrated circuit, ultimately a capital-saving technology, required huge investments in chip fabrication facilities and equipment. The economic returns realized from advances in knowledge thus depend on the rate of capital investment.

Human capital performs a similar function. Subsistence farming demanded strong backs; the modern economy demands strong minds. Innovation is change, and only education prepares the work force to understand and adapt to it. The number of white-collar jobs began an abrupt increase after 1890.[85] At the other end of the spectrum, farm labor and unskilled day labor declined sharply in response to mechanization.[86] School systems had to respond to these shifts in demand at every level. Germany led in curricular reform, replacing ancient languages with sciences and history at the high school level and establishing technical colleges and the teaching of modern disciplines in the universities. In the words of Kaiser Wilhelm II, "It is our duty to educate men to become young Germans, and not young Greeks and Romans."[87] Meanwhile, Great Britain clung tightly to an elitist and outmoded educational system. Germany's rise in Europe was not coincidental. "[T]he German secret was an open secret. . . . They were simply, and for the particular need of the time, better educated."[88] As were the Americans, who quickly adopted German curricular reforms and added universal primary and secondary education. World economic leadership devolved upon these two nations early in the twentieth century largely because they trained themselves for it.

ENOUGH OF A GOOD THING. All of which would suggest that the advanced economies can pave the road to further progress with the right mixture of tangible and intangible capital. That formula lacks just two ingredients for success—supply and demand.

Capital begins with saving, and saving has permanently dropped out of fashion. The net savings rate in the United States has declined steadily since the 1950s, from an average of 8 percent of gross national product during the 1960s, to about 7 percent during the 1970s, to about 3 percent during the 1980s, with a corresponding reduction in net national investment. The 1990s began with a further decline.[89] Despite much high-level hand wringing, "[n]obody is sure why personal savings fell so much, or whether it will bounce back."[90] Efforts to reverse this trend have proven futile.

Americans are saving less because they have less reason to save. People save when they can *and* need to. Postponing gratification is rarely the spontaneous response to surplus funds; people need a reason to do it. Some saving is in the nature of insurance against economic mishap (loss of a job, temporary disability) or against known eventualities (college education for children). The social safety net—including unemployment insurance, disability benefits, and free or highly subsidized tuition to state colleges and universities—now cushions such shocks. These programs are (at best) funded on an ongoing basis and therefore accumulate no capital.

76   Wealth is an even more effective guarantor against economic insecurity, and thus an even better deterrent to saving. Rising incomes enhance the ability to save, but the accumulated savings, in turn, decrease the incentive to save more.[91] While incomes are commensurate with the needs of daily life and wealth remains modest or restricted to a privileged few, the income effect dominates, producing higher savings rates. But ever rising incomes must eventually shift the balance: the resulting wealth begins to depress saving more effectively than the higher incomes lift it.

Saving thus becomes self-limiting at some point, as saving accumulates into wealth that discourages further saving.

The United States has clearly passed that point. As of 1988 (*after* Black Monday and before the runup that pushed the stock market to record highs in 1992), about 1.5 million American households (out of a total of ninety million) were worth at least $1 million, with half of those worth more than $2 million.[92] Despite inflation, $1 million covers most eventualities comfortably and supplies a retirement annuity of about $100,000 per year, enough in most situations to afford an adequate if not lavish life-style. At a less exalted level, eight million households with over thirty million people had net worths in excess of $250,000,[93] which, if not independent means, is certainly enough money to dull any impulse to save. This wealth is concentrated in the high-income households that necessarily produce most of an economy's net savings.[94] The spending and saving habits of these households therefore have a disproportionate impact. Falling saving rates have coincided precisely with this rise and spread of wealth.

The rising affluence of America's elderly[95] may also be rippling outward to affect their children, as the expectation of an inheritance saps the incentive to save for retirement. As of 1988, one seventh of all households headed by a person sixty-five years of age or older had a net worth in excess of $250,000; more than 40 percent had net worths of more than $100,000.[96]

America's economic rivals only recently began to share the "problem" of widespread wealth. Their incomes lagged behind those in the United States from the late nineteenth century onward, and they suffered horrendous devastation in the two world wars.[97] Sharply rising incomes lifted the savings rates of every major economy in the world except the United States between 1955 and 1969.[98] Increasing wealth has now exactly reversed that trend, as every advanced nation experienced a decline in its savings rate in the 1980s compared to the 1970s,[99] producing a commensurate reduction in worldwide investment.[100] Even occasional deviations from this downward trend serve only to confirm the dominance of wealth over income in controlling the rate of saving. American savings rates rose in 1988 directly in response to the loss of wealth from the October 1987 stock market crash. Japanese savings rates responded identically to the bursting of the real estate and stock market bubbles in 1990 and 1991.[101] These upticks are no cause for celebration: they merely verify that wealth, the inevitable by-product of saving, discourages further saving, a dynamic that virtually precludes a return to the savings rates of the 1960s.

Spreading affluence has provided a measure of economic security to the nonwealthy as well. Social Security is the best-known example. The average monthly Social Security retirement benefit rose from $29 per month in 1950 to $492 per month by 1987. Even after adjusting for inflation, the increase has been more than threefold in little more than a generation.

Private-sector arrangements have tended in the same direction. As of 1987, assets of private and public pension plans totaled more than $2.2 trillion. More than half of all full-time employees in the private sector, and approximately 85 percent of those earning more than $50,000 per year, have some pension plan. Pension savings account for more than one quarter of the total, compared to one tenth in 1950.[102] Unlike Social Security, pension plans at least produce savings from current income. But not much of this saving will ever become part of society's permanent capital patrimony. Defined benefit pension plans, easily the most popular form, effectively annuitize savings, allowing the elderly to maintain a higher standard of living without fear of outliving their capital, but also consuming the accumulation that could otherwise have been transmitted to the next generation.[103] Pensions thus facilitate not only the creation but also the rapid dissipation of savings.

The impact of rising Social Security payments and pension outlays has been obvious and direct. The poverty rate among the elderly has fallen from the highest of all age groups to nearly the lowest.[104] The larger incomes of senior citizens have dulled the interest in saving for

78   retirement,[105] as well as the fear of spending those savings during retirement.

Finally, some evidence suggests that the need for more productive capital is itself approaching limits in advanced economies. Capital productivity (i.e., the output realized from additional capital) declined materially after 1973 in OECD countries, suggesting that highly productive uses for additional physical capital may not be abundant.[106] This decline reversed a trend of increasing output per unit capital that had persisted in the United States since at least 1889.[107] As discussed in Chapter 4, many capital-intensive industries had excess capacity throughout the 1980s. By the middle of the decade, the Japanese saving machine was increasingly forced to invest its surplus funds in high-profile, speculative real estate projects, in sharp contrast to its historical preference for investments in primary and secondary sector production. The 1990s began with short-term borrowers paying interest that barely exceeded the rate of inflation, despite severely depressed saving levels. All of these harbingers suggest that an existing surfeit, or at least sufficiency, of physical capital may be depressing returns on capital investment in advanced economies. If so, even the unlikely event of a return to past savings rates would not yield the same level of tangible benefits.

The productive potential of more education is also reaching obvious limits. Despite widely publicized concerns over the number of dropouts at the secondary level, high school graduation rates are nearly 90 percent in the United States (about the same as in other leading economies). As a result, the average American adult has had more than twelve years of formal education (compared to less than ten years in 1950).[108] Further progress will necessarily be incremental.

College enrollments reflect the same trends, and the same limits. More than half of all high school graduates in the United States enroll in college. This may already be too many. Deficiencies in attitude, aptitude, or basic skills prevent many of them from acquiring anything that could fairly be described as higher education. Some large state university campuses look like panoramic beer commercials suddenly sprung to life: fitness, fun, and suntans are on prominent display, and study is not often permitted to disrupt the happy picture. The libraries are heavily used—they serve as convenient social gathering points for students taking a break from eating or working out.

Only a relative handful of graduates complete a rigorous academic   *79*
major. Even in narrowly utilitarian terms, the experience is often
wasted. Graduates find a marked surplus of applicants for desired
positions in many fields; more than a quarter of them take jobs that
do not require a degree.[109] Newly minted advanced degrees in law,
business, the social sciences, and liberal arts face comparable gluts in
their job markets. In short, higher education has reached saturation
levels.

Capital accumulation thus faces real, if necessarily ill-defined, limits. Ever deeper and wider affluence has begun to discourage rather
than to promote saving and investment and to reduce rather than to
enhance the opportunities for further productive investment. Even
human capital has only limited potential for further expansion. Policy
initiatives designed to emulate the successes of the past will therefore
prove self-defeating over any but the shortest term.

NOTES

1. As the economic recovery from the 1990–91 recession faltered, many observers blamed a lack of consumer confidence that produced debt reduction and saving rather than spending. A rise in consumer spending moves the economy closer to its productive capacity. But debt reduction and saving represent capital accumulation, one of the three sources of long-term progress. See also *Wall Street Journal,* May 18, 1992, p. A1, on the tension between productivity and employment.

2. Economists' inability to explain, and consequent disinterest in, the processes of long-term progress is widely if quietly acknowledged. See, for example, Irving Kristol, *Reflections of a Neoconservative: Looking Back, Looking Ahead,* p. 183, Basic Books, 1983; R.M. Hartwell, "C.E. Ayres on the Industrial Revolution," p. 58, in Breit & Culbertson (eds.), *Science and Ceremony,* Univ. of Texas Press, 1976; Geoffrey Wyatt, *The Economics of Invention,* pp. 147–50, St. Martin's, 1986. The most prominent twentieth-century exception was Joseph Schumpeter, who first described the processes of "creative destruction" in the economy.

3. See, for example, *Economist,* 4–10 Jan. 1992, pp. 15–18, discussing recent efforts to adapt neoclassical economic theory to explain growth.

4. For readers reasonably comfortable with Greek-letter economics, Paul Romer, "Endogenous Technological Change," *Journal of Political Economy,* Vol. 98, p. S71, Oct. 1990, sets forth a formal economic model that largely coincides with the description of progress in the text. Romer's model posits innovation resulting from investment in research and development and human capital. (This is referred to as endogenous technological change. The standard neoclassical model assumes exogenous, or externally given, technology, which makes it nearly useless for the analysis of progress.) Knowledge can be shared by all (i.e., it is "nonrival"), but an inventor is entitled to exclude others from the commercial use of new technology (i.e., technology is partially excludable or partially appropriable). The model predicts, among other things, a form of monopolistic competition, with innovators charging more than the perfect competition equilibrium price; nondiminishing ("nonconvex") returns to investment in technology; suboptimal investment in technology and in human capital; and increased output from market expansion (in addition to the effect of comparative advantage), most of which conforms to the discussion in the text and, not so coincidentally, reality.

5. Writers on technology sometimes distinguish among invention (an increase in

knowledge), innovation (first application of knowledge in a production function), *81* and diffusion (the spread of a new technique, process, or product). A nearly parallel classification, primarily used in national income accounts and factor analysis, distinguishes among basic research, applied research, and development. These distinctions are not material to the current discussion and are therefore ignored.

6. An agreement with other sellers to restrict output and raise prices is inherently unstable. Every firm, whether within or outside the cartel, has an incentive to expand output by pricing just under the cartel price. See Richard Posner, *Antitrust Law*, Ch. 4, especially pp. 47–55, Univ. of Chicago Press, 1976. The fragility of cartels was forcefully illustrated by the collapse of the OPEC-supported price of oil as soon as the United States ceased controlling the price of energy.

7. The cost-reducing innovator thus does not (as is commonly assumed) add his profit to the price; the market fixes the price. Rather, he takes it out of the cost. See John Chamberlain, *Roots of Capitalism*, Ch. 7, Liberty Press, 1959.

8. "Only in disequilibrium are there opportunities for entrepreneurial profit. . . . In equilibrium all profits have been squeezed out, costs and prices have become fully adjusted." Israel Kirzner, *Perception, Opportunity, and Profit*, Ch. 7, p. 110, Univ. of Chicago Press, 1979. In economic terms, innovation creates a form of imperfect competition, so called in order to distinguish it from the perfectly competitive market of many identical firms selling a fungible product. The terminology is unfortunate, as the imperfection benefits the consumer. See Joseph Schumpeter, *Capitalism, Socialism, and Democracy*, Ch. 8, p. 106, Harper & Row, 3d ed., 1975: in fostering the long-term expansion of the economy, "perfect competition is not only impossible but inferior, and has no title to being set up as a model of ideal efficiency"; Kristol, *Reflections of a Neoconservative*, p. 187: "it is only *imperfect* competition and *dis*equilibrium that permits the marketplace to function at all."

9. In reality, of course, firms do not wait for a breakthrough by a competitor and then seek to catch up. Many firms seek to innovate continuously in the hope of becoming the leading firm that earns the economic profits. The process is described *seriatim* in the text solely for didactic purposes.

10. J. Tracy Kidder, *The Soul of a New Machine*, Little, Brown, 1981, chronicles the process of competitive innovation in the computer industry.

11. "The success of Western economies in assimilating Western technology is . . . a consequence of . . . firms that can gain much by commercializing new ideas more quickly than their rivals can." Rosenberg & Birdzell, "Science, Technology and the Western Miracle," *Scientific American*, Nov. 1990, p. 42, at p. 53.

12. Nicholas Rescher, *Scientific Progress: A Philosophical Essay on the Economics of Research in Natural Science*, Ch. 4, Table 5, Univ. of Pittsburgh Press, 1978; *Statistical Abstract of the United States 1989*, Table 970.

13. Christopher Wills, *Exons, Introns, and Talking Genes: The Science Behind the Human Genome Project*, Ch. 4, p. 82, Basic Books, 1991.

14. Elizabeth Corcoran, "Redesigning Research," *Scientific American*, June 1992, p. 102 at p. 104 (data from graph). See also *Statistical Abstract of the United*

82 *States 1989,* Table 970. Total research and development expenditures in other advanced countries are comparable. See *Statistical Abstract of the United States 1989,* Table 973.

15. F.M. Scherer, *Innovation and Growth: Schumpeterian Perspectives,* Ch. 16, MIT Press, 1984, estimates that the decline in research and development spending during the 1970s resulted in a prolonged loss of from 0.2 to 0.4 percentage points in productivity growth per year. See also Baily & Chakrabarti, *Innovation and the Productivity Crisis,* Ch. 2, pp. 39–42, Brookings Inst., 1988. *Wall Street Journal,* Nov. 7, 1990, p. A1, describes the intensifying competition for research grants and the inability to obtain funding for some apparently meritorious projects.

16. The argument in the text follows Rescher, *Scientific Progress.*

17. "[D]iscoveries tend to come in areas that become available for study as the result of new observational techniques." Gerald Feinberg, "Progress in Physics: The Game of Intellectual Leapfrog," Ch. 7, p. 170, in Almond, Chodorow & Pearce (eds.), *Progress and Its Discontents,* Univ. of California Press, 1982. Empirical observation may anticipate theory or vice versa. In either case, the need for observation beyond the realm explained by the prior theory is the same.

18. See James Watson, *The Double Helix: A Personal Account of the Discovery of the Structure of DNA,* Atheneum, 1968.

19. Thomas Simpson, "The New Pythagoreans: Reflections on the Idea of Science in Our Time," p. 162, at p. 192, in *The Great Ideas Today 1988,* Britannica. Simpson was referring to the Stanford Linear Accelerator Center, a relatively simple and cheap particle accelerator by current standards. CERN's budget of over $500 million per year is supported by thirteen European member states. Lederman & Schramm, *From Quarks to the Cosmos: Tools of Discovery,* Ch. 7, Scientific American Books, 1989, lists some past, present, and proposed particle accelerators. Accelerator and particle detector technologies are described in I.S. Hughes, *Elementary Particles,* Ch. 1, Cambridge Univ. Press, 2d ed., 1985; Peter Watkins, *Story of the W and Z,* Chs. 7–9, Cambridge Univ. Press, 1986; and Myers & Picasso, "The LEP Collider," *Scientific American,* July 1990, p. 54. Charles Mann, "The Massive Search for Mass," *Smithsonian,* March 1989, p. 106, describes the work of particle physicists engaged in a collider experiment.

20. See Freeman Dyson, *Infinite in All Directions,* Ch. 8, p. 139, Harper & Row, 1988.

21. Robert Routledge, *Discoveries and Inventions of the Nineteenth Century,* p. 2, 1890, reprinted by Crescent Books, 1989.

22. Roger Penrose, *The Emperor's New Mind: Concerning Computers, Minds, and the Laws of Physics,* p. 151, Oxford Univ. Press, 1989.

23. The standard model is the product of decades of leapfrogging by nuclear theorists and experimentalists. It is very forbidding territory. Lederman & Schramm, *From Quarks to the Cosmos,* Ch. 4, provides a comprehensible, if necessarily simplified, description.

24. Gerald Feinberg, *Solid Clues: Quantum Physics, Molecular Biology, and the Future of Science,* Ch. 3, p. 104, Simon & Schuster, 1985. Feinberg is a professor of physics at Columbia and longtime experimenter at CERN.

25. Feinberg, *Solid Clues,* Ch. 3, pp. 75–78.

26. *Scientific American,* Feb. 1990, pp. 18–19; Ed Regis, *Who Got Einstein's Office?: Eccentricity and Genius at the Institute for Advanced Study,* Ch. 7, Addison-Wesley, 1987.

27. See Dennis Flanagan, *Flanagan's Version: A Spectator's Guide to Science on the Eve of the 21st Century,* p. 19, Knopf, 1988 (advanced physics uses only a small fraction of mathematics).

28. Baily & Chakrabarti, *Innovation and the Productivity Crisis,* Ch. 6, p. 115, notes the lack of contact between research and practical applications in some disciplines, resulting in "an academic community that is too self referenced."

29. Clifford Will, *Was Einstein Right? Putting General Relativity to the Test,* Basic Books, 1986, describes the various empirical verifications of the validity of general relativity. Richard Feynman, *QED: The Strange Theory of Light and Matter,* Princeton Univ. Press, 1985, contains the only reasonably accessible treatment of quantum electrodynamics.

30. Feinberg, "Progress in Physics," Ch. 7, pp. 169–70, in Almond, Chodorow & Pearce (eds.), *Progress and Its Discontents.*

31. Quoted in Rescher, *Scientific Progress,* Ch. 2, p. 23n.

32. Gunther Stent, *Paradoxes of Progress,* Ch. 2, W.H. Freeman, 1978, argues that the sciences have limits and that, given the accelerated rate of scientific discovery, those limits must soon be reached.

33. "When science finishes disproving theories, the survivors often huddle so close together that the gap between them makes no practical difference." K. Eric Drexler, *Engines of Creation,* Ch. 3, p. 49, Doubleday, 1986.

34. "[A]s technological advances made possible by the application of the results of scientific research vanquish all threats to human survival . . . further scientific research appears to have arrived at the point of ever-decreasing utility. Thus it seems possible that there could occur a waning of the present high social interest in supporting the sciences." Stent, *Paradoxes of Progress,* Ch. 2, p. 48. Stent first advanced this forecast in 1969, before the declining trend in research and development expenditures became evident.

35. See Margaret Jacob, *The Cultural Meaning of the Scientific Revolution,* Ch. 7, p. 237, Knopf, 1988.

36. "[S]cientific progress represents one of the great creative challenges of the human spirit. . . . A society that spends many billions of dollars on a varied cornucopia of deleterious trivia . . . assumes an uncomfortable moral posture in deciding that science—even big and expensive science—is a game that's not worth the candle." Rescher, *Scientific Progress,* Ch. 15, p. 264.

37. Rescher, *Scientific Progress,* Ch. 15, p. 263.

38. Rescher, *Scientific Progress,* Ch. 15, p. 252. This is not intended to suggest that innovation depends entirely on continued scientific advances. New products or processes may be developed from long-known science in response to an increase in demand caused, for example, by market expansion or shifts in the prices of competing or complementary goods. The pace of innovation is a function of such changes in demand, spending on research and development, and the technological

84 opportunities presented by broad advances in scientific understanding. For a discussion of the respective roles of supply and demand in the innovation process, see Nathan Rosenberg, _Perspectives on Technology_, Ch. 15, Cambridge Univ. Press, 1976. Efforts to segregate and quantify the effect of each of these factors empirically have not been notably successful. Despite these qualifications, Rescher's assertion that a deceleration in the pace of scientific progress will, other things being equal, significantly slow technological progress is not open to serious dispute. In any event, investment in new products based on old science is also susceptible to diminishing returns. "[T]he cost of seeking the final increment of improvement that separates the best from the merely excellent may not be worth paying." Drexler, _Engines of Creation_, p. 156.

39. A.B.C. Whipple, _The Challenge_, William Morrow, 1987, describes the era of the clippers and includes an extensive bibliography on the subject.

40. The true forerunner of modern steam vessels, I.K. Brunel's _Great Britain_, survived eleven months in the Irish surf after running aground in 1846 and was finally returned to Bristol from the Falklands in 1970, still intact. Increased size also produced important efficiencies, as capacity rises faster than the cost of building the ship, crew size, or water resistance. (For the mathematically minded, cargo capacity is a function of volume and therefore rises as the cube of size as a ship is scaled up. Cost and water resistance vary with surface area and therefore rise as the square of size.)

41. Rinman & Brodefors, _The Commercial History of Shipping_, p. 64, Rinman & Linden, 1983.

42. Joel Mokyr, _Lever of Riches_, Ch. 6, p. 130, Oxford Univ. Press, 1990. Steam reduced the cost of sending freight upriver even faster. See Paul Johnson, _The Birth of the Modern: World Society 1815–1830_, Ch. 3, p. 196, HarperCollins, 1991.

43. Angus Maddison, _The World Economy in the Twentieth Century_, Table D-8, p. 145, OECD, 1989.

44. Mokyr, _Lever of Riches_, Ch. 6, p. 124, notes the role of the telegraph in coordinating international markets.

45. The effect of smaller products on the volume of foreign trade was noted by Alan Greenspan, _Wall Street Journal_, Oct. 24, 1988, p. A14.

46. Sources on world trade volume include W.W. Rostow, _The World Economy: History & Prospect_, Table II-8 and Appendix A, Univ. of Texas Press, 1978 (indexed world trade estimates from 1720 to 1971); _Economist_, 21–27 April 1990, p. 86 (increase in world trade since 1971); and _Wall Street Journal_, Mar. 7, 1990, p. A18 (annual rates of increase in world merchandise trade volume for ten-year periods beginning in 1953). The rise in world trade actually occurred in two separate segments: two world wars sandwiching the Smoot-Hawley tariff left trade volume essentially unchanged from 1913 to 1948.

47. Angus Maddison, _World Economy in the Twentieth Century_, Table D-6, p. 143, and Rostow, _World Economy_, Appendix A.

48. _Economist_, 21–27 April 1990, p. 86, and 7–13 July 1990, "Survey of the European Community," p. 6. _Economist_, 22–28 Sept. 1990, "Survey of World Trade," p. 6, shows trade flows among the major trading regions of the world.

49. Note that a trade advantage need only be "comparative." If the United States is much better than Korea at making pharmaceuticals and only slightly better at making cloth, both benefit from having Koreans exchange their cloth for American drugs. Thus the oft-repeated bogey that a nation may lose its trade advantage in everything is gibberish. In the case of automobiles, of course, Japan's advantage is more than just relative.

50. Johnson, *Birth of the Modern*, Ch. 7, pp. 576–77. Sigvard Strandh, *The History of the Machine*, Ch. 2, pp. 55–57, Dorset Press, 1989, describes and depicts Brunel's innovative machines.

51. Trevor Williams, *A Short History of Twentieth-Century Technology c. 1900– c. 1950*, Ch. 15, pp. 180–81, Oxford Univ. Press, 1982.

52. John Rae, *The American Automobile*, Ch. 4, p. 58, Univ. of Chicago Press, 1965.

53. Thomas Hughes, *American Genesis: A Century of Invention and Technological Enthusiasm 1870–1970*, Ch. 5, Viking, 1989, describes Taylor's work.

54. Frank Gilbreth, a disciple of Taylor, tripled the number of bricks laid per shift simply by having unskilled workers responsible for filling movable, height-adjustable scaffolding with bricks, so that the skilled masons did not interrupt their work to fetch or move bricks or even bend over.

55. Ford may have been inspired by Armour's late-nineteenth-century pork-packing plant in Chicago. Overhead trolleys formed a sort of disassembly line, carrying pork carcasses from one worker to the next, each worker performing one or two tasks in butchering or dressing the meat.

56. Table 3.2 is from Womack et al., *The Machine That Changed the World*, Fig. 2.1, p. 29, Rawson Assocs., 1990. See also Alfred Chandler, "Technology and the Transformation of Industrial Organization," Ch. 3, at p. 67, in Colton & Bruchey (eds.), *Technology, the Economy, and Society: The American Experience*, p. 6, Columbia Univ. Press, 1987.

57. Peter Drucker, "The Changed World Economy," *Foreign Affairs*, Spring 1986, Vol. 6, p. 768, at p. 778.

58. "In many industries the level of output was so high at [the minimum efficient] scale that a small number of plants were able to meet existing national and even global demand." Chandler, "Technology and the Transformation of Industrial Organization," Ch. 3, at p. 62, in Colton & Bruchey (eds.), *Technology, the Economy, and Society*.

59. Hughes, *American Genesis*, Ch. 4, discusses the transition to specialized corporate research and development.

60. See, for example, Scherer, *Innovation and Growth*, Chs. 9 and 11.

61. Quoted in Scherer, *Innovation and Growth*, p. 13.

62. Some investments in physical capital exhibit the same positive returns to scale (and therefore market size) as research and development spending. The cost of a canal, for example, varies little with the number of boats that use it. The difference is that most physical capital has a capacity limit, which an innovation may not.

63. See Baily & Chakrabarti, *Innovation and the Productivity Crisis*, Ch. 6, p. 107. Chapter 6 discusses the recent stagnation in productivity.

86   64. Arabic progress in mathematics and Chinese inventions of gunpowder, paper made from cloth, and movable print are two ancient examples. Gregor Mendel's mid-nineteenth-century work in genetics essentially vanished, not to resurface until shortly after 1900. Some such narrowly confined discoveries may have sunk without a trace, wasting not only the expense of later rediscovery (including the expense of failed attempts at discovery), but also the benefits that would have been gained from the knowledge in the interim.

65. The accelerated diffusion of technology in the twentieth century is noted in Myron Ross, *A Gale of Creative Destruction: The Coming Economic Boom, 1992–2020,* Ch. 4, Praeger Publishers, 1989, and Alvin Toffler, *Future Shock,* Ch. 2, Random House, 1970, from which the time-lag estimates in the text are taken.

66. An externality is a cost or a benefit resulting from a transaction (broadly defined) that is not borne by either party to the transaction. Pollution is a negative externality. The creation and use of intellectual capital often generates positive externalities.

67. Studies indicate that the social rate of return on patented inventions (consumer surplus plus resource savings divided by research and development investment) is more than double the private rate of return. See, e.g., Edwin Mansfield, "Micro-economics of Technological Innovation," pp. 310–11 in Landau & Rosenberg (eds.), *The Positive Sum Strategy: Harnessing Technology for Economic Growth,* National Academy Press, 1986; Scherer, *Innovation and Growth,* Ch. 15, p. 280; and Edwin Mansfield et al., *The Production and Application of New Industrial Technology,* Ch. 8, W.W. Norton, 1977.

68. Romer, "Endogenous Technical Change," *J. Polit. Econ.,* Vol. 98, at p. S73.

69. The news is not all bad on trade matters. Positive developments include the free-trade agreement between the United States and Canada and the pending agreement with Mexico, the prospects for increasing participation in the world market by Eastern Europe, and liberalized trade policies in Mexico and Brazil.

70. *Wall Street Journal,* Jan. 13, 1992, p. A8.

71. Note that a world market price can prevail even when it is uneconomic to ship a product worldwide from one location. If, for example, United States cement producers compete with both South Korean and British producers, cement will sell at similar prices in Great Britain and South Korea even if their producers do not compete directly.

72. *Economist,* 23–29 June 1990, p. 67, and 24–30 Aug. 1991, p. 57. Edward Graham, "Foreign Direct Investment in the United States," *Science,* Vol. 254, p. 1740, 20 December 1991, discusses recent trends in foreign investment in the United States.

73. Robert Reich, *The Work of Nations: Preparing Ourselves for 21st Century Capitalism,* Knopf, 1991, especially Chs. 10, 11, and 12, maintains that economic integration has proceeded so far that the nationality of large corporations and asset owners has ceased to be meaningful. Whether or not that fairly extreme contention is accepted, the fact that it can be plausibly maintained suggests how thoroughly the world economy has been integrated.

74. Drucker, "The Changed World Economy," *Foreign Affairs*, Vol. 6, p. 768, at p. 782, Spring 1986. The further increase in the volume of world currency transactions since 1985 is not material to the present discussion.

75. *Fortune*, May 18, 1992, p. 16. *Economist*, 27 June–3 July 1992, p. 78, cites even lower projections of a 0.5 percent gain in world income from a successful Uruguay compromise, ranging up to a 1 percent gain from a radical reduction of trade barriers.

76. See Friedrich Hayek, *The Constitution of Liberty*, Ch. 3, p. 47, Univ. of Chicago Press, 1960.

77. Hayek, *Constitution of Liberty*, Chs. 2 and 3, and Jude Wanniski, *The Way the World Works*, Ch. 4, Simon & Schuster, 2d ed., 1983, discuss the development of human capital.

78. John Langbein, "The Twentieth-Century Revolution in Family Wealth Transmission," *Occasional Papers from the Law School*, Univ. of Chicago, No. 25, p. 8, 1989.

79. Kristol, *Reflections of a Neoconservative*, p. 174. See also Milton & Rose Friedman, *Free to Choose*, p. 52, Harcourt Brace, 1979, contrasting the attitudes of ethnic Indians living outside of the country with those remaining in India.

80. The use of certain forms of intellectual property is restricted for limited periods by patent, copyright, and trade secrecy. The protection afforded by these laws is, however, fairly meager both in scope and duration, and many significant developments fall into gaps between these laws and receive no protection. See C.O. Paepke, "An Economic Interpretation of the Misappropriation Doctrine: Common Law Protection for Investments in Innovation," *High Technology Law Journal*, 55, Spring 1987. The potential for foreign exploitation of scientific discoveries and technological developments, arising in part from the ineffectiveness of intellectual property protection, tends to discourage investment in innovation. "[T]he very success of the countries that are catching up [in technology] erodes the return to the pioneer. Even when the United States had a clear lead in technology, inventors and innovators received only a fraction of the social return from their activities. Once other countries made up the gap in technology, U.S. innovators found many additional foreign competitors poised to take advantage of whatever they did." Baily & Chakrabarti, *Innovation and the Productivity Crisis*, Ch. 6, p. 106.

81. Hayek, *Constitution of Liberty*, p. 24.

82. On the difficulties of attempting to quantify intangible capital, see John Kendrick, *The Formation and Stocks of Total Capital*, National Bureau of Economic Research, No. 100, General Series, 1976.

83. Jacob Schmookler, "Technological Change and Economic Theory," reprinted in Schmookler, *Patents, Invention, and Economic Change*, p. 60, Harvard Univ. Press, 1972. On the roles of Konrad Adenauer and Ludwig Erhard in promptly reinstating a free market (despite a marked lack of enthusiasm among the Allies), see Richard Nixon, *Leaders*, Ch. 5, Warner Books, 1982.

84. See Dale Jorgenson, "The Embodiment Hypothesis," *Journal of Political*

88 *Economy,* Vol. 74, p. 1, Feb. 1966. See also Ralph Landau, "U.S. Economic Growth," *Scientific American,* June 1988, p. 44, at p. 47.

85. Church & Sedlak, *Education in the United States: An Interpretive History,* p. 290, Macmillan, 1976.

86. R.F. Butts, *Public Education in the United States: From Revolution to Reform,* p. 320, Holt, Rinehart & Winston, 1978.

87. James Russell, *German Higher Schools: The History, Organization and Methods of Secondary Education in Germany,* Ch. 4, p. 106, Longmans, Green, 2d ed., 1910. Charles McClelland, *State, Society, and University in Germany 1700–1914,* Ch. 8, Cambridge Univ. Press, 1980, describes the establishment of modern university curricula.

88. G.M. Young, *Portrait of an Age: Victorian England,* p. 164, Oxford Univ. Press, 1977 ed.

89. *Economist,* 27 June–3 July 1992, p. 27, citing General Accounting Office data.

90. Paul Krugman, *The Age of Diminished Expectations: U.S. Economic Policy in the 1990s,* Ch. 6, p. 68, MIT Press, 1990. The supply-side explanation is probably the most persuasive on its face. Income taxes (including the tax on capital gains) apply to nominal returns on investment, without adjusting for inflation. Thus, a 30 percent tax rate on an 8 percent rate of return during a period of 5 percent inflation leaves a real rate of return of only 0.6 percent, too small an incentive to save. See *Wall Street Journal,* Nov. 21, 1988, column by Martin Feldstein. Although tax policies surely affect savings rates, the facts flatly contradict this explanation for the secular decline in saving: both the marginal tax rate and inflation were substantially higher in the 1970s, as was the savings rate. The worldwide decline in savings rates during the 1980s (see below) sinks any uniquely American explanation.

91. In economic terms, saving as a percentage of earned income increases with rising income level but decreases with rising wealth. See, e.g., Hendershott & Peek, "Household Saving, an Econometric Investigation," Ch. 4, especially Table 4-6, in Hendershott (ed.), *The Level and Composition of Household Saving,* Ballinger, 1985; William Hamburger, "The Relation of Consumption to Wealth and the Wage Rate," *Econometrica,* Vol. 23, p. 1, Jan. 1955 (consumption as percentage of wage earnings rises linearly with wealth as multiple of wage earnings).

92. Kevin Phillips, *The Politics of Rich and Poor,* Ch. 6, pp. 157–63, Random House, 1990. Phillips, Robert Reich, Paul Krugman, and others treat the rising wealth of the top 1 or 5 percent of the income distribution primarily as a morbid by-product of Reagan administration economic policies, a theme popularized by Governor Clinton's campaign. The merits of that position are irrelevant to the present discussion. However the wealth is divided, the rising tide must eventually push enough of those at the top of the distribution past the point of indifference to depress the overall rate of saving. The decline of savings during the 1970s suggests that the wealth effect was already being felt in that more egalitarian America.

93. U.S. Bureau of the Census, *Current Population Reports,* Series P-70, No. 22, Household Wealth and Asset Ownership: 1988, Table 3 (1990). See also *Statistical Abstract of the United States 1989,* Table 746.

94. "Upper-income taxpayers do a lopsided share of the accumulating." Phillips, *Politics of Rich and Poor,* Ch. 1, p. 11. For a quantitative treatment, see Daphne Greenwood, "Age, Income, and Household Size: Their Relation to Wealth Distribution in the United States," in Wolff (ed.), *International Comparisons of the Distribution of Household Wealth,* Table 6.6, p. 136, Oxford Univ. Press, 1987 (highest decile in money income owns half of national net wealth; 1973 data).

95. See Strauss & Howe, *Generations: The History of America's Future, 1584 to 2069,* William Morrow, 1991.

96. U.S. Bureau of the Census, *Current Population Reports,* Series P-70, No. 22, Household Wealth and Asset Ownership: 1988, Table 5 (1990).

97. World War I is estimated to have cost 32 percent of the accumulated national wealth of England, 30 percent of that of France, and 22 percent of that of Germany. Michel Beaud, *A History of Capitalism 1500–1980,* p. 148, Macmillan, 1984. World War II destroyed 43 percent of Japan's capital. Kotkin & Kishimoto, *The Third Century: America's Resurgence in the Asian Era,* Ch. 4, p. 125, Ballantine Books, 1988.

98. Rostow, *World Economy,* pp. 282–83.

99. Ralph Landau, "U.S. Economic Growth," *Scientific American,* June 1988, pp. 44, 50; *Economist,* 3–9 Feb. 1990, p. 13, and 16–22 June 1990, p. 94. The continued high savings rate of Japan despite its increasing wealth does nothing to undermine the analysis in the text. First, the savings rate in Japan has been higher than in the West through most of the twentieth century, presumably due to cultural factors, but the trend was downward through most of the 1980s. Moreover, Japan's consumer prices are well above world levels. By one estimate, prices are 60 percent higher in Japan than in the United States. See *Economist,* 18–24 May 1991, p. 81. As a consequence, the Japanese may perceive themselves to be far less wealthy than the economic statistics would suggest.

100. The annual compound growth rate of fixed capital stock in the five leading free-market economies averaged 4.72 percent from 1950 to 1973, but only 3.22 percent from 1973 to 1984. Maddison, *World Economy in the Twentieth Century,* Table 6.5, p. 74 (data from U.S., Japan, Germany, France, and U.K.). The average ratio of gross domestic investment to GDP for the same five countries declined from 26.2 percent in 1973 to 20.4 percent in 1986. Maddison, Table 6.6.

101. See *AMEX Bank Review,* 16 Jan. 1991, and *Economist,* 9–15 Feb. 1991, p. 69.

102. Sheng-Cheng Hu, "The Growth of Pension Saving," in Hendershott (ed.), *Level and Composition of Household Saving,* Ch. 9. This rise in pension saving is likely to slow in response to the same forces as other forms of saving. *Wall Street Journal,* Dec. 17, 1991, p. A1, reports that 60 percent of employees polled would accept a reduced pension in exchange for increased health benefits.

103. Langbein, "The Twentieth-Century Revolution in Family Wealth Transmission," *Occasional Papers from the Law School,* Univ. of Chicago, No. 25, pp. 18, 23–25, 1989.

104. See Strauss & Howe, *Generations,* pp. 28, 261–78. The trend is the same in

90   Britain, where the portion of the lowest income group that is elderly declined by more than half during the 1980s. See *Economist*, 2–8 May 1992, p. 67.

105. Hendershott & Peek, "Household Saving, an Econometric Investigation," pp. 89–90.

106. Maddison, *World Economy in the Twentieth Century*, Tables 1.5, 6.10, and 7.5 and p. 89; John Kendrick, *Interindustry Differences in Productivity Growth*, Tables 5 and 7, American Enterprise Institute, 1983 (showing absolute declines in output per unit capital, 1973–79 and 1979–81); and *Economist*, 3–9 August 1991, p. 18 (capital productivity declined during 1980s in all of the largest economies except Britain).

107. Harold Vatter, "Technological Innovation and Social Change in the United States, 1870–1980," in Colton & Bruchey (eds.), *Technology, the Economy, and Society*, Ch. 2 at p. 46.

108. Maddison, *World Economy in the Twentieth Century*, Table C-12, p. 136. The data for other affluent nations reflect similar trends.

109. *Economist*, 24–30 Aug. 1991, p. 25.

Chapter Four

PLATEAUS AND CEILINGS

More than twenty years ago, *Future Shock* popularized the thesis that change has accelerated, stressing people barely able to maintain pace with events. That idea has since traded its novelty for universal acceptance. Madison Avenue, the ultimate authority on public sentiment, has added its imprimatur: the pace of change sells investment service, headache remedies, leisure travel, mobile telephones, psychological counseling, political candidates, and almost everything else that sex does not. The historical record fully justifies this emphasis. The rate of change has outstripped even utopians' imaginations. Julian West, who slept from 1887 to 2000 in Edward Bellamy's *Looking Backward,* awoke to a society that would have seemed positively familiar next to the one that actually exists. After millennia of virtual stagnation, people remade their world in a mere two centuries. And that change has been overwhelmingly beneficent, the cavils of perennial social critics notwithstanding.[1]

Such progress cannot continue at anything like its pace of the last two centuries. Past advances have so vastly improved the technological and economic ability to satisfy people's material desires that the scope available for further improvements is quite limited. Future progress will be confined to a small and shrinking increment between the state of the art and the limits of the possible.

In assessing such limits, it is crucial to focus on the underlying human ends, not on the present means of achieving those ends.

92   Horses have scarcely improved since first being tamed, but the railroad could still revolutionize transportation in the nineteenth century. Simon Kuznets, a pioneer in studying the role of technology in growth, concluded that little additional progress was possible in textile manufacturing just before the invention of synthetic fibers. The basic oxygen process similarly dispatched Kuznets's analysis of steelmaking.[2]

Unforeseen advances in technology are, as a class, predictable, and they will continue to occur, which makes any analysis based on the present means of production quite fragile. The underlying human needs and wants, by contrast, change very little. People have always moved about; the airplane is merely the most recent vehicle for that purpose. The question posed by this chapter is how much better any advances, whether foreseeable or not, could satisfy those needs and wants. In each instance, the answer is: not much.

FOOD PRODUCTION

Food has everywhere and always been primary among these needs. It also provides a clear and simple illustration of the external limits to continued progress. Food production, once the dominant activity of society, has been permanently relegated to the margin.

The trends that produced this transformation are readily identified. One was mechanization. The subsistence farmer scratched the earth with a few hand tools and, if he was comparatively prosperous, an ox-drawn plow. Contrast modern agribusiness. A grain combine harvests more than one hundred acres of grain in a day, compared to about one acre for a man with a scythe. Such combines, rare as recently as 1920, numbered more than a million in the United States by 1960.[3] Tractors represented nearly as great an improvement over horses for plowing. Milking machines reduced the required labor per dairy cow fourfold. Mechanization brought similar gains across a broad range of farming, ranching, and fishing activities.

Meanwhile, improvements on nature sharply increased output. Chemical fertilizers are higher in plant nutrients and cheaper to apply than manure and other organic fertilizers. Worldwide usage now exceeds 100 billion pounds annually (about twenty pounds for each person on the planet), not only raising yields, but also reducing the need for crop rotation in advanced economies.[4] This allowed increased scale and specialization, but at the cost of providing a banquet for insects. DDT and other organic insecticides greatly alleviated this problem after World War II. But the largest improvements were in the crops themselves, as America began and then exported the "Green Revolution." Semidwarf hybrid wheats, with thick, short stalks to support heavier heads of grain, replaced marquis wheat, itself a hardy Canadian hybrid, beginning in the 1960s.[5] Corn hybrids, almost unknown in 1930, were nearly universal by 1980. Fast-maturing, disease-and insect-resistant semidwarf rice hybrids followed in the 1960s. Together, these advances have raised yields from threefold to tenfold over nineteenth-century levels. Selective breeding has similarly doubled average milk production per dairy cow since the 1930s and halved the amount of grain consumed by chickens per pound of meat produced since the 1940s.

The following table indicates the impact of such advances on farming efficiency.[6]

4.1 U.S. FARM LABOR PRODUCTIVITY, 1925–86

	1925–29	1960–64	1982–86
Wheat man-hours/100 bu.	74	12	7
Corn man-hours/100 bu.	115	11	3
Milk man-hours/100 lbs.	3.3	1.2	0.2
Chickens man-hours/100 lbs.	8.5	0.8	0.1

In each instance, labor productivity has risen more than tenfold. This rise has steadily reduced prices. A bushel of wheat averaged $1.05 during the 1870s.[7] An equivalent price in the 1980s would have been about $12 per bushel, about three times the actual price.

Enhancement of crops will continue. Genetic engineering offers many of the same opportunities as cross-fertilization and cross-breeding, but with much greater speed and flexibility.[8] Tomato plants have already been altered to produce fruit that rots less quickly. Scientists have recently developed methods for implanting heritable foreign

94 genes into monocots, which comprise the most important food crops.[9] One early use of this technology will be to improve the nutritional value of corn by inserting the genes for the two essential amino acids it lacks. Work is proceeding on increasing the resistance of several crops to insects, herbicides, and plant diseases. It may be possible to give food crops the rhizobium bacterium's ability to convert atmospheric nitrogen into ammonia, drastically reducing the need for fertilizer.[10] Although genetically engineered crops have yet to be harvested, several bioengineering projects are moving from laboratories into field testing.[11] Scientists may eventually be able to bypass traditional crops altogether by engineering microbes to produce edible proteins, carbohydrates, or oils without normal cultivation.

But the impact of these or any other advances, whether foreseeable or not, will be comparatively minor. In the eighteenth century, agricultural production occupied approximately 60 percent of the total population.[12] Americans employed in agriculture now account for only 2.6 percent of the work force, or 1.3 percent of the total population. Even these few are more than enough; they produce large surpluses for export and government stockpiles.[13] Past progress has thus reduced the need for farm labor by about 98 percent. Future advances will be directed toward saving some fraction of the remaining 2 percent. Even if food could be produced with no labor at all, the savings would be tiny compared to those already achieved. The other resources used in agriculture border on insignificance. Expenditures on all forms of pesticides, for example, total about $15 billion. Overall, the farm value of food consumed in America accounts for less than 4 percent of consumer expenditures.[14] Even halving those expenditures would produce barely noticeable savings. Progress may continue, but its tangible benefits cannot be anything other than paltry compared to past gains. Agriculture has reached the meaningful limits of productivity.

CONSTRUCTION

The Industrial Revolution began with construction techniques little changed from Roman times. Skilled carpenters fashioned complex joints to fasten heavy timbers, while designers used elaborate systems of secondary columns, posts, and trusses to compensate for wood's lack of strength. Stone provided the strength needed for larger buildings, but the costs of quarrying, transportation, and construction labor were staggering. Only by subjugating much of the population in slavery could Rome and Egypt afford to build their magnificent and nearly indestructible edifices. Even the best roads of the eighteenth century (excluding the few stone-paved roads surviving from Roman times) were made of gravel over compacted dirt, vulnerable to both weather and wear. Bridges consisted of timber spans between timber pilings.

New materials opened new design possibilities.[15] Cheaper iron first widened the use of nails and other quick fastenings in place of finely fitted joints, beginning an evolution that produced the typical frame houses of the present.[16] Interior iron beams began to substitute for massive timbers in factories, theaters, train stations, and anywhere else that strength or fire resistance was at a premium. Joseph Paxton, gardening superintendent for the Duke of Devonshire, demonstrated iron's larger potential with the Crystal Palace, the main hall for the Great Exhibition of 1851.[17] Its structure consisted of thousands of identical iron columns supporting miles of iron trusses. Construction on site consisted of little more than assembly. Paxton completed the building less than nine months after the design was accepted, with only four months occupied on site. The result was a glass box enclosing over eighteen acres. The iron structure was so thin as to seem fragile and gossamerlike to nineteenth-century eyes accustomed to massive wood and masonry members, but it was more than strong enough. When the exhibition ended, promoters disassembled and reerected it at Sydenham, where it stood until destroyed by fire in 1936.

This substitution of a metal skeleton for thick load-bearing walls was the inspiration behind the skyscrapers that began to appear in the United States in the 1880s. With the completion of the Empire State Building (1931), the design had achieved its full potential. It was ready for occupancy little more than a year after groundbreaking. (Westminster Palace, with its stone structure, required thirty years to complete in the mid-nineteenth century, and some cathedrals built in the Middle Ages occupied generations of builders.) A B-25 bomber

96   answered any question about the strength and integrity of steel frame construction in 1945 by crashing into the seventy-eighth and seventy-ninth floors without causing any structural damage.

The 1824 invention of portland cement solved another set of construction problems.[18] Concrete offered most of the qualities of stone at much lower cost. The builder could quickly pour a foundation or column in any desired shape at the building site. Steel reinforcement and prestressing with steel cables added resistance to tensile and shearing stresses, creating composite structural members that combined the differing strengths of the materials. This combination of versatility and low cost made concrete the most widely used construction material in the world.

The substitution of power equipment for labor has been the other basic trend in construction. Bulldozers, power shovels, and other earth-moving equipment have substantially replaced the gangs of pick-and-shovel men so long a feature of every construction site. Cement mixers deliver ready-mixed concrete for foundations. Forklifts, elevators, and cranes raise heavy loads far better than the muscle power supplemented by elaborate pulleys and hoists used since Roman times. Power saws, drills, and sanders, nail and staple guns, and paint sprayers are the standard tools of home builders everywhere.[19]

These advances have combined with increasing affluence to construct a new world in just two centuries. But little more will be done in the developed economies, simply because so little remains to be done.

Roads and bridges illustrate the point. As recently as 1900, the United States had only about two hundred miles of paved roads outside the few large cities.[20] Highways now radiate in all directions from even the smallest hamlets. New roads are comparatively rare, simply because it is hard to conjure up a need. Through the nineteenth century, roads commonly stopped at any wide, deep, or navigable river, because trussed timber bridges could span no more than two hundred feet between pilings. Traffic waited for ferries, creating long delays, even on heavily traveled routes. (Ferries linked Brooklyn and Manhattan until 1883, and the George Washington Bridge was the first across the Hudson at New York in 1931.) Iron, steel, and reinforced concrete stretched the maximum span length to more than five hundred feet, and suspension bridges carry light traffic over even longer distances. Multimile bridges connect the Florida Keys and cross Lake Pontchartrain and Tampa Bay. Concrete arches span gorges hundreds of feet deep in the western United States and the Alps. The absence of a bridge across any obstacle now indicates not an engineering constraint, but a lack of potential traffic. Similarly, undammed rivers are those that have no potential for water impoundment or hydroelectric power generation (or where the environmental costs are too great for current sensibilities). Substantially all of the major dam projects in recent years have been in less developed countries, where suitable damsites remain to be exploited.[21]

Surfeit or sufficiency characterizes most other kinds of construction as well. Most cities in the United States are awash in high-rise office and retail shopping space.[22] New buildings may reduce rents or lure some tenants away from older buildings; they rarely reflect any shortage of suitable space. In housing, the United States has more dwelling units than households, and the units provide, on average, about six hundred square feet of living space per occupant. The housing stock of most other advanced nations is comparable, if a bit less generous. Further amenities can always be added, but the improvement over living conditions of the past, with extended families living in rude shelters covering a few hundred square feet of beaten earth floor, certainly cannot be repeated or even approached.

The existing housing surplus contrasts sharply with the impression conveyed by the media, which regularly fill slow news days with stories about the homeless or the fading American dream of homeownership. In a few places, the problem is rent control or antigrowth zoning that produces a genuine (although factitious) local housing shortage. More generally, the affordability of housing is simply a political choice, although rarely articulated as such. City councils levy taxes, impose density and use restrictions, and require developers to provide ever more and better roads, sidewalks, utilities, parks, and other off-site improvements. Apparently contrary to expectations, buyers, rather than the tooth fairy, must pay for these niceties: less than half of the price of a single-family home goes toward building the actual structure.[23] Any city that wants more owners and less renters can grant its own wish by lightening these burdens. The result will be affordable housing, albeit with fewer amenities. As for the

98 homeless, their problem is not lack of housing, but poverty. They could equally be described as carless or phoneless. Another million or two houses or apartment units would still leave them on the street. When they have enough income to afford a dwelling, it will be there, waiting. In short, these are not problems that more or better construction can address.

Two conclusions flow from these observations. First, the great construction surge of the nineteenth and twentieth centuries is over in advanced economies. Both residential and commercial construction, although considered depressed by those in the industry since the late 1980s, has in fact exceeded the needs of the slowly expanding United States population. Given the multidecade useful life of most construction, the construction sector will almost certainly shrink in relative importance, with maintenance and upgrading forming a larger portion of the work.

Second, future improvements on current design, engineering, and construction techniques will necessarily be incremental and modest in comparison to such enabling advances as the use of iron and steel, reinforced concrete, and power equipment. Indeed, progress during the last generation has been conspicuously lacking. Measured productivity in the U.S. construction sector is less than in 1948, the only sector to experience an absolute decline.[24] Little if any potential exists for reversing that trend.

TRANSPORTATION

Railroads and steamships severely undermined the tyranny of distance in the nineteenth century. Automobiles and airplanes overthrew it completely in the twentieth. After a victory this sweeping, relatively little remains to be accomplished.

The Model T combined the speed of a train with the flexibility of a wagon, at a price the masses could afford.[25] Ford sold over sixteen million of them between 1908 and 1927. By the end of that run, other manufacturers had adopted Ford's mass production methods to keep costs down while greatly enhancing the product. Electric starters, low-pressure tires, automatic transmissions, and radios first appeared in luxury vehicles, then percolated rapidly downmarket.

Higher-performance engines and limited-access highways combined to double cruising speeds. These improvements cost essentially nothing: the average price of U.S. automobiles, adjusted for inflation, was about the same in 1959 as in 1919.[26] Total U.S. registrations rose from eight million to sixty million during the same period, making autos almost universally available. Ordinary people enjoyed a mobility greater than the wealthiest nobles of the eighteenth century.

The aviation equivalent of the Model T was the DC-3, a twin-engine 170-mile-per-hour monoplane that dominated scheduled commercial service after 1935.[27] It was reliable and durable, if a bit Spartan, with its unpressurized cabin and cramped seating. World War II telescoped the inevitable improvements into little more than a decade. Aircraft derived from military designs and flown by former military pilots filled airlines' expanding fleets. Radar was quickly adapted from air defense to civilian air traffic control. The quest for faster fighter aircraft brought an infusion of public funds for research into jet engines, a form of gas turbine that converts heat energy into thrust rather than mechanical work. Practical engine designs arrived too late to affect the course of the war, but just in time to boost the postwar surge in commercial aviation. By the mid-1960s, airlines scheduled New York–Los Angeles flights for five hours, less than one third of the time needed for the DC-3, at less than half the cost.[28] Since then, speed has plateaued, but rising fuel efficiency,[29] larger airplanes, and deregulation have combined to push down ticket prices.[30] Each year, more than one third of all American adults fly,[31] compared to only twenty million civilian passengers worldwide in 1947.[32]

In many respects, this technology already exceeds the demands of the market. Commercial airlines fly the present generation of subsonic jets far below top speed to conserve fuel and extend engine life. The failure of the Concorde demonstrates the limited demand for faster aircraft. The British and French governments had to pay for the few airplanes ever put into service. Its builders frankly concede that no new supersonic transport will leave the ground without similar governmental subsidies. Supporters of the hypersonic spaceplane have dropped any commercial application as patently infeasible.[33]

Ground travel presents the same situation. Many automobiles sold in the United States would cruise comfortably at one hundred miles

100   per hour or more, speeds that are also within the design limits of most interstate highways. Nevertheless, speed limits in the United States are sixty-five miles per hour or less. The clamor for raising these limits has been decidedly muted. With the public willingly forgoing a 50 percent increase in speed, enhancing the technology further would be pointless.[34] This multidecade plateau in the speed of both ground and air transportation suggests that still-faster travel is not high on many people's agendas.[35] Nor is it easy to imagine how comfort or reliability could be much enhanced.

More fundamentally, the absolute potential for future progress is almost insignificant compared to that previously achieved. Cost and speed are the dominant considerations. The next generation of commercial aircraft will be still more fuel-efficient, but even 100-percent-efficient engines would reduce ticket prices comparatively little. High-speed passenger trains could fill a niche between automobiles and airplanes on some densely traveled routes, although politicians and the media have greatly exaggerated their market potential.[36] Automotive fuel efficiency may continue to rise slightly as polymer composites and other advanced materials lower vehicle weights,[37] while improved ceramics finally permit the introduction of gas turbine engines.[38] Compact gas turbines would also open the possibility of turboelectric automobiles, reducing air pollution locally in metropolitan areas.[39] Advances even in these areas could not compare to those of the recent past; 1990 model year vehicles sold in the United States emitted far less pollution and used far less fuel than those from 1970.[40]

If cost savings could be important anywhere, it would be in freight transportation. Freight charges weigh most heavily on low-value, high-volume bulk shipments. Trucking such freight five hundred miles costs no more than a penny or two per pound, representing a few percent or less of the delivered price. Shipment by rail is even cheaper. Transatlantic bulk shipment costs in the range of $5 to $10 per ton. Tanker transport adds only a few cents per gallon of gasoline. High-value, perishable, and other priority shipments can absorb even air freight, at slightly over $1 per ton-mile in the United States (less than one fifth of the cost in 1970, adjusted for inflation). Even a substantial percentage decline in the transportation cost component would thus not represent a significant saving on most goods. The advent of global assembly lines and the existence of world markets in so many products demonstrate that freight costs have become a relatively minor consideration.

In moving people, speed outweighs other considerations.[41] Sailing across the Atlantic in the early nineteenth century required six weeks. By 1906, luxury liners had reduced that time to five days. The same trip on subsonic commercial jets occupies about six hours and on the Concorde slightly over three hours. The irreducible ground time (traveling to and from airports, checking in, waiting, taxiing, clearing customs) may equal or exceed the time actually spent in transit. The progress in overland travel has been even greater. The Western settlers' trek from St. Louis to California or Oregon by wagon required approximately four months. Completion of the transcontinental railroad condensed that trip to four days by 1870. Jets cross the same distance in a few hours.

Thus, people now complete the overwhelming majority of their trips in half of a working day or less. Even if speeds were to double or triple, trip times would decline only slightly.[42] By this or any other measure, the potential for future progress in transportation appears puny compared to the advances of the last two hundred years.

MANUFACTURING

Progress in manufacturing has also advanced far into the realm of diminishing returns.

Since Ford's introduction of the assembly line, machinery has continued to replace physical labor, with robotics the most recent extension of the trend.[43] The first generations of robots, introduced through the early 1980s, were rigidly programmed machine tools that excelled in such repetitive tasks as welding and painting. Current designs use more intelligent programming techniques and tactile and visual sensing systems to achieve greater flexibility. The fastest-growing application is assembly. Prototype factories produce electric starter motors and dishwashers with essentially no manufacturing labor; the few workers in the plant monitor and maintain the robots. The leading memory chip fabricators virtually exclude workers from the confines of the factory, both for efficiency and to avoid contami-

102   nation of the wafers. Improved robots will substitute for blue-collar production labor in performing an ever wider range of tasks, particularly in high-wage economies.

The other pervasive trend in twentieth-century manufacturing has been the development of synthetic materials with combinations of qualities not found in nature. Efficient large-scale processes for producing inorganic chemicals began to appear in the nineteenth century. With Germany in the lead, an expanding chemical industry supplied acids, caustics, and chemical fertilizers in huge volumes at steadily lower prices.[44]

The emphasis soon shifted to organic chemistry, using coal tar and later petroleum as feed stocks. Manufacturers had long sought a substitute for natural rubber, but the incomplete understanding of polymers discouraged a systematic attack on the problem. The threatened loss of natural rubber supplies with the outbreak of World War II added urgency to the effort, producing the first synthetic rubbers, some cheaper than natural rubber, others with qualities natural rubber cannot match. Rigid polymers (particularly polyethylene and polyvinyl chloride) followed after the war.[45] Manufacturers can mold or extrude them into virtually any shape and vary their properties by introducing additives. They substitute for metal, wood, or paper in a wide range of applications, usually at a fraction of the cost, and perform some functions for which no satisfactory alternatives exist.[46] Annual thermoplastic production in the United States alone now exceeds sixty billion pounds.

The long linear structure of polymers also suggested their use as synthetic fibers. Du Pont, recognizing the opportunity, lured a reluctant Wallace Carothers from the Harvard chemistry department. Carothers delivered, converting his discoveries in polymer chemistry into nylon, a polyamide that can be extruded and drawn into fibers.[47] Nylon's excellent flex, water and abrasion resistance, and strength made it an immediate commercial success, even though it was initially twice as expensive as silk. Full-scale production began in 1938; 64 million nylon stockings were sold the following year. Polyester followed in 1941 and quickly became a mainstay of the apparel industry. By 1987, worldwide synthetic fiber production exceeded thirty billion pounds.

A new generation of synthetic materials is gaining importance in manufacturing.[48] The most common of these are the plastic-fiber composites, in which synthetic fibers are embedded in a thermoplastic matrix. Carbon-fiber-reinforced plastic provides strong and light structural components in recent generations of jet airplanes. More exotic materials include metal matrix composites, which are produced by pouring molten metal into a preform of metal (e.g., silicon carbide) fibers. The fibers resist both deformation and stress cracking, the source of catastrophic failure when metal becomes fatigued. In ceramic composites, metal "whiskers" (monocrystalline fibers a few microns or less in length) are added to ceramic powders before processing. Such composites have the strength and heat resistance of ceramics without their tendency to shatter. New heat-resistant fibers (e.g., silicon carbonitride) may open the way to reinforcing ceramics with longer fibers. Homogenous "nanophase" materials (processed to reduce their grain to a fineness of a few billionths of a meter) exhibit some of the same properties as composites. Nanophase metals may be three to five times harder than ordinary samples; ceramics become more ductile and less prone to fracture. With processing advances[49] and declining costs, sales of composites and other advanced materials are projected to increase tenfold during the 1990s with worldwide sales of $400 billion by the year 2000.[50]

But neither these nor any other advances can begin to rival past progress in manufacturing, for several reasons.

First, and contrary to generations of experience, productivity gains may no longer produce more total output. Whether the product was cotton cloth, steel, automobiles, radios, or microwave ovens, the cycle has always been the same: higher productivity reduces costs, lowering prices, increasing sales, and raising output. But many major industries now operate at well below capacity, regardless of the business cycle. The world automotive industry, for example, can efficiently produce sixty million cars and light trucks annually, eight to ten million more than it can sell, even in a boom year.[51] The steel industries of both the United States and Europe consistently operated at less than 80 percent of capacity during the 1980s, despite the closure of plants formerly accounting for many tens of millions of tons of annual output. Unused capacity commonly means that the cost of producing one additional unit (another car or ton of steel) would be less than the average cost of producing the preceding units, because the factory and other fixed costs are essentially free. The manufacturer could therefore lower its average cost per unit without any change in technology or added investment.[52] This suggests that, despite the longest worldwide economic expansion on record, output was constrained by demand, not supply. If so, incremental cost reductions from new technology or investment would add little to output.

Second, the shifting mix of manufactured goods sharply limits the benefits to be realized from further advances in manufacturing processes. An $8,000 personal computer costs about $800 to manufacture,[53] compared to perhaps $4,000 for an $8,000 automobile. Fiber-optic cable is cheaper to make than copper wire of equal message-carrying capacity, as is plastic compared to steel of equal strength. Extreme cases include new microprocessors, software, and pharmaceuticals, for which the cost of production is a negligible fraction of the purchase price. Personal computers, fiber-optic cable, software, and other knowledge-intensive products constitute an ever-increasing portion of the world's total manufacturing mix, while automobiles, copper wire, steel, and other such early-industrial-age products are in relative if not absolute decline. The same dynamic operates to a lesser extent even within the traditional manufacturing industries, as, for example, integrated circuits come to represent an ever larger fraction of the value of an automobile. With manufacturing cost a declining factor in the changing mix of goods and services in the economy, further efficiencies will yield decremental economic gains.

Finally, past progress has left comparatively little room for improvement. The first wave of mechanization in many industries reduced the required labor by 80 percent or more. These gains continued even into recent decades as mechanization intensified and materials improved. The number of vehicles produced per production worker doubled between 1948 and 1978, and has risen another 40 percent since then. Japanese manufacturers require only about twenty man-hours to assemble an average automobile (either in Japan or in transplant factories in the United States).[54] With production labor accounting for only 20 to 25 percent of the cost of an automobile (less than the combined costs of distribution, marketing, and warranty repairs), further productivity gains would yield only small and diminishing returns. This example is not isolated. Western steel producers faced with Japanese competition doubled their labor productivity between 1982 and 1989.[55] The most efficient mini-mills now use only about two hours of production labor per ton of output.[56] Overall, the quantity of blue-collar labor required per unit of manufacture declined by 60 percent in the United States between 1973 and 1988.[57]

Employment data reflect these realities. In the 1920s, one third of the American work force was manufacturing labor.[58] That proportion declined to one fourth by the 1950s, and to one sixth by the mid-1980s. The payroll of production workers declined from more than one tenth of gross national product in 1949 to less than one twentieth at present.[59] During this period, total manufacturing output has risen manyfold. Since the Korean conflict, manufacturing output in the United States has accounted for a relatively steady percentage of a rapidly rising gross national product. Between 1973 and 1985 alone, United States manufacturing production in constant dollars rose by almost 40 percent, while the manufacturing work force declined by five million. Thus, media reports of the manufacturing sector's imminent demise have been, at a minimum, premature; only manufacturing *employment* is declining, a "victim" of rising productivity.[60] This trend is firmly established in every advanced economy, despite sporadically intense resistance by organized labor and in government. But the trend has an obvious and absolute limit: manufacturing employment cannot decline to zero. As advanced economies approach that limit, the tangible benefits from productivity gains will continue to diminish.

Intense price competition in a world economy marked by overcapacity virtually assures further mechanization and innovation in manufacturing processes. But those advances lack any potential to be the driving forces of material progress that they have been for the last two hundred years.

ENERGY AND POWER

The announcement of cold fusion caused great excitement. "The greatest discovery since fire," the sober and objective assessment of

106 one Utah politician, seemed to capture the popular sentiment. It would deliver another industrial revolution, only larger and less gritty than the original. With this buildup, the story's unraveling[61] may have been for the best: it substituted a quick, sharp disappointment for the drawn-out disillusionment that would have resulted when cold fusion made no appreciable difference. Even in its fairy-tale form, it could have done no more than to make energy cheap and abundant. Past progress has long since done that.

Watt's steam engine barely began the shift from muscle to mechanical power. High-pressure compound engines increased thermal efficiency and multiplied the uses of steam power through the nineteenth century. By 1896, worldwide steam capacity had risen to 66 million horsepower, more than three times the combined power of water, wind, wood, draft animals, and people at the end of the eighteenth century.[62] But even the most advanced reciprocating engines suffered from vibration and mechanical stress. Several inventors tried to circumvent these shortcomings by adapting existing water turbines to steam. For most of the nineteenth century, they failed: steam accelerated to far greater speeds than flowing water, regularly destroying experimental turbine wheels. Charles Parsons, an English engineer, finally overcame this difficulty in 1884 by decompressing the steam gradually through many turbine stages.[63] Parsons's turbines achieved an overall thermal efficiency of 20 percent and delivered their power in the form of rapid rotation, eighteen thousand revolutions per minute for the first turbine, compared to perhaps a thousand for reciprocating engines. Parsons graphically demonstrated the potential of the new power source at Queen Victoria's Diamond Jubilee by dancing his *Turbinia* around the British fleet at an unheard-of thirty-four knots, revealing the proud flagships as so many lumbering dinosaurs doomed by changing technology. By 1906, Cunard's luxurious *Mauretania* and ill-fated *Lusitania* were crossing the Atlantic in five days, powered by their seventy-thousand-horsepower turbines.[64] The internal combustion engine would soon deprive all steam power of its pride of place in small and mobile applications, but Parsons's turbines lived on in electric power generation.

Internal combustion engines were inherently smaller and lighter than steam, but they introduced design and engineering problems that strained the limits of nineteenth-century technology. Fuel and air needed to be mixed in precise ratio, compressed, and ignited, all inside a cylinder that had to operate reliably and durably under extremes of temperature and pressure. Nikolaus Otto cleared the basic hurdles in 1876 with his four-stroke engine, which "wasted" two strokes drawing the fuel-and-air mixture into the cylinder and compressing it. Otto built these engines solely for stationary uses. His technical director, Gottlieb Daimler, realized that locomotive applications would best exploit their small size. He therefore quit the firm in 1885 and began mounting engines on carriages and bicycles. The nascent automotive industry brought surging demand, producing frequent improvements in engine performance and efficiency. The less esoteric of these have included shortening the piston stroke to reduce friction losses, substituting fuel injection for carburetors to improve distribution of fuel in the cylinders, replacing mechanically regulated ignition by electronic ignition, and supercharging or turbo charging to increase oxygen in the cylinder at high engine speeds. These advances have produced engines of diverse and impressive capabilities, including some that squeeze fifty miles of highway cruising from one gallon of gasoline and others that pull thirty tons of freight.

Internal combustion engines required liquid fuels in unprecedented quantities. Whale oil had supplied most of those needs before the industrial era. As the demand for synthetic lighting grew, it confronted a distinctly inelastic supply, with predictable results. Between 1675 and 1721, seven thousand Dutch whaling expeditions killed 33,000 whales in the Spitsbergen area alone, effectively depopulating the once-rich feeding ground.[65] Just as with the earlier firewood shortage, a fossil fuel was the needed replacement.

Oil debuted modestly enough in 1859, when Edwin Drake drilled near some surface seepage in Titusville, Pennsylvania, and struck a deposit that yielded twenty-five barrels per day. As such surface pools were exhausted, geologists began to understand the kinds of structures likely to bear oil. British earthquake research in Japan produced the seismograph in 1880, which permitted subsurface mapping of geologic formations (a positive externality from research of the kind noted in Chapter 3). In 1889, as the internal combustion engine emerged from the workshop, oil production in the United States had risen to 35 million barrels. Most of this was distilled to obtain kerosene for use in lighting. Gasoline was a dangerous by-product, which the distillers carefully discarded. This erstwhile nuisance was quickly recognized as the optimal fuel for the new engines. The popular success of the Model T shifted the demand balance, and most crudes yielded far more kerosene and other heavy fractions than could be sold. Petroleum refiners therefore began enhancing the output of gasoline by "cracking" large molecules at high temperature and pressure without air. Catalytic cracking followed in the 1930s, producing better yields of high-grade fuels at lower cost.[66] The reaction vessels and tall fractionating columns (for separating the fractions of oil on a continuous basis) represented huge investments. Economies of scale required constant, high-volume throughput, which contributed as much to the concentration of the industry as Rockefeller's machinations. As gasoline engines became pervasive in both transportation and industry, petroleum production spiraled upward, from 150 million barrels in 1900[67] to 250 million metric tons in 1938,[68] an elevenfold increase.

Electricity has been the other signature power source of the twentieth century. Michael Faraday, an English chemist, recorded the first results of practical value. In 1831, Faraday discovered that a changing magnetic field induces a current in a conductor, the basis of both the electrical generator and the electric motor. (The practical significance of induction may not have been immediately apparent, except to Faraday. William Gladstone, later prime minister, skeptically asked at a demonstration, "What good is it?" Faraday is supposed to have replied: "Soon you will be able to tax it.")[69]

The crucial early battle over the spread of electrical power involved the transition to alternating current. Edison based his work at Menlo Park and the original Pearl Street lighting system on direct current. When George Westinghouse and the eccentric genius Nikola Tesla began to champion alternating current, Edison reacted with a savage propaganda campaign, exploiting his almost legendary stature and public concern over the safety of electricity generally. As late as 1900, direct current remained the principal form of electrical service.[70] But alternating current enjoyed one clear advantage—it can be generated and transmitted at very high voltages, then stepped down to safer levels near the point of usage. This allows the primary transmission lines to carry more power over long distances without excessive resistance losses. Westinghouse's thirty-kilovolt transmission line from Niagara Falls to Buffalo convincingly demonstrated this advantage, and alternating current soon dominated.

Long-distance transmission allowed utilities to make the most efficient use of their huge capital investments in power generation and distribution. Generating capacity must satisfy maximum demand. Expanding the system across broad regions diversifies the customer base and thus tends to level the load curve, resulting in more efficient use of capital and lower cost power. This self-reinforcing dynamic drove rapid consolidation of electric utilities early in the new century, with Samuel Insull playing the role of Rockefeller.[71] At its peak, Commonwealth Edison and interconnected utilities controlled by Insull served customers in thirty-two states.

Altogether, electricity usage in the United States and worldwide roughly doubled during each of the first eight decades of the twentieth century. Consumption of all forms of energy followed a similar if slightly less dramatic trend, rising more than fivefold between 1925 and 1972.[72] A nation's energy use per capita correlates almost perfectly with its degree of economic advancement, a correlation that has held for more than a century.[73] Abundant and ever cheaper energy has quite literally fueled material progress during the industrial era.

But these trends cannot continue, as a moment's thought on the glimmering potential of cold fusion will demonstrate. The principal use of cold fusion would have been to generate electricity. Graph 4.2 on the next page reflects the results of past advances:[74]

After this 80 percent price reduction, the potential for further gains is negligible. Generation equipment, the distribution system, maintenance, management, and customer service account for most of the remaining cost. Cold fusion would not have reduced any of these. On the best assumptions, it might have saved a penny or two per kilowatt-hour.

Real energy technologies fare no better than imaginary ones on this analysis. Solar power has for decades been the dream of those disenchanted with fossil fuels and nuclear power. Tangible progress toward realizing that dream has been slight: the "fuel" is free, but the capital cost of collecting it remains prohibitive. Electricity from a commercial-scale photovoltaic facility would currently be four to five times

4.2 PRICE OF ELECTRICITY, U.S. RESIDENTIAL 1920–88
(cents per kwhr, constant 1980$)

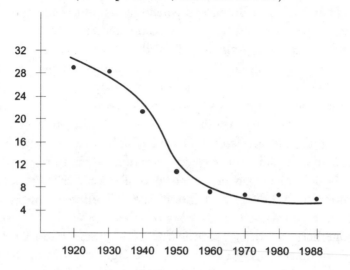

more expensive than from a coal-fired generator.[75] Recent developments have the potential for making solar cells more efficient and cheaper.[76] But technology cannot circumvent a basic limitation: the sun delivers no more than one kilowatt of power per square meter to the surface of the Earth, and that only at relatively low latitudes for about eight hours per day.[77] To replace a one-thousand-megawatt generating station, even assuming improved conversion efficiencies and favorable operating conditions, would require about thirteen and a half square miles of solar cells.[78] Cloud cover, moisture, natural particulates, and pollutants sporadically reduce the available power. These fluctuations in output would require maintaining conventional generating capacity of nearly peak requirements or massive power storage devices. The resulting capital costs would almost certainly dwarf the fuel savings. As a result, solar power is not likely to become cost-competitive with fossil fuel or nuclear power generation. The director of the Solar Energy Research Institute, not one inclined to disparage the potential of solar power, implicitly acknowledges this fact when he asserts that the sun could supply appreciable amounts of electricity in the United States within the next fifty years if "governmental policies . . . require a rapid displacement of fossil fuels without respect to cost, that is overrid[e] normal 'free market' processes."[79] As Dennis Flanagan, longtime editor of *Scientific American,* has observed about the prospects for solar (and wind) power: "In the long run . . . scarcely anyone wants to pay a larger electric bill for sentimental reasons."[80] Solar power will remain restricted to a few niche applications.[81]

"Hot" fusion suffers from several difficulties that the cold version was supposed to avoid. All the possible methods of initiating the reaction require huge expenditures of energy; none has yet approached the breakeven point (where recoverable energy output equals the initiating energy).[82] Even after that point is reached, any form of fusion would produce localized temperatures higher than those at the center of the sun, creating daunting engineering problems. After forty years of basic research and the expenditure of more than $6 billion in the United States alone, few observers believe that fusion holds any practical promise for many decades, if ever.[83] Support for continued research is waning. And, of course, even if all the problems were overcome, the potential gains could not exceed those imagined above from cold fusion.

Fission is a real and already viable energy source, stymied in the United States (although not elsewhere) by misplaced safety and environmental concerns.[84] Passive safety features may revive the technology.[85] Metallic-alloy fuel elements, for example, expand when overheated, automatically stopping the reaction. An alternative is pelletized uranium encapsulated with a shell that can withstand core temperatures even during a total loss of coolant accident. Gravity-feed flooding is another way to achieve safety without relying on human or mechanical intervention. At best, however, nuclear power would be only slightly cheaper than power from conventional sources. The reduction in air pollution from replacing coal-fired generators is potentially more significant than the cost savings.

High-temperature superconductors are also real and likely to produce useful applications within a few decades. Transportation is among the areas that may be affected. Superconducting coils create a powerful magnetic field with no loss of power from resistance. Such magnetic fields can be used to levitate trains, permitting high-speed travel without friction losses, or to propel ships with "jets"

112   of seawater.[86] But any contribution of superconduction to the large-scale generation or distribution of electrical power would necessarily be minor because efficiencies are already so high. Modern generators are more than 98 percent efficient in converting mechanical to electrical energy, and large electric motors are more than 90 percent efficient in the reverse conversion. High-voltage aluminum transmission lines dissipate less than 10 percent of generated electricity in distribution to customers.[87] Reducing these losses still further with the new superconductors would produce only trivial savings.[88] The same is true of other improvements on the existing technology, whether currently foreseeable or not. The present generation of turbines is about forty times more efficient than Watt's steam engine, and the Carnot limit severely restricts the potential for further gains.[89] In power distribution, amorphous iron alloys are replacing crystalline iron in transformer cores, sharply reducing waste heat, but the savings represent a minuscule fraction of total power flow.

The largest potential energy gains almost certainly lie in the realm of conservation, but here too limits are evident. The first oil crisis spurred industry efforts to use energy more efficiently. These efforts plus the declining relative importance of heavy manufacturing[90] reduced the amount of raw energy consumed per $1,000 of national product in every advanced economy between 1973 and 1986, with the sharpest decreases achieved in Japan (40 percent) and the United States (27 percent).[91] The potential savings from conservation have thus already been substantially squeezed in the industrial sector.

The gains that remain available in the residential and consumer sector seem significant on a percentage basis, but barely matter in practical terms. New technologies and designs offer improved energy efficiency, particularly in lighting, heating, and refrigeration, but buyers have displayed little enthusiasm.[92] Fluorescent tubes, for example, have been adapted to fit into standard light sockets. They are five times more efficient than incandescent bulbs, and pay for themselves several times over in reduced electricity and replacement costs. Consumers have ignored them in droves. Activists' explanations for this lack of interest—that people just need to be educated or that they cannot afford the higher initial cost—can scarcely be taken seriously.

Consumers had no difficulty learning about VCRs or finding hundreds of dollars to pay for them. Buyers simply do not care about saving a few kilowatt-hours, because electricity costs so little. Automobiles, one of the less efficient uses of energy, illustrate the basis for this indifference nicely. Driving fifty thousand miles over five years in a typical compact, a commuter spends $2,500 or less for gasoline, a small amount compared to the purchase price of the car and even smaller compared to the owner's income.[93] (Taxes would account for much of this cost. The typical expense in Europe would be more because of higher taxes.) Little wonder that buyers routinely opt for quick acceleration and comfort over fuel efficiency (to the constant bewilderment and frustration of the enlightened few, who benevolently urge regulations to overturn the consumers' expressed preferences and call it consumer advocacy).

The market is, as usual, more perceptive than the experts. Energy is not scarce and precious, but abundant and cheap. The returns from further advances are diminishing, if not vanishingly small, compared to the gains of the past.

COMMUNICATIONS

Communication illustrates the limits of progress in an especially stark manner. Changes and even some improvements continue, but the close approach of absolute physical limits precludes further meaningful gains.

Through the eighteenth century, information traveled as a tangible commodity. Most communications rated no better than a packet in a coach or a note entrusted to a passing traveler. Mechanical signaling proved too expensive and unreliable for ordinary use. Relays of horseback messengers carried the most urgent dispatches at speeds of 150 to 180 miles per day. By this means, for example, London learned of Wellington's victory at Waterloo after only four days, then a record time for news from the Continent.

Since then, communication has progressed by regular and predictable cycles. A scientific advance (electricity, electromagnetic waves, solid-state electronics, rocketry, or photonics) spurs inventors to

114   develop a new technology, which provides faster, cheaper, or more powerful communications. Capital investments allow the technology to spread. Along with the direct benefits, markets widen, which further increases the demand for the new medium.

Electricity initiated the first of these cycles. Traveling faster than could then be measured and requiring only a minimal energy expenditure, it was the ideal communications medium. Samuel Morse was the first to exploit this potential in 1837.[94] In its simplest form, the Morse telegraph consisted of two switches (telegraph keys) connected by a conducting line, each with an associated battery and electromagnet. Depressing one key would close the circuit between the battery at that end and the electromagnet at the other. The electromagnet would then snap the other key shut, creating the tapping sound familiar from Western movies, to be transcribed by the telegrapher. Morse code and, later, International Morse code assigned a sequence of dots and dashes (shorter and longer durations of contact) to each letter, the more frequently occurring letters receiving the faster sequences. A skilled telegrapher sent about twenty-five words per minute. With the use of automatic relays, the signal could travel any distance almost instantaneously.

Consumer response was predictable. Traffic in England increased from ten million messages in 1870 to approximately forty million in 1885 and ninety million in 1900. Further inventions accommodated this rapid rise in traffic. Thomas Edison developed duplexing, to allow one line to carry signals in both directions simultaneously. A punched-paper-tape-driven transmitter, first introduced in 1858, increased transmission speeds on high-volume lines to sixty to one hundred words per minute. Investors, sensing the immense commercial potential, poured capital into the new enterprises, quickly stringing lines to every city and town. Within a few decades, the continent of Europe had over seventy thousand miles of wire, the United States alone nearly fifty thousand miles. Oceans proved to be more formidable barriers, as the resistance and capacitance of long underwater lines without relays weakened and spread the signal, and the sheer weight and bulk of cable insulated and armored for strength and durability stretched the manufacturing technology of the time. Efforts to lay a transatlantic cable failed expensively in 1857, 1858, and 1865. The fourth attempt finally succeeded in 1866.

In one step, the telegraph brought information and people formerly separated by days, weeks, or months together within hours. Few inventions in history have had more impact.

The success of the telegraph naturally spurred inventors to attempt direct voice transmission by electricity. But the sound of a human voice is far more complex than the simple on-off that serves for telegraphy. The limited nineteenth-century understanding of the nature of sound provided would-be inventors with few clues. As a result, efforts to transmit voices electrically failed for more than thirty years. Given this history, Bell's successful instrument, first demonstrated in 1876, was surprisingly simple. He used a metal diaphragm, vibrating in response to sound waves, to induce a weak electric current, which caused the same vibrations in the diaphragm in the other instrument, reproducing the sound. Edison promptly improved on Bell's device with a form of transmitter that used carbon's varying electrical resistance under pressure to superimpose sound waves on a current supplied by a battery.

The telephone provided universality, the ability to communicate directly without employing intermediaries to code and decode the message. Its success was immediate. By 1887, only ten years after commercial introduction, there were 140,000 subscribers in the United States, 26,000 in Britain, and 22,000 in Germany. Automatic exchanges began appearing in 1897 in response to increasing traffic.[95] The number of subscribers in the United States passed one million in 1900.[96] Vacuum-tube signal repeaters, introduced in 1915, gave the signal essentially unlimited range. Transatlantic service (initially by shortwave radio) began in 1926. By 1934, there were about 33 million telephones worldwide, about half of them in the United States, where vast continental markets demanded them and deep capital resources made them possible. (The telephone system, with a separate line and instrument for each household instead of each town, required much more capital than the telegraph.) By shortly after World War II, telephone service was essentially universal in the United States and expanding rapidly in other Western nations. Instantaneous communication had become an established feature of everyday life.

Radio soon broadened the range of such communication by eliminating the need for a conductor between transmitter and receiver. In

116   perhaps the most important theoretical work of the nineteenth century, British physicist James Clerk Maxwell described electrical and magnetic fields and predicted the existence of invisible electromagnetic radiation. Heinrich Hertz verified this prediction in 1887. Guglielmo Marconi promptly converted this advanced science into a practical communications medium. By 1896, he was sending Morse code signals over distances of a few kilometers with his wireless telegraph. In 1899 he bridged the English Channel, and in 1901 the Atlantic Ocean.[97] The American inventors (and bitter enemies) Lee De Forest and Edwin Armstrong added vacuum-tube rectifiers and amplifiers, allowing transmission on a single, stable frequency.[98] Voice transmission then required little more than to replace the key in the transmission circuit with a microphone, a device similar to Edison's carbon transmitter for the telephone.

Radio supplemented but did not supplant the telegraph and the telephone. Its earliest important practical use was in marine communications. But its real promise lay in point-to-multipoint or broadcast communications; it was a natural mass medium. Commercial broadcasting began in 1920, the first radio network in 1926. Receiving sets quickly became household fixtures; sales in the United States increased from approximately 200,000 units in 1923 to nearly five million in 1929.[99]

Television added pictures. The technical problems had been solved in principle by the 1930s, but World War II interrupted commercialization.[100] After the war, television rapidly became the dominant mass communications medium. By 1960, there were more than eighty million receivers in the United States alone, and nationwide programming networks flourished in every developed country. Television has become the principal source of news and entertainment for more people in advanced nations than radio, newspapers, and periodicals combined.

The effects of such mass communications media were profound. News became instantly accessible to anyone within range of a transmitter. Widespread awareness of most major events anywhere in the world trailed the occurrence of those events by a day or less. Producers and consumers could immediately adapt their behavior to droughts, political changes, wars, scientific or natural-resource discoveries, and any other event with implications for the balance of supply and demand. The time lags and uncertainties in the flow of basic information had all but disappeared. Sellers could market and promote their goods nationally, accelerating trends toward standardization of product offerings, increased scale of production, and faster acceptance of new products. The result was accelerating integration of world markets.

Two further advances have dominated and will continue to dominate progress in communications: satellites and fiber optics.

Electromagnetic transmissions travel in (almost) straight lines. The curvature of the earth thus places definite and relatively restrictive limits on the range of wireless communications.[101] A satellite, however, may be placed within the line of sight of most of a hemisphere. It is the functional equivalent of a transmitter on a mast thousands of miles tall. The early satellites had little capacity and, being placed in low orbit, were only intermittently available. More powerful rockets began placing the satellites in geosynchronous orbit in 1964, allowing continuous communications. Since then, advances in electronics (particularly the development of high-speed gallium arsenide chips) have multiplied capacity. The Intelsat 6 generation of satellites, for example, can carry up to 120,000 telephone calls and three television signals simultaneously. This capacity has found or created numerous commercial applications. The high-capacity broadcasting capability has been particularly useful for continental and transoceanic television transmissions. A movie channel, superstation, or news report can be "uplinked" from one location to the satellite, then "downlinked" to subscribers across continents and oceans. The wider availability of satellite communications has thus been instrumental in the rapid spread of cable television systems.

The next generation of satellites, currently projected to be launched in 1993, will combine higher power with digital data compression technology. Flat antennas about the size of a handkerchief and costing about $300 will be able to receive the signals on rooftops, window sills, or trucks. This technology will likely boost direct broadcast of television entertainment as competition for cable service. Another probable application will be increased video teleconferencing to reduce business travel.

For point-to-point communication, fiber-optic technology is superior. In principle, optical communication links are the same as digital

118   electronic communications: photons replace electrons, and an ultra-pure silica glass fiber, or wave guide, replaces the copper conductor. In practice, fiber optics enjoy huge advantages. The fiber is much thinner and consequently lighter and less expensive to install. Silica, the raw material for the fiber, is more abundant and cheaper than copper. The signal travels farther with less attenuation, reducing the need for repeaters. By far the most important advantage, however, is signal-carrying capacity. Photons travel about three times faster than electrons in wire[102] and can be spaced closer together than electrons. The transatlantic fiber-optic telephone cable installed by AT&T in 1992 (the TAT-9) carries up to eighty thousand telephone conversations simultaneously on three fiber pairs, more than eight times the capacity of the most recent copper cables.

New fiber-optic technology promises yet another quantum jump in transmission rates. The combination of self-amplifying fibers and soliton pulses (wave forms that retain their shape over long distances) can produce transmissions that will cross the Atlantic without a repeater, with ten to twenty times the capacity of the current genera-tion of fibers.[103] Processing this volume of data with conventional electronics has been likened to sucking up the Mississippi River with a drinking straw. Newly developed hybrid (electro-optic) compo-nents are widening although not eliminating this bottleneck.[104] Sig-nificantly faster processing may require development of completely photonic switches, an ongoing quest of Bell Laboratories that has begun to produce some results.

The improvement and spread of fiber-optic technology could radi-cally alter the present communications infrastructure.[105] Fiber-optic-based, broadband integrated services digital networks (BISDNs), capable of carrying a gigabit per second, would make full-motion video and direct long-distance computer links possible. A single network may thus be able to subsume all the consumer and commer-cial applications currently served by telephone and cable television systems and add others, all at lower cost.

Despite these and other predictable advances, the important prog-ress in telecommunications clearly lies in the past.[106] Existing tech-nologies provide instantaneous voice, data, and video commu-nications worldwide. Capacity is, for practical purposes, already unlimited: a single state-of-the-art optical fiber could, in theory, carry all the long-distance telephone traffic in the United States or transmit the *Encyclopaedia Britannica* in a few seconds. The combined capacities of the existing U.S. long-distance networks vastly exceed demand. Expense is not a serious impediment. The cost of a three-minute telephone call from Los Angeles to Tokyo has declined from $30 in 1934 (by radio) to $6.34 in 1964 (copper cable) to $3.78 in 1990 (fiber-optic cable), a decrease of more than 98 percent measured in constant dollars.[107] Portable satellite antenna "uplinks" have made even video communications, by far the most data-intensive form of transmission, essentially instantaneous throughout the world. In 1989 alone, television viewers in the United States watched live video of one revolution succeeding in Eastern Europe and another failing in China.[108]

Every event of political, economic, scientific, or social significance occurring anywhere in the world is known or readily knowable in all advanced countries by the following day. Any further improvement, whatever the advances in technology, will pale in comparison to that achievement.

INFORMATION PROCESSING

Information processing would seem a severe, even slightly unfair, test for the thesis of this chapter. Progress in computing is, after all, the stuff of legend, with various measures of performance doubling every few years, while costs decline. Acceleration, not slowdown, seems to be the defining trend of this progress.

The course of solid-state electronics illustrates this trend in its most dramatic form. The vacuum-tube triode had held center stage in communication technology for nearly forty years until Bell Laboratories invented the transistor in 1947.[109] Without more, this was a modest advance, but it opened the way to integrating circuits on a single silicon chip at a minuscule fraction of the cost of the separate components.[110] The electronics industry pursued these economies with a vengeance. In 1960, the most advanced chips included about one hundred transistors. Thirty years later, that number had risen into the millions. The progression of standard semiconductor memory

120   chips (dynamic random access memories, or DRAMs) reflects these trends. Every few years, these chips quadruple in capacity, with little or no increase in the cost per chip.[111] As a result, the cost of one megabit of semiconductor memory decreased from $25,000 in 1975 to $10 in 1985 to less than $5 in 1991.[112]

Storage media underwent a similar transformation. Each generation of magnetic media more than doubled the data storage density of its predecessor, speeding access and increasing capacity.[113] Ordinary personal computers often include one hundred megabytes (about fifty thousand pages) of available storage at a cost of a few hundred dollars. Optical disks are available for even-higher-volume storage.

These advances brought quantum jumps in computer performance. The comparisons are familiar, but bear repeating. The ENIAC, the most powerful computer in the world when it was finished in 1946, had eighteen thousand vacuum tubes, occupied three thousand cubic feet, and drew 140 kilowatts of power, not counting the air conditioning needed to dissipate the heat that its tubes produced.[114] Current personal computers fit comfortably on a desktop, consume a few watts of power, and are incomparably more powerful. Indeed, the personal computer is more powerful in virtually every respect than the third-generation mainframe computers of the early 1970s, at less than 1 percent of the cost.

Improvements will continue. New ultraviolet and X-ray lithographic techniques will permit transistor dimensions as small as one tenth of a micron, which represents a theoretical limit for semiconductor-based devices in any event.[115] Designers may combine these smaller features with wafer scale integration to place trillions of transistors on a single chip.[116] In data storage, optical disks have a theoretical density limit of about one square micron per bit, which would allow the *Encyclopaedia Britannica* to be recorded on a single disk. "Flash" chips, which do not need constant power to retain their data and are about a hundred times faster than magnetic or optical storage media, will provide an alternative for high-performance applications. Improvements in real-time data compression will further reduce the cost of storage, whatever medium is used. Ongoing research into photonics, quantum-effect devices, and ceramic superconductors could provide even smaller and faster components if the limits on existing technologies ever began to pinch.[117] Ample room thus remains for improving several aspects of computer performance.[118]

Apart from performance improvements in individual components, computing power will continue to rise through improved system architecture. Most current computers work on tasks serially, executing each instruction in sequence. Many problems consist of separable elements, on which the computer could work simultaneously, thereby reducing processing time. Both theoretical and practical problems have impeded implementation of this simple idea. The parallelism believed to be lurking in many tasks has often proved difficult to isolate or exploit. Software written for serial computers would have to be substantially rewritten to function in a parallel-processing environment. Parallel architecture requires vastly more communication links. Nevertheless, most supercomputers now incorporate some degree of parallelism, and the most recent generation of mainframe computers uses from four to eight central processors.[119] The potential gains are substantial: in 1988, Sandia National Laboratories announced the development of a parallel-processing technique that increased processing speed on certain scientific problems a thousandfold, the largest such gain ever achieved.

A dizzying history of performance advances and promising prospects on several technology fronts hardly suggest closely approaching limits. But here as elsewhere, the tasks to be performed, not the technology, define the limits. The hype surrounding the Information Age tends to obscure the fact that computing is rarely an end in itself. Its worth lies in facilitating the performance of other tasks, as the director of the MIT Laboratory for Computer Science has observed:

> [I]nformation has economic value to people only if it can lead them to the acquisition of tangible goods. . . . Rich nations must . . . remember that if they become enamored of and blinded by the glamour of the information era and neglect to produce and improve tangible wealth—such as food, manufactured goods, natural resources and human services—the information colossus will lead to

nothing and so will collapse. Information is, after all, secondary to people's principal needs.[120]

Existing technology more than satisfies essentially all these needs. Word processing is a familiar example. The Intel 80386–based generation of personal computers provided more than ample power, memory, and storage for even the most demanding clerical tasks. Most offices refuse to pay any premium for 80486 machines, even three years after their introduction, because the substantially increased power has little value to them.[121] The technology has simply outstripped the need. Accounting, spreadsheet, and database management applications followed similar paths. Early products were starved for processing power, memory, or storage capacity, but a later generation of machines supplied the deficiency. Thereafter, hardware improvements were of little consequence. Modestly priced RISC-based engineering workstations greatly exceed most users' needs, even for applications previously considered demanding, such as computer-aided design and manufacturing (CAD/CAM) and complex graphics. Increasing computing power another tenfold would thus confer only the slightest tangible benefit on the vast majority of users. Indeed, economic data suggest that even the present generation of computers has added little to measured productivity in most sectors.[122]

This does not imply that improved computer performance will go begging. Declining costs are always welcome, and more power is better than less for any computing application. "Excess" power is already being devoted to enhancing the user interface, giving less sophisticated users access to higher-level functions.[123] Some scientific problems require still more computing power. Useful weather models, for example, necessarily include many equations that require difficult numerical solutions, with huge volumes of data that must be processed nearly in real time. Enhanced computer performance should improve the accuracy of predictions. Fluid dynamics, quantum mechanics, and econometrics are among the other fields likely to profit from more computing power. From a utilitarian perspective, however, such applications must be considered peripheral. The pervasive impact of past advances in computer technology is unlikely to be repeated.

. . .

Material progress has thus reached or is closely approaching external limits on every front, limits that would withstand any combination of astute policymaking, human ingenuity, effort, sacrifice, and even luck. In reality, however, these limits may scarcely be tested, because the goods and services that consumers in the affluent nations already enjoy leave little motivation to do so.

1. Mistrust of, and even hostility toward, material progress has been a distinguishing mark of the intellectual elite since World War II. "Writers nowadays who value their reputation among the more sophisticated hardly dare to mention progress without including the word in quotation marks. The implicit confidence in the beneficence of progress that during the last two centuries marked the advanced thinker has come to be regarded as the sign of a shallow mind. Though the great mass of the people in most parts of the world still rest their hopes on continued progress, it is common among intellectuals to question whether there is such a thing, or at least whether progress is desirable." Friedrich Hayek, *The Constitution of Liberty,* Ch. 3, p. 39, Univ. of Chicago Press, 1960. On intellectuals' twentieth-century retreat from the idea of progress, see Robert Nisbet, *History of the Idea of Progress,* Ch. 9, Basic Books, 1980, and Peter Medawar, *The Hope of Progress,* p. 13, Methuen, 1972.

2. See Kuznets, *Secular Movements in Production and Prices,* Ch. 1, Houghton Mifflin, 1930, and *Economic Change,* Ch. 10, W.W. Norton, 1953 (first published in 1941).

3. *Changes in Farm Production and Efficiency,* USDA Statistical Bulletin No. 561, 1976, Table 30.

4. Trevor Williams, *The Triumph of Invention,* Ch. 31, p. 286, Macdonald, 1987 (fertilizer usage in 1970).

5. Dennis Flanagan, *Flanagan's Version: A Spectator's Guide to Science on the Eve of the 21st Century,* p. 182, Knopf, 1988, estimates a tenfold gain in worldwide wheat yields between 1960 and 1980 because of widespread use of hybrids, fertilizer, and pesticides.

6. The data in Table 4.1 are from *Historical Statistics, Colonial Times to 1970,* Series K 445–485, and *Statistical Abstract of the United States 1989,* Table 1110. The data for chickens in the first column are for 1935–39, as earlier data are unavailable.

7. *Encyclopaedia Britannica,* 11th ed., Vol. 1, p. 418, 1910. The price of wheat in the United States was consistently above $1 per bushel between 1810 and 1854. W.W. Rostow, *The World Economy: History & Prospect,* Table III-10, p. 124, Univ. of Texas Press, 1978.

8. The *Chicago Tribune,* April 9, 1990, Section C, p. 1, surveys genetic engineering developments in agriculture.

9. For announcements of successful genetic alteration of monocots, see *Scientific American*, Apr. 1990, p. 24; *Wall Street Journal*, April 19, 1990, p. B1, and Jan. 24, 1990, p. B2.

10. Researchers at Cornell University have isolated bacteria that fix nitrogen (like the rhizobium) but obtain their energy requirements from solar radiation rather than from the plant to which they are attached.

11. See *Wall Street Journal*, Aug. 1, 1991, p. B1, and *Scientific American*, May 1990, p. 81. A number of genetically altered microbes promise biological control of crop damage. An early example is "ice minus," a modified bacterium that protects tomatoes and similar crops that are susceptible to damage during mild frosts. See Yvonne Baskin, "Getting the Bugs Out; Agricultural Use of Genetically Altered Bacteria," *Atlantic Monthly*, June 1990, p. 40. Field testing continues to be opposed by Jeremy Rifkin and other activists who have made virtual careers of legislative and judicial opposition to almost every aspect of genetic research and modification. As one example, Rifkin's Foundation on Economic Trends opposes the use of genetically engineered bovine growth hormone, proven safe for human consumption, ostensibly because it could harm the cattle. *Scientific American*, Nov. 1990, p. 26. (A steer's prognosis is presumably bleak, with or without injections of growth hormone.) The increasingly tangible benefits of progress in this field have weakened the appeal, but not the ardor, of these most recent avatars of Ned Ludd.

12. See, for example, Carlo Cipolla, *Economic History of World Population*, Ch. 1, Tables 1, 2, Barnes & Noble, 7th ed., 1978; *Encyclopedia Britannica*, 15th ed., Vol. 13, p. 181. In Russia as recently as 1914, 80 percent of the population derived its livelihood from agriculture. Paul Kennedy, *The Rise and Fall of the Great Powers*, Ch. 5, p. 235, Random House, 1987. Nations that continue to use prescientific methods continue to need a large portion of the labor force for agriculture.

13. Government agricultural policies artificially inflate the number of farm workers, especially in Europe and Japan. A free and unsubsidized world market in farm products would probably reduce farm employment below 1 percent of the population in advanced economies, with no further investment or changes in technology.

14. See *Statistical Abstract of the United States 1989*, Table 1104, and U.S. Dept. of Labor, Bureau of Labor Statistics, *Consumer Expenditure Survey, 1989*, USDL 90-16, Nov. 30, 1990.

15. Except as otherwise noted, the discussion of construction technology in the text is based on Carl Condit, *American Building: Materials and Techniques from the First Colonial Settlements to the Present*, Univ. of Chicago Press, 2d ed., 1982, and Henry Cowan, *Science and Building: Structural and Environmental Design in the Nineteenth and Twentieth Centuries*, Wiley & Sons, 1978.

16. The light or "balloon" frame appeared in Chicago in 1833, a child of necessity. A builder with a contract to construct the first Roman Catholic church in that city lacked the skilled manpower needed to complete the job. He therefore nailed together a framework of many light studs and joists, in lieu of heavy posts and beams with individually crafted joints. Purists scoffed, but the church was completed in half the projected time at half the anticipated cost. Martin Mayer, *The*

126   *Builders: Houses, People, Neighborhoods, Governments, Money,* Ch. 11, p. 254, W.W. Norton, 1978.

17. Folke Kihlstedt, "The Crystal Palace," *Scientific American,* Oct. 1984, p. 132, describes the design and construction of the Crystal Palace. P.W. Kingsford, *Builders and Building Workers,* Ch. 3, Edward Arnold, 1973, describes Paxton's career.

18. Concrete had long been used, but it varied in quality and could not withstand long exposure to water. Portland cement provided uniformity and water resistance (the latter quality produced by the presence of silicon and aluminum oxides).

19. The other major trend has been increasing off-site prefabrication. Gypsum wallboard is, in effect, a prefabricated wall. Wood siding arrives cut, finished, and often painted, doors and windows prehung in their frames. All of these save expensive and often inefficient on-site labor. Mayer, *Builders,* Ch. 10, describes the "assembly-line" production of entry-level housing.

20. John Rae, *The American Automobile,* Ch. 1, p. 5, Univ. of Chicago Press, 1965.

21. The *Britannica Book of the Year* annually lists major dam projects completed and in progress worldwide in a table under "Engineering Projects."

22. See *Wall Street Journal,* May 17, 1991, p. A1; *Economist,* 15–21 June 1991, pp. 21–26; and *Fortune,* May 18, 1992, pp. 70–83.

23. Mayer, *Builders,* Ch. 11, p. 256.

24. See, for example, Baily & Chakrabarti, *Innovation and the Productivity Crisis,* Table 1–3, p. 4, Brookings Institute, 1988. Several factors may explain the lack of measured progress in construction. Unionization and restrictive work rules in the construction trades may be an impediment to efficiency and progress, as may stricter building codes. Improved worker and building safety would make no direct contribution to measured productivity. Regardless of such factors, however, it is apparent that the state of the art in construction has not enjoyed the rapid progress of other sectors during the postwar era.

25. Rae, *American Automobile,* Ch. 4, Table 1.

26. Rae, *American Automobile,* Ch. 12, Table 4, and Ch. 14, Table 7.

27. Roger Bilstein, *Flight in America 1900–1983: From the Wrights to the Astronauts,* Johns Hopkins Univ. Press, 1984, and Carl Solberg, *Conquest of the Skies: A History of Commercial Aviation in America,* Little, Brown, 1979, describe the DC-3 and the subsequent evolution of air transportation.

28. Miller & Sawers, *The Technical Development of Modern Aviation,* Ch. 7, Tables 2 and 12, Routledge & Kegan Paul, 1968.

29. The U.S. commercial air fleet consumes about 40 percent less fuel per seat-mile flown than in 1970. *Statistical Abstract of the United States 1989,* Table 1044.

30. See *Statistical Abstract of the United States 1989,* Table 1044, and *Economist,* 10–16 March 1990, p. 73, estimating a 20 percent decline in U.S. ticket prices (after inflation) during the 1980s.

31. *Wall Street Journal,* Jan. 13, 1989, p. A10. *Statistical Abstract of the United States 1989,* Table 1044, provides detailed passenger and passenger-mile data for 1970 to 1987.

32. Trevor Williams, *Triumph of Invention,* Ch. 35, p. 317.

33. The proposed National Aerospace Plane (NASP, or X-30) would be about the size of a Boeing 727, powered by air-breathing, hydrogen-burning "scramjets" (supersonic-combustion ramjets) integrated into the airframe for improved lift and reduced drag, and designed for a top speed of Mach 25 (17,000 miles per hour), ten times the speed of the Concorde and more than fast enough to achieve earth orbit. The investigation of the X-30 is under the auspices of the Defense Advanced Research Projects Agency (DARPA). The only proposed uses of the X-30 are for military, national security, and space exploration applications. The projected cost of $4 billion per plane plus operating costs of $1 million to $9 million per flight would render a spaceplane uneconomic for the few civilian uses that may be imagined. See Thomas Heppenheimer, "The National Aerospace Plane," *1990 Britannica Yearbook of Science and the Future,* p. 26, and *Wall Street Journal,* June 19, 1989, p. A1. Development of the spaceplane is exceedingly unlikely in the current international and budgetary environment. For a harrowing description of one of the flights that led to abandonment of earlier Air Force efforts to achieve transatmospheric flight, see Tom Wolfe, *The Right Stuff,* Ch. 15, Farrar, Straus & Giroux, 1979.

34. The electorate's failure to demand an increase in speed limits may reflect a rising risk aversion that is symptomatic of the encroaching limits of material progress. See Chapter 6.

35. The same is true of freight transportation. Railroads could run trains faster by investing more in track and rolling stock. But speed is of secondary importance for rail freight; shippers would refuse to pay a premium for minor reductions in shipment times.

36. High-speed trains have long existed: the present Japanese "bullet trains" operate at more than one hundred miles per hour. That such trains are not in wider use is as much due to lack of demand as to shortcomings in the technology. Advances in superconduction may produce levitating trains that operate virtually without friction. Gary Stix, "Air Trains," *Scientific American,* Aug. 1992, p. 102, provides a balanced report on the potential of this maglev technology. Beyond typical commuting distances, such trains would compete primarily with airplanes. Airplanes will retain a substantial speed advantage in this competition because the aerodynamic drag at cruising altitudes is a small fraction of that at sea level. In addition, levitating trains represent a huge capital investment; guideways are projected to cost between $8 and $60 million per mile. *Scientific American,* Feb. 1992, pp. 104–5. The successors to the bullet trains are projected to cost at least $25 billion. *Economist,* 16–22 June 1990, p. 38. Such trains may serve some market niches, primarily as links between pairs of cities separated by a few hundred miles or less (see *Scientific American,* Feb. 1992, pp. 104–5, and *Economist,* 3–9 Feb. 1990, pp. 19–22, for some possible routes), but their overall impact on transportation will be slight.

37. See Compton & Gjostein, "Materials for Ground Transportation," *Scientific American,* Oct. 1986, p. 93.

38. See Thomas Canby, "Advanced Materials," *National Geographic,* Dec. 1989, p. 746, at pp. 763–67.

_128_ 39. The Advanced Energy System Program, Second Annual Report, Gas Research Institute, Rep't No. 89/0080, describes a compact gas turbogenerator prototype.

40. Karen Wright, "The Shape of Things to Go," _Scientific American,_ May 1990, p. 92.

41. Safety would, of course, be an issue, except that air crashes rank with lightning and alligators as causes of death. Cost is occasionally a factor in travel; witness the failure of supersonic transports in commercial aviation. In general, however, the value of time saved makes the fastest form of transportation the most efficient. A person may, for example, take a trip of five hundred miles by airplane in slightly over an hour, or by bus in a day. If the person's time is valued at a modest $20 per hour, the lost opportunity cost would dwarf any out-of-pocket savings from taking the bus. To similar effect is Miller & Sawers, _Technical Development of Modern Aviation,_ Ch. 7, estimating the value of the time saved by the transition from prop to jet airplanes.

42. The diminishing returns of increasing speed have already become apparent. The transition from propeller to jet propulsion, a relatively major advance, reduced transcontinental trip times by less than three hours and left scheduled transit times for some shorter trips almost unchanged. Jet engines did, however, significantly improve airline productivity, particularly on the longer routes.

43. Raymond Kurzweil, _The Age of Intelligent Machines,_ Ch. 8, pp. 312–17, MIT Press, 1990, discusses robotic technology.

44. Solomon Fabricant, _The Output of Manufacturing Industries, 1899–1937,_ Appendix B, pp. 489–90, National Bureau of Economic Research, 1940.

45. Polyvinyl chloride was developed in 1928, polystyrene in 1930, polyethylene in 1933, and polyurethane in 1937. The war delayed mass production, as chemists concentrated on rubber substitutes for tires. Trevor Williams, _A Short History of Twentieth-Century Technology c. 1900–c. 1950,_ Ch. 11, pp. 140–45, Oxford Univ. Press, 1982, describes the development of synthetic polymers.

46. Plastic's raw material cost (including energy) is about half that of the sheet steel it replaces. Peter Drucker, "The Changed World Economy," _Foreign Affairs,_ Spring 1986, Vol. 6, p. 768, at p. 774.

47. Carothers's success story had a tragic ending. Du Pont wanted all of his attention focused on developing the great commercial potential of nylon, while Carothers wanted to continue his pure research. The strain snapped Carothers's already tenuous mental balance, resulting in his suicide. Thomas Hughes, _American Genesis: A Century of Invention and Technological Enthusiasm 1870–1970,_ Ch. 4, pp. 175–80, Viking, 1989, and Jewkes et al., _The Sources of Invention,_ W.W. Norton, 2d ed., 1969, describe the invention of nylon and other synthetic fibers.

48. Canby, "Advanced Materials," _National Geographic,_ Dec. 1989, p. 746, and "Materials for Economic Growth," _Scientific American,_ Oct. 1986, discuss composites and other advanced materials.

49. General Electric has developed a process for transforming condensation polymers into rings, which then flow more easily around the fibers. After the material fills the mold, a catalytic reaction cuts the rings and reforms the original polymer

chains. See *Scientific American,* Dec. 1989, p. 102. The new process is expected to be commercialized rapidly and to increase the uses of polycarbonates and other plastics in engineering applications.

50. See *Wall Street Journal,* Dec. 26, 1989, p. B4; U.S. Dept. of Commerce, Technology Administration, *Emerging Technologies: A Survey of Technical and Economic Opportunities,* p. 30, Spring 1990.

51. *Economist,* 3–9 Aug. 1991, p. 64. The overcapacity in the automotive industry is by no means restricted to American manufacturers. Toyota's newest assembly line was running only one shift per day during the first half of 1992. *Wall Street Journal,* May 19, 1992, p. A1.

52. In the standard economic models, the situation described in the text—unused capacity resulting in marginal costs materially below average costs—could not persist. But it clearly existed in major chemical process industries, including polyvinylchloride and polyethylene production, as well as the automobile and steel industries, through most of the 1980s. The author is unaware of any economic studies that have investigated or attempted to explain this seeming anomaly. The saturation discussed in Chapter 5 may help to explain the persistence of overcapacity.

53. Robert Reich, *The Work of Nations: Preparing Ourselves for 21st Century Capitalism,* Ch. 7, p. 86, Knopf, 1991 (citing IBM officials).

54. Womack et al., *The Machine That Changed the World,* Ch. 4, particularly Fig. 4.7, Rawson Assocs., 1990; Reich, *Work of Nations,* Ch. 12, p. 146, and Ch. 17, p. 214; and Drucker, "The Changed World Economy," *Foreign Affairs,* Spring 1986, p. 768.

55. *Wall Street Journal,* Feb. 9, 1990, p. A1 (USX); *Economist,* 10–16 March 1990, p. 69 (British Steel). See also *Fortune,* April 6, 1992, p. 79 (total operating costs at USX per ton of steel produced declined by 20 percent from 1985 through 1991).

56. *Fortune,* May 18, 1992, p. 88.

57. Peter Drucker, *The New Realities,* Ch. 9, p. 123, Harper & Row, 1989.

58. Drucker, "Changed World Economy," *Foreign Affairs,* Spring 1986, p. 776.

59. Johnson et al., *Workforce 2000: Work and Workers for the 21st Century,* Ch. 1, p. 27, Hudson Inst., 1987.

60. In addition to the works cited above, see Baumol et al., *Productivity and American Leadership: The Long View,* Chs. 6 and 7, MIT Press, 1989.

61. Although several reputable research institutions report excess heat generation from the heavy water electrochemical cells, the evidence has not established fusion as the source of that heat.

62. Compare Cipolla, *The Economic History of World Population,* Ch. 2, Table 3, and Rostow, *World Economy,* Table III-22, p. 155, to Fernand Braudel, *The Structures of Everyday Life,* Ch. 5, pp. 371–72, Harper & Row, 1981.

63. W. Garret Scafe, "The Parsons Steam Turbine," *Scientific American,* April 1985, p. 132, describes the development and design of the steam turbine.

64. The *Queen Mary,* launched in 1936, boasted 160,000-horsepower turbines.

130 By then, regenerative feed heating, using the spent steam to preheat feed water entering the boiler, had further raised overall thermal efficiency.

65. Braudel, *Structures of Everyday Life*, p. 220.

66. The products of cracking are reintroduced into the fractionating columns for separation into their components. The development of catalytic cracking is described in Jewkes et al., *Sources of Invention*, pp. 235–37.

67. Williams, *Short History of Twentieth Century Technology*, Ch. 2, p. 24.

68. Rostow, *World Economy*, Table III-45, p. 232.

69. Faraday's exchange with Gladstone is quoted in Flanagan, *Flanagan's Version*, p. 208.

70. See *Encyclopaedia Britannica*, 11th ed., Vol. 28, p. 193–200, 1910.

71. Thomas Hughes, *American Genesis: A Century of Invention and Technological Enthusiasm 1870–1970*, Ch. 5, pp. 226–43, Viking, 1989, describes Samuel Insull's pioneering efforts in load management. Eastern financiers and the Depression ultimately broke Insull, who was prosecuted and acquitted on charges of securities fraud.

72. Rostow, *World Economy*, Table VI-2, p. 595.

73. See Claasen & Girifalco, "Materials for Energy Utilization," *Scientific American*, Oct. 1986, p. 103, and especially the graph on p. 104. See also Kennedy, *Rise and Fall of the Great Powers*, Table 16, p. 201 (table of energy usage by country from 1890 to 1938), and Rostow, *World Economy*, p. 802, Table N-36.

74. The data for Graph 4.2 are from *Historical Statistics of the United States*, Series S116, and *Statistical Abstract of the United States 1990*, Table No. 788.

75. Photovoltaic power is not inherently complex or difficult to achieve. Two layers of a semiconductor, one doped to collect electrons (the n-type semiconductor) and the other doped to repel them (the p-type semiconductor), are bonded together. Light striking near the junction may free electrons from their associated atoms. The n-type semiconductor collects most of these free electrons. It becomes negatively charged relative to the p-type semiconductor. If conductors attached to each layer are connected, current flows and continues flowing as long as light strikes the cell.

76. Yoshihiro Hamakawa, "Photovoltaic Power," *Scientific American*, Apr. 1987, p. 86, and H.M. Hubbard, "Photovoltaics Today and Tomorrow," *Science*, Vol. 244, p. 297, 21 Apr. 1989, survey recent developments and current commercial prospects for the technology.

77. Israel Dostrovsky, "Chemical Fuels from the Sun," *Scientific American*, Dec. 1991, p. 102, shows the geographic distribution of sunlight falling on the planet.

78. Flanagan, *Flanagan's Version*, p. 179.

79. Hubbard, "Photovoltaics Today and Tomorrow," *Science*, Vol. 244, p. 297, 21 Apr. 1989.

80. Flanagan, *Flanagan's Version*, p. 180. Another darling of alternative energy advocates is power from the sea. The options currently under study are described in Penney & Bharathan, "Power from the Sea," *Scientific American*, Jan. 1987, p. 86, and "Energy from the Ocean," *1989 Britannica Yearbook of Science and the Future*, p. 98. Little practical potential has yet been demonstrated.

81. Some practical confirmation of the limited potential of solar power comes from the withdrawal by ARCO Solar, a joint venturer in the largest solar-power-generating station built to date, from the entire field of photovoltaics. Focused solar power can also be used to heat a working fluid, which generates steam, which drives a conventional turbine. See the description of pilot plants operating in the Mohave Desert in *1988 Britannica Yearbook of Science and the Future,* p. 320. Another possible approach is to use solar heating to produce chemical fuels for use in transportation or industrial applications. See Dostrovsky, "Chemical Fuels from the Sun," *Scientific American,* Dec. 1991, p. 102. The basic limitation imposed by the relatively low power density of sunlight applies equally to either of these approaches.

82. American and European magnetic fusion reactors have now been able to produce approximately 0.2 percent of the energy needed to heat the plasma. This is actually regarded as promising, because a fuel mixture richer in tritium is expected to lift energy output near the breakeven point. See *Science News,* Oct. 13, 1990, p. 230.

83. See *Scientific American,* Feb. 1989, pp. 25–28, for an assessment of current fusion methods.

84. At the end of 1988, forty-seven nuclear reactors were under construction (none of them in the United States). *Wall Street Journal,* Mar. 7, 1989, p. A4. France and Belgium generate most of their electricity from nuclear plants, and enjoy low rates as a result. See also Freeman Dyson, *Infinite in All Directions,* pp. 140–47, Harper & Row, 1988, attributing the decline of nuclear power in the United States to a misguided quest for size, leading to complex designs that proved too slow and expensive to build.

85. John Taylor, "Improved and Safer Nuclear Power," *Science,* Vol. 244, p. 318, 21 Apr. 1989, and Peter Miller, "A Comeback for Nuclear Power? Our Electric Future," *National Geographic,* Aug. 1991, p. 60, survey recent advances in reactor technology. See also *Wall Street Journal,* Dec. 1, 1988, p. B4, and Golay & Todreas, "Advanced Light-Water Reactors," *Scientific American,* Apr. 1990, p. 82.

86. When an electric charge passes through an ionic fluid in a strong magnetic field, the fluid accelerates. Electrical energy can thus be converted directly to fluid thrust, with no moving parts to dissipate energy as heat. This magnetohydrodynamic propulsion is a potentially elegant approach for ocean shipping, because seawater is ionic. Japanese companies have produced a prototype SEMP (superconducting electromagnetic propulsion) vessel using traditional low-temperature superconductors. See *Economist,* 27 April–3 May 1991, p. 90. The *New York Times,* May 15, 1990, Section C, p. 1, describes ongoing research on magnetohydrodynamic propulsion.

87. Wolsky et al., "The New Superconductors: Prospects for Applications," *Scientific American,* Feb. 1989, p. 61.

88. The largest potential of high-temperature superconductors for power generation may be in the form of large-scale storage rings (if current density limits can be overcome). These would permit the lowest-cost power to be generated off-peak

132 and saved for later use. Even here, the capital cost would largely negate any savings in the cost of generating capacity.

89. Williams, *Short History of Twentieth Century Technology*, Ch. 6, pp. 68–70, and Williams, *Triumph of Invention*, Ch. 24, p. 22, discuss past advances in steam turbine technology. Sadi Carnot, a nineteenth-century French physicist, proved that only a portion of heat energy can be converted to mechanical energy. This limit is based on the second law of thermodynamics. It applies to any kind of heat engine and is fixed by the upper and lower temperatures at which the engine operates. The recent flattening of the electricity price curve shown in Figure 4.2 reflects the fact that the technology has approached the Carnot efficiency. See Baily & Chakrabarti, *Innovation and the Productivity Crisis*, Ch. 4, p. 81.

90. Fiber-optic cable, for example, requires only about one twentieth as much energy to produce as copper cable of the same capacity. The comparison of plastic composites to steel is similar.

91. Angus Maddison, *World Economy in the Twentieth Century*, Table 7.4, p. 90, OECD, 1989. To similar effect are *Wall Street Journal*, Mar. 6, 1989, p. A5, and *1989 Britannica Yearbook of Science and the Future*, pp. 336, 350–51.

92. Rosenfeld & Hafemeister, "Energy-Efficient Buildings," *Scientific American*, Apr. 1988, p. 78, describes some of the available technologies and their potential energy savings.

93. Gasoline and motor oil accounted for only 3.5 percent of U.S. consumer expenditures in 1989. See U.S. Dept. of Labor, Bureau of Labor Statistics, *Consumer Expenditure Survey*, 1989. That percentage was even lower for upper-income groups.

94. Robert Routledge, *Discoveries and Inventions of the Nineteenth Century*, "The Electric Telegraph," 1890 ed., reprinted by Crescent Books, 1989, is a nearly contemporary discussion of the evolution of the telegraph.

95. Williams, *Short History of Twentieth Century Technology*, Ch. 25, p. 304.

96. Data on the spread of telephones are from Williams, *Triumph of Invention*, Ch. 25, pp. 235–36.

97. Transatlantic radio transmission required what was then a wholly unsuspected phenomenon. Electromagnetic radiation travels in (almost) straight lines; hence, the curvature of earth should have prevented transmissions across an ocean. The ionosphere, however, reflects radiation in the "radio" frequency range, so that a signal can "skip" a great distance around the earth, albeit with some interference.

98. Hughes, *American Genesis*, Ch. 4, pp. 139–50, describes the work of De Forest and Edwin Armstrong and their bitter and protracted contests over priority, contests that ultimately resulted in Armstrong's suicide.

99. Fabricant, *The Output of Manufacturing Industries, 1899–1937*, Appendix B, pp. 573–74.

100. For a description of the invention and early development of television, see Jewkes et al., *Sources of Invention*, pp. 307–10.

101. Unfortunately, the communications frequencies that reflect off the ionosphere have the least bandwidth, and such reflection is a variable phenomenon.

102. Kurzweil, *Age of Intelligent Machines,* Ch. 10, p. 417.

103. The new optical-fiber technology is surprisingly simple in concept. Self-amplifying fibers, announced by Bell Laboratories in 1989, are doped with erbium or some other rare earth element. A laser pulse passing through the fiber excites electrons in the outer shell of the rare earth atoms, causing some of them to jump to a higher energy level. The signal pulse causes some of these high-energy electrons to fall, boosting the signal. With the proper combination of doped fiber and signal frequency, the passage of the signal pulse itself temporarily increases the speed of light through the fiber. As a result, the trailing photons always travel slightly faster than the leading ones, keeping the signal pulse bunched in a soliton. Solitons and rare earth doping of optical fibers are reported in Emmanuel Desurvire, "Lightwave Communications: The Fifth Generation," *Scientific American,* Jan. 1992, p. 114; *Scientific American,* Apr. 1992, p. 143; *Wall Street Journal,* June 25, 1991, p. A1; and *Economist,* 6–12 July 1991, p. 87. *Wall Street Journal,* June 3, 1992, p. B3, reports the successful test of the optically amplified system that will be able to carry 600,000 telephone calls simultaneously across the Pacific.

104. Light of the proper frequency striking the junction between two differently "doped" layers of gallium arsenide dislodges electrons, which flow across the junction, producing a pulse of current. This direct conversion from light to electricity, combined with gallium arsenide's ability to switch its electronic state several billion times per second, has produced a set of chips that transmit and receive data over a single filament at a rate of more than one gigabit per second. Gallium arsenide components can also be finely "tuned" to a particular frequency by substituting atoms of another metal (commonly aluminum or indium) for some of the gallium atoms. The principles of this "band gap engineering" are explained in J.M. Rowell, "Photonic Materials," *Scientific American,* Oct. 1986, p. 147. Mare Brodsky, "Progress in Gallium Arsenide Semiconductors," *Scientific American,* Feb. 1990, p. 68, describes the potential uses (as well as the weaknesses and engineering difficulties) of gallium arsenide components. Even higher-speed quantum well laser diodes are now under development. See Elizabeth Corcoran, "Diminishing Dimensions," *Scientific American,* Nov. 1990, p. 122.

105. Vinton Cerf, "Networks," *Scientific American,* Sept 1991, p. 72, describes the spread of long-distance, high volume communications networks.

106. The translating telephone, long a staple of science fiction, is likely to be realized early in the next century. See Kurzweil, *Age of Intelligent Machines,* Ch. 10, pp. 405–6. Although the device will have widespread application in an increasingly integrated world economy, the language barrier presently prevents only a tiny fraction of communications that people have or desire to have. The practical impact on communications will therefore be small. Solid-state digital television systems will supplant existing analog, vacuum-tube technology within two decades. Although likely to be commercially important, this advance will alter the state of communications little if at all. Existing television provides adequate pictures with excellent reliability at relatively low cost.

107. Partly as a result of decreasing prices, the volume of international telephone

_134_ traffic has soared. Calls by Americans to Japan increased from less than 300,000 hours in 1977 to nearly three million hours by 1987. The price decreases are a direct result of falling costs. Between 1975 and 1989, the cost of commercial optical fiber declined more than 95 percent per meter, and even more measured on the basis of message-carrying capacity.

108. The spread of satellite video technology may also have had a role in _causing_ the sweeping political upheaval in the communist world. One of the imperatives for maintaining a totalitarian state is to monopolize the sources of information. "Everything which might cause doubt about the wisdom of the government or create discontent will be kept from the people. The basis of unfavorable comparisons with conditions elsewhere, the knowledge of possible alternatives to the course actually taken, information which might suggest failure on the part of the government to live up to its promises or to take advantage of opportunities to improve conditions—all will be suppressed." Friedrich Hayek, _The Road to Serfdom,_ Ch. 11, p. 160, Univ. of Chicago Press, 1944. Western satellite television broke this monopoly with a thoroughness that Radio Free Europe and its ilk could never approach. As the gaps in living standards and personal and political freedoms became palpable, widespread discontent was predictable.

109. Braun & Macdonald, _Revolution in Miniature,_ Cambridge Univ. Press, 2nd ed., 1982, describes the invention of the transistor and the subsequent evolution of semiconductor electronics.

110. Each wire on a printed circuit board costs about 10 cents, each connection on a chip a few millionths of a cent. George Gilder, _Microcosm: The Quantum Revolution in Economics and Technology,_ p. 346, Simon & Schuster, 1989.

111. Gelbach's law: every chip ends up costing $5.

112. Gilder, _Microcosm,_ p. 160; _Economist,_ 23 Feb.–1 Mar. 1991, p. 64. Altogether, memory costs only one hundred millionth as much as it did in 1950. Kurzweil, _Age of Intelligent Machines,_ Ch. 10, p. 401.

113. Mark Kryder, "Data-Storage Technologies for Advanced Computing," _Scientific American,_ Oct. 1987, p. 117, explains the evolution of magnetic storage technologies.

114. Braun & Macdonald, _Revolution in Miniature,_ Ch. 3, p. 32. The ENIAC was itself a major advance over the Harvard Mark I, an electromechanical computer built by IBM for wartime needs. It could multiply two numbers in about five seconds, its relays sounding "like a roomful of ladies knitting." Current-generation personal computers are about a million times more powerful. Kurzweil, _Age of Intelligent Machines,_ Ch. 10, p. 402. (One lasting legacy of the Mark I is the verb "to debug." An early failure was traced to a moth inside one of the relays.) For descriptions of the early computers, see Herman Goldstine, _The Computer from Pascal to von Neumann,_ Princeton Univ. Press, 1972; Stan Augarten, _Bit by Bit: An Illustrated History of Computers,_ Ticknor & Fields, 1984 (which includes an extensive bibliography); Joel Shurkin, _Engines of the Mind: A History of the Computer,_ W.W. Norton, 1984; or Ed Regis, _Who Got Einstein's Office? Eccentricity and Genius at the Institute for Advanced Study,_ Ch. 5, Addison-Wesley, 1987 (describing the role of John von Neumann).

115. Transistors smaller than 0.1 micron would short-circuit themselves. See James Meindl, "Chips for Advanced Computing," *Scientific American,* Oct. 1987, p. 78, at pp. 81–82.

116. A prototype wafer scale memory chip has been produced using one-megabit DRAM design rules, with storage capacity of two hundred megabits. With four-megabit design rules, capacity would increase to nearly a gigabit.

117. On alternatives to semiconductors for data-processing components, see Wolsky, "The New Superconductors: Prospects for Applications," *Scientific American,* Feb. 1989, p. 61, and Robert Bate, "The Quantum-Effect Device: Tomorrow's Transistor?" *Scientific American,* Mar. 1988, p. 96.

118. Advancing technology may also finally replace the venerable cathode ray tube (CRT) as the principal means of electronic display. The CRT is the only significant species of vacuum tube technology remaining in use, and it suffers the normal shortcomings of the genus, namely, excessive size, weight, and power consumption. The exponential increase in the number of transistors per chip makes separate and simultaneous control of each pixel on the display screen feasible. Several candidates exist for the flat screen itself, including electroluminescent phosphors and semiconducting plastics. See Burroughes et al., "Light-Emitting Diodes Based on Conjugated Polymers," *Nature,* Vol. 347, p. 539, 11 Oct. 1990; *Wall Street Journal,* June 11, 1992, p. B7.

119. Denning & Tichy, "Highly Parallel Computation," *Science,* Vol. 250, p. 1217, 30 Nov. 1990, and Fox & Messina, "Advanced Computer Architectures," and David Galernter, "Programming for Advanced Computing," both in *Scientific American,* Oct. 1987, survey progress and prospects in parallel architectures. Cray's 1990 announcement that it is developing a massively parallel supercomputer and NCR's 1991 announcement of the first massively parallel mainframe computer confirm the trend toward parallelism. Worldwide sales of parallel processing computers by U.S. companies rose from negligible levels in 1987 to $140 million by 1990 and are expected to triple by 1994. *Economist,* 18–24 May 1991, p. 80.

120. Michael Dertouzos, "Communications, Computers and Networks," *Scientific American,* Sept. 1991, p. 62, at pp. 64–65.

121. Buyers will begin to choose '486 machines for office use when they cost essentially the same as '386 machines—that is, after '586 machines become established.

122. The measured productivity of clerical, white-collar, and information workers (except in communications) has not increased with the spread of computer technology. Baily & Chakrabarti, *Innovation and the Productivity Crisis,* Ch. 5, discusses possible explanations for this puzzle. These include the possibility that qualitative improvements in service are not being measured, that computers are used for unproductive competitive and distributional purposes rather than to enhance productivity, and that expanding computer staffs are offsetting savings elsewhere. Whatever the explanation, it is unlikely that productivity enhancement will suddenly materialize from technological advances with few practical applications.

123. The ultimate user interface will be speech recognition, the direct machine transcription of normal speech. Systems for limited applications (for example,

136   specialized vocabularies or discrete speech) appeared during the 1980s. Large-vocabulary, continuous speech recognition systems should be in common use by the end of this decade, an outgrowth of artificial intelligence research. The resulting saving of clerical time represents one of the few remaining tangible benefits to be realized from advances in computer technology. Kurzweil, *Age of Intelligent Machines*, Ch. 7, describes the technology of speech recognition.

Chapter Five

ENOUGH

William Randolph Hearst was born in 1863, sole heir to his father's vast mining fortune. His father indulged Hearst's interest in journalism, buying him the *New York Morning Journal* when he was twenty-four. Hearst later acquired the failing *San Francisco Examiner*. Within a relatively short time, Hearst had reversed the fortunes of these moribund newspapers and founded a thriving, highly profitable journalistic empire. His already formidable wealth increased.

Hearst spent much of that wealth building and furnishing "Hearst Castle" on an estate spanning forty-two miles of California's central coast. Construction began in 1919 and continued for eighteen years. Hearst lived there periodically until shortly before his death. (The castle had by then sadly diminished his personal estate, to less than $60 million.) His family later deeded the buildings to California as a state historical monument.

Each year, approximately one million people tour Hearst Castle. Some go to see Hearst's priceless art, collected from throughout the world. For most, however, the principal attraction is a glimpse into the life-style afforded by fabulous wealth. Terrazzo and ceramic tile terraces dot the landscaped grounds, with fountains and decorative lighting for visual interest. Three guest houses surround the main house. There are two swimming pools and lighted tennis courts. The castle even includes a private screening room, where Hearst and his guests watched both major studio releases and home movies featuring

138   Hearst's many celebrity friends. Hearst's was wealth without practical limitation, spent without restraint. Most visitors are suitably impressed.

For a view of such creature comforts, however, they could have saved the trip: comparable amenities and more would be found within a few miles of their homes. Houses boasting many thousands of square feet of living space plus guest accommodations are fairly common in affluent suburban neighborhoods. Those in the sunbelt generally have swimming pools, and rather fewer have private tennis courts only because a nearby club provides them in abundance. Every home in the neighborhood has at least one videocassette recorder, giving the occupants a private screening room for both home movies and a greater variety of studio releases than Hearst would have dreamed possible, despite his extensive holdings and connections in the entertainment field. Hearst Castle is thus little more than an upper-middle-class home of the present, writ large.[1]

In other respects, of course, Hearst Castle could not compete with the most ordinary tract house. Television did not exist when Hearst Castle was built, much less the satellite and cable transmissions that deliver fifty or more channels. Modern air conditioning would have been welcome on those summer days when the ocean winds flagged. The tour guides say that Hearst and his guests dined simply. He may have been making a virtue of necessity. Fresh food from outside California would rarely have been available, and frozen foods were only just being developed.

Examples could be multiplied, but the point is obvious. The modestly affluent of the present can, in many respects, match the living standards of the fabulously wealthy of less than two generations past, and enjoy some amenities not then available at any price.[2]

By comparison, those living today will have little to envy their grandchildren in material terms. The limits described in the preceding two chapters would force the rise in living standards to slow down: consumption cannot long outrun production. But consumption also faces intrinsic limits. Abundance already extends over such a wide range of needs and wants that further gains matching those of the past would be difficult to envision, if not fanciful. Affluence has, in practical if not in absolute terms, reached saturation. These limits would compel a similar outcome even if, by some unsuspected agency, the advanced economies were able to regain their past rates of progress.

MEASURED STANDARD OF LIVING

Living standards are too often described in terms of economic statistics. For whatever the figures are worth, the best historical estimates place European GNP per capita in the range of a few hundred dollars per year in the opening decades of the nineteenth century,[3] compared to more than $10,000 in the leading economies today (in constant dollars). This translates to slightly less than a doubling in income each generation.

But this increase greatly understates the real improvement. Economic statistics capture only the cost, not the value, of a good or service.[4] "The difference between treating pneumonia with poultices instead of penicillin nowhere appears in the national product figures."[5] A typewriter sold in 1960 added about the same amount to the gross national product as a personal computer sold in 1990, but the computer delivered much more to the buyer. Such new products are anything but peripheral to the economy; most firms traded on the major stock exchanges are engaged in businesses that did not exist even a century ago.

Improvements in existing products generate the same effect, if less dramatically. The Volkswagen Beetle provided reliable and low-cost (albeit Spartan and unexciting) transportation to millions and was justly renowned for its value. It sold for $1,999 in the United States in 1972, $5,431 in 1987 dollars. The 1987 Hyundai Excel, a spiritual avatar of the Beetle, sold for $4,995.[6] The sale of the Hyundai thus counted for less in the statistics, although its better performance, fuel economy, and safety, as well as more and better amenities, made it distinctly more valuable to the consumer.[7] The measured increases in per capita income omit this added value.

The arrival of new products and improvements in old ones thus all but destroy the utility of economic statistics for measuring actual living standards over extended periods. History, however, supplies what economics cannot. A glimpse at how some aspects of life-style

140 have changed during the modern era suggests the immense gains in
material prosperity.

DIET

More and better food has always been the first evidence of a rising
standard of living. In premodern economies, the mass of the people
commonly lived on gruel and coarse-grained bread, occasionally supplemented by meat, salted fish, and dairy products. Most vegetables
were rare. Fruit, sugar, and tea or coffee were luxuries.

With progress in farming during the late eighteenth century, bread
replaced gruel as the dietary staple, and milled wheat replaced rye,
oats, and barley as the principal bread corn. Potatoes (originally from
the New World) came into general use in Northern Europe. The diet
of common people nevertheless remained wretched through the first
half of the nineteenth century.[8] A typical London family in 1841
consumed some fifty pounds of bread and potatoes weekly. Agricultural workers fared even worse. This meager sustenance consumed
not less than half of the household budget. The diet of the affluent
was more varied, with larger quantities of meat, fresh fish, and dairy
products, but still claimed as much as 40 percent of a professional's
income.

Rising prosperity radically altered this diet. In England, real wages
rose sharply with the spread of industrialization (first among the
middle class, later among ordinary wage earners), while the cost of
staples declined with advances in farming and inexpensive food imported from the Americas. Rural and working-class families began
eating regularly, if not yet well. Variety and nutrition also started to
improve with rising consumption of meat, fish, dairy products, fruit,
vegetables, and eggs. Railroads, refrigerated steamers, and steam
trawlers packed with ice brought perishables from the English countryside, beef and mutton from America and Australia, and cod from
Icelandic shoals. The American diet was even better, with railroads
making fresh meat, vegetables, fruit, and dairy products readily available through much of the country before 1900.[9]

In this century, diet became a function less of necessity, more of
choice. Improved preservation techniques lowered the cost and re-

duced the seasonality of many foods. Pasteurization made milk safer and less perishable. Commercial canning became reasonably reliable and economical with the advent of the autoclave for producing super-heated steam (1870s), automated canning lines (1880s), and machine-made sanitary tin-plated cans (1900s).[10] Industrial-scale canning of meats, vegetables, fruits, and condiments began in the 1880s and grew steadily and rapidly through World War II. Clarence Birdseye's 1929 discovery that quick freezing preserves vegetables without destroying their flavor or texture[11] launched an industry that has altered postwar single life-styles no less than the Pill. By 1934, the average British family spent twice as much on fruit and vegetables as on bread and flour.[12] This trend away from starchy staples continued after the war, with rising consumption of fresh meat and fish, dairy products, eggs, and fruits and vegetables.[13] Technology and affluence had converted luxuries into staples.

The principal remaining dietary problem in the developed nations is excess. Daily adult food intake in the United States has risen to 3,500 calories, more than twice the minimum energy intake needed for survival.[14] Other developed nations are at similar levels. Consumption of inexpensive staples continues to decline, replaced by fresh and frozen fish, poultry, cheese, fresh fruits, and other foods once reserved for the privileged few. Despite this shift, the cost of eating has trended consistently downward: the food served in American homes accounts for less than one tenth of total consumer expenditures.[15]

Attitudes toward food are even more telling. The paramount concern is to *reduce* caloric intake (without, of course, resorting to the unpleasant expedient of eating less). Artificial sweeteners, low-fat milk, light beer, frozen diet entrees, and many other innovations of the last few decades succeeded for one reason—they allow people to eat and drink more without gaining weight. Minimizing energy intake while maximizing food consumption would have seemed bizarre behavior to people whose only, and often elusive, objective was to find enough calories to sustain life. That fat has replaced hunger as the principal concern is an unmistakable symptom of saturation.

HOUSING AND CONSUMER GOODS

As hunger recedes, people divert their surplus income into more lasting forms of consumption.

Housing is one of the first areas to improve.[16] Conditions remained execrable for the great majority through the first half of the nineteenth century. Wattle-and-daub cottages with thatch or turf roofs, one window, an open fire, a beaten-earth floor, and only a few hundred square feet of enclosed space sufficed for large families (sometimes accompanied by farm animals) throughout the English countryside. The cellar dwellings and tenement houses of the urban masses were as bad as the worst Third World slums. Conditions in France were no better.[17] The housing stock in America was somewhat newer than that in Europe, but equally lacking in space, comfort, and amenities.[18] The petitions of social reformers to the contrary notwithstanding, economic necessity largely dictated these conditions. Neither legislation nor moralistic urging would free the resources needed to create decent housing so long as food consumed the majority of the household budget. "[A]t its roots, the housing problem was a problem of poverty."[19]

Higher wages were therefore the principal antidote. Dwellings grew and included more bedrooms, while the average number of occupants per unit declined. Separate kitchens and bathrooms with running water were standard in houses built near the end of the century. Central heating appeared in custom-built homes for the affluent in the 1860s and gradually percolated downmarket. The lower cost of machine-made furniture improved the comfort of working-class housing.

Man's material aspirations have rarely extended beyond decent shelter and an adequate diet, even in the most advanced countries.[20] As the burden of securing these necessities eased, technology and affluence added a panoply of new goods, which have since become so commonplace as to be thought indispensable. As electricity spread through cities and towns after 1900 and began to penetrate rural areas in the 1920s, electric vacuum cleaners and other small appliances followed in its wake.[21] Gas or electric hot water heaters were common in middle-class homes by World War I, as were permanent tubs in bathrooms. These and other conveniences and amenities reflected not only the triumph of technology, but also enough affluence to afford a degree of domestic comfort. The expense of indoor plumbing, central heating, and wiring added 25 to 40 percent to the cost of building a house.[22] An ordinary complement of appliances adds thousands of dollars more. Only twentieth-century incomes allow twentieth-century amenities.

The United States now has about 100 million dwelling units, nearly two thirds of them owner-occupied, most of them built since 1960. Most are single-family detached homes and include a patio or balcony and a garage or carport. About five million Americans own second homes. Altogether, there are about nine million more dwellings in the United States than domestic households to put in them,[23] without counting millions of hotel rooms and other temporary accommodations. The idea of extra dwellings, standing vacant, waiting for occupants, would have been utterly unthinkable before this century.

These houses have comforts and conveniences that would have exceeded the experience and defeated the imagination of earlier generations. Children typically have their own bedrooms and bathroom. Public water supplies are nearly universal. The restriction of car washing or lawn watering during a drought merits featured treatment on the television news, suggesting how prodigal ordinary usage is. Cost is minimal, with water consuming less than 1 percent of household budgets. The refrigerator, the electric or gas range, and the oven are not considered amenities; their ownership is automatically assumed in every household. Yet, each of them would have been almost miraculous just one hundred years ago. Refrigeration equipment was still limited to bulky, commercial units; the freons and small electric motors that made home refrigerators feasible lay in the future. Many homes even lacked iceboxes; regular delivery of ice was an expensive luxury. For most town dwellers, shopping remained a daily chore. The brick oven (heated by coals that were raked out before the baking began) and the cast-iron stove (with a small fire built inside) defined the state of cooking technology until late in the century, when appliances fired by coal gas became more common. Thermostatic control was a twentieth-century development. Central heating has become nearly universal. Almost all dwellings located in the South

144 and Southwest have central air conditioning, a post–World War II development. The vast majority of all households include a vacuum cleaner (first made practical in the 1920s), washing machine, and dryer, and about half include a dishwasher. Complaints about today's housework would seem ridiculous to those accustomed to the unrelenting drudgery and hard physical labor of any earlier century.

Residential telephone service was still a mark of fairly considerable affluence in 1900. It has now reached saturation levels: 93 percent of all households in the United States have at least one telephone. Almost all of these are private lines. The party line slipped into history as affluence spread and people became unwilling to tolerate the inconvenience of sharing. Most households have at least two telephone sets, and many have two or more separate lines, with one for business calls or for the use of children. Answering machines eliminate the dreaded possibility of missing a call.

Electronics created a new set of twentieth-century necessities. Radios are ubiquitous, and television sets outnumber households in the United States by two to one. As of 1990, more than nine out of ten households in the United States owned an audio system; more than eight out of ten had a microwave oven; more than seven out of ten a videocassette recorder. Only about a quarter of all households owned a personal computer, but this was quite clearly due to a lack of consumer interest, as major manufacturers had been offering inexpensive and easy-to-use machines for years.

Such abundance is certainly not limited to the home. Practicality has become decidedly secondary to fashion and appearance in most clothing purchases. Clothing is rarely worn out; it simply ceases to be worn. Even so, it accounts for only 5 percent of consumer expenditures in the United States[24] and less than 10 percent in all advanced economies.[25]

Automobiles are another obvious example of saturation. They had become commonplace, but hardly ubiquitous, before World War II. As recently as the early 1960s, a single generation past, the two-car family was comparatively rare, and an adolescent with an automobile was a mark of considerable affluence or of an aspiring mechanic. Any middle-class teenager of the 1990s without instant access to a car feels deprived. Over 140 million vehicles are registered in the United States, about 550 per thousand population, or slightly less than one for every licensed driver. A household with no vehicle is a rarity; it bespeaks either unusual circumstances or fairly severe poverty. (Many households below the official poverty line own automobiles.) That the next generation will have even more and better vehicles is not to be doubted. But easy mobility is already nearly universal; future improvements will be incremental and relatively insignificant by comparison.

Until recently, only the United States enjoyed this cornucopia of consumer goods, in part because two world wars had devastated the other advanced nations. For example, in 1950, when the United States had over thirty million civilian vehicles, no other country had as many as two million. As recently as 1954, less than one British or French household in twelve had a refrigerator. That gap in living standards has since narrowed sharply, as the following table indicates.[26]

5.1 CONSUMER GOODS OWNERSHIP, SELECTED COUNTRIES (% HOUSEHOLDS)

	United States	West Germany	Japan	United Kingdom
Automobiles	85	68	75	64
Telephones	93	93	99	83
Televisions	98	99	99	98
Refrigerators	100	99	98	95

Foreign ownership of consumer goods is not limited to such "essentials." Almost all Japanese households own washing machines and vacuum cleaners, more than two thirds own VCRs and microwave ovens, and almost half own compact disc players.[27]

Such saturation does not rule out qualitative improvements. Horses, after all, could have reached saturation levels in some areas during the nineteenth century. New consumer goods regularly appear, some of which become great commercial successes. But the prospect of improvements rivaling those of the last hundred years appears remote. The automobile allows trips by anyone anywhere at any time, at speeds constrained by law, not technology, with relative comfort, safety, and convenience and at low cost. Short of "beaming" from place to place in the fashion of *Star Trek*, which is not in

146 the offing, the room for qualitative improvement is slight. The telephone provides immediate and relatively inexpensive communication between any two people in the world. Furnaces, air conditioners, and electric lights maintain a uniform environment almost automatically and at minimal expense. Washing machines clean clothes with little human intervention. The refrigerator prevents food from spoiling for days or weeks, the freezer for months, and the microwave cooks it in minutes. Television constantly provides video entertainment at no cost.[28] Compact discs reproduce sound with a fidelity that approaches the limits discernible by the human ear. Even the VCR, probably the least refined of these goods, provides easy access to five decades of Hollywood's best efforts in a reasonably high-quality and low-cost form. New technology could enhance or even replace any of these appliances, but it is difficult to envision any way to perform the underlying task in a qualitatively better manner. Innovation will continue to deliver commercial successes, but the tangible benefits to consumers will be measured in ever finer increments.

HEALTH AND MEDICINE

"[I]t was not until a few decades ago that patients stood a better than even chance of being helped by a physician's therapy."[29] Doctors offered not cures, but comfort. As Tolstoy observed of nineteenth-century Russian doctors, "their usefulness did not depend on making the patient swallow substances for the most part harmful (the harm was scarcely perceptible, as they were given in small doses), but . . . because they satisfied a mental need of the invalid and of those who loved her . . . for hope of relief, for sympathy, and that something should be done."[30] Restoring sick people to health was simply not within medical competence. "[T]he only difference between a young and an old physician was that 'the former will kill you, the latter will let you die.' "[31] The results were high infant mortality, short life expectancy, and periodic contagion.

The first significant salient into the sea of disease occurred with little understanding of the underlying pathology. Smallpox was one of the most common of the fatal diseases in Europe during the eighteenth century. It is estimated that as of 1775, as much as 95 percent of the population of France had been infected by smallpox. One in seven of those infected died.[32] It became fairly common to infect healthy patients with what was hoped to be a mild case of smallpox in order to prevent a later and more severe occurrence. Unfortunately, the infection often did not prove to be mild.[33] "Between 1 and 5 percent of the people subjected to the procedure died of induced smallpox. Such were the ravages of the disease, and the fear it engendered, that this was considered an acceptable risk."[34]

Edward Jenner, an English country surgeon and biologist, observed that persons infected with cowpox, a harmless disease carried by cattle, did not thereafter contract smallpox. In 1796, Jenner inoculated a patient with matter from a cowpox lesion. The patient promptly developed cowpox. When Jenner thereafter inoculated the patient with smallpox matter, no infection resulted.[35] By 1801, all British sailors were receiving the cowpox vaccine, with results so favorable that the navy awarded Jenner a medal. Within a few decades, the procedure spread throughout the Western world, and the incidence of smallpox decreased markedly.

Jenner, of course, could not know what caused smallpox or how his vaccine worked. Systematic progress in immunology began after the discovery of pathogenic bacteria. Louis Pasteur played a leading role. While investigating a lethal chicken disease, Pasteur inoculated a chicken with a culture weakened by long storage. It had little effect. Recognizing his error, and not wanting to waste the chicken, Pasteur inoculated it again, using a fresh culture. Still the bird would not die. Pasteur had discovered that effective vaccines could be produced from attenuated strains of the disease causing organisms themselves. A vaccine for typhoid prepared from killed typhoid bacilli was introduced in 1897. A diphtheria toxoid and a tuberculosis vaccine followed in the 1920s and 1930s.

Progress was slower in the prevention of viral diseases, largely because many viruses are too small for effective study using optical microscopes. Viral epidemics thus remained a substantial public health threat through the early twentieth century. The 1918–19 Spanish flu pandemic, for example, infected about one billion people worldwide, killing twenty-two million, including twenty-five million infected and five hundred thousand dead in the United States, more than the combined battlefield deaths of all the wars of the twentieth

148 century.[36] Increased understanding led to vaccines for the prevention of yellow fever, poliomyelitis, various strains of influenza, and measles. Routine vaccination of children and supplementary inoculation of susceptible segments of the population after the initial outbreak of a disease have effectively eliminated the threat of contagion from advanced countries.

Doctors naturally searched for means to cure as well as to prevent disease. That search, at least in its initial form, was not notably successful. Inorganic chemicals capable of killing infectious agents, such as arsenic, iodine compounds, and alkaloids, frequently proved just as toxic to human cells. The first widely useful advance was the isolation and synthesis of sulphonamide, or sulfa, drugs, introduced in 1935. They greatly reduced deaths due to disease and infection during World War II and continue to be used in treating some tropical diseases.

More important in the long run was the discovery of antibiotics, natural products of living organisms that are toxic to bacteria and other microbes. Sir Alexander Fleming discovered in 1928 that the penicillium mold secretes a bactericidal substance, a useful evolutionary adaptation for an organism that competes with bacteria for food. After a decade of repeated failure and frustration, a crash Allied research effort at the outset of World War II finally brought the drug into mass production.[37] It proved effective against a range of bacteria and almost entirely harmless to human tissues. Streptomycin (the first antibiotic effective against tuberculosis), tetracycline (which can be taken orally), cephalosporin derivatives, and various other natural and synthetic antibiotics soon followed.

Pathogenic bacteria also began to explain the mystery of disease transmission. Cholera had become increasingly prevalent with the growth and concentration of cities.[38] John Snow, a London physician, studied the historical progression of cholera outbreaks from India to Europe over several centuries and correctly conjectured that contaminated public water supplies were the common source. When cholera broke out in London in 1854, Snow traced the disease to a single public well that had been contaminated by leakage from a nearby sewer. This led cities to begin discharging wastes into storm sewers, where the next rain carried them into the river. Victor Hugo, for one, scorned this measure as an inexcusable waste of fertilizer,[39] but the epidemics stopped. As the role of bacteria in causing disease became more widely appreciated, authorities began protecting water supplies prophylactically by chlorination. Researchers also began to uncover animate disease vectors. Ronald Ross, a British bacteriologist, discovered the malarial parasite in the gut of mosquitoes in 1898, winning one of the first Nobel Prizes for his efforts. Two years later, Walter Reed, a United States Army pathologist serving in Cuba, proved that infected mosquitoes carried yellow fever. Eliminating stagnant pools and other potential breeding sites halted the outbreak within a few months. (This discovery was instrumental in completing the Panama Canal, where the disease had devastated digging crews, halting an earlier French effort.)

The combined result of these advances has been the almost complete control of infectious diseases in the developed world. Through the nineteenth century, these regularly claimed more than 1 percent of the population each year. In Japan in 1989, the death rate from communicable disease was less than one per ten thousand population. The death rate from infection was slightly higher in the United States almost solely because of AIDS, which arrived on the scene too recently for a vaccine or cure to have been developed yet. It will shortly follow polio, smallpox, diphtheria, and dozens of other infectious killers into history.[40]

Pasteur's work also laid the foundation for modern surgery. Through the mid-nineteenth century, suppuration of wounds was the norm, frequently followed by septicemia and death. Hospitals, with their crowded collection of bacterial breeding grounds, perversely presented the greatest risks. The surgeons themselves carried infection, as neither scalpel, nor ligature, nor clothing was sterilized or even cleaned between patients.[41] Major surgery was so often fatal that patients rarely considered it if there was any other chance for survival.

In 1865, Joseph Lister, then a leading Glasgow surgeon, hypothesized that Pasteur's microorganisms caused postoperative infection. He decided to test that hypothesis on compound fractures, where sepsis had historically been high and the survival rate correspondingly low. Lister applied dressings soaked in carbolic acid directly to the wounds. Ten of the first eleven patients lived, nine of them with retention of the fractured limb, an unprecedented success rate. (Their appreciation may have been somewhat tempered by the agony of

150   having an open wound treated with carbolic acid. Lister later discovered that dilute solutions of the acid are equally effective antiseptics and cause far less tissue damage.) Lister rapidly extended his discovery to general surgery, combining aseptic surgical procedures, an antiseptic mist of dilute carbolic acid playing on the area of the incision during the surgery, and antiseptic dressings. Postoperative mortality dropped to a small fraction of prior rates. Of equal importance, the range and complexity of surgical procedures that could be undertaken with reasonable prospects for success broadened dramatically. Doctors began to operate on patients who would previously have been considered hopeless.

Anesthesia was the other prerequisite for surgery. Stupefaction, using alcohol, opium, or any of various herbs, was widely practiced, but was of limited effectiveness except for superficial operations and had adverse side effects. Lengthy and invasive procedures were practically impossible. Strength, speed, and decisiveness were prized as the most important qualities of the surgeon. The intoxicating effect of breathing ether fumes became known at least as early as 1815. Amazingly, the only use of the discovery for three decades was recreational, so-called ether frolics. Several American dentists finally exploited the medical potential of ether in 1846. Within a few months, London surgeons were using ether for general anesthesia. The search began for other anesthetics, leading to the discovery of chloroform in the following year.

The widening range of surgery made blood loss a recurrent concern. By 1875, direct blood transfusions from donor to recipient were sometimes being used in emergencies such as postpartum hemorrhage. But clotting and other immune responses were frequent, prompting the substitution of weak saline solution for blood. Saline restores blood volume, thereby preventing shock, but does not replenish oxygen-carrying capacity or perform any of the other functions of blood. Karl Landsteiner's discovery of the major blood types in 1900 explained the most common adverse reactions to the donor's blood. By World War I, transfusion was part of the accepted treatment for loss of blood due to wound or surgery.[42]

Procedures now exist for the repairing of virtually every part of the body, and for the replacement of many by transplants or prostheses. Microsurgical techniques allow the repair of practically invisible structures, speeding recovery and minimizing permanent damage. Arthroscopic surgery is now standard for most injuries to connective tissues, vastly reducing required rehabilitation and loss of function. Measures once desperate, such as surgery on the heart or brain, have become routine. For an individual over the age of fifty to have had surgery for some otherwise fatal or disabling condition barely occasions comment.

Only two causes of death continue to figure prominently in the mortality tables of developed nations. Diseases of the circulatory system now kill about 375 people and cancer about two hundred people per hundred thousand population in the United States each year.[43] The next largest cause of death is accidents and violence, at approximately sixty deaths per hundred thousand. The statistics from other advanced countries are similar, except that mortality due to heart disease is much lower in Japan.

Progress continues against the two major killers. Angioplasty and bypass surgery have become routine operations for coronary arteries constricted by fatty deposits. Beta blockers prevent or reduce excitation of the sympathetic nervous system, thereby reducing the risk of second heart attacks. Calcium channel blockers ameliorate angina by blocking a harmful feedback in which an onset of pain triggers the release of neurotransmitters that constrict blood vessels, worsening the angina. Thrombolytic agents (clot dissolvers) limit the damage to the heart muscle caused by a blockage if promptly administered. High-risk patients increasingly use drugs that control serum cholesterol levels, either by inhibiting production of low-density lipoproteins (which form plaques on arterial walls) or by increasing high density lipoproteins. As a result of these and other therapies, as well as better diets and the reduction in smoking, deaths due to heart disease in the United States and most other advanced countries have generally declined since the mid-1960s and will continue to do so.

Similar progress is occurring in cancer treatment. The three standard therapies—surgery, radiation, and chemotherapy—have sharply increased survival rates for many malignancies. Advances in molecular genetics will continue that progress. Detailed investigations of the medical histories of large families, coupled with painstaking chromosome mapping, are beginning to uncover cancer's genetic origins.[44] These studies have shown several malignancies, including such com-

152   mon killers as breast and colon cancer, to be strongly associated with a flaw in a single gene.[45] Such discoveries will aid in the identification of high-risk individuals, resulting in preventive measures, earlier detection, and increased survival.

Genetic research has also begun to yield useful therapies.[46] One approach is immunotherapy, increasing the activity of the body's immune system against cancer cells. White blood cells cultured with interleukin-2 have shown experimental effectiveness in attacking some malignant tumors.[47] Another approach is to alter cancer cells genetically to make them sensitive to a drug, then inject the cells back into the tumor, where they multiply. Tests on mice indicate that the drug then kills both the altered cells and at least some of the original cancer cells, which acquire susceptibility to the drug by an unknown mechanism.[48] Human tests of this "suicide gene" therapy should begin shortly. Scientists have also altered animals, plants, and bacteria to mass-produce monoclonal antibodies, identical antibodies that attack specific kinds of cancerous cells.[49] The current challenge is to circumvent the response of the human immune system, which identifies the antibodies themselves as invading proteins and destroys them. One promising approach is to use altered human cells, either *in vitro* or implanted in genetically modified mice, to manufacture the desired antibodies. Using these and other production techniques, researchers have achieved promising results against several forms of malignancy, including some for which no effective treatment currently exists.[50] In the longer term, doctors may be able to correct genetic predispositions to cancer by introducing cultured cells with properly functioning genes or using vectors to insert properly functioning genes into existing cells.[51]

Medical research thus remains a fertile field, where breakthroughs promise Nobel Prizes and profitable patents. Nevertheless, the tangible impact of future advances will be paltry compared to the progress of the past.

In 1900, life expectancies in advanced countries throughout the world averaged forty-nine years.[52] They now average seventy-six years.[53] Most people survive into their seventies, eighties, or beyond. Some still die in their sixties. Death at any earlier age is considered unusual or even tragic. In 1900, surviving into old age was the aberration. But the lucky few who reached the age of sixty in 1900 could expect to live nearly as long as their counterparts (many more in number) of the present, as the following table indicates:[54]

5.2 U.S. LIFE EXPECTANCIES, 1900 TO 1986
(AVERAGE AGE AT DEATH)

	At Birth	At Age 60
1900	48	75
1950	69	78
1986	75	80

Thus, by the 1980s, surviving the first sixty years of life lengthened the total life expectancy by only five years. The convergence of these two columns shows that medicine has succeeded in curing or treating almost every cause of death except old age.[55] At seventy-six years, life expectancy is approaching the natural limit of the human life span, with infant mortality and accidents accounting for much of the gap. Medicine's ability to narrow that gap further is slight. Even complete elimination of circulatory disease and cancer as causes of death would increase life expectancies at birth by only five to ten years,[56] with social consequences that would almost certainly be negative on balance. By the most basic of measures, life and death, medicine has already reached its limits: children born in the 1970s and 1980s will live, on average, only a few years longer than their parents.[57] With relatively few exceptions, and until scientists begin manipulating the life span itself (see Chapter 11), the future effort in medical research will be focused on reducing morbidity rather than achieving slight delays in mortality. The quantum jumps achieved during the last two centuries cannot be repeated.

EDUCATION AND INFORMATION

Literacy remained uncommon long after the printing press had broken the Church's control over information.[58] The reasons were primarily economic. Parents placed little value on the ability to read, as the work of common people required no knowledge acquired from books. The costs of schooling were far more apparent and weighed far more heavily than the nebulous and uncertain benefits of liter-

154   acy.[59] This competition between child labor and education was, of
course, not an invention of the industrial era. Children had long
worked on farms from a very early age, with full-time labor beginning
before adolescence. Child labor in the mines and factories was thus
only the continuation of a traditional pattern in a new setting.

The nineteenth century brought both more opportunity and more
demand for schooling. Rising wages enabled more English workers
to forgo a child's potential earnings through the age of twelve or
fourteen. Experience with a market-based and increasingly industrial
economy provided evidence of the advantages of education. Employers frequently expressed a preference for literate employees, even for
positions in which reading was not required. Within the rapidly
advancing sectors of the economy, "the accelerating pace of innovation demanded workers capable as never before of mastering new
techniques and processes."[60] The clerks, managers, shopkeepers, and
shippers needed in a market economy had to work with written
communications and accounts. As a consequence, literacy became a
prime determinant of upward social mobility,[61] producing a positive
correlation between education and income.[62] Such incentives predictably drew children from the factories and fields into the classroom.
Compulsory education laws followed late in the century, but these
largely confirmed what the forces of modernization had already accomplished.[63] By 1900, illiteracy had all but disappeared from advanced nations (excluding the oldest population segments).[64]

The twentieth century saw the same forces reshape secondary
schooling. Widening affluence provided the tax dollars needed for
public high schools and allowed more families to support children
into their teens.[65] At the same time, the demand for adolescent labor
declined, as industries mechanized the many routine operations that
youths had previously performed.[66] The shift away from farming and
mining and toward industry and service jobs expanded the need for
workers educated beyond basic literacy and numeracy skills.[67] A high
school education was becoming the prerequisite for entrance into the
employment market. Secondary school attendance rose from 1 percent in 1880 to 10 percent in 1900 to nearly half in 1930.[68] The
emphasis gradually shifted from simply obtaining some secondary
schooling to graduating from high school. By 1950, half of the
seventeen-year-olds completed four years of high school, a propor-

tion that increased to 75 percent in the 1970s and 85 percent in the 1980s.[69] Western Europe and Japan trailed the United States by several decades in this broadening of secondary education, but enrollment rates now generally exceed 80 percent.

Higher education has traveled far along the same path. The nineteenth century began the process with curricular reform, as theology, metaphysics, and rote repetition of classical texts gave way to the sciences, history, and other modern subjects and an emphasis on active scholarship and research.[70] College enrollments soon responded, rising from less than 2 percent in the United States before 1900 to 10 percent in 1925 and more than 30 percent in the 1970s and 1980s.[71] Twenty percent of the population over the age of twenty-five has a college degree, compared to 11 percent in 1970 and less than 8 percent in 1960.[72] (This percentage includes the older population segments that have relatively few college graduates. It will therefore continue to rise for several decades, even without any further increase in college enrollments.) Higher education is also becoming more widespread in other advanced nations, although few have yet approached the numerical levels reached in the United States.[73] These enrollment levels are creatures of prosperity: even if the demand had been present earlier, the resources would have been unavailable. Expenditures on college and university education in the United States totaled $124 billion in 1988,[74] an amount that, adjusted for inflation, would have accounted for 8.5 percent of the country's gross national product in 1950 (compared to the slightly more than 1 percent of GNP actually spent on postsecondary education in that year).

This history of widening educational opportunity has reached an obvious endpoint. Primary and secondary education are free and nearly universal.[75] Public colleges and financial aid programs have made higher education easily accessible to most qualified (and some not so qualified) students. More than half of all high school graduates in the United States enroll in college. Most of the remainder have chosen, in one way or another, not to do so. Genuine financial inability is a rarity. Many campuses and faculties are operating at well below capacity. Thus, despite generous subsidies to encourage attendance, supply already exceeds demand. Higher education has reached saturation levels.

156   So have other sources of learning. Commercial and public radio
and television provide an endless stream of news and informational
programming. Commercial, computerized databases provide instant
access to vast stores of current and specialized information. About
fifty thousand books are published annually in the United States,
along with more than ten thousand newspapers and eleven thousand
periodicals.[76] Other advanced nations produce a comparable flood.
The stacks of any major university library reflect the triumph of
knowledge. Dozens of titles cover even the most obscure topic. This
accumulation greatly exceeds both people's interest and their ability
to learn. Leonardo da Vinci commanded most of the world's knowledge, making him the original Renaissance man, but any reasonably
bright teenager of the present would have much to teach him. As
recently as the Victorian era in England, "science, fast as it was
growing, was not yet either so extensive or minute that its achievements could not be followed and borne in mind."[77] Intervening
accretions and the present pace of discoveries make anything approaching comprehensive knowledge of nature or the world a fanciful
aspiration. Scientists, academics, and other knowledge workers generally confine themselves not only to a field, but to a narrow specialty
within a field.[78] Even the best-educated and most curious take the
accumulated knowledge of the world for granted, resigning themselves to ignorance outside of the few areas they need to command
for their jobs or daily lives.[79] This ascent from the pervasive ignorance, superstition, and speculation that held almost unchallenged
sway until the industrial era to the current super-abundance of knowledge will not be duplicated.

LEISURE AND ENTERTAINMENT

The same is true of entertainment, where the current wealth of
options contrasts sharply with the meager and distasteful choices
available at the beginning of the industrial era.

Representations of life in Merrie Auld England often depict towns-
folk engaged in quaint, bucolic, and harmless pastimes. These no
doubt existed. But those with the most appeal were so brutal as to
tax modern credulity.[80]

One favorite category of entertainment encompassed various methods of torturing animals to death. Cock scailing was traditional and popular at wakes, fairs, and other celebrations. A cock would be tethered to a stake in the ground. Participants would pay to throw a heavy stick (the scail) at the bird from a short distance. The one who killed the bird was the winner. The objective of the early throws would be to render the cock immobile by breaking its legs. A lucky blow might have ended the contest quickly on occasion. One imagines, however, that the cock more often succumbed to repeated bludgeoning. Another popular sport was bull baiting. Participants bred bulldogs for ferocity and insensitivity to pain specifically for this pastime, a concrete indication of its popularity. A dog would be set on a bull tethered by a short rope. A dog that succeeded in sinking its teeth into the bull could be shaken loose only at the cost of the flesh it had seized. On occasion, a dog got under a bull and seized its "pendulous organs." The bull's predictable reaction was a particular crowd favorite. The bull sometimes succeeded in throwing a dog to its death. Dogs, however, were in ample supply. A strong and agile bull might linger, but it would not last. Bear and badger baiting were variations on this theme.[81] Dog fighting, cock fighting, and ratting were among other popular blood sports.

Human contestants fared little better. Boxing matches proceeded essentially without rules. Fighters could be hit while down. Butting was a favored tactic. There was no set limit to the duration of a fight. A serious contest could last dozens of rounds and ended only when one fighter was beaten senseless and could not be revived by those who had bet on him. Football (an amalgam of what later became soccer and rugby) was little more than an organized brawl. As more violent means were undeniably effective, they tended to predominate, especially with the liberal consumption of alcohol that accompanied most games.

> [T]he requirement that some sort of ball be kicked, run with or thrown was the only common denominator in what was in the modern sense hardly a sport at all. At Derby there could be as many as 1,000 a side playing in the annual Shrove Tuesday match. . . . Indeed, many football matches appear to have been more like battles than sport. . . .[82]

158 A Frenchman witnessing one such game remarked that "if English-men called this playing, it would be impossible to say what they would call fighting."[83] This was a precursor not of twentieth-century foot-ball, but of twentieth-century gang wars. Not surprisingly, the game was considered too uncivil for gentlemen and was condemned by middle-class reformers.

By 1900, the forces of modernization had eradicated or utterly transformed all these popular eighteenth-century pastimes. England's middle classes and opinion leaders, whether out of smugness or simple self-awareness, perceived themselves as the leading edge of a new era of civilization, to be marked by enlightenment, intellect, humanity, and prosperity.[84] Senseless and wanton pastimes had no place in this image. "[T]he 'march of intellect' should be overpower-ing such primitive practices."[85]

Blood sports were the first casualties of the new attitudes.[86] When Parliament enacted the Cruelty to Animals Act in 1835, all but a few of its targets had already passed into history; the act merely ratified an existing consensus within the opinion-making segments of society. Progress, manifested by a growing revulsion and a shrinking band of enthusiasts, abolished most blood sports years before Parliament did.[87]

Athletics lost much of their brutality, received a graft of the ethic of self-improvement, and became respectable, even desirable.[88] The modern rules of soccer were fixed in 1863, those of rugby in 1871. The public schools increasingly encouraged these sports not only for fitness but to teach the virtues of teamwork, self-discipline, compli-ance with rules, and sportsmanship. Prizefighting generally fell in repute, but survived in a much diluted form under the London Prize Ring Rules (1839), which outlawed kicking, butting, biting, low blows, and the like. The late-nineteenth-century emergence of tennis and golf reflected the growing refinement of athletics. The rules required self-officiating, and etiquette required that the opponent be afforded every courtesy. The Victorians had legitimized and co-opted sports.

Reading became a middle-class religion. Victorian culture exalted ideas and knowledge, and reading was the avenue to understanding in a world increasingly explained in rational and empirical terms. Technology provided a boost in the form of reduced printing costs.[89]

The reading public in England increased from perhaps eighty thousand in the 1790s to several million by the 1830s.[90] Novels were the most popular form. The number of novels appearing in England increased fourfold from 1820 to 1850 and another threefold by 1864. Newspapers increased in popularity, with the circulation of the *Times* growing from five thousand in 1815 to fifty thousand by 1850. One hundred new magazines appeared in London in the 1820s, compared to twenty between 1801 and 1810. Some of these had a distinctly intellectual cast, inspired by the *Edinburgh Review* (first published in 1802) and the *Quarterly Review* (1809), which enjoyed wide circulation among opinion leaders.

Other intellectual and self-improving activities proliferated. The middle class attended and supported lectures, exhibitions, and museums. They formed gardening clubs, choral groups, and literary and debating societies. In short, they gamely and consciously distanced themselves from anything base or common and molded themselves to the ideals of modernism, humanism, and rationality.

The predictable, if less admirable, sequel was to impose this ethic on the working class. Opinion leaders increasingly disapproved the coarse, drink-centered leisure of the workingman and fretted over evidence of the potentially decaying effects of industrialism and urbanization. The solution, self-evident to the reformers if not to their intended beneficiaries, was the rational recreation movement, founded to inculcate the working class with middle-class values and a desire to participate in improving recreations.[91] Laborers and their families would spend their leisure time reading poetry, science, and other edifying works, attending lectures and concerts, walking in parks, appreciating nature, and touring museums and exhibitions.

Judged by its own terms and standards, the rational recreation movement failed. Workingmen stubbornly displayed a greater appetite for enjoyment than for improvement. But the end result was positive. Entertainment remained the focus of leisure, but in more civilized forms.

Workingmen's clubs illustrate this dynamic.[92] The vision of the evangelical and upper-class reformers who founded these clubs reflected the temper of the age. Workingmen would gladly abandon the pubs to sip tea, read, and hear improving lectures, all for the benefit of their eternal souls, their minds, and their finances, in that order.

160   Contributions proved easier to attract than members. The few clubs that defied their founders and began selling beer and providing games, music, and other diversions prospered. The message was clear. The membership voted to become self-sustaining and self-governing. Freed from the restraints and the stigma of temperance and upper-class patronage, clubs proliferated and membership grew rapidly, from less than 100,000 in 1874 to more than 500,000 by 1883.[93] Despite the fears of the founders, the clubs retained a sober and restrained atmosphere. The men continued lectures and trips to exhibitions and museums, interspersed with picnics, band concerts, and pleasure excursions. Thus, "literate and intellectual interests coexisted with the more boisterous traditional recreations among a working class whose culture had been as much stimulated as disrupted by economic upheaval and social conflict."[94] Workers were receptive to improvement, if not to condescension or boredom.

Reading also percolated through society, penetrating at least to the stratum of skilled labor. The *Daily Telegraph,* first published in 1855, brought the daily newspaper within working-class means, and its circulation, which soon exceeded that of the *Times,* attests to its success in that market. Popular journalism on the American model appeared late in the nineteenth century with tabloids specifically directed to a working-class readership. Books were initially too expensive for workers' budgets, but privately donated libraries, subscription libraries, and later public libraries made novels and other popular works widely accessible. An estimated 81 percent of the users of the Leeds library in the 1870s were of the working class.[95] Many workers also attended zoos, exhibitions, and museums, played in brass bands, and kept gardens.

Professional theater grew rapidly as railways made national touring companies feasible.[96] Impresarios sought to attract customers from lower on the social scale to fill more and larger theaters, bringing a rise in melodrama and spectacle and a deterioration in audience behavior. The upper strata of society initially reacted by migrating to opera, a trend that was predictably short-lived. Straight drama experienced a revival and social pressure improved the behavior of working-class audiences.

But the music hall epitomized late-nineteenth-century working-class entertainment.[97] Elaborate structures, with permanent stages,

proscenium arches, and fixed seating for more than a thousand patrons, began to appear in the 1860s and 1870s. Drink continued to
be applied liberally as a social lubricant, but the show had become the
focus of the establishment. The entertainment was professional, consisting of singers, comedians, cancan dancers, trapeze artists, and a
variety of other acts. Stars appeared nationally and commanded large
salaries. The content of the entertainment stretched the bounds of
propriety severely, and the music halls became a common target of
middle-class reformers. But with the London halls alone selling 25
million tickets annually, their popularity had obviously transcended
their working-class origins, which tempered Parliament's enthusiasm
for regulation. The objections, in any event, lacked the moral force
of earlier reform efforts. The atmosphere of the halls was boisterous,
but controlled. That risqué humor and scantily dressed women had
replaced suffering animals as the entertainment vices of the working
class is a measure of both the commercialization and the civilization
of leisure during the nineteenth century.

The twentieth century has added technology to the entertainment
mix. Recorded music appeared as early as Edison's phonograph in
1877, but reasonable convenience and sound quality appeared only
with high-fidelity (1946) and stereo recording (1958). Few households lack a stereo system, and combined sales of records, tapes, and
compact disks are approaching one billion units annually in the
United States. Motion pictures introduced mass video entertainment
and became the largest single form of commercial entertainment
shortly after the addition of sound. Those living in cities or suburbs
may choose among perhaps a dozen major studio movies within
convenient driving distance on any evening, or among thousands of
titles on local video store shelves.

But the signature entertainment of the twentieth century has been
broadcasting. Radio brought professional music, comedy, drama, and
other entertainment daily to ordinary households. Its immediate success, with six hundred commercial broadcasting stations and one
million listeners in the United States by 1922, demonstrated the
potential of true mass market entertainment.[98] The impact of television has been even greater. The number of broadcast television
stations increased from 559 in 1960 to 1,362 in 1988,[99] giving most
viewers access to independent and public television stations along

162 with the four networks. Even this selection evidently proved insufficient for many viewers, as the number of cable television subscribers rose more than tenfold between 1970 and 1990. Sixty percent of all American households now subscribe.[100] Most cable systems offer thirty-five or more channels, presumably enough choices to satisfy even the most avid viewer. Critics, commentators, and informed opinion regularly decry the quality and value of television programming. The popular judgment is otherwise. Large segments of the American population watch thirty or more hours of television each week, making it overwhelmingly the favorite form of entertainment. The alternative uses of leisure time remain available; people simply prefer to watch television. Popular opinion has thus concluded that television is the best form of entertainment ever devised.

Although eclipsed in commercial importance by broadcast media and movies, live theater and music continue to be popular, with revenue from ticket sales in the United States (adjusted for inflation) more than doubling since 1970.[101] Most large cities boast major league professional sports franchises, access to major college football and basketball, and one or more racetracks. The six hundred major amusement and theme parks in the United States attracted approximately 250 million admissions in 1989.[102]

Eating out has become another leading pastime. Restaurants number more than 300,000 in the United States, or about one for every 250 households. Any urban or suburban dweller has dozens of alternatives, representing an almost equal number of ethnicities, located within a few minutes. The lure of such convenience and variety has easily overcome such deterrents as relatively high cost and frequent warnings by nutritionists. More people are employed preparing and serving food in commercial establishments than in growing it on the farm or selling it at grocery stores.[103] Total sales exceed $100 billion annually, with food prepared away from home accounting for more than 40 percent of total food expenditures.[104] In some affluent urban and suburban neighborhoods, the meal prepared at home has become a relative rarity.

These do not, of course, exhaust the alternatives, but they are enough to establish that most people have easy access to many more entertainment options than they could hope to try. Some of these will fade away, and the constant search for novelty will generate still more in the future.[105] But enough already exist to fill every leisure minute many times over. The improvement from the crude and meager entertainments of the past will not be repeated.

TRAVEL

From ancient times through the early nineteenth century, the well-to-do traveled in coaches. Fifty miles was a day-long journey, and passengers arrived dirty, sore, and tired. Ordinary people, on the other hand, did not travel at all: horses and drivers were simply too expensive.[106] Even the next village was often several hours away by foot. Travel was thus impractical except on extraordinary occasions.

Railways shattered this isolation beginning in the 1840s, trimming coach trip times by two thirds or more and fares by as much as 80 percent, making travel possible even for those with limited leisure time and funds. The Great Exhibition of 1851 demonstrated the potential of this newfound mobility. With the Crystal Palace housing displays showing England's great scientific, technological, and industrial achievements, the Exhibition was the quintessential improving recreation. Six million people attended during the five and one half months it was open, an attendance level that only the widening rail net made possible. Cheap rail excursions to the Exhibition were within workers' means. The excellent comportment of ordinary laborers improved their reputation among the elite, while the Exhibition itself strengthened national pride (and correspondingly weakened any class identity) among the workers. Queen Victoria's hope, expressed on the occasion of the reopening of the Crystal Palace at Sydenham, "that this wonderful structure, and the treasures of art and knowledge which it contains, may long continue to elevate and instruct, as well as to delight and amuse the minds of all classes of my people," was already being realized.[107]

With the extension and improving efficiency of railroads, the seaside holiday became a staple of Victorian leisure.[108] Seaside resorts had long existed, but had been the almost exclusive preserve of the wealthy. Brighton, the resort in closest proximity to London, required six hours to reach by coach at a cost far beyond the means of wage earners. The railroad line (completed in 1841) soon reduced the

164   trip time by two thirds and the cost by three quarters. The result was predictable: visitors to Brighton rose from 117,000 in all of 1835 to 73,000 in one week by 1850.[109] The 1851 census showed the seaside towns as a group to be the fastest-growing in England. Many of the visitors were day-trippers, but an increasing number of white-collar workers could afford longer stays. With the spread of two weeks' paid holiday in the 1870s and 1880s, annual extended vacations became an accepted fixture of middle-class life, with the seaside remaining one of the favored destinations.

Travel exploded in the twentieth century as automobiles added flexibility and airplanes added speed. Air carriers in the United States enplane nearly one half billion passengers each year, almost a three-fold increase just since 1970.[110] Hotel and motel revenues total more than $50 billion annually. Americans take over 1.2 billion trips of one hundred miles or more per year, an average of five per person.[111] About one fifth of these represent business travel, which is likely to plateau or decline with cheap and accessible video conferencing.

Nothing would prevent more pleasure travel, now or in the future, except that few people may find more travel to be a pleasure. Among even the modestly affluent, it is not generally the costs but the time constraints, conflicting commitments, fatigue, and flagging desire that discourage additional trips. With much of the populace already saturated, further decreases in fares or increases in disposable income would not appreciably expand the amount of travel.

PUBLIC GOODS AND INTANGIBLES

It is fashionable among some intellectual elites to scorn the consumer bounty that progress has delivered. Part of this reaction is simply the contempt of familiarity: affluence receives much more respect from those who have experienced poverty. Equally important to this attitude is the assumption, often articulated but rarely examined, that people have made a Faustian bargain, purchasing material progress at the expense of higher values.

The facts are precisely to the contrary. The impact of material progress has been overwhelmingly beneficent, not only in the marketplace, but in all aspects of life. Indeed, progress is beginning to push against effective limits in many of the areas thought to have suffered from its influence. Two examples may illustrate the point.

CULTURE. The American penchant for self-criticism is nowhere more evident than in the cultural arena. "Wasteland" is a fairly representative description, particularly among those with an interest in raising the level of support for cultural activities. The reality appears far different, at least if judged by availability.[112]

The United States has 4,400 museums of art, history, natural history, science, and the like.[113] They commonly keep the cost of admission quite low, and attendance exceeds 300 million annually. The performing arts are also quite accessible, with more than fifteen hundred symphony orchestras and twelve hundred opera companies in the United States.[114] In addition, public television and radio regularly broadcast live musical performances of leading orchestras and opera companies featuring world-renowned conductors, principals, and soloists. Most other advanced nations offer similar or superior cultural opportunities. This ready accessibility is the product of progress; promoting the arts among peasants and laborers was not high on any eighteenth-century agenda.

The number and availability of cultural outlets suggest that people can easily satisfy their taste for the arts, and the financial status of cultural institutions confirms that the supply outstrips the demand. Almost without exception, they depend heavily on charitable contributions and direct or indirect governmental support. That is, patrons are demanding significantly less of these institutions' services than is already being provided. This is more than saturation; it is surfeit.

THE ENVIRONMENT. With other consumer demands increasingly satisfied, environmentalists have received growing support, a trend that became particularly evident in the 1980s. The failure to espouse environmentalism became political suicide in many democratic countries. Legislatures continue to pass new laws, while stricter limits of earlier laws gradually take hold. The "Greens" increasingly reject as anathema any notion of a balancing between economic development and conservation: owls' nesting preferences and piscine spawning habits must enjoy absolute priority over logging or dam building. Prosecutors more often seek severe criminal sanctions in

166   enforcement actions. Concerns over the possibilities of global warming, damage to the ozone layer, acid rain, and other putative environmental crises have received widespread and sympathetic circulation, often without much critical examination, suggesting imminent environmental apocalypse to the casual observer.

The reality, however, is that previous legislation and favorable economic and technological trends were improving environmental quality even before the most recent spate of measures. Rising energy costs in the 1970s encouraged efforts to reduce fuel consumption in both transportation and industry. Improving fuel efficiency automatically reduces the emission both of conventionally defined pollutants and of the "greenhouse gas" combustion products. In addition, several emission-control technologies have matured. As a consequence, 1990-model-year automobiles sold in the United States emit 96 percent less pollutants per mile than 1970-model-year vehicles.[115] During the same period, the electric power industry reduced its emissions 60 percent per kilowatt-hour produced.[116] By any measure, average air quality has improved significantly since the 1970s, as the following table indicates.[117]

5.3 U.S. AIR POLLUTANT CONCENTRATIONS, 1977–86

	Carbon Monoxide	Sulfur Dioxide	Suspended Particulate	Nitrogen Dioxide	Lead
1977	10.7	0.16	62.9	0.029	1.16
1986	7.2	0.12	48.4	0.025	0.15

This decline in emission and pollution levels would have continued even without further measures. Water pollution is also decreasing. Earlier laws substantially eliminated discharges of raw sewage and untreated industrial waste, routine as recently as the 1960s. Farmers, motivated by both economic and environmental concerns, have curtailed agricultural chemical usage, reducing water contamination caused by surface runoff.[118] The benefits of these past improvements are only beginning to be realized. The trends are similar in other developed nations.[119] Eastern Europe and Russia, long among the world's worst polluters, will begin to clean up as the transition to a market economy takes hold, and the signs are also favorable in Mexico. Further technological, economic, and legal changes may accelerate the pace of these advances, but the direction has long been fixed.

Progress thus produces a predictable metamorphosis: goods and services once unavailable at any price become the luxuries of one generation, middle-class amenities in the next, and necessities in the following. Repetition of this cycle for more than two centuries has utterly transformed daily life. This is not to suggest that society has arrived at a material Utopia of effortless abundance. Most households must continue to restrain their indulgence to live within their budgets. Time may somewhat relax those restraints and provide still more and better material comforts. It is not, however, Panglossian to observe that the ordinary consumer now lives better than any king or nobleman before the industrial era.[120] Indeed, any eighteenth-century observer would quickly be driven to miraculous explanations for the present human condition, which would surely seem the gift of a suddenly generous God, particularly given the comparatively easy labor needed to sustain it. The potential for further improvement pales in comparison to that historic victory of plenty over want.

1. Thomas Aidala, *Hearst Castle*, Crown Publishers, 1984, provides a photographic tour and brief history of Hearst Castle.

2. See D.C. North, *Structure and Change in Economic History*, pp. 158–62, W.W. Norton, 1981; Paul Johnson, *The Birth of the Modern: World Society, 1815–1830*, Ch. 11, p. 879, HarperCollins, 1991.

3. See Paul Bairoch, "Europe's Gross National Product: 1800–1975," *J. European Economic History*, Vol. 5, p. 273, 1976, various tables.

4. Mancur Olson, writing in the *Wall Street Journal*, Dec. 22, 1988, p. 12, highlights the rise in living standards by asking whether a consumer would choose an annual income of $25,000 currently, or the same income in 1932, worth perhaps $200,000 today. "[O]ne could readily afford a Rolls-Royce, the best seats in the theater, and the care of the best physicians in the country. But the 1932 Rolls-Royce, for all its many virtues, does not embody some of the desirable technologies available today in the humblest Ford. Nor would the imposing dollars of 1932 buy a TV set or a home videocassette recorder. And if one gets an infection, the best physicians in 1932 would not be able to prescribe an antibiotic."

5. Moses Abramovitz, "The Retreat from Economic Advance: Changing Ideas About Economic Progress," Ch. 12, pp. 256–57, in Almond et al. (eds.), *Progress and Its Discontents*, Univ. of Calif. Press, 1982. To similar effect is Jude Wanniski, *The Way the World Works*, pp. 60–68, Simon & Schuster, 2d ed., 1983. The same process can operate in reverse. The selling price of Monets and of first-growth Bordeaux soared during the 1980s, the result not of any sudden surge of art or wine appreciation but of the intervening accumulation of wealth. The higher price brought the consumer no added increment of pleasure or utility. Similar distorting effects are apparent in everyday transactions. Whether in clothing, automobiles, consumer electronics, vacation resorts, or restaurants, the latest or the most fashionable commonly commands a premium in the marketplace that no objective difference in quality or performance would justify. The dollar value attached to novelty, stylishness, luxury, prestige, and other intangibles tends to rise with increases in disposable income. Thus, the limits discussed in this chapter may not be reflected accurately in the economic statistics.

6. Price decreases resulting from technological and production innovations are not limited to recent years. Between 1882 and 1953, the price of aluminum declined almost 99 percent in constant dollars. For this and similar examples, see John Chamberlain, *The Roots of Capitalism*, Ch. 10, Liberty Press, 1959.

7. An automobile made in 1972 would also have the disadvantage of being illegal today. Since that date, federal law has mandated better pollution controls, stronger bumpers, and better passenger restraints, among other changes. The Appendix describes the contribution of product improvements to the consumer surplus more formally.

8. John Burnett, *Plenty and Want: A Social History of Diet in England from 1815 to the Present Day*, Chs. 1–4, Scolar Press, rev. ed., 1979, describes the early-nineteenth-century English diet. See also Reay Tannehill, *Food in History*, Stein & Day, 1973.

9. Harvey Levenstein, *Revolution at the Table: The Transformation of the American Diet*, pp. 23, 26, 30, and 101, Oxford Univ. Press, 1988. As one example of the impact of improved transportation, fresh milk production rose from two billion pounds in 1870 to eighteen billion pounds by 1900. Levenstein, p. 31.

10. Trevor Williams, *A Short History of Twentieth-Century Technology c. 1900–c. 1950*, Ch. 17, Oxford Univ. Press, 1982, and Levenstein, *Revolution at the Table*, Ch. 3, discuss the major advances in food-processing technology during this period.

11. Earlier freezing methods allowed the formation of large ice crystals that broke cells, producing mush upon cooking.

12. Burnett, *Plenty and Want*, pp. 299–300. To similar effect is James Johnston, *A Hundred Years Eating: Food, Drink and the Daily Diet in Britain Since the late Nineteenth Century*, pp. 22–23, McGill-Queens Univ. Press, 1977.

13. Burnett, *Plenty and Want*, comparing Table 26 at p. 300 with Table 44 at pp. 339–40.

14. Unless otherwise indicated, food consumption data in the text are from *Statistical Abstract of the United States 1989*, Tables 194–97.

15. U.S. Dept. of Labor, Bureau of Labor Statistics, *Consumer Expenditure Survey, 1989*, USDL 90-16, Nov. 30, 1990. The *Economist*, 12–18 May 1990, p. 22, provides similar data for European countries.

16. John Burnett, *A Social History of Housing 1815–1985*, Methuen, 2d ed., 1986, surveys British housing during the modern era.

17. See Roger-Henri Guerrand, "Private Spaces," in Michelle Perrot (ed.), *A History of Private Life*, Vol. IV: *From the Fires of Revolution to the Great War*, Belknap Press, 1990.

18. Gertrude Fish (ed.), *The Story of Housing*, Ch. 2, Macmillan, 1979, describes American housing in the nineteenth century.

19. Burnett, *Social History of Housing*, Ch. 3, p. 96.

20. "A life of poverty is a life in which survival is the first and almost only order of business." Rosenberg & Birdzell, *How the West Grew Rich: The Economic Transformation of the Industrial World*, Ch. 1, p. 4, Basic Books, 1986.

170 21. Ruth Cowan, *More Work for Mother,* Chs. 4 and 6, Basic Books, 1983, describes the twentieth-century spread of household technology. See also Williams, *Short History of Twentieth-Century Technology,* Ch. 30.

22. Clifford Clark, *The American Family Home, 1800–1960,* p. 162, Univ. of North Carolina Press, 1986.

23. *Statistical Abstract of the United States 1989,* Tables 58 and 1241. *Britannica 1990 World Data Annual,* pp. 842–47, contains housing data for other countries.

24. *Statistical Abstract of the United States 1989,* Table 693.

25. *Britannica 1991 World Data Annual,* pp. 848–53.

26. The data in Table 5.1 are from *Britannica 1991 World Data Annual* and various reports of consumer surveys and government studies, including *Wall Street Journal,* Sept. 6, 1990, p. B1, June 4, 1990, p. A1, and Sept. 19, 1989, p. B1, *Times,* June 5, 1990, Overseas News, and Asahi News Serv., Mar. 16, 1990.

27. *Economist,* 13–20 April 1991, Consumer Electronics Survey, p. 5.

28. High-definition television (HDTV) or digital television is likely to supplant the existing analog CRT technology within a generation. But sharper picture definition and better sound hardly compare in significance to the original invention and spread of television, or even of color television.

29. *New York Times,* July 15, 1986, p. C3, arguing that AIDS returns doctors to their traditional role of care-giving, without any means of curing. To similar effect is Peter Medawar, *The Hope of Progress,* pp. 57–58, Methuen, 1972.

30. *War and Peace,* Book 9, Ch. 16.

31. Johnson, *Birth of the Modern,* Ch. 9, p. 746.

32. Fernand Braudel, *The Structures of Everyday Life,* Ch. 1, p. 79, Harper & Row, 1981.

33. "She was inoculated for the small-pox and had it beautiful fine." Thomas Hardy, *The Woodlanders,* Ch. 4.

34. Christopher Wills, *Exons, Introns, and Talking Genes: The Science Behind the Human Genome Project,* Ch. 10, p. 234, Basic Books, 1991.

35. The source of Jenner's inoculation is memorialized in the word "vaccine." In Latin, *vacca* means cow.

36. For an account of the Spanish flu epidemic, see *Smithsonian,* January 1989, p. 131. Apart from countless human tragedies, one actuary estimated that the epidemic cost ten million productive man-years in the United States alone.

37. The penicillium mold naturally produces only enough antibiotic to suppress bacterial growth in its vicinity, resulting in a very low concentration of the drug in culture. The solution was to irradiate cultures of the mold with X-rays. Some of the resulting mutant strains had lost the natural mechanisms regulating antibiotic output.

38. Prior to modern times, religious proscriptions of "uncleanliness" were the primary public health measures. See Deuteronomy 23: 12–14.

39. *Les Miserables, Jean Valjean,* Book 2, Ch. 1, p. 1054, Modern Library edition.

40. The absence of a vaccine or cure makes it easy to overlook how rapid progress has been against AIDS. Epidemiologists quickly traced the method of transmission, making the disease almost completely avoidable. (Only the pampered modern critic would lightly discount this achievement. Any eighteenth-century doctor who had offered reasonable life-style means of avoiding smallpox or diphtheria would have been hailed as a savior.) Researchers have since worked out the life cycle of the virus and picked out several points at which it may be attacked. Although it may be small comfort to those already afflicted, this is considerable progress against a disease that was first isolated little more than a decade ago.

41. The first advance in aseptic procedures actually occurred without any understanding of the underlying pathology. Childbed fever, a bacterial infection of the uterus or birth canal following childbirth, was a common killer in hospitals through the first half of the nineteenth century. In 1847, Ignaz Philipp Semmelweis deduced that doctors were transmitting the fever from one patient to another. By the simple expedient of requiring handwashing in a chlorinated lime solution, he reduced the mortality rate from puerperal fever from an almost unbelievable 18 percent to 2 percent. Guy Williams, *The Age of Miracles: Medicine and Surgery in the Nineteenth Century,* p. 86, Constable, 1981. That Semmelweis died from an infection of his finger was a bitter and ironic injustice.

42. See John Keegan, *The Face of Battle,* Ch. 4, p. 266, Dorset Press, 1976.

43. *Britannica 1992 World Data Annual,* pp. 764–69. These statistics likely overstate the social significance of heart disease and, especially, cancer. Both diseases fall disproportionately on the elderly. Most victims are thus nearing the completion of full life spans. An adjustment of the statistics (for example, to estimate the years of life lost to a particular category of disease instead of the number of deaths caused) would still show heart disease and cancer as the two principal health problems in all advanced nations. Any such adjustment would merely strengthen the point that relatively little socially important progress remains in medicine because few people live significantly less than a full life span.

44. Wills, *Exons, Introns, and Talking Genes,* Chs. 11 and 15, and White & Lalouel, "Chromosome Mapping with DNA Markers," *Scientific American,* Feb. 1988, p. 40, describe the process of identifying the genetic sources of disease by chromosomal mapping. Genetic research is not limited to cancer. One inherited cause of circulatory disease has been found to be a genetic defect that produces a variant LDL form of cholesterol, which the liver fails to remove from the bloodstream. Some alcoholics have a genetic abnormality that apparently interferes with the action of dopamine, a neurochemical that induces feelings of pleasure and well-being, and creates a predisposition to heavy drinking to produce those feelings. See *Wall Street Journal,* July 15, 1991, p. B1.

45. See, for example, Malkin et al., "Germ Line p53 Mutations in a Familial Syndrome of Breast Cancer, Sarcomas, and Other Neoplasms," *Science,* Vol. 250,

172   p. 1233, 30 Nov. 1990, identifying the genetic origin of Li-Fraumeni syndrome, a rare inherited susceptibility to several forms of cancer.

46. *Scientific American,* June 1992, pp. 112–14, and Culver et al., "Gene Therapy," *1993 Britannica Yearbook of Science and the Future,* p. 126, report on the status of gene therapies.

47. On tumor-infiltrating lymphocytes, see Steven Rosenberg, "Adoptive Immunotherapy for Cancer," *Scientific American,* May 1990, p. 62. The FDA has approved the use of interleukin-2 against kidney cancer. See *Wall Street Journal,* Jan. 20, 1992, p. B6.

48. *Science News,* Vol. 140, p. 69, Aug. 3, 1991, describes the results of suicide gene animal tests.

49. The most common technique for producing monoclonal antibodies has been to inject a mouse with the antigen (a molecular identifying characteristic) of the targeted cancer cell. The mouse's immune system begins producing the appropriate antibodies. Antibody-producing cells are removed from the mouse's spleen and fused with a melanoma cell *in vitro,* producing a hybridoma (hybrid melanoma). The hybridoma is immortal. It will continue dividing and producing the desired antibody indefinitely. Use of altered bacteria instead of mouse cells is described in Ward et al., "Binding Activities of a Repertoire of Single Immunoglobulin Variable Domains Secreted from E. coli," *Nature,* Vol. 341, p. 544, 12 Oct. 1989. Hiatt et al., "Production of Antibodies in Transgenic Plants," *Nature,* Vol. 342, p. 76, 2 Nov. 1989, and *Scientific American,* Feb. 1990, p. 62, describe research into "plantibodies."

50. See, for example, *Wall Street Journal,* July 10, 1989, p. A1, reporting promising results against lymphoma and colon, liver, and pancreatic cancer.

51. Human tests of somatic cell gene therapy have begun. Some of the techniques are surveyed in Inder Verma, "Gene Therapy," *Scientific American,* Nov. 1990, p. 68, and described in more detail in Theodore Friedmann, "Progress Toward Human Gene Therapy," *Science,* Vol. 244, p. 1275, 16 June 1989.

52. Angus Maddison, *The World Economy in the Twentieth Century,* Ch. 1, p. 18, OECD, 1989; *Encyclopaedia Britannica,* 11th ed., Vol. 22, p. 98, table, 1910.

53. Maddison, *World Economy in the Twentieth Century,* Ch. 1, p. 18; *Britannica 1992 World Data Annual,* pp. 764–69. Infant mortality skews these data. More than 1 percent of infants born in the United States, for example, do not survive their first year. Although relatively few in number, these deaths have a disproportionate impact on the average life expectancy.

54. The data in Table 5.2 for 1900 and 1950 are from Carlo Cipolla, *The Economic History of World Population,* Ch. 4, Table 16, Barnes & Noble, 7th ed., 1978. Data for 1986 are from *Statistical Abstract of the United States 1989,* Table 109.

55. "[L]ife expectancy has increased, but the human life span has remained virtually unchanged since recorded history." Leonard Hayflick, "Prospects for Increasing Human Longevity," in Johnston (ed.), *Perspectives on Aging: Exploding the*

Myths, Ballinger, 1981, Ch. 2, p. 29. Hayflick represents the narrowing gap between life expectancy and life span with the following graph.

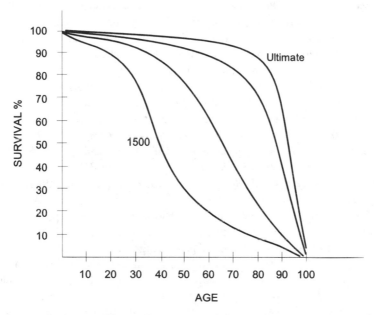

(Figures approximate.) The "ultimate" survival curve represents the theoretical situation in which old age is the only cause of death, that is, the elimination of death due to accident, illness, or genetic defect. The advances in nutrition and medicine have brought reality reasonably close to that theoretical limit. Chapter 11 discusses the prospects for extending the human life span.

56. See Olshansky et al., "In Search of Methuselah: Estimating the Upper Limits to Human Longevity," *Science,* Vol. 250, p. 634, 2 Nov. 1990, concluding that it is "highly unlikely" that life expectancy would exceed eighty-five years, even if cancer and heart disease were substantially eliminated as causes of death.

57. The cost effectiveness of current health care presents another and increasingly pressing issue, but not one that progress can resolve. The problem is uniquely American: the United States spends 12 percent of its national output on health care, compared to about 7 percent for other advanced nations. Aggressive care of the terminally ill is a principal difference. One seventh of all U.S. medical spending is on people in the last six months of their lives. *Wall Street Journal,* Feb. 26, 1992, p. A10. This is an allocation of economic resources that needs to be evaluated critically. Contrast Japan, where, for example, only one heart transplant has ever been performed, but the life expectancy is the highest in the world. Technology, affluence, and a professional mind-set fixated on prolonging life, however briefly and at whatever cost, are largely responsible. As long as patients can continue to receive any level of medical care at little or no expense to themselves and regardless of the tangible benefit from the treatment, progress will push the cost of medical

174   care higher, not lower. Some form of rationing, preferably by the price system, is the only possible solution. For a harbinger of the coming debate on applying cost-benefit analysis to health care, see *Economist,* 20–26 Oct. 1990, pp. 17–20.

58. Literacy data before the nineteenth century are neither comprehensive nor reliable. They most often reflect the ability to sign either the public marriage register or a will. Of course, not everyone married or left a will, and those who did may not have been representative of the population. More fundamentally, the ability to sign one's name hardly demonstrates literacy in any practical sense. For whatever the information is worth, between 30 and 60 percent of brides and grooms were able to sign the marriage registers in most towns and rural districts in England from 1754 to 1804. W.B. Stephens, *Education, Literacy and Society, 1830–1870: The Geography of Diversity in Provincial England,* Tables 1.1 and 1.2, pp. 6–9, Manchester Univ. Press, 1987. Similar literacy rates prevailed in France. Fernand Braudel, *Perspective of the World,* Ch. 4, p. 340, Harper & Row, 1984. Literacy was generally higher in the United States.

59. "[T]he widespread opportunities for child labour, and the apparent lack of demand for literacy skills, meant that parents saw no economic advantage, either to themselves or to their children, of prolonging school life and foregoing the child's earnings. The contribution of the child's earnings to the family economy was important even in the better paid occupations of mining and ironmaking: while in the poorer-paid jobs like nailing, a child's earnings even from a very young age might be crucial." Jacqueline Grayson, "Literacy, Schooling and Industrialization: Worcestershire, 1760–1850," Ch. 5, at p. 64, in W.B. Stephens (ed.), *Studies in the History of Literacy: England and North America,* Univ. of Leeds, 1983.

60. David Vincent, *Literacy and Popular Culture: England 1750–1914,* p. 105, Cambridge Univ. Press, 1989.

61. Vincent, *Literacy and Popular Culture,* Tables 4.6–4.9 and accompanying text, pp. 129–31.

62. Soltow & Stevens, *The Rise of Literacy and the Common School in the United States: A Socioeconomic Analysis to 1870,* Table 4.10 and accompanying text, pp. 125–26, Univ. of Chicago Press, 1981 (showing data from 1867 Pennsylvania study).

63. R. Freeman Butts, *Public Education in the United States: From Revolution to Reform,* p. 69, Holt, Rinehart & Winston, 1978.

64. For literacy rates in England and Wales through the late nineteenth century, see T.W. Heyck, *The Transformation of Intellectual Life in Victorian England,* Table 7.1, p. 199, St. Martin's Press, 1982.

65. Church & Sedlak, *Education in the United States,* pp. 289–90, Macmillan, 1976.

66. Church & Sedlak, *Education in the United States,* p. 289. The increase in secondary school enrollments was slower in rural areas because of the continuing need for adolescent labor during planting, harvesting, and other busy periods.

67. Geraldine Clifford, "The Impact of Technology on American Education, 1880–1980," Ch. 10, at p. 264, in Colton & Bruchey (eds.), *Technology, the*

Economy, and Society: The American Experience, Columbia Univ. Press, 1987. The connection between economic development and education is also apparent from data showing the strong correlation between per capita income school enrollment ratios. See W.W. Rostow, *The World Economy: History & Prospect,* Table II-3, pp. 56–57, Univ. of Texas Press, 1978.

68. Church & Sedlak, *Education in the United States,* p. 289; Butts, *Public Education in the United States,* p. 182.

69. Butts, *Public Education in the United States,* pp. 319–20; *Statistical Abstract of the United States 1989,* Table 211.

70. Germany led in this curricular reform (see Charles McClelland, *State, Society, and University in Germany 1700–1914,* Cambridge Univ. Press, 1980), with the United States following closely behind. The immense prestige of Oxford and Cambridge slowed adoption of the new curricula in England, eventually producing a shift in the center of industrial innovation. "[W]hile England was the locale of revolutionary discoveries in many scientific fields, England also was falling behind in the industrial . . . applications of science," an observation chillingly familiar to American ears. G.M. Young, *Portrait of an Age: Victorian England,* p. 82, Oxford Univ. Press, 1977 ed.

71. Church & Sedlak, *Education in the United States,* p. 294; Butts, *Public Education in the United States,* p. 319; and *Statistical Abstract of the United States 1989,* Table 245.

72. *Statistical Abstract of the United States 1989,* Table 212; Butts, *Public Education in the United States,* p. 319.

73. *Britannica 1990 World Data Annual,* pp. 882–87. As of 1980, the average years of formal education in the adult population ranged from 9.4 years in Germany to 10.8 years in Japan, compared to 12 years in the United States. Maddison, *The World Economy in the Twentieth Century,* Table C-12. That gap has since narrowed slightly.

74. *Statistical Abstract of the United States 1989,* Table 200.

75. The quality of secondary education in the United States is much more in doubt than its availability. The symptoms of declining performance are too well known to need recounting here, and the causes are much debated. For the current analysis, the only salient fact is that the problem is not caused by a lack of resources, most of the educational establishment to the contrary notwithstanding. Educational expenditures in the United States equal or exceed those in other advanced nations and, by any measure, have risen throughout the period of declining performance. See, for example, Clifford, "The Impact of Technology on American Education, 1880–1980," Ch. 10, at p. 254, in Colton & Bruchey (eds.), *Technology, the Economy, and Society* (fivefold spending increase in constant dollars between 1950 and 1980). The salaries of public-school teachers rose more on the average during the 1970s and 1980s than those of accountants. Parochial schools deliver a better education than most public schools at much lower cost. The problems are thus institutional; material progress will not resolve them.

76. *Statistical Abstract of the United States 1989,* Tables 382, 913.

176   77. Young, *Portrait of an Age: Victorian England,* Sec. 28, p. 159.

78. "[F]ew scholars . . . call themselves mathematicians or physicists or biologists without restriction. A man may be a topologist or an acoustician or a coleopterist." George Gilder, *Microcosm: The Quantum Revolution in Economics and Technology,* p. 278, Simon & Schuster, 1989.

79. "Man prides himself on the increase of his knowledge. But, as a result of what he himself has created, the limitations of his conscious knowledge and therefore the range of ignorance significant for his conscious actions have constantly increased." Friedrich Hayek, *The Constitution of Liberty,* Ch. 2, p. 26, Univ. of Chicago Press, 1960.

80. Robert Malcolmson, *Popular Recreations in English Society 1700–1850,* Chs. 1 and 3, Cambridge Univ. Press, 1973, describes English recreation through the eighteenth century.

81. Ken Follett, *The Pillars of the Earth,* Ch. 10, William Morrow, 1989, graphically describes a bear baiting.

82. Golby & Purdue, *The Civilisation of the Crowd: Popular Culture in England 1750–1900,* Ch. 1, p. 23, Schocken Books, 1985.

83. Peter Bailey, *Leisure and Class in Victorian England: Rational Recreation and the Contest for Control, 1830–1885,* Ch. 1, p. 8, Univ. of Toronto Press, 1978.

84. "The Englishman . . . knew that in the essential business of humanity, the mastery of brute nature by intelligence, he had outstripped the world. . . ." Young, *Portrait of an Age,* Sec. 2, p. 27.

85. Malcolmson, *Popular Recreations in English Society,* Ch. 7, p. 136. Early industrialists also opposed many traditional recreations on the narrow ground that they conflicted with the secular ethic of productivity. "[C]oncern for economic growth allowed slight sympathy for activities not obviously productive. . . . [W]hat was of doubtful economic value could only be deplored." Malcolmson, Ch. 8, p. 159. See also James Walvin, *Leisure and Society 1830–1950,* Ch. 1, p. 5, Longman, 1978: "[T]he pre-industrial calendar of frequent and varied holidays was simply consumed by the encroaching national commitment to useful toil." Another important source of opposition was Evangelicalism, as to which see Young, *Portrait of an Age.* Evangelicals' general antipathy to leisure and recreation outside the home ultimately proved unpalatable; the secular spirit of the Enlightenment was more influential in shaping modern leisure.

86. Some reformers of the time and since have urged the abolition of all hunting as simply another barbaric pastime. Whatever the merits of that contention, a basic distinction between hunting and the animal recreations of the eighteenth century cannot be ignored. In hunting, the objective is a "clean" kill, in which the animal does not suffer. The essence of many early recreations was to torture the animals to death. See Golby & Purdue, *Civilisation of the Crowd,* Ch. 2, p. 55: "It is often pointed out that in the long war against blood sports it was the most plebeian activities . . . which were the first to go under and that those sports with gentry and upper class support survived. It would be more correct to say that it was the most pointless and purely cruel pastimes which went first. . . ."

87. The end of the Stamford bull running illustrates the importance of shifting public opinion. This annual event continued after 1835 in defiance of special magistrates and dragoons imported to enforce the new law. It was stopped in 1840 by respectable citizens of the Stamford area, who simply strolled the streets of Stamford on the accustomed day of the running. Their presence tangibly expressed community disapprobation, and no further bull running occurred. See Malcolmson, *Popular Recreations in English Society,* Ch. 7, pp. 126–35.

88. The transformation of sports during the nineteenth century is described in Bailey, *Leisure and Class in Victorian England,* Ch. 6, and Lowerson & Myerscough, *Time to Spare in Victorian England,* Ch. 8, Harvester Press, 1977.

89. "The world of publishing was a manifest result of the new technical age which made possible cheap, mass-produced literature." Walvin, *Leisure and Society,* Ch. 4, p. 56. The printing advances of this era included the all-metal press; stereotyping, in which a block of type was cast as a single mold to allow recycling of the type during printing; the steam-powered press; and the cylindrical press, which reduced the total pressure needed to form an impression.

90. Heyck, *Transformation of Intellectual Life in Victorian England,* Ch. 2, p. 25.

91. The rational recreation movement is discussed in Hugh Cunningham, *Leisure in the Industrial Revolution c.1780–c.1880,* Ch. 3, St. Martin's Press, 1980, Bailey, *Leisure and Class in Victorian England,* Ch. 2; and Golby & Purdue, *Civilisation of the Crowd,* Ch. 4.

92. Workingmen's clubs are discussed in Bailey, *Leisure and Class in Victorian England,* Ch. 5.

93. Bailey, *Leisure and Class in Victorian England,* Ch. 5, p. 118. The number of clubs rose from 245 in 1873 to 550 in 1883. Cunningham, *Leisure in the Industrial Revolution,* Ch. 5, p. 183.

94. Bailey, *Leisure and Class in Victorian England,* Ch. 1, p. 11.

95. Cunningham, *Leisure in the Industrial Revolution,* Ch. 5, p. 154.

96. On nineteenth-century developments in theater, see Cunningham, *Leisure in the Industrial Revolution,* Ch. 1, pp. 28–29, and Ch. 5, p. 159; Golby & Purdue, *Civilisation of the Crowd,* Ch. 3, pp. 70–74; and Lowerson & Myerscough, *Time to Spare in Victorian England,* Ch. 5.

97. Victorian music halls are described in Bailey, *Leisure and Class in Victorian England,* Ch. 7; Golby & Purdue, *Civilisation of the Crowd,* Ch. 7, pp. 172–78; and Cunningham, *Leisure in the Industrial Revolution,* Ch. 5, pp. 164–170.

98. Williams, *Triumph of Invention,* p. 237.

99. *Statistical Abstract of the United States 1989,* Table 900.

100. *Economist,* 15–21 Feb. 1992, p. 25.

101. *Statistical Abstract of the United States 1989,* Table 377.

102. *Christian Science Monitor,* May 21, 1990, p. 9.

103. *Statistical Abstract of the United States 1989,* Tables 642, 657.

104. See U.S. Dept. of Labor, Bureau of Labor Statistics, *Consumer Expenditure Survey, 1989,* USDL 90-616, Nov. 30, 1989; *Statistical Abstract of the United States 1989,* Table 1104.

105. Virtual reality is beginning to migrate from defense research and pilot training into amusement parks. As the technology declines in price, it will move into arcades and eventually the home. The commercial potential is substantial. This development will provide one more option for the use of leisure time. Even those who welcome that option will not likely judge it a watershed event in the history of entertainment.

106. Johnson, *Birth of the Modern*, Ch. 3, pp. 169–76, describes the rigors and expense of pre-mechanical travel.

107. Cunningham, *Leisure in the Industrial Revolution*, Ch. 5, p. 156; see also p. 157: "The Crystal Palace was an enduring ideal of what the nation's leisure might be; it could civilise, improve and unite the people."

108. The growth of seaside vacations is described in Lowerson & Myerscough, *Time to Spare in Victorian England*, Ch. 2; Walvin, *Leisure and Society*, Chs. 2 and 6; and Cunningham, *Leisure in the Industrial Revolution*, Ch. 5, pp. 160–64.

109. Walvin, *Leisure and Society*, Ch. 2, p. 19.

110. Reduced fares because of deregulation account for some of the increase in air travel since 1970. That change has been fully assimilated, and no comparable further reduction is in the offing.

111. *Statistical Abstract of the United States 1989*, Table 408.

112. Consistent with the theme of the chapter, the text argues that affluent societies are saturated with cultural outlets. Gunther Stent, *Paradoxes of Progress*, Ch. 2, W.H. Freeman, 1978, suggests another kind of limit: artistic exhaustion. At the risk (if not certainty) of oversimplifying, Stent argues that music, painting, and other arts have undergone a progressive relaxation of compositional rules (or canons, in Stent's terminology). Each generation of artists has found the existing canons too confining because, Stent suggests, geniuses of the previous generation exhausted their potential, and any later artist of talent would scorn imitation. The progression from the tight structure of Bach's fugues through the atonality and seeming temporal chaos of Schoenberg and other modern composers is thus, on Stent's analysis, a one-way trip that has now reached its end, the freedom from any canons having become the defining value of the work.

113. *Britannica 1990 World Data Annual*, pp. 888–93.

114. *Statistical Abstract of the United States 1989*, Table 397.

115. For example, Karen Wright, "The Shape of Things to Go," *Scientific American*, May 1990, p. 92. Total automotive pollution has not, of course, decreased to the same extent, because of the continuing use of older vehicles and increased total traffic.

116. *Economist*, 8–14 Sept. 1990, "A Survey of Industry and the Environment," p. 26.

117. The data in Table 5.3 are from *Statistical Abstract of the United States 1989*, Table 344. Concentrations are stated in parts per million, except for particulates and lead, which are in micrograms per cubic meter. Declining ambient pollutant concentrations are a direct result of declining emissions, as shown by the following data from Table 345.

	Carbon Monoxide	Sulfur Oxides	Suspended Particulates	Nitrogen Oxides	Lead
1970	98.7	28.3	18.5	18.1	0.20
1980	76.1	23.9	8.5	20.3	0.07
1986	60.9	21.2	6.9	19.3	0.01

All figures are annual emissions in the United States in millions of metric tons.
118. Synthetic organic pesticide usage in the United States declined by 30 percent between 1980 and 1986. *Statistical Abstract of the United States 1989,* Table 351.
119. *Economist,* 23–29 May 1992, p. 79, shows the decline in emissions in OECD countries between 1970 and 1988, citing a World Bank Development Report.
120. Joel Mokyr, *The Lever of Riches,* Ch. 12, p. 303, Oxford Univ. Press, 1990. "[E]xisting society opens an astounding range of choice to the poor man—a range greater than that which not many generations ago was open to the wealthy." Friedrich Hayek, *The Road to Serfdom,* Ch. 7, pp. 89–90, Univ. of Chicago Press, 1944.

Chapter Six

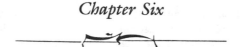

SYMPTOMS OF THE LIMITS

No single insurmountable barrier blocks further material progress. The world economy may become a bit more integrated; technology can always squeeze out a little more production; tax changes may motivate some people to save and invest more of their earnings. A complete cessation of progress may never occur, and certainly has not yet arrived. But the leading economies have already traversed the easy ground, and the obstacles become steadily more formidable as they try to advance further. The result is a gradually worsening slowdown in the rate of progress, visible first in the most advanced economies. Symptoms of this confrontation with the future are everywhere; indeed, they are so pervasive that they tend to blend into the background of daily events. This chapter highlights some of the early portents.

THE PRODUCTIVITY COLLAPSE

"Productivity isn't everything, but in the long run it is almost everything."[1] Temporarily leaving aside the many complications inherent in a market economy, people can consume only what they make. Having more thus starts with making more, which in turn requires either (1) working harder or (2) producing more from the same amount of effort. Nonstop toil looks good in the national income accounts, but it is hardly a prescription for improving the quality of life. Real material progress therefore means extracting more or better output (products or services) from the same inputs (labor, capital, or raw materials).[2] That is increased productivity. Productivity data thus provide the best single economic measure of the rate of progress.

Those data clearly show that progress is slowing. Productivity in the United States rose almost without interruption from the mid-nineteenth century, when statistics began to be maintained, until 1973.[3] Since then, total factor productivity has been essentially flat;[4] expansion of the work force plus some small additions to capital accounted for virtually the entire increase in measured output. Labor productivity exhibits the same trend.[5] Output per man-hour in the United States rose at a rate of only 1.2 percent per year from 1973 to 1986, half the rate achieved from 1950 to 1973. Labor productivity actually fell in 1989 and 1990 and recovered only about half its loss in 1991.[6] Efforts to blame this fall on the business cycle must contend with an inconvenient fact: no postwar recession gave rise to a three-year period in which productivity declined.

Stagnant productivity begets flat or falling wages. Average weekly pay in the United States, after adjusting for inflation, was 15 percent lower in 1989 than in 1973,[7] and still had not recovered by 1992. Such a decline is, again, unprecedented. The sharp increase in two-income households maintained median family income at earlier levels, but only barely.[8] Even that cheerless statistic rests on a flaw in the economic data, which place no value on the leisure time or the uncompensated services (cleaning, nurturing, volunteer work) lost when both spouses work. Potential further gains from that source are, in any event, negligible—the huge reservoir of nonworking wives that existed in the 1950s and 1960s has been sucked nearly dry. Falling wages make for some stirring rhetoric by political candidates, labor leaders, and trade and class warriors, but the reality is depressingly simple: to make more money, American workers must make more stuff, and that they have essentially failed to do for twenty years.

The United States enjoyed the dubious honor of leading a world-wide parade toward lesser productivity gains. The growth of both total factor productivity and labor productivity of every advanced economy, notably including Japan, has slowed since 1973.[9] Only the newly industrialized countries, such as South Korea and Singapore, maintained or increased their productivity growth during the 1970s and 1980s, largely by exploiting innovations earlier pioneered in the advanced economies. Total output has naturally flattened along with productivity, with the rise in output per capita falling by half in the developed nations after 1973.[10] Compounded over a span of decades, these sagging growth rates profoundly affect living standards.[11]

Arguments over the cause of this stagnation have generated more heat than light. A common early reaction was denial. Flat productivity could not be happening because it had never happened; it was a statistical fluke of no particular long-term significance.[12] The persistence of the trend through nearly two decades and across several business cycles has convincingly buried that position.

Liberal politicians and opinion leaders are as quick to blame the economic policies of the 1980s for productivity problems as for everything else, but this theory requires that the facts be ignored. The trend had clearly begun by the mid-1970s. Indeed, the Reagan administration was acutely aware of the problem from the outset and sought to address it with a number of plausible policies. Reducing marginal tax rates decreases tax-induced distortions in the economy and rewards incremental effort. A lower tax rate on capital gains encourages saving and capital investment. Antitrust policies better informed by economics (in both the Justice Department and the Supreme Court) allow efficient mergers and market arrangements. Reduced regulation decreases unproductive expenditures. Lower inflation eliminates the distorting effects of rapidly changing price levels. The thirteen million jobs added between 1980 and 1988 testify persuasively to the success of these policies; productivity remained sluggish not because of them, but in spite of them. Moreover, the global scope of these trends belies this or any other uniquely American explanation. Lamentations about the loss of American competitiveness and menacing imprecations over foreign scheming are misdirected for the same reason.

A more sophisticated school of thought focuses on two events at the threshold of the slowdown: an OPEC-initiated rise in the price of oil and the final collapse of the Bretton Woods international monetary accord.[13] But energy costs have since returned to historically low levels (after adjusting for inflation) without triggering a resurgence of growth. The instability of exchange rates resulting from the inconsistent and unchecked political aims of the major trading countries is a genuine problem, but it lacks much force in explaining the post-1973 stagnation. Exchange rates affect only the importing and exporting sectors of the economy, which were quite small in the United States in 1973 compared to Japan and West Germany, both of which fared much better at least through the 1970s. Any loss of American economic vitality caused by fluctuating exchange rates would have been evidenced (1) by declining or at least flat international trade volumes and (2) largely in those industries most heavily involved in the world market. Instead, the intervening years have seen a disproportionate rise in world trade, with the smallest declines in productivity gains occurring in the economy's international sectors.[14]

As the facts eliminate the usual suspects, economists have been forced to admit that they know neither the source nor the cure for the productivity slump.[15]

The cause is the general slowdown in material progress, for which there is no cure. Progress is not produced by and can scarcely be affected by economic policy. In the past, innovation, market expansion, and capital accumulation could be relied upon to reduce the labor and other inputs needed to produce a given output. Those forces are largely spent, and the progress they generated has limited the scope available for further productivity gains.

Agriculture is the paradigm. The rising productivity of American farmers provided the labor needed for manufacturing and other expanding sectors in the nineteenth and early twentieth centuries. But ever-increasing efficiency has since reduced the economic role of farming to virtual insignificance.[16] Another doubling of agricultural productivity would now free only about 1 percent of the work force, producing a comparable gain in overall productivity. The same limitation increasingly applies to manufacturing: improved productivity saves too little labor to provide much boost to the economy as a whole.[17] Thus, "brilliant productivity performers may actually be condemned by their . . . achievements to 'burn themselves out.' "[18] Through this process, stagnant sectors assume an enlarged role simply by remaining in stasis; hence the increasing relative importance of retail trade and of services generally in the United States and other advanced economies.[19] This shift dilutes the effect of any continuing advances in the most progressive sectors.

184   Rising productivity is a creature of material progress. They came and passed together, and they will not return.

CUTTING THE PIE

An era's living symbols of wealth speak volumes about its defining values and dynamics. Stanford, Rockefeller, Carnegie, and Ford, for all their flaws, built fortunes out of railroads, oil, steel, and factories, the vehicles of progress for their age. Consider some of the comparable symbols of the 1980s: Michael Milken, Henry Kravis, Donald Trump, Joseph Flom, Joe Jamail, and even Michael Jackson. Their fortunes arise not from building or making, but from manipulating.[20] Carl Icahn was no expert in railcar leasing, textiles, or airlines, as events quickly proved. But he had few peers in redirecting existing wealth and income from others to himself and those aligned with him.

This is "the 'rent-seeking' society, in which the tax lawyer and the political lobbyist have replaced the inventor and the engineer and the entrepreneur's main instruments towards higher profits."[21] Agriculture, manufacturing, and construction have occupied steadily smaller portions of the civilian work force since 1970.[22] Meanwhile, the number of new law-school graduates in the United States roughly doubled during the 1980s. Accountants, investment advisers, stockbrokers, and real estate agents have also multiplied. These are typically people of considerable energy and intellect, "diverted from productive contribution in pursuit of their share of the available pool of rent."[23] The damage they do while rent seeking, although considerable, is less troubling than the loss of their talents from the tasks of production and progress.[24]

Corporate takeovers and buyouts were among the most visible reshufflings of wealth during the 1980s. With vast income flows and capital accumulations at stake, tiny reallocations could be worth tens or even hundreds of millions of dollars, many times what the productive effort of a lifetime could earn. Huge rewards awaited individuals able to influence the outcome of these transactions. These rewards naturally attracted many talented and energetic people. Their daring and brilliant maneuvers and the riches they received are the stuff of best-sellers, but they contributed little if anything to the wealth of society. Any efficiency gains that arose from most takeovers were incidental to the overriding objective, the transfer of wealth from creditors, managers, employees, suppliers, and other stakeholders to deal makers and shareholders.[25] This corporate purse snatching creates nothing.

The world capital of rent seeking, however, is not New York, but Washington, D.C. The United States reached a milestone of sorts in 1992, with more Americans working in government than in manufacturing for the first time. The Senate had only 365 paid lobbyists as recently as 1960; in 1990, it had 33,704.[26] They earn their keep by securing favorable (or preventing unfavorable) redistributions of the national income. The federal budget is a catalog of their successes. Even when they fail, they consume the time and energy of people who could otherwise do something useful.

But the failures pale in comparison to such triumphs as the sugar program.[27] Most American sugar growers cannot compete with producers from the Caribbean, Central and South America, and other areas with ideal climates and cheap labor. Economics textbooks and the politically naive would suggest that they grow something else. But sugar growers, like most rent seekers, have a more refined appreciation of the public interest.[28] Their solution to their lack of competitiveness is to exclude foreign sugar through an ever-shrinking import quota. Like all such solutions, this one carries a cost: sugar growers' political action committees contributed $2.6 million to Congressional campaigns between 1985 and 1990. But they got more than their money's worth: the sugar program cost the other 240 million Americans $3 billion in 1988.[29] Any attempt to curtail the program invariably meets sustained, well-financed, and lethal resistance. In 1990, for example, farm-state senators and representatives easily defeated an attempt to roll back the United States sugar price to a mere 180 percent of the world market price, compared to the 200 percent sought (and obtained) by the sugar lobby.[30] Proponents of the rollback, knowing a lost cause, did not bother to attack the program's obvious economic irrationality, arguing instead that the quota increased coca cultivation in South America and pollution from sugarcane processing in Florida. This inability even to address the real merits of the issue suggests the difficulty that democratic governments experience in dealing with rent-seeking special interests.

The ill effects of the sugar subsidy do not end at the high price paid

186   by consumers.[31] Producers of cake mixes and other packaged foods containing sugar could not compete with foreign competitors paying the world market price, requiring import protection for those products as well. Food processors have substituted corn syrup in soft drinks and other sweetening applications to avoid the high cost of domestic sugar. The subsidy assures American sugar beet producers enough profits to outbid other farmers for available land, producing a steady rise in domestic sugar production, despite declining demand. The sugar program thus transfers productive resources from soybean and corn growers, who enjoy a comparative advantage in world markets, to sugar growers, who are not even close to competitive in those markets. Kansas could, with equal rationality, tax its wheat farmers to subsidize fish canneries. Such market distortions are just part of the price that must be paid to guarantee a few sugar growers that their princely incomes will continue.

From modest beginnings during the Depression, farm programs have grown steadily. The direct cost of the programs to taxpayers swelled to more than $25 billion by 1987. The total cost to American taxpayers and consumers during the past decade has been estimated at $300 billion.[32] Farmers received some of this bounty; most of it was wasted. Congress annually votes to pay farmers not to grow crops, perhaps the highest tribute to the effectiveness of the farm lobby and clear evidence that the American polity has become oblivious to special-interest legislation. A drought thus becomes good news, because it reduces the total payments to farmers. Such perversity suggests the extent to which policy and common sense have parted company.

But farm programs are merely one outrageous example of a larger phenomenon. Social welfare outlays and other transfer payments now approach $1 trillion annually in the United States, dwarfing all other categories of government spending combined. This trend is global; social welfare spending rose sharply in every Western nation between 1960 and 1990, pushing taxes and deficits to dizzying heights.[33] Most of these programs have some fairly plausible justification, but they consume real resources and deaden progress at every level. Lobbyists and politicians seek to expand such programs, from a variety of motives, and are opposed by other lobbyists and politicians seeking to restrict the same programs. Recipients stand in lines and fill out forms to receive their shares. Potential recipients may modify their behavior, usually unproductively, to qualify for payments. Civil servants process the payments and monitor for fraud or abuse. "To be sure, a great nation can indulge [such] little extravagances . . . but a long enough series of little extravagances . . . can add up to a stagnating if not crippling economic burden."[34]

The dream of receiving something for nothing is not unique to the postwar period, but its widespread fulfillment is. The explanation is surfeit. The vast quantities of existing wealth and income make prospecting for some share of it a viable livelihood for much of the population. The sustained superabundance of food and manufactured goods[35] weakens the social and economic pressure for more production. The most prosperous economy of even one generation past could not have tolerated the present scale of transfers and deadweight losses. But tens of billions of dollars can slip through the cracks almost unnoticed when GNP approaches $6 trillion. Widespread affluence makes this sort of diversion of resources possible, predictable, even easy. Rent seeking is thus an inevitable but poisonous by-product of progress. Even at their uncommon best, government, finance, law, and the like merely facilitate and soften the economic process. They did not generate progress in the past, nor will they in the future.

WORK ETHIC

Some provincial Japanese politicians call it laziness. Some American employers no doubt think the same, but instead feel constrained to speak in such neutral terms as attitude, motivation, absenteeism, and priorities. Its real name is affluence. Affluence and toil are ill-suited and uncomfortable companions, ready to part at the first excuse.

The balance between work and leisure varies widely, depending on several factors. One is the level of pay. At the margin, higher pay makes the additional hour of work more valuable than the hour of leisure forgone. This is, of course, the rationale for higher overtime rates, and for supply-side economics. But increased incentives at the margin usually translate into sharply higher total income. At some point, the worker achieves an income or, more precisely, a standard of living such that still more income declines in value.[36] A person may work hard to be able to afford a house in a fashionable neighborhood, a luxury automobile, a second automobile, an athletic club membership, and an annual vacation, but be unwilling to work still harder for a second house, another vacation, or weekly gardening service. How many and which life-style components are important vary among individuals, but most people's appetite for still more must begin to wane at some level of income.[37]

Such income effects are not limited to some minuscule group of the "idle rich." A household in the United States with a gross annual income of $150,000 (two nice salaries or one very nice one) keeps about $100,000 after taxes. That translates to $8,300 each month for housing, food, transportation, clothing, education, insurance, entertainment, vacations, and the like. People can and do find ways to spend such amounts. But another $1,000 per month (a hefty $20,000 raise, after taxes) would scarcely make a difference in the household's standard of living from that level. The willingness to sacrifice in order to earn this increment of income would be correspondingly small. In other words, income effects would likely have overcome incentive effects.

Another perspective may illustrate the same point. The same household lives modestly, spending only $40,000 and saving $60,000 each year. After ten years, the resulting accumulation would continue to yield a return of approximately $40,000 per year for a lifetime. That is, the wage earner(s) could stop working and still maintain the same standard of living. For such people, a lifetime of maximizing income has become optional. A modest inheritance would shorten the needed working span still more.

Few people actually target a level of income and expend just the amount of effort needed to attain it or work hard for a decade or two and then retire. The changes and uncertainties of life would make too fine a calculation very risky. But the ability to construct these scenarios, using realistic assumptions, establishes two points:

1. Paying more begins to *dis*courage rather than encourage work at some level; and

2. That level is within reach of a large and expanding group of people.

Quantifying where income effects may begin to outweigh incentive effects is not now possible, and may never be.[38] That point would vary significantly among individuals. For some households with mod-est needs in low-cost-of-living areas, the level may be less than $100,000 annually; for others, twice or three times that amount. Whatever the level, rising prosperity has obviously begun to push against it. Census Bureau figures from 1989 show one household in twenty-five making more than $100,000 per year in income, one in eleven above $75,000, and one in four above $50,000.[39] This distri-bution may, of course, already reflect significant income effects. Fur-ther rises would bring them ever more widely and strongly into play. Such affluence must undermine the willingness of at least some people to strive and sacrifice. "The uniform, constant, and uninter-rupted effort of every man to better his condition" observed by Adam Smith and firmly embedded in the foundations of economic theory ever since can no longer be assumed.

Anecdotal evidence suggests that the traditional work ethic is already dissolving, even among employees situated well below the highest income brackets. More managers and professionals are re-moving themselves from the "fast track" of rapid advancement to accommodate family and leisure activities,[40] that is, voluntarily re-nouncing the prospect of greater incomes in order to work less. Indeed, one survey reported that 70 percent of those earning more than $30,000 per year would willingly forgo one fifth of their salaries to have one additional day of leisure per week.[41] The notorious unreliability of such surveys warns against accepting such statistics as literal truth, but the erosion of the work ethic is still clear. Overall, between 1973 and 1986, the average number of hours worked per person per year declined in every OECD country.[42] In the United States, the decrease was from 1710 to 1609 hours per year. Workers are also choosing to retire earlier, despite longer life expectancies, better health, and new laws against age discrimination. The percent-age of men aged fifty-five to sixty-four who have left the work force rose in all the leading economies during the 1980s.[43] These choices are not irrational or even surprising for individuals whose current income and wealth are sufficient to guarantee material security. The change is that rising levels of affluence have afforded many more people the luxury of making that choice.

A society's increasing affluence reduces the incentives even of its lowest income segments, albeit by a different mechanism. People necessarily endure and tolerate poverty where it is pervasive. Those so

190   stricken must find their own salvations. The means simply do not exist to relieve their hardships. Not so in affluent societies. Governments establish various assistance programs to supply at least the minimal material needs. (Minimal is, of course, a relative term; a household at the poverty line in the United States enjoys a standard of living that most people in South America, Africa, and Asia could only envy.) The income provided, although low, is reasonably competitive with that of entry-level or unskilled jobs. And, of course, gainful employment typically ends eligibility for the governmental relief. Such programs thus leave the recipient with little incentive to seek work,[44] and attempts to condition eligibility for assistance on efforts to do so have rarely proven effective.

The consequences are readily observed. Throughout the 1970s and 1980s, and most notably during the eight-year economic expansion that began in 1983, unemployment in the United States consistently remained above 5 percent. To be classified as "unemployed," an individual must be in the work force and out of a job, someone who claims to want, to be looking for, and to be capable of performing full-time productive work. That is, out of every twenty people employed full-time, one supposedly could not find work, not counting those who admitted that they were not looking. But this is simply ridiculous, as Robert Reich, no apologist for laissez-faire capitalism, has candidly admitted: "The truth is that by the last decade of the twentieth century, almost all Americans who wanted to work could find a job."[45] At any point in the economic cycle, and certainly during the later stages of an expansion, hundreds or thousands of fast-food establishments, retail outlets, construction sites, shippers, cleaning services, and factories in every American city advertise in a futile effort to fill entry-level positions. To many of the unemployed, and to those who choose not to be in the work force at all, these jobs are simply not worth taking. The work requires no skill, it is hard or tedious, or it pays little. The preferred alternative is to coast, waiting for something better to present itself, while depending on governmental doles in money or in kind, savings, family, or some combination thereof. It is a sensible and predictable choice, given the social availability of the resources to support it.

Rising affluence thus impairs incentives across the entire spectrum of incomes. Those incentives nourish and sustain the work ethic that involves each individual in the process. Material progress could not long survive its passing. As Victor Hugo observed, "By wishing to sit down, we may stop the progress even of the human race."[46]

FRIVOLOUS CONSUMPTION[47]

Pollsters regularly report on people's satisfaction (or lack thereof) with their material situations and prospects. "I make more money than I have any real use for" is not one of the more common responses, despite the data presented in the previous section. But what people do better reflects their feelings than what they say. How they spend their money is particularly revealing about the prospects for continued progress.

Trendy and luxury items command exorbitant prices, even in the midst of a recession. A designer dress or purse may cost $1,500 or more. Many brand-name athletic shoes retail for over $100. Gold and platinum credit cards provide most customers no meaningful increment of service in return for their higher annual fees. Some brands of watches regularly sell for $1,000 to $6,000 or more, which, for perspective, is about the same price range as for used cars. Whatever drives these purchases, it is clearly not intrinsic value.

Entertainment expenditures are, by definition, unnecessary. They are also among the most costly. A pair of choice season tickets for professional football may cost $1,000 or more, for professional basketball, as much as $2,000.[48] Tickets to one championship sporting event are likely to cost several hundred dollars. A pair of tickets to a successful Broadway show cost over $100. In all, recreation (excluding restaurant meals and leisure travel) accounts for more consumer spending than household utilities and gas and oil *combined*.[49] The bill for dinner for two at any of several dozen popular restaurants in most cities is over $100, more than enough to feed a family for a week. Even at ordinary restaurants, the price of a meal is several times the cost of dining at home, which does not, of course, discourage many people from dining out regularly. Leisure travel consumed $313 billion in the United States in 1988, 6.5 percent of the gross national product, and has been growing at a rate of 9 percent per year.[50] Millions of people pay a monthly fee to belong to health clubs. Relatively few often use those clubs, still fewer for any exercise they could not perform at home.

192   Affluence is not the exclusive province of some thin upper stratum of society. Even ordinary, middle-class neighborhoods offer ample evidence of surplus income. Recreational vehicles typically cost hundreds of dollars per day of use. Third television sets and second videocassette recorders are becoming commonplace, as is a separate telephone line for one or more children. More than 200,000 Jacuzzis are sold annually in the United States. Cellular telephone antennas, once seen only on luxury automobiles, now sprout from Toyotas, Mazdas, and Buicks, despite the high purchase price and usage charges. Couples and their parents routinely spend many thousands of dollars on a wedding and its various accouterments. Women in middle- to upper-income brackets may own several dozen pairs of shoes. Cosmetic surgery and adult orthodontia, once restricted to celebrities, have become routine and accepted responses to trivial flaws in appearance, flaws often discerned only by the patient. Stores sell water, slightly flavored or with carbonation, at three to four times the price of gasoline. Shopping has become a principal leisure activity for many. Such profligacy absolutely astounds visitors from the Third World, but it is so commonplace in advanced economies as to escape notice altogether.

The means of many, many people obviously exceed their needs, however earnestly they may assert the contrary; otherwise, indulging in such expenditures would be irrational. This excess makes such people difficult to motivate, because they can already afford not only what they need, but a lot else besides. Even a decline in income would entail little hardship. Their tolerance for long hours, monotony, failure, excess travel, or any of the other disamenities of work may be limited, along with the motivational potential of higher compensation. Saving does not rank high among the priorities of people who spend their incomes in these ways. They greet pleas for hard work, saving, sacrifice, and other such anachronisms not with action or assent, but with incomprehension.

PLAYING IT SAFE

The first American colonists died in droves. Disease, starvation, accidents, and the myriad other hardships served up by a harsh land often claimed half of the settlers before a colony became established. Two centuries later, the Founding Fathers' pledge of their lives and fortunes was no empty rhetoric. Failure of the Revolution would surely have meant ruin or death for many of them; even success carried a steep price for some. Western pioneers chanced the hazards of the trail and the hardships of the frontier against the prospect of cheap land and fresh opportunity. Successive generations of immigrants risked life and limb digging coal and building railroads and bridges. Pilots' lives paid for the early advances in aviation.[51] Pioneers in industry similarly risked economic ruin with their new ventures. Almost all the early car builders went broke at some time, and many of them died that way.[52]

These people were not idle thrill seekers. Death threatened everyone constantly, whatever they did, and few people enjoyed any material security. They accepted some additional risk as the price for the chance to better their lives and those of their children. Their willingness to do so built a nation.

Willingness to assume risk is not one of the distinguishing marks of contemporary America. Alar residues on apples that pose less danger than peanut butter sparked a national furor. Even remote or speculative environmental hazards outweigh almost any economic impact. The Food and Drug Administration demands something approaching absolute proof of safety before approving new food additives or drugs. OSHA inspectors routinely cite factories for workplace safety violations that could only charitably be described as trivial. The Federal Aviation Administration and the Consumer Product Safety Commission intensively regulate (at considerable cost) toward an apparent objective of zero risk. The sixty-five-mile-per-hour speed limit, mandatory passive restraints, and motorcycle helmet laws protect people even from themselves. Any mishap is cause for a lawsuit, reflecting the belief that nothing bad should ever happen.

The wisdom of any of these policies may be debated. The point for current purposes is that the public endorses or at least accepts them, demonstrating a pervasive aversion to risk.

The preference for certainty over risk is neither new nor surprising. No one of ordinary means wagers $10,000 on a coin flip, even though the bet neither raises nor lowers the anticipated worth of the participants. People routinely pay liability insurers' administrative

194 costs and profits to guard against financial catastrophe. The change from the past is simply that more people now have enough money to indulge their taste for safety and security.

Affluence is the natural enemy of risk-taking.[53] People become cautious when they can afford to be and when their desire for further material gain begins to subside. The comfort of a secure income discourages an established employee from risking a new position. An existing fortune makes additional wealth less enticing as an incentive, and the prospect of living without the cushion of wealth more troubling. Even more so, only a dire financial condition is likely to induce someone to risk life or health for more income. The goals of an increasingly affluent society inevitably shift away from betterment, with its attendant risks, and toward conservation.[54]

But safety and certainty are expensive. Pollution control and air bags cost money. Speed limits and other risk-reducing measures commonly sacrifice efficiency in some form. Drug and product safety testing and the threat of liability discourage innovation. And progress in any form, whether the building of a new factory or pioneering of a new product or process, requires a willingness to assume financial risks. Playing it safe is a strategy for stability and quiescence, not progress.

SOCIAL BEHAVIOR

The fastest growing large American city of the 1980s was Las Vegas. During 1988, Americans legally gambled more than $200 billion,[55] roughly $1,000 for every person over the age of thirteen. The newest form of gambling, state-sponsored lotteries, consumed $17 billion.[56] Gambling produces nothing: the winners win what the losers lose, less the expense of running the game. Money itself, the distillation of economic productivity, becomes the plaything, which reveals much about the society's attitude toward useful effort.

Illegal drugs are not only unproductive and expensive, they are dangerous and illegal as well. By any measure, however, drug use exploded in the United States and, to a lesser extent, in European countries beginning in the early 1960s. Once a pathology of the ghetto, drugs became a common recreation of the affluent beginning in the 1970s and even approached social acceptability before the reaction set in.

More than half of all first marriages in the United States end in divorce. The costs of the legal proceedings, child care, lost work time, and additional housing generally lower living standards of divorced parents by about 30 percent, even without taking the human toll into account. The total of abortions and illegitimate births approaches the number of legitimate births nationwide, and is higher in some areas. The rise in unwanted pregnancies coincided almost exactly with the arrival of convenient and effective contraception, marking the problem quite clearly as social and not technological. Other advanced countries exhibit similar trends, although cultural differences produce significant variations in the pattern.

These are isolated manifestations of what is increasingly recognized as a debilitating tendency in American society. It is a decline in the sense of individual responsibility, a breakdown of social restraints, a loss of direction and purpose. George Gilder has captured it as well as any:

> [Beginning in the 1970s], the United States launched a campaign against family roles and rules, achieved unparalleled rates of crime and drug addiction, nourished a media and intellectual counterculture hostile to business and technology, and taught more students sex education and psychology than physics or calculus. . . . The United States ignited a national fever of litigation and a national obsession with claims of "rights" and a national disdain for duties.[57]

None of this would have been possible or long tolerated without widespread affluence. Societies struggling to rise above subsistence are notorious for their rectitude. Work largely occupies their time and energies, and even leisure time is employed constructively, or at least inexpensively, harmlessly, and inoffensively. Social and community pressures restrain deleterious behavior before it even approaches the threshold of criminality. A society that spends hundreds of billions of dollars annually on gambling and recreational drugs, in which stability of the family unit is a secondary concern, has scant interest in bettering its condition and little inclination to defer gratification. It has become largely indifferent to further material progress.

TRADE DEFICITS

The 1992 election produced no shortage of explanations and proposed solutions for the persistent American trade deficit. All of them were wrong. At its core, the trade deficit is nothing more (or less) than another symptom of the limits of material progress.

Every city in the United States has its wealthy suburbs and exclusive neighborhoods. Such communities include many people who, by hard work, talent, inheritance, luck, or otherwise, have accumulated far more wealth than their fellows, enough wealth to supply their needs and those of their dependents for a generation or more. This wealth enables them to buy more goods and services from people aspiring to affluence in nearby areas than people in those areas buy in return. Wealthy communities thus transfer some of the proceeds of their wealth to productive but less wealthy surrounding communities. This transfer is so automatic, natural, and obvious that it is not noticed, and would not merit comment if it were.

The United States is a wealthy nation. Many of its people have accumulated far more wealth than all but a handful of the citizens of other nations, enough wealth to supply their needs and those of their dependents for a generation or more. This wealth enables Americans to buy goods manufactured in other countries by workers, managers, and capitalists aspiring to become wealthy themselves. The citizens of those less affluent countries buy fewer goods and services from the United States. Thus, the United States, to maintain its life-style, must transfer some of the proceeds of its wealth to other productive but less wealthy countries.

This equally automatic, natural, and obvious transfer of wealth is called a trade deficit and is thereby transformed into a great evil. It elicits a response sometimes bordering on hysteria. Lee Iacocca whines; presidents and presidential wannabes promise and posture; Congressional committees investigate; trade negotiators alternately cajole and threaten; commentators wring their hands. The leeches regularly prescribe two cures for the disease: retaliatory trade barriers and devaluation of the dollar. Neither one achieves anything positive.

Trade barriers are intended to and do in fact punish those nations with the temerity to embrace capitalism and offer high-quality goods at low prices. But the main victims of such measures are invariably American consumers.[58] Those who buy Mazdas and Vouvrays believe (not without some justification) that they represent better quality or value than Dodges or Chenin Blancs. Discouraging the exportation of goods from the City or the East Bay to Marin County would make no less sense.

And the follow-on effects can be disastrous. Trade wars rarely end with the first salvo. Japanese buy few American cars; Americans watch even fewer Japanese movies. Why is one a ground for trade reprisals and the other not? "There is a tendency for every nation to see itself as unfairly disadvantaged by world competition in sectors in which it is doing poorly while taking for granted its success in sectors where it is doing well."[59] With each nation judging its own trade cause, the potential for spreading protectionism is great. The Smoot-Hawley tariff of 1930, for example, precipitated retaliatory tariffs worldwide. Not only the imports but also the exports of the United States declined by 70 percent between 1929 and 1932. The not so coincidental result was worldwide depression. Purporting to restrict retaliatory measures to "predatory" trade is a meaningless limitation: "The successful always appear predatory."[60]

The effect of trade barriers depends entirely on the responses of the affected countries. If those countries retaliate, or even if they do nothing, a heightened trade barrier is clearly detrimental. The woeful history of trade sanctions imposes a heavy burden on anyone who would claim to be capable of predicting those responses.

Currency manipulation can claim no better record of results. The common litany in favor of devaluation is that it makes foreign goods more expensive (and, hence, less desirable) in the United States, and American goods cheaper abroad. But the trade balance is measured in money, not in physical units. After devaluation of the dollar, every American product sold in Japan fetches less yen, and every Japanese product bought in this country costs more dollars. The deficit thus increases, an increase that may or may not be counterbalanced later by a favorable shift in unit exports and imports.[61] History provides little encouragement. Mexico, with its regular devaluations during the 1970s and much of the 1980s, should have accumulated a massive trade surplus under this theory. The opposite was, of course, true. During the 1980s, America's large trade deficit with Japan persisted

198   through years when the dollar was grossly overvalued relative to the yen, and years when the yen was grossly overvalued relative to the dollar. Altering the unit of exchange does little to affect the fundamental positions or interests of buyers or sellers, foreign or domestic.

Analyzed in terms of the sweep of progress, the current trade deficit is easily explained. Beginning in the late nineteenth century, the United States led the world in increasing productivity. That lead plus the destruction in Europe and Japan during two world wars made Americans substantially wealthier than anyone else. The gap in productivity began to close after 1950,[62] but the difference in accumulated wealth is naturally slower to disappear. The concentration of wealth in the United States, no longer balanced by a commensurate lead in productivity, creates a financial osmosis—some of the money automatically flows from Americans to foreigners in return for goods and services. Wealthy Americans feel free to spend all or substantially all of their earned income, while less wealthy foreigners save and invest.[63] The less wealthy devote the effort, take the risks, and make the sacrifices necessary to enhance their material positions or those of their children; the wealthy are more complacent. The differing attitudes and motivations prevalent in other nations are readily observed in the palpably superior work ethic of most immigrants. As one (understandably anonymous) Labor Department specialist noted: "You see exhortations all the time to hire the handicapped, minorities, women. But did you ever see an ad campaign to hire an immigrant? Apparently there is no need."[64] Korean immigrants defended their little shops in areas of Los Angeles that the police had conceded to the mobs; try to imagine middle-class suburban store owners doing the same. Such differences are no more sinister, and should be no more unsettling, than the same differences between old money and the upwardly mobile in this country.

Japan's shifting trade balance illustrates this dynamic perfectly. Japan ran a sizable trade deficit through the 1960s and much of the 1970s. Its lagging productivity forced it to import the goods needed to rebuild its economy. By the 1980s, its hardworking labor force, modern factories, lean manufacturing methods, and zealous quality control had raised its productivity to (and sometimes above) American levels in many of the tradable sectors. But the Japanese people had not become wealthy in any meaningful sense. Cultural preference could conceivably explain paper walls and *tatami,* but not the widespread lack of flush toilets.[65] Leisure remained almost nonexistent. Exorbitant housing costs and prices some 60 percent higher than in the United States kept the affluent life-style out of reach even for many successful Japanese.[66] Despite Japan's economic surge, Japanese consumers probably remained, certainly felt, and therefore acted much less prosperous than their American counterparts. Japanese families returning from extended assignments in the United States often remarked on the difficulty of the transition back to a more Spartan life-style. These differences began to erode by the late 1980s, and Japan's trade surplus predictably declined, gradually but steadily, from 1987 through 1989.[67] Japan's property and stock markets then crashed, much of its paper wealth vanished at a stroke, and the trade surplus jumped. Exchange rates, trade barriers, dumping, the *kei-retsu,* and structural impediments are largely media and political diversions. Trade with Japan will move toward balance as the Japanese approach American levels of affluence, and not before.

The Japanese will thus follow the path of the Europeans. The American trade balance with Western Europe, which showed a sharp deficit through most of the 1980s, has since moved to a modest surplus. The overall American trade deficit has also shrunk, as the wealth gap between the United States and the rest of the world has narrowed. As the wealthy nations settle into a more balanced trade position among themselves, they will continue to run trade deficits with newly emerging industrial economies (South Korea, Singapore, etc.),[68] although with no single dominant economy, those deficits may be smaller for any one country than they have been for the United States in recent years. In the meantime, the trade deficit is a symptom not of maladroit American trade negotiators or of malevolent scheming by foreigners, but of the limits of progress faced by all advanced nations.

Plausible alternative explanations exist for several of these symptoms, and some of them have occurred before in isolation. But their current convergence, and their resistance to time-honored remedies, is no coincidence. They are signs of the end of material progress, with little independent significance. Efforts to treat them outside of that context will continue to fail.

1. Paul Krugman, *The Age of Diminished Expectations: U.S. Economic Policy in the 1990s*, Ch. 1, p. 9, MIT Press, 1990.

2. The discussion in the text focuses on labor and capital as the principal factors of production. The quantity of raw materials required per unit of output has also decreased, by approximately 60 percent since 1900. The decrease in Japan has been 40 percent just since 1973. Peter Drucker, "The Changed World Economy," *Foreign Affairs*, Vol. 6, at p. 773, Spring 1986. To similar effect is W.W. Rostow, *The World Economy: History & Prospect*, p. 98, Univ. of Texas Press, 1978.

3. See Angus Maddison, *Economic Growth in the West: Comparative Experience in Europe and North America*, Tables H-1, H-2, and I-7, Twentieth Century Fund, 1964, showing steady growth in output per man and per man-hour in the United States, the United Kingdom, and Germany between 1870 and 1960.

4. Angus Maddison, *The World Economy in the Twentieth Century*, Table 1.5, p. 22, OECD, 1989 (1973–84 data); Baily & Chakrabarti, *Innovation and the Productivity Crisis*, Ch. 1, Brookings Inst., 1988; Landau, "U.S. Economic Growth," *Scientific American*, June 1988, p. 44, 46; and *Wall Street Journal*, Jan. 11, 1989, p. A14 (column by Lindley Clark).

5. Labor productivity data, although widely reported, are potentially misleading, because they effectively attribute the return from added physical capital to labor. Thus, a poor investment in machinery (one, for example, that yielded only a 1 percent return) would nevertheless appear as a gain, because workers could produce slightly more output with the equipment than without it. The same investment would be correctly reflected as a decline in total factor productivity. The data that follow in the text are from Maddison, *World Economy in the Twentieth Century*, Table 7.2, p. 88, and *Wall Street Journal*, which reports labor productivity data at least quarterly. See also Baily & Chakrabarti, *Innovation and the Productivity Crisis*, Ch. 1, Tables 1-1 and 1-2.

6. *Wall Street Journal*, May 4, 1992, p. A4.

7. *Economist*, 10–16 Nov. 1990, p. 19; *Wall Street Journal*, Mar. 20, 1989, p. A1. Weekly income per worker fell from $366 in 1972 to $312 in 1987 (in constant 1987 dollars). Kevin Phillips, *The Politics of Rich and Poor*, Ch. 1, p. 15, Random House, 1990.

8. *Economist*, 10–16 Nov. 1990, pp. 19–20; Phillips, *Politics of Rich and Poor*,

Ch. 1, p. 15. See also *New York Times,* May 3, 1987, p. F2 (median family income doubled from 1947 to 1973, then declined through 1984).

9. Maddison, *World Economy in the Twentieth Century,* Tables 6.10, 7.2, and 7.5 (data through 1984); Baily & Chakrabarti, *Innovation and the Productivity Crisis,* Ch. 1, Table 1–2; Landau, "U.S. Economic Growth," *Scientific American,* June 1988, pp. 44, 46, 50. See also *Wall Street Journal,* Oct. 6, 1988, p. A1, noting the lack of productivity growth or wage gains in Britain notwithstanding the successes of Prime Minister Thatcher's economic policies in other respects.

10. The growth of real gross domestic product per capita in the OECD countries averaged 3.8 percent between 1950 and 1973, but only 1.9 percent between 1973 and 1987. Maddison, *World Economy in the Twentieth Century,* Table 3.2, p. 35. To similar effect is Ralph Landau, "U.S. Economic Growth," *Scientific American,* June 1988, p. 44.

11. An Urban Institute economist estimated that median family income in 1990 would have been $47,000 instead of $35,000 if productivity had not flattened after 1973. *Wall Street Journal,* May 4, 1992. Economics is not arithmetic, and this kind of calculation contains many unstated and questionable assumptions, but it does suggest the magnitude of the effect.

12. One careful and detailed attempt to explain away flat productivity as a temporary statistical aberration is Baumol, Blackman & Wolff, *Productivity and American Leadership: The Long View,* Ch. 4, MIT Press, 1989, which concluded that the U.S. data through 1984 did not establish a meaningful trend because of the wide variability of measured productivity over time. Continuing stagnation had dispatched the statistical-anomaly "explanation," along with the authors' hope for a return to 3 percent annual productivity increases through 2020, before it appeared in print.

13. See Maddison, *World Economy in the Twentieth Century.* Robert Bartley, editor of the *Wall Street Journal,* has focused particularly on the disruption of price signals caused by currency fluctuations as the underlying cause. See "The Great International Growth Slowdown," *Wall Street Journal,* July 10, 1990, p. A16. The resort to such explanations is driven by the pervasive, natural, but erroneous premise that "technological possibilities are stupendous, promising a new industrial revolution." The technology is indeed stupendous, but its contributions to economic gains cannot match those of earlier high-growth eras for any extended period.

14. "[I]t is the nontradable sector that has suffered the biggest productivity problem." Baily & Chakrabarti, *Innovation and the Productivity Crisis,* Ch. 6, p. 107.

15. Krugman, *Age of Diminished Expectations,* Ch. 1, p. 13; James Galbraith, *Balancing Acts: Technology, Finance and the American Future,* Ch. 1, p. 10, Basic Books, 1989. Peter Drucker, writing in the *Wall Street Journal,* July 25, 1989, p. A16, has suggested a strategy for reinvigorating productivity growth. Mr. Drucker notes that service and support groups (e.g., clerical, maintenance, transportation) account for ever larger portions of total costs (up to 40 percent) in large organiza-

202 tions and that they typically operate inefficiently. He calls this "a central productivity problem of advanced economies." His solution ("the next productivity breakthrough") is to "unbundle" (i.e., contract out) many such service and support functions, leading to lower-cost performance of those services. Without questioning either the diagnosis or the prescription, the potential gains (some fraction of 40 percent) are surely a pale imitation of the kind of multifold productivity increases that have characterized past progress, several of which Mr. Drucker himself noted in "The Changed World Economy," *Foreign Affairs*, Spring 1986, pp. 772–78.

16. The agricultural value-added component of gross domestic product in OECD nations dropped from an average of 39 percent in 1870 to only 4 percent in 1987. Maddison, *World Economy in the Twentieth Century*, Table 1.4, p. 20.

17. U.S. manufacturing productivity rose smartly through the mid-1980s, reacting to intensified foreign competition, rebounding from the slump of the late 1970s and the sharp recession that began the decade, and benefiting from a reduced regulatory burden. This burst had little overall impact, despite the jubilance of some observers, largely because of the diminished manufacturing work force.

18. Baumol, Blackman & Wolff, *Productivity and American Leadership*, Ch. 6, p. 116.

19. Services produced 13.6 percent of national income in 1978, compared to 9.4 percent in 1955. During the same period, agriculture declined from 4.6 to 2.9 percent of income, and manufacturing from 32.6 to 26.4 percent. Walton & Robertson, *History of the American Economy*, Table 27-1, p. 583, Harcourt Brace, 5th ed., 1983. During that period, total factor productivity rose rapidly in manufacturing and farming (due largely to continuing technological advances) and was essentially stagnant in services. John Kendrick, *Interindustry Differences in Productivity Growth*, Table 1, American Enterprise Institute, 1983.

20. Phillips, *Politics of Rich and Poor*, Ch. 6, pp. 182–83.

21. Joel Mokyr, *The Lever of Riches*, Ch. 7, p. 181, Oxford Univ. Press, 1990. Economists classify an activity as "rent seeking" or, more descriptively but less felicitously, directly unproductive profit seeking or DUP if they "yield pecuniary returns but produce no goods or services that enter a conventional utility function directly or indirectly." D.C. Colander (ed.), *Neoclassical Political Economy: The Analysis of Rent-Seeking and DUP Activities*, p. 18, Ballinger, 1984. The economist's definition of rent seeking is, however, generally restricted to activities that are unambiguously social-welfare-reducing and that arise from artificially created economic rents. Colander, p. 8; Robert Tollison, "Rent Seeking: A Survey," *Kyklos* 35:575 (1982). Thus, lobbying for food stamps would not be classified as rent seeking, even when undertaken by the farm lobby, because the egalitarian effect of the measure could be considered a social good. The discussion in the text is not limited by this restrictive definition. For discussions of several aspects of the theory of rent seeking, see Edward Wolff, *Growth, Accumulation, and Unproductive Activity*, Cambridge Univ. Press, 1987, and Buchanan et al. (eds.), *Toward a Theory of a Rent-Seeking Society*, Texas A&M Press, 1980.

22. *Statistical Abstract of the United States 1989*, Tables 620, 645, and 655;

Historical Statistics of the United States, Series D170 and D174; and *Economist,* **203** 10–16 Nov. 1990, p. 22.

23. Baumol, Blackman & Wolff, *Productivity and American Leadership,* Ch. 12, p. 276.

24. See Robert Reich, *The Work of Nations: Preparing Ourselves for 21st Century Capitalism,* Ch. 15, pp. 190–91, Knopf, 1991.

25. "[E]ven if there are some efficiency gains from a takeover, they may pale by comparison with the transfers of wealth." Shleifer & Summers, "Breach of Trust in Hostile Takeovers," Ch. 2, at p. 42, in Alan Auerbach, *Corporate Takeovers: Causes and Consequences,* Univ. of Chicago Press, 1988.

26. *Economist,* 10–16 Nov. 1990, p. 22.

27. Clifton Luttrell, *The High Cost of Farm Welfare,* Ch. 10, Cato Inst., 1989, and *Wall Street Journal,* June 26, 1990, p. A1, describe the sugar program. On farm programs generally, see James Bovard, *The Farm Fiasco,* ICS Press, 1989, and *Economist,* 27 June–3 July 1992, pp. 21–24.

28. "Single-cause pressure groups . . . may define the mission of America as high subsidies for a few thousand tobacco farmers in North Carolina." Peter Drucker, *The New Realities,* Ch. 7, p. 102, Harper & Row, 1989.

29. *Wall Street Journal,* July 29, 1991, p. A2.

30. *Wall Street Journal,* July 24, 1990, p. A8, and July 25, 1990, p. A12, reported the "debate" over renewal of the sugar program.

31. The ill effects of the sugar program do not even stop at the U.S. border. It costs the world economy an estimated $300 million to $500 million, with the Caribbean nations bearing the lion's share. *Economist,* 27 June–3 July 1992, p. 24. The ability to sell sugar into the United States at world market prices would contribute more to the quality of life in the Caribbean than any form of aid. The present quota system threatens to swamp a natural paradise with poverty and seething resentment.

32. *Economist,* 27 June–3 July 1992, pp. 21–24.

33. See *Statistical Abstract of the United States 1989,* Table 567, and *Economist,* 19–25 May 1990, p. 11. The trend toward higher governmental expenditures began early in the twentieth century. See Maddison, *World Economy in the Twentieth Century,* Table 6.3, p. 71 (total government expenditures as percentage of GDP in six leading countries from 1913 to 1986). Every OECD country increased governmental transfer payments as a percentage of gross national product between 1955 and 1969. See Rostow, *World Economy,* pp. 282–83, and Tables III-65 and IV-15.

34. William Buckley, *Up from Liberalism,* p. 216, Hillman Books, 1961.

35. "The world of excess supply of almost everything that commenced in the early 1980s should still be in effect in ten years." *Wall Street Journal,* Feb. 27, 1989, p. A1 (quoting A. Gary Shilling and Co.). See also Drucker, "The Changed World Economy," *Foreign Affairs,* Spring 1986, pp. 770–78.

36. Gunther Stent, *Paradoxes of Progress,* W.H. Freeman, 1978, advances a similar argument in psychological rather than economic terms. Stent posits that maintain-

ing the goal of striving for success (which he equates with the Nietzschean will to power) requires an ambiance of economic insecurity. Thus, "accession to economic security, a secular consequence of progress, will ultimately brake progress because it is inimical to the . . . transmission of the will to power." Stent, Ch. 2, p. 35. As a consequence, progress is, "by its very nature, by its very dependence on the will to power, self-limiting." Stent, Ch. 1, p. 25.

37. "Money is worth nothing to the man who has more than enough." George Bernard Shaw, quoted in Simon James, *A Dictionary of Economic Quotations*, p. 132, Barnes & Noble, 2d ed., 1984.

38. "We simply do not know at what levels of income per capita, as we arbitrarily measure that concept, human beings will decide, on average, that enough is enough and diminishing relative marginal utility will set in for real income itself." Rostow, *World Economy*, pp. 563–64. A 1992 Roper Organization survey asking Americans how much annual income they would need to fulfill all their material wishes produced a median response of $77,000, although participants above that income level predictably quoted higher figures.

39. U.S. Bureau of Census, *Money Income and Poverty Status in the United States: 1989* (Advance Data from the March 1990 Current Population Survey), Current Population Reports, Series P-60, No. 168. Preliminary 1990 data show more than 5 percent of all families having annual incomes above $100,000. See also Phillips, *Politics of Rich and Poor*, Ch. 1, p. 15, citing Congressional Budget Office estimates for the average incomes of the top 10 percent and 1 percent of American families. *Wall Street Journal*, May 12, 1992, p. B1, shows about sixteen million American households (about one sixth of the total) with incomes above $75,000 and net worth above $300,000 in 1991, citing an unofficial source. If accurate, these figures would show that the portion of the population potentially subject to income effects grew even during a recession.

40. *Wall Street Journal*, June 13, 1989, p. B1.

41. *Wall Street Journal*, Aug. 5, 1991, p. B1.

42. Maddison, *World Economy in the Twentieth Century*, Table C-8, p. 132.

43. *Economist*, 25–31 July 1992, p. 60.

44. Expanding social welfare programs also alter incentives for the productive sectors of society, by raising tax rates to pay the bills.

45. *Work of Nations*, Ch. 16, p. 203. This pithy statement of an infrequently acknowledged reality is nestled somewhat uncomfortably in a chapter devoted entirely to bemoaning sharp disparities in American incomes.

46. *Les Miserables, St. Denis*, Book 1, Chapter 2. See also Jude Wanniski, *The Way the World Works*, p. 163, Simon & Schuster, 2d ed., 1983: "If . . . there are human institutions capable of having individuals extend themselves for the commonweal first, and their self interest second, such institutions have not yet been found."

47. The term "frivolous" may imply an unintended censoriousness. People are, of course, entitled to spend their money however they wish. "Frivolous consumption" is here merely shorthand for purchases made with little regard to their utilitarian value.

48. This level of demand for entertainment translates into the multimillion-dollar-per-year salaries commanded by star athletes and other entertainers, people who otherwise might earn one hundredth as much.
49. U.S. Dept. of Labor, Bureau of Labor Statistics, *Consumer Expenditure Survey, 1989,* USDL 90-616, 30 Nov. 1990; *Statistical Abstract of the United States 1989,* Table 693.
50. *Wall Street Journal,* Oct. 3, 1989, p. B1.
51. Thirty-one of the first forty pilots hired by the Post Office to fly mail died in crashes within six years, with no interruption in service. Roger Bilstein, *Flight in America 1900–1983: From the Wrights to the Astronauts,* p. 52, Johns Hopkins Univ. Press, 1984.
52. See John Rae, *The American Automobile,* Chs. 2–7, Univ. of Chicago Press, 1965, for a description of the many initially promising automotive ventures that did not survive.
53. See Reuven Brenner, *History—The Human Gamble,* Ch. 1 and Appendix 1.1, Univ. of Chicago Press, 1983. Brenner seeks to explain innovation and other risky behavior as a response to an actual or anticipated loss of wealth (by the individual or a group with which he identifies) relative to society as a whole.
54. Herman Kahn, *World Economic Development: 1979 and Beyond,* Ch. 3, pp. 153–56, Westview Press, 1979, analyzes the social and cultural forces behind increasing risk aversion in affluent nations. See also Irving Kristol, *Reflections of a Neoconservative: Looking Back, Looking Ahead,* p. 243, Basic Books, 1983, attributing the social democratization of Western Europe to an "increasingly intense focus on satisfying the demands of a 'risk aversive' society."
55. *Time,* July 10, 1989.
56. *Time,* July 10, 1989. State governments that sponsor lotteries (thirty-two as of 1988) display a rare form of pathological schizophrenia—two distinct personalities manifested by the same entity. One arm of the government buys expensive television advertising and otherwise encourages conduct indistinguishable from that which another prosecutes, conduct outlawed on the ground that it is morally impermissible and erodes the fiber of society. Gambling is either socially detrimental, in which event the state should not sponsor and encourage it, or it is not, in which event it should not be criminal. The dubious ethical underpinnings of state-sponsored gambling have been mooted at least since the huge state lotteries and tontines of the late eighteenth and early nineteenth centuries. The 1808 British Select Committee on Lotteries concluded that the State Lottery increased "idleness, poverty and dissipation . . . [a]nd this unseemly state of things is to continue, in order that the state may derive a certain annual sum from the partial encouragement of a Vice." Quoted in Golby & Purdue, *Civilisation of the Crowd: Popular Culture in England 1750–1900,* p. 86, Schocken Books, 1985. The state lotteries were finally outlawed in 1825, to be revived in the United States in the 1970s.

One explanation for their return is that a significant change in the individual's wealth relative to others' may have an independent value. See Brenner, *History—The Human Gamble,* Ch. 1. This explanation, even if correct, does not purport to

206 account for most gambling (on horse races, football games, blackjack, and the like), which offers no prospect of a material change in wealth. Moreover, Brenner's formulation must assume a small marginal utility of money in order for the expected utility of engaging in an unfair (i.e., losing) gamble to be positive. See his Appendix 1.1, equation 7b.

57. George Gilder, *Microcosm: The Quantum Revolution in Economics and Technology*, p. 340, Simon & Schuster, 1989.

58. "Other countries that impose restrictions on international trade do hurt us. . . . [I]f we impose restrictions in turn, we simply add to the harm to ourselves and also harm them as well. Competition in masochism and sadism is hardly a prescription for sensible international economic policy." Milton Friedman, *Free to Choose*, Ch. 2, p. 42, Harcourt Brace, 1979.

59. Guile & Brooks (eds.), *Technology and Global Industry: Companies and Nations in the World Economy*, p. 10, National Academy Press, 1987.

60. Jagdish Bhagwati, *The World Trading System at Risk*, p. 28, Princeton Univ. Press, 1991.

61. *Wall Street Journal*, June 15, 1989, p. A11, Dec. 13, 1989, p. A10, and Jan. 22, 1990, reported temporary decreases of the U.S. trade deficit with Japan because of the rise in value of dollars relative to yen. A "J-curve" (a temporary decline followed by a larger rise) is traditionally used to describe export earnings after a currency devaluation. But "U-curves" and "mirror-image J-curves" are about equally common. Extrinsic factors determine the long-term effect. See *Wall Street Journal*, June 2, 1989, p. A14, on the shakiness of the statistical correlation between devaluation and the trade balance.

62. Output per man-hour of other OECD nations rose from an average of 43 percent of that of the United States in 1950 to 76 percent in 1986. Maddison, *World Economy in the Twentieth Century*, Table 7.3, p. 89. Interestingly, Japan ranks fairly low by this measure; its per capita income is the product of the highest number of working hours per man-year. See Maddison, Table C-8, p. 132. See also Baily & Chakrabarti, *Innovation and the Productivity Crisis*, Ch. 1, Table 1 4, showing GDP and manufacturing output per hour worked for France, Germany, and Japan relative to the United States.

63. "The only way for an economy to spend more than it earns . . . is to import more than it exports—to run a deficit." Krugman, *Age of Diminished Expectations*, Ch. 4, p. 46. To similar effect is Baily & Chakrabarti, *Innovation and the Productivity Crisis*, Ch. 6, p. 130: "The current economic crisis in the United States is associated with a large gap between the rate at which spending has been expanding and the rate at which production has been expanding. According to our spending behavior, we are living . . . with growth of 4 percent a year. But production . . . is growing only 2.8 percent a year. The nation refuses to accept the consequences of a productivity slowdown for living standards. The gap between production and spending is being met by foreign borrowing. . . ."

64. Quoted in Kotkin & Kishimoto, *The Third Century: America's Resurgence in the Asian Era*, Ch. 6, p. 178, Ballantine Books, 1988.

65. "[Japanese] living standards, measured in material terms, continue to be remarkably low for so wealthy a nation." Baumol, Blackman & Wolff, *Productivity and American Leadership,* Ch. 9, p. 181.

66. *Economist,* 18–24 May 1991, p. 81. One estimate of GDP per capita adjusted for purchasing power ranked Japan *thirteenth* in income among nations. *Fortune,* July 27, 1992, p. 68.

67. Japan's merchandise trade surplus with the United States in 1989 was $45 billion, down slightly from 1988 and 1987. Its trade surplus with all of the rest of the world was less than $20 billion. *Wall Street Journal,* Jan. 22, 1990, p. A1.

68. Throughout 1988, 1989, and the first half of 1990, while the U.S. trade deficit with Japan and the rest of the world steadily declined, its deficit with the newly industrialized countries (Singapore, Hong Kong, Taiwan, and South Korea) increased. See *Wall Street Journal,* June 16, 1989, p. A2.

Chapter Seven

THE NEW WORLD ORDER

The cessation of material progress is a global event. As the world's leading economy, the United States confronted the limits first and most severely, but the same trends are now clearly evident in Japan and Western Europe. Recognition of these limits and their differential impact on continued progress could help to defuse some unnecessary and potentially damaging international tensions.

U.S. LEADERSHIP

The dreaded "decline of American leadership (or competitiveness)" is a pack of solutions in search of a problem. Democrats urge trade barriers, an industrial policy, and increased government spending. Republicans favor pro-business measures and unleashing the free market. (The disease obviously has no relevance to the prescriptions.) The mood ranges from jingoistic frenzy to despair. But American competitiveness has not suddenly evaporated. Workers in the United States are still the most productive, and its manufactured exports rose sharply in the last half of the much-maligned 1980s.[1] Foreign rivals have not spurted ahead, they have merely shortened America's lead. The United States remains the most prosperous nation in the world, but it is no longer in an economic class by itself.

This narrowing of the gap was a minor and inevitable side effect of the slowdown in progress. The United States emerged from World War II the dominant economic power in the world. History provided no reason to expect this dominance to erode. Throughout the industrial era, the leading nations had often gone from strength to strength, maintaining or extending their leads over their economic rivals for decades.[2] The accepted postwar wisdom among economists of all stripes foresaw the United States widening its leads in technology and productivity indefinitely.[3] But America arrived at the front of the wave just as it rolled into the barriers to further progress, which slowed the advance of the leading edge, while the rest of the wave continued nearly unimpeded. Hence the gradual convergence of living standards among the leading economies. Bashing the Japanese for this convergence is both pointless and stupid: Japan is this country's second-largest customer (after Canada), its capital infusions surely enhanced American competitiveness in the 1980s, and it is just one of several developed economies to have narrowed America's lead.

The recent rise of anti-American sentiment in Japan shows that the United States has no monopoly on such stupidity. Japan's rapid postwar progress was an estimable achievement, but it was an advance over easy ground, much of it beaten smooth by America's earlier passage. The obstacles suddenly loom large. Japan's lean manufacturing methods are very lean indeed, leaving scant room for further progress. Many in newly prosperous Japan no longer wish to outwork and outsave the world; younger workers favor more leisure and consumption, to the dismay of the immediate postwar generation of adults.[4] The perennial government scandals reflect the predictable rise of rent seeking in an increasingly affluent society. The bubble economy of the 1980s only briefly concealed underlying trends (in saving and productivity, for example) that would bring Japan's growth rates back down to earth. Stock market and real estate prices predicated on continued rapid progress collapsed as investors began to sense this sea change, with the stock market losing more than half of its value after 1989 and the property market still groping for a bottom as this book goes to press. Slower growth brought the cyclical correction that began in late 1991 into sharp relief; the rapid underlying rate of progress masked similar corrections through the 1970s and 1980s. Japan will never again sustain the rate of advance it enjoyed from the 1950s through much of the 1980s, simply because the impediments

210 to further progress have become so much more severe.[5] Japanese frustration as this new reality dawns is understandable, but blaming the ineffectual and misguided measures of a few American trade warriors and their Congressional spear carriers is neither plausible nor productive.

Western Europe naturally faces the same limits. The postwar gains of West Germany and France in particular brought those countries near American levels of prosperity. Those gains have since slowed sharply. The symptoms are clear and, by now, familiar. Vacations lengthen, working hours shorten, saving declines, productivity gains slow. Polities fragment, with tiny interest groups single-mindedly pursuing narrow goals. The current political response—which consists largely of circling the wagons to exclude the world's best automobiles, consumer goods (except Mickey Mouse), and bananas—harms consumers and is unhealthy for the economy, but it does suggest some awareness of the larger trends. Competition with Japanese automakers or American farmers would force Europeans to work more like their Japanese or American counterparts, a result that many European politicians see no reason to encourage. Barring a reversal of these attitudes, Western Europe will settle into a comfortable, if not very dynamic, economic niche, near but never quite at the top.

Most of the world does not share the "problem" of the economic leaders. Antiquated production methods and pervasive poverty leave ample room for further progress. But a rise to uniform prosperity is not in prospect. Some nations (with South Korea and Taiwan likely in the vanguard) will join the favored few now at the top. Most will continue to languish.

THE ROAD FROM SERFDOM

Several of the newly prosperous nations will likely emerge from Eastern Europe.

The postwar economic performance of the Comecon nations has been woeful, an open embarrassment to socialists and economic planners everywhere. Per capita income figures were unreliable because of the limited convertibility of the Eastern Bloc's currencies, but the following rough-and-ready indicators of prosperity provide a fair comparison between some Eastern European nations and their Western counterparts.[6]

7.1 WESTERN VS. EASTERN EUROPE; SELECTED INDICATORS

	Housing: Persons Per Room	Cars Per Capita	Telephones Per Capita
West Germany	0.5	0.47	0.67
France	0.6	0.39	0.59
Austria	0.6	0.35	0.53
East Germany	0.9	0.22	0.23
Czechoslovakia	0.9	0.17	0.24
Hungary	0.8	0.17	0.15
Poland	0.9	0.11	0.12

The Comecon economies had managed to fall decades behind in economic development and living standards just since the end of World War II, and the gap has continued to widen.

With the sweeping arrival of democracy and capitalism, however, the ingredients are in place to make Eastern Europe the premier economic growth area in the world:

(1) Free markets. Planned economies lack the self-adjusting allocative efficiency of free markets. Official edict and inconvenience ration scarce goods. The dictates of the plan or planner drives production, training, and investment. The result is predictable: too few of some kinds of goods, workers, or machines, too many of others.

The transition to a market-based economy has already begun. Poland and Hungary have substantially freed pricing from bureaucratic meddling. Small shops and street vendors actually have goods to sell because they charge what the market will bear. Producers are shifting their focus from making quota to making items they can sell for a profit at market prices. The changes naturally produce inflation, unemployment, and other transitional hardships, but they are essential to tap the efficiencies of the price system.

In the longer term, economic freedom will release the productive energies of the people. Workers are learning to associate job performance with their ability to buy new cars or their own homes.[7] Managers

212 and entrepreneurs seeking profits are gradually supplanting apparatchiks seeking security. The economy and, with it, the entire society are becoming more fluid and dynamic.

(2) Technological advances.   The Soviet Bloc has lagged badly in technology throughout the postwar period, not only in electronics and other high-visibility technologies, but also in the thousands of smaller inventions and techniques that mean competitiveness in a modern economy. Endemic shortages of goods have assured buyers for all production, eliminating the incentives for quality control and innovation. Reducing the labor force has never been a permissible objective, so mechanization and automation have yielded little efficiency. Energy and raw materials are wasted.[8] Few of the products or production methods of Eastern Europe approach world market standards.

This technology gap should narrow rapidly. Germany is pouring world-class manufacturing technology into its Eastern zone. The relaxation of Western technology export restrictions began with Hungary in 1992. Poland, Czechoslovakia, and others will soon follow. Western companies are bringing current technology and standards to ventures formed with salvageable enterprises, with General Electric's acquisition of half of Hungary's Tungsram a leading example. Some indigenous companies are hiring foreign managers and technical experts to survive in the newly competitive markets. Capable students and key employees will study and work in Western Europe and return with new know-how and attitudes. The process taxes the patience of the populace and exceeds the attention span of Western media, but the result should be a productive base equipped with up-to-date technology and expertise.

(3) Increased capital.   Struggling Eastern European economies have not generated the operating surplus required to accumulate productive capital. Fictive markets and currencies have discouraged outside investment. At the individual level, low per capita incomes, severe restrictions on the accumulation of wealth, and the absence of any investment opportunities have sharply limited household savings. The little capital available has been misallocated to excessive military expenditures and inefficient state-owned firms, all of which starved the few potentially productive sectors for capital.

With the fall of the communists from power, Western deal-makers and multinationals eager to establish a presence descended on the Eastern European capitals. This investment frenzy produced the predictable false starts, unmet expectations, and retrenchments, but also occasional successes. The privatization of thousands of state-owned enterprises in Czechoslovakia, Poland, and Hungary is also spawning some bootstrap capitalism, as farmers, workers, and budding entrepreneurs squeeze a bit more production from worn-out or converted equipment. Capital markets will gradually mature and allocate savings more efficiently. The turmoil in the meantime wastes some resources, but it is a healthy sign of economies stirring to life after decades of hibernation.

(4) Expanded markets. The Comecon countries have formed an insular and insignificant trading bloc since World War II.[9] Few Eastern European firms produced goods that could sell in world markets. Unrealistic official exchange rates foreclosed even those few from competing effectively. The Soviet Union frequently dictated the direction and terms of trade within the bloc for political and strategic reasons. The net effect was a self-imposed blockade, a formidable economic weapon, enforced more effectively than any outside agency could have hoped.

Outside trade will naturally expand rapidly, as Eastern Europe seeks capital equipment, technology, and some manufactured goods from the West. Eastern Europe has one precious commodity to offer in return: inexpensive, educated, skilled labor. Germany, with strong Central and Eastern European cultural ties and some of the highest labor costs in the world, has already begun outsourcing labor-intensive fabrication and assembly work to the former Comecon countries.[10] Other Western nations will follow this lead. Foreign exchange from such undertakings will be reinvested in higher-level production until a mature trade pattern emerges. This market expansion will generate economies of scale, the use of more advanced technologies, and efficiencies due to increasing specialization.

The dominant themes of the news from Eastern Europe are dislocation and hardship. These will quickly fade from memory. Whenever and wherever in history these four conditions have coincided, rapid and sustained growth has followed. Barring a loss of nerve in the new governments, Eastern Europe will not be the first exception.

It would be pleasant to report that all the underdeveloped economies share in this rosy future. The limits to progress do not directly affect those economies. They could advance while the privileged few already near the limits mark time. This would be a relatively painless process for arriving at the greater material equality so fervently urged in the never-ending North-South economic conferences. But it will not occur. A few other nations, particularly in Central and South America and Southeast Asia, may move toward the developed world's level of prosperity. Most will not. Progress in the developing world has always moved in tandem with that in the leading economies: any loss of vitality at the top quickly slows the momentum of those further down the scale.[11] Understanding why requires a brief digression on the roles of inequality in promoting progress.

A free market produces inequality.[12] Joseph Schumpeter described the process in characteristically stark terms: "[The market] appeals to, and . . . creates, a schema of motives that is unsurpassed in simplicity and force. The promises of wealth and the threats of destitution that it holds out, it redeems with ruthless promptitude."[13] The wealthy and the destitute are scarcely equal. The rewards for success and the penalties for failure create the incentives for the requisite effort, sacrifice, or utilization of abilities or resources. The world market performs the same function internationally, reinforcing national policies and business strategies that foster economic efficiency and deterring those that discourage it. (The worldwide collapse of communism demonstrated this deterrence in dramatic fashion. If the Soviet Union and Eastern Europe had been economically competitive with the West, the Communist Party would remain in power there today.) Interfering with the process or nullifying the outcome attenuates these incentives at both ends of the spectrum. Mitigating inequality thus reduces effort and, with it, prosperity. Even the most fervent advocates of redistribution commonly accept some measure of inequality as a necessary evil on this basis.[14]

But inequality is more than an unavoidable consequence of the incentives necessary for progress; it is also an independent cause of that progress. "The rapid economic advance that we have come to expect seems in large measure to be the result of this inequality and to be impossible without it."[15] Progress is the product of trial and error. At least as many ideas fail as succeed, and even the successes are expensive until methods and processes are refined, know-how spreads, and production quantities increase. The wealthy fund this experimentation by investing capital in novel and risky ventures in the hope of earning above-market returns. What is more important, they buy the untried innovations, thereby paying for the privilege of being test subjects. Only German luxury sedans costing as much as some condos had air bags and antilock brakes in the early 1980s. Many of those sedans remained on the road in 1992, when the same features began to appear on Chevy compacts. "The rich are thus doomed to prepare the future life of the poor. It is, after all, their justification: they try out the pleasures that the masses will sooner or later grasp."[16] The affluent also pay for the errors in the process of trial and error: the eight-track tape player is a recent example.

This process requires not just wealthy people, but wealthy nations. A telephone is just a desk ornament until most people and businesses have them. A television set has something to receive only with enough viewers to support commercial broadcasting. Electrical appliances need cheap electricity from large generating stations and automobiles need roads and service stations. Even the videocassette recorder, seemingly the most personal of inventions, achieved mass appeal only because the market would support tape rental outlets every few blocks. These advances evolve into a practical and useful form over decades, subsidized by the economies that are willing and able to afford the development expense and inevitable mistakes. The United States and Europe paid for all the early advances in automotive and aviation technology, steelmaking, electrical generation, vacuum tubes, synthetics, and pharmaceuticals. They built extensive telegraph systems and direct-current electrical systems that became superfluous within a generation. The lagging nations simply skipped such preliminaries and assimilated the perfected technologies, settling comfortably into territory that the pioneers had fought hard to win.[17]

The most familiar recent example is postwar Japan's efficient exploitation of technologies already substantially developed in the United States. Between 1956 and 1978, Japanese companies paid only $9 billion for licenses to technologies that cost the United States

216   between $500 billion and $1 trillion to develop, an astonishing saving in both percentage and absolute terms.[18] This allowed Japan to move immediately to the forefront of sophisticated manufacturing without spending scarce capital on research and development. Western European countries pursued a similar economic strategy. The growth rates of all of these countries slowed in the 1980s with the virtual exhaustion of the United States' technological inventory.[19] The same process helps to explain the more recent emergence of South Korea, Taiwan, and the other Asian tigers.[20]

The leading nations also provide the means and the opportunities for the laggards to progress. Excess capital leaves affluent nations in search of untapped labor pools and new markets for their output. Their imports of food and raw materials supply a basis for exchange. Secondhand and surplus equipment provides developing nations with productive capital at a fraction of its original cost.[21] Progress in the leading economies also creates niches that others can profitably fill. The destruction of old industries and the creation of new ones, the discovery and application of new technology, and demand for an ever-changing mix of goods and services characterize advanced economies while they retain vitality. This ferment creates opportunities elsewhere. Virtually every major early advance in semiconductor technology occurred in the United States; Japan nevertheless dominates consumer electronics, memory chips, and other key commercial sectors. The leaders in microcomputer sales and technology are in the United States and Japan, but much of the fabrication and subassembly occurs in South Korea, Singapore, and other developing nations. If developed economies stagnate, the process loses its dynamism and flexibility, and these opportunities become rare. The same process can be observed domestically. Many high-technology companies originally clustered around San Francisco, Boston, and other affluent cosmopolitan centers, but manufacturing facilities quickly scattered into areas with larger and cheaper labor pools.[22] "Trickle-down" may be much derided in political debate, but it is a palpable truth in the real world.

But progress on the cheap is available only to less-developed nations, with no pretensions to leadership. If a developing nation would close the gap on the leaders, rather than following comfortably in their wake, it must compete successfully, head-to-head, in high-value-added industries in which those leaders remain actively interested. This is a much riskier and more expensive proposition. The nation aspiring to leadership must generate surplus capital, so that some of it can be wasted on untried processes and inventions. It must also establish world-class universities, squandering scarce talent on teaching rather than doing. Its businesses must be weaned from the safe and nurturing subcontracting work that the leading firms bestow on their suppliers, but rarely on their competitors. And all this must occur not in one industry or sector, but across much of the economy, because islands of affluence surrounded by a sea of underdeveloped poverty places too great a strain on the social fabric.

This is not an easy trick. It requires the happy coincidence of all the forces of progress, plus an extraordinary exercise of will, accepting decades of challenge and sacrifice for the uncertain prospect of making unborn generations wealthier. Few nations will make the attempt. Fewer still will succeed.

The slowing of progress at the leading edge will thus ripple through to the less affluent with little delay; selective progress, bringing most of the world to Western levels of affluence, is not a likely outcome. Some leveling will occur automatically, as additional technologies become accessible to less-developed nations, but the process will naturally stop well short of material equality.[23] Such equality could be forced, either domestically or internationally, but it would be the equality of subsistence, not of plenty.[24]

1. See *Economist*, 18–24 Jan. 1992, pp. 13–14 and 65–68, and *Wall Street Journal*, April 21, 1992, p. A18, on the strange failure of American confidence in the face of these and other favorable international trends.

2. In economic terms, there was no evidence of international convergence before World War II, contrary to the reported results of some early studies. Those results were fatally flawed by the criterion used to select the countries studied: they were chosen on the basis of having achieved economic prosperity, guaranteeing that they had converged. Baumol, Blackman & Wolff, *Productivity and American Leadership: The Long View*, Ch. 5, p. 94, MIT Press, 1989. See also Paul Romer, "Increasing Returns and Long Run Growth," *J. of Polit. Economy*, Vol. 94, p. 1002, 1986. Countries chosen on the basis of their economic status at the beginning, rather than the end, of the period under study showed little tendency toward convergence until after World War II.

3. Volcker and Gyohten, *Changing Fortunes: The World's Money and the Threat to American Leadership*, Ch. 1, Times Books, 1992.

4. Bill Emmott, *The Sun Also Sets: The Limits to Japan's Economic Power*, Chs. 2 and 3, Simon & Schuster, 1989, describes the rise of Japanese consumerism and leisure travel. On the changing work ethic of the *sararimen*, see also *Economist*, 2–9 May 1992, p. 81.

5. Paul Kennedy, *The Rise and Fall of the Great Powers*, Random House, 1987, attributes America's relative decline to "global overstretch," i.e., the leading power's assumption of too many expensive and distracting foreign and military commitments. This thesis leads to the conclusion (to which Kennedy essentially subscribes in Chapter 8, pp. 458–71 and 514–35) that Japan, which is legendary for its avoidance of foreign commitments, will vault past the United States to become the leading economic power of the twenty-first century. The "limits to progress" thesis, on the other hand, has Japan achieving no more than rough economic parity with the United States, barring a self-destructive frenzy in Washington. The evidence is not yet decisive, but Japan's slowdown in savings rates and productivity growth and its sudden loss of economic momentum put the "limits to progress" ahead on points.

6. The data for Table 7.1 are from *Britannica World Data Annual 1990*.

7. *Wall Street Journal*, May 18, 1992, p. A1, describes Polish workers moving into the private sector and beginning to taste the fruits of the marketplace.

8. The following table shows the quantities of energy (in kilograms of coal equivalent) and steel (in kilograms) used per $1,000 GDP in certain Eastern and Western European nations in 1979–80:

	Coal	Steel
West Germany	565	52
East Germany	1,356	88
France	502	42
Hungary	1,058	88
Britain	820	38
Czechoslovakia	1,290	132

Kennedy, *Rise and Fall of the Great Powers,* Ch. 8, Table 46. Kennedy used official GDP figures in compiling this table, and he therefore suspected that it understated the actual disparity. See Kennedy, n. 136.

9. "After 1945, under communist rule, with strong autarchic biases and, in most cases, under pressure to channel a high proportion of trade to the Soviet Union, the trading position of Eastern Europe declined despite rapid industrialization." W.W. Rostow, *The World Economy: History & Prospect,* Ch. 7, p. 74, Univ. of Texas Press, 1978. As just one example, East German imports in 1987 totaled $29 billion, of which 65 percent came from the Soviet Union and Eastern Europe, compared to West German imports of $251 billion (1988). *Britannica World Data Annual 1990,* p. 842.

10. Oddly, Germany's decision to raise wage scales in the East to those of the West may have slowed the progress toward economic equality. At their former wages, East German labor was cheap. At West German rates, it is dear. This will push more foreign ventures to other countries.

11. W.A. Lewis, "The Slowing Down of the Engine of Growth," *American Economics Review 1980,* p. 555.

12. Edward Wolff (ed.), *International Comparisons of the Distribution of Household Wealth,* Oxford Univ. Press, 1987, discusses the distribution of wealth in the United States and several Western European nations. For a more polemical treatment, see Kevin Phillips, *The Politics of Rich and Poor,* Random House, 1990. Robert Nozick, *Anarchy, State and Utopia,* Ch. 7, pp. 160–74, Basic Books, 1974, demonstrates that voluntary transfers among individuals will upset any patterned distribution, such as equality. This point, although rarely acknowledged, is not seriously doubted. Even Phillips, who preaches against material inequality with the fervor of the newly converted, acknowledges that liberty and equality are complementary: more of one means less of the other. See Phillips, p. 73.

The inequality of result inherent in free-market economies should not be taken to imply that controlled markets yield less inequality in living standards. Indeed, the opposite is more often true. See Milton Friedman, *Free to Choose,* p. 137, Harcourt Brace, 1979. The difference in living standards between peasant and seigneur was almost certainly greater than the difference between the upper and lower classes in any advanced economy. Inequality of income in South and Central America greatly

220 exceeds that in the advanced economies of the West or the developing economies of Asia. See Angus Maddison, *World Economy in the Twentieth Century,* Table 6.4, p. 71, OECD, 1989 (1970 data); and *Economist,* 18–24 Apr. 1992, p. 11.

13. Schumpeter, *Capitalism, Socialism, and Democracy,* Ch. VI, p. 73, Harper & Row, 3d ed., 1975.

14. Politicians and social scientists seem a great deal more concerned with material inequality than its supposed victims are. "Inequality, one gets the impression, is an important issue for today's social scientists *despite* the fact that such importance escapes all empirical verification. . . . [T]he subtlety with which [economists] measure income trends in the quintiles or deciles of the population is matched . . . by the utter lack of interest of the average American in their findings." Irving Kristol, *Reflections of a Neoconservative: Looking Back, Looking Ahead,* pp. 195–97, Basic Books, 1983. The last few candidates who sought to ride the fairness issue into the White House have vanished without a trace.

15. Friedrich Hayek, *The Constitution of Liberty,* Ch. 3, p. 42, Univ. of Chicago Press, 1960, from which much of the ensuing discussion is also drawn.

16. Fernand Braudel, *The Structures of Everyday Life,* Ch. 2, p. 184, Harper & Row, 1981.

17. "Not only are the countries of the West richer because they have more advanced technological knowledge, but they have more advanced knowledge because they are richer. And the free gift of the knowledge that has cost those in the lead much to achieve enables those who follow to reach the same level at a much smaller cost. Indeed, so long as some countries lead, all the others can follow, although the conditions for spontaneous progress may be absent in them." Hayek, *Constitution of Liberty,* Ch. 3, p. 47.

18. Robert Reich, "The Quiet Path to Technological Preeminence," *Scientific American,* Oct. 1989, p. 41, at p. 43.

19. "After the end of World War II , , , Japan and most of the countries of Europe followed a strategy of diffusion and catch-up. They became very good at it and grew quite rapidly until their leading industries rivaled U.S. industries in levels of productivity. . . . As they approached the frontier, Japan and Europe faced an inevitable slowdown." Baily & Chakrabarti, *Innovation and the Productivity Crisis,* Ch. 6, pp. 104–5, Brookings Inst., 1988. To similar effect is Angus Maddison, "Comparative Analysis of Productivity Situation in the Advanced Capitalist Countries," Ch. 2, p. 60, in Kendrick (ed.), *International Comparisons of Productivity and Causes of the Slowdown,* Ballinger, 1984 (Europe and Japan "are ceasing to enjoy the 'opportunities of backwardness' because they have now drawn close to U.S. productivity levels [and are] operating closer to the frontier of technology").

20. "[T]he most profound current advantage of the contemporary developing nations lies in the enormous backlog of technology available to them. . . ." W.W. Rostow, *The Stages of Economic Growth,* Appendix A, p. 181, Cambridge Univ. Press, 2nd ed., 1971.

21. See, for example, *Economist,* 4–10 July 1992, p. 52, describing Third World purchases of used industrial machinery.

22. This is not a recent phenomenon. Adam Smith noted that material well-being of the working class depends on progress in an economy at least as much as on the absolute level of affluence in *Wealth of Nations,* Book 1, Chs. 8 and 11.

23. Herman Kahn, *World Economic Development: 1979 and Beyond,* Ch. 2, Westview Press, 1979, projects that the transfer of technology, capital, and know-how will gradually "close" the gap between rich and poor nations, meaning that per capita incomes of rich nations will be only ten to forty times as high as those of poor nations. This definition presumably does not correspond to that of supporters of the New International Economic Order.

24. "Giving away all we have to the poor spells starvation for the poor just as much as for us. And universal starvation is no high aim." D.H. Lawrence, *Lady Chatterley's Lover,* Ch. 13.

Part II

The

BEGINNING
of
PROGRESS

As one era of progress ends, another begins. The next century will very much resemble the last few decades of this one in material terms, especially in the developed nations, where the potential for further progress is so slight. Change will continue at a somewhat superficial level. Some sectors will rise as others fall. Inventions will benefit some companies at the expense of others. A new household item or entertainment source will occasionally catch the public's fancy. But such froth cannot long conceal the lack of real progress. The children of the 1980s and 1990s will exert about the same effort during their lifetimes, and will have their needs and wants satisfied to about the same degree, as their parents. (If this forecast sounds less than momentous, recall that such a stagnation in living standards has not occurred in the United States, or many other places in the Western world, for over two hundred years. Progress itself has been the only enduring status quo during the industrial era.) Man's material state has arrived at its practical limits.

But the species itself remains subject to considerable improvement. People rarely have occasion to ponder their limitations very deeply. The presence of lower animals and the absence of higher ones reinforce a comfortable sense of superiority. And natural abilities have remained fixed in a sea of change for uncounted centuries, virtually compelling a belief in their immutability.[1] But a moment of detached reflection suggests the breadth and depth of human shortcomings.

226 People must spend a third of their lives unconscious to function adequately in the remaining two thirds. Evolution has allotted a life span just long enough for its own purposes: aging and mortality begin to force unwelcome choices within a decade or two after adulthood begins. Scholars need years of dedicated study to master just one subspecialty, representing the tiniest fraction of the world's knowledge. Technology has conquered awesome external challenges and compensated for severe physical limitations, but has barely touched other (and more important) human deficiencies.

As progress increasingly tames the outer frontiers, the focus naturally turns inward, toward the means for overcoming these deficiencies. The needed technologies, long relegated to the realm of science fiction,[2] are beginning to emerge from the laboratories. Genetic engineers first modified _E. coli_ in 1973; laboratories now house patented strains of mice, and the National Institutes of Health is claiming ownership of newly discovered sequences of human DNA. DNA Alley has begun to challenge Silicon Valley for pride of place in American high technology. Thought, the least understood function of the human body, has become the subject of intense research, with the 1990s appropriately named the Decade of the Brain. The exorbitant cost of health care is beginning to focus attention on the ultimate in preventive medicine, the postponement of old age. And artificial intelligence is increasingly allowing machines to substitute for brain power, as well as muscle power.

These technologies are already assuming commercial importance, and they will continue to expand rapidly. For the reasons discussed in earlier chapters, they will not usher in the often promised second industrial revolution. But they will be the weapons in an even more fundamental revolt, against natural human limitations.

NOTES

1. Julius Stone, *Social Dimensions of Law and Justice*, Ch. 12, pp. 550–51, Stanford Univ. Press, 1966, describes this tendency to believe that what has long existed must be inherent and right ("a tendency from which not even great minds have been immune") as "the normative tendency of the factual."
2. As recently as 1977, biochemist and Nobel laureate Ernst Chain foresaw no likelihood that genetic engineers would be able to modify mammalian cells in a controlled way. He was proved wrong in about a decade. See Robert Shapiro, *The Human Blueprint: The Race to Unlock the Secrets of Our Genetic Script*, Ch. 19, p. 366, St. Martin's Press, 1991.

Chapter Eight

BRAVE NEW BRAINS

William Shockley was right, at least in one respect. A Nobel laureate and one of the founders of Silicon Valley, he clouded the last twenty years of his life with a quixotic foray into the heritability of intelligence. This embroiled him in a pointless and endless "debate" (mostly reminiscent of people shouting at each other in different languages) about racial and cultural biases in psychometric intelligence testing and the role of environment in mental ability.

To those not blinded by political and social agendas, inherited differences in aptitude are obvious beyond the necessity of argument. All men are not created equal in their mental endowments. Some suffer from organic mental deficits, while others possess truly extraordinary gifts. John von Neumann joked with his father in classical Greek at the age of six, mentally performed complex calculations in minutes that required hours of paperwork for ordinary mathematicians and physicists, and apparently memorized pages of text after a single reading.[1] Albert Einstein published four papers during his twenty-sixth year. The first explained Brownian motion of particles in a fluid. The second described the quantum properties of light. The third set out the special theory of relativity. The fourth mathematically formulated the equivalence of energy and matter. Any one of these would have marked its author as a giant of physics. Erwin Schrödinger established the cornerstones of quantum mechanics, held important academic appointments in philosophy, and was one of the first proponents of a molecular theory of genetics. The mathematical ability of Richard Feynman humbled the Nobel Prize–winning physicists around him. Mozart began composing at the age of five. By his death at thirty-five, he had completed sixteen operas, forty-one symphonies, and forty concerti. Such mental feats far exceed the capacities of ordinary people. Genius is not learned.

Heredity's influence is not limited to a few people on the fringes of the distribution. Serious investigators no longer question its leading role in determining mental ability. Studies of identical twins raised apart from infancy (same heredity, different environment)[2] and of adoptive siblings raised together from infancy (different heredity, same environment) indicate that heredity accounts for 50 to 70 percent of measured differences in intelligence.[3] This leaves ample scope for family, nutrition, education, culture, affluence, and the other influences worshiped by the thralls of political rectitude. But genetic differences alone matter more than all those factors combined. This has long been a source of frustration, because it placed the largest component of ability beyond the range of human intervention.[4]

The meteoric rise of genetic engineering is converting that roadblock into an opportunity. Researchers first cloned a segment of DNA in 1973. As recently as 1976, the Cambridge, Massachusetts, city council could declare a moratorium on all recombinant DNA experiments.[5] The same moratorium would now strike many of the academic laboratories in that city like a neutron bomb: the buildings would still be standing, but no one would be in them. Biotechnology start-ups, once the most speculative of investments, are now actively pursued by pharmaceutical industry leaders as the most likely source of new wonder drugs. In 1991 alone, thirty-six American biotechnology firms obtained stock market listings, and the industry raised $3 billion from the sale of new shares.[6] In all, U.S. biotechnology industry revenues rose from about $1 billion in 1989 to $4 billion in 1991, heading toward an estimated $40 to $60 billion by 2000. The figures will cease to mean much by then, because the products and technology of genetic engineering will have permeated medicine, agriculture, and other traditional sectors of the economy too thoroughly to retain their separate identity.

For the present purposes, the lengthening scientific reach of bio-

230   technology is even more significant. Genetic alteration has progressed
from bacteria and viruses to field crops and mammals. Researchers
have inserted genes that produce human and rat growth hormones
into embryonic mice, some of which grow to twice normal size. Drug
companies are experimenting with using the mammary glands of
sheep to produce human antibodies. The next and most important
subject of genetic engineering will be people, with the Human
Genome Project providing the needed road map.

MOLECULAR GENETICS

Modern genetics began in 1866, when Gregor Mendel, an Augus-
tinian monk, published the first and second laws of genetics. There
genetics languished for generations. In the early decades of the twentieth century, geneticists explored and extended Mendel's laws
through ever more elaborate crosses, in higher organisms, and in
connection with more traits. This research shed little light on the
biological source of these laws.[7] One clue came from Thomas Hunt
Morgan's fruit fly research, in which he discovered that the fly's
different traits are combined or linked in four groupings. Two traits
within the same grouping tend (with varying probabilities) to be
inherited together, while the co-inheritance of traits in different
groupings occurs only randomly. This observation suggested that
parents transmit genetic information to their offspring in discrete
packets and, further, that the genetic bases for traits are regularly
organized within each packet. Studies of one-celled organisms finally
identified the chromosomes (literally "color bodies," so named because of the stains originally used to make them visible under the
microscope) as the cellular sources of these packets. Chemical analysis
established that each chromosome consists of a deoxyribonucleic acid
(DNA) molecule, along with protein and water packaging.

A major breakthrough came in 1953, when James Watson and
Francis Crick described the structure of the DNA molecule.[8] DNA
takes the form of a spiral staircase (a double helix). The steps consist
of only four chemicals, adenine, guanine, cytosine, and thymine,
abbreviated by their initials A, G, C, and T. Two molecules, bound
to sugar molecules on each side, form a step in the staircase. Each

sugar-plus-half-step combination is referred to as a nucleotide, a complete two-molecule step as a base pair. The nucleotides always form the same pairs: C links only with G and A only with T. This complementary base pairing allows the cell to replicate a DNA molecule from a single strand during cell division.

Almost incredibly, this four-letter alphabet is enough to spell out all the life on the planet. Each DNA molecule includes thousands of genes. Each gene is a DNA segment that acts through several ribonucleic acid (RNA) intermediaries to "code" for the synthesis of a single protein. (The Appendix describes the process.) The sequence of nucleotides in the gene precisely determines the composition and structure of one protein. Proteins, in turn, largely define the organism. They are the primary components not only of structural and connective tissues, but also of the enzymes, hormones, neurotransmitters, and receptors that are responsible for initiating and regulating most biological functions.[9]

Each cell in an organism contains two complete sets of chromosomes, one from each parent, except gametes (sperm and egg cells), which contain only a single set of chromosomes. Each chromosome in the gamete is a spliced composite of that parent's pair of chromosomes. When the egg and sperm fuse to form a single cell, the chromosomes are again paired. This process of genetic exchange and mixing vastly multiplies the number of possible genetic patterns in offspring, accounting for the great variability that can exist even between siblings.

This description applies to most of the life on the planet. In moving from lower to higher life forms, basic cellular genetics changes little, the total genetic code simply becomes larger. It is, not unexpectedly, largest in man. Each human cell has twenty-three pairs of chromosomes. The smallest has about fifty million nucleotides; the largest, 250 million. There are estimated to be 100,000 pairs of genes in the human genome, spread over about three billion nucleotide pairs. Charting this vast molecular *terra incognita* is the mission of the Human Genome Project.

HUMAN GENOME PROJECT[10]

On first impression, the Human Genome Project seems daunting, even overwhelming. Its objective is to determine the sequence of nucleotides contained in human chromosomes. The completed code will cover about one million pages, all printed in the mind-numbing four-letter alphabet of DNA. Jointly orchestrated and funded by the National Institutes of Health and the Department of Energy, the project was originally projected to require fifteen years and $3 billion to complete. (Cost estimates have since declined somewhat with improvements in the technology, but various experts still quote substantially different figures.)[11] It has become a career project for thousands of scientists. It is, in sheer scale, the most ambitious (or grandiose, according to its critics) biological research ever undertaken.

By the standards of modern science, however, the project could be considered trivial. When President Kennedy first declared that the United States would place a man on the moon during the 1960s, the technology to accomplish that feat simply did not exist. Redeeming that pledge required thousands of advances, many to solve problems that appeared only during the program. Sequencing the genome, on the other hand, requires only time and money. Adequate technology already exists, even without the improvements that the project itself will engender. And other Big Science projects easily exceed this one in terms of the resources required. The superconducting supercollider would cost twice as much just to build, before the first particles annihilate each other. The completion of the project is thus inevitable; political vicissitudes may affect the timing and cost, but not the outcome.

The immediate motivation for the project is to aid in the search for the defective genes that cause hereditary diseases. Doctors have identified hundreds of such diseases, many of them fatal. Blind man's buff would aptly describe the present process for locating the responsible genes.[12] Researchers study inheritance patterns of the disease in large family groups, searching for some known trait or marker with which the disease tends to be co-inherited. Such a correlation fixes the chromosome on which the gene is located. Researchers then test every known marker on that chromosome to find the one or two with which the disease is most often linked, which fixes the region in which the target gene will be found. Starting from that marker, they must painstakingly work their way along the nucleotide ladder, past long stretches of meaningless sequence, looking for segments that form part of a gene (i.e., code for protein) and are inherited in the same pattern as the disease. Finally, they compare candidate segments between healthy and diseased members of the family to determine which nucleotides differ, establishing the source of the disease at the molecular level. The process frequently ends in failure, and even the successes often require years of effort and consume tens of millions of dollars.

The Human Genome Project will obviate these efforts in the future by producing a complete map and sequence of human chromosomes. Mapping is the top-down approach, beginning with a complete chromosome and locating genes and other landmarks on it, to be used as reference points for still further markers. Sequencing is the bottom-up approach, the determination of the exact nucleotide sequences of individual segments located by reference to those markers.

Mapping is already producing useful results in medicine. Researchers have developed several approaches.[13] They differ considerably in detail, but follow the same overall outline.

1. Pick a chromosome and produce a working sample of it.
2. Separate the DNA molecules from their protein-and-water packing.
3. Break the molecules into segments, doing it in such a way that the segments from each molecule will vary in length and will overlap with segments from other molecules.
4. Insert the segments into bacteria or other simple organisms to clone copies of them.
5. Locate and mark particular nucleotide sequences on the segments using fluorescent or radioactive probes.
6. Use any previously identified genes or other markers on the segments to fix their general positions on the chromosome.
7. Compare the patterns of markers on different segments to detect overlaps, which identify adjacent segments. (See the Appendix and the sources referenced there for more detail on both mapping and sequencing.)

234   Gradually, as researchers arrange segments along the length of the chromosome, a fairly contiguous map of markers emerges. Doctors searching for a disease gene, for example, may then be able to bracket it with known markers, roughly fixing its location. Each added marker improves the resolution of the map.

The ultimate map, with a resolution of one nucleotide, is a DNA sequence. Sequencing begins with the same four steps as mapping, yielding millions of identical copies of the segment to be sequenced. The crucial step is then to produce fragments from that segment, all of which begin at one end and end with the same nucleotide (T, for example). Doing this with each of the four nucleotides yields four samples of fragments that vary in size from just one base pair to the entire length of the segment. Well-known methods of physical chemistry allow molecules to be sorted by size. If the smallest fragment is from the sample known to end in T, and the next-smallest from the sample ending in A, and the next-smallest from the sample ending in G, the sequence begins TAG, and so on.

Not surprisingly, results are harder to achieve in the laboratory than to describe on paper. Literally thousands of technicians worldwide toil daily at mapping and sequencing, jobs that soon become tedious beyond imagining. (One biologist has suggested that the work be done in penal colonies.) The logistics are formidable. Leading centers of genome research must maintain living libraries of chromosomes, segments, fragments, and probes for their own use and to lend to other researchers. The international Human Genome Organization (HUGO) serves as a clearinghouse for mapping information, consisting primarily of known locations of genes and markers. Johns Hopkins University maintains another mapping database, with funding from the Human Genome Project. The human genome center at Los Alamos maintains GenBank, a database of DNA sequences worked out by researchers worldwide. In all, computerization of the data may consume 30 percent of the total project funds.[14] Repetition, wasted effort, and errors are inevitable. But the progress is inexorable.

Because of its immediate medical applications, mapping has received the greatest attention. The molecular biologists who first proposed the possibility of mapping the chromosomes in 1980 began with about two dozen markers then known. That number had risen one hundredfold by 1991,[15] enough to provide crude maps of most of the chromosomes.[16] The resolution of those maps will improve to the level of a few hundred thousand nucleotides by 1995.

GenBank's sequence database passed seventy million base pairs by the beginning of 1992, with improving technology and increasing resources doubling that number every two years.[17] The database should include sequences of all the genes and many other important segments by the end of the decade, with the remaining stretches filled in by 2005. Long before the complete million-page listing arrives on laboratory computers, however, scientists will have begun to decipher its code.

INTERPRETING THE GENOME

Evolution can be a very sloppy designer. Rather than labeling genes or at least organizing them for ease of explication, it throws them together somewhat haphazardly. Only a few percent of the genome actually codes for proteins. Researchers have also identified some regulatory sequences, which encode signals for activating or inactivating transcription of genes. But most DNA is apparently without any function, "junk" accumulated and never quite discarded over millions of years. Separating this dross from the genetic gold and discerning biological meaning in the endless pages of nucleotide sequences will be crucial to making the Human Genome Project worthwhile.

That task has begun on the sequences already completed. Computer analysis of DNA sequences can ordinarily reveal which stretches constitute genes.[18] Animal studies assist in this process and in identifying regulatory and other important sequences that are located outside the genes. Evolution tends to conserve functional segments with little change because species need them to survive, while the junk can mutate or disappear without any harm. Segments preserved essentially intact in, for example, the mouse, the dog, and the human genome are thus likely to serve some important function, as parts of genes or otherwise. Researchers will therefore focus their attention on noncoding segments of the human genome that match segments in lower animals.

Once the computers identify a gene sequence as such, animal

studies may also assist in ascertaining the role of the gene. The DNA of humans and chimpanzees differs by only about 1 percent,[19] and considerable overlap also exists with other mammals. By selectively crippling genes in laboratory animals, researchers can establish the role(s) of those genes clinically. Conversely, splicing uniquely human genes into lower animals may provide clues to function. Advances in physical chemistry could obviate such time-consuming biological studies. The DNA sequence of a gene reveals the precise composition of the protein for which it codes. In principle, scientists could simply assay the different tissues of the body to find where a gene is active and what function it serves, or search nucleotide sequences to find the origin of a protein of known structure and function. At present, the ability to predict a protein's structure from its amino acid sequence is too crude to be useful as a tool, but evolving computer techniques may soon resolve this difficulty.[20]

Knowing the role that a particular gene or other sequence performs will not by itself explain how variations in that sequence affect its performance. The Human Genome Project will produce a picture of a *representative* genome. Chromosomes from different people differ in about one out of every thousand nucleotide pairs.[21] These differences are called polymorphisms; each different form of a gene is called an allele. Every inherited difference between people reflects one or more such polymorphisms. Tracing observed differences to their genetic sources (or alleles to their resulting traits) will be a massive undertaking.

To date, geneticists have accomplished this only with a handful of discrete genetic diseases.[22] Researchers have, for example, traced cystic fibrosis, the most common serious genetic ailment of Caucasians, to a three-nucleotide deletion on chromosome 7.[23] The genetic origins of such broader traits as memory will be harder to uncover because they could stem from differences in many genes. Preliminary estimates indicate that fifteen to twenty thousand genes may be active only in the central nervous system,[24] suggesting that they play some role specific to the structure or function of the brain. (How many of these genes vary significantly between individuals is not yet known.) This will rule out direct cause-and-effect linkages, at least initially, dictating instead a statistical approach.

[T]he genetic quest is to find not one or two major genes responsible for genetic influence on intelligence, but rather the many genes . . . that decrease or increase intelligence in a probabilistic rather than predetermined manner.[25]

With a large enough population sample, researchers will be able to tease out correlations between measured mental abilities and polymorphisms (either singly or in combination) in genes and regulatory sequences pertinent in some way to brain function. Genetic differences that appear significant may then be tied to specific neurophysiological consequences to explain (or in some cases debunk) the correlation.

From the present state of knowledge, the complexities and uncertainties of such an investigation seem impenetrable. Nevertheless, it will ultimately succeed. The relationships between particular nucleotide sequences and inherited mental abilities are an unchanging (if currently obscure) reality. The evidence necessary to discover those relationships is abundantly accessible. Nothing about the subject places it beyond the reach of human understanding. Whether by a few conceptual breakthroughs or by slow accretion of detail, researchers will uncover the genetic bases of intelligence.[26] As they do, improvements will follow.

HUMAN GENETIC ENGINEERING

The stated purposes of the Human Genome Project are to improve diagnosis and treatment of genetically caused or predisposed diseases and to enhance understanding of the biology of all living things at their most fundamental level, both of which it should certainly accomplish. Eugenic applications of the same knowledge are studiously ignored in public discussions, probably out of fear that the resulting controversy would jeopardize funding.[27] But human genetic engineering on a massive scale will be the greatest legacy of the project, whatever its supporters' stated intentions.

The improvement process will begin with simple selection. *In vitro* fertilization has become a fairly routine procedure for couples unable to conceive children naturally. The physician "harvests" a number of

238 eggs, fertilizes them with sperm from the husband or other donor, and implants one or more zygotes in the uterus, either discarding the extras or freezing them for future use. Allowing the fertilized eggs to divide a few times (into four, eight, or sixteen cells) before implantation does no harm. Neither does extraction of one of those cells; an embryo that begins with the implantation of seven cells instead of eight apparently develops quite normally. But the DNA in one extracted cell contains a complete genetic picture of the person that the embryo would become. Even with current technology, scientists can produce millions of copies of specific DNA segments within a few hours. Without more, this makes it feasible to select embryos for implantation based on the absence of discrete genetic defects.[28] Increasing knowledge of the genome will expand parents' options to include height, hair color, breast size, and myriad other characteristics, both important and trivial. In a Darwinian struggle among selection criteria, however, those bearing on the brain will quickly prevail. Physicians could routinely extract and read one or two dozen segments of the chromosomes known to correlate with memory, abstract reasoning, musical ability, or other mental attributes.[29] Parents then could (and surely would) choose to implant the fertilized egg(s) with the favored genetic profile(s). The prospective advantages to the child would so overwhelm the inconvenience and expense of the procedure in the minds of many parents that it could quickly become the standard means of conception.[30] Siblings exhibit wide variations in ability. Endowing every child with the innate intelligence of the most capable in the family, and thereby truncating the lower portion of the intelligence curve, will obviously raise the average considerably.

But selection will be only the beginning. Rarely if ever would one of the crop of fertilized eggs contain precisely the combination of sequences that the parents would choose. As the process ceases to inspire awe, their demands will become more exacting. The result will be a natural and almost imperceptible shift from mere selection to detailed design.

The blueprints will be readily at hand. The current genetic lottery turns out a few conspicuous winners, people with vastly greater mental ability than their fellows. These winners have, in effect, tested and proved the merit of certain genetic combinations. After research has identified the portions of the DNA that bear most heavily on intelligence, crucial fragments from the chromosomes of hundreds or thousands of such winners could easily be cloned and maintained as library sequences.

With current recombinant DNA technology, such libraries would be useful only for research (i.e., refining the understanding of genetic origins of intelligence). Using such libraries to provide children with desired traits requires the ability not just to insert foreign DNA, but to reliably replace specific genes with versions having the desired sequences. Researchers have achieved such targeted replacement (or "homologous recombination") experimentally, but only crudely, with one gene at a time and not with a high rate of success. (See the discussion of recombinant DNA technology in the Appendix.) But the current rate of improvement in genetic engineering techniques virtually assures that the needed ability will exist before scientists have gained enough understanding of the genome to use it.

Parents may begin by filling in some of their child's genetic characteristics from a library of their own DNA sequences instead of relying on random genetic exchange. This by itself would be more powerful than simple selection from among fertilized eggs, each of which would include a mix of desired and unwanted traits. Inevitably, however, some parents will conclude that their children deserve better genes than those that nature gave them, and will have doctors splice in the desired sequences from an outside donor. Depending on the sophistication of the technology, parents may be able to select complete sets of genes from a library or other outside source, using their own DNA as a framework or not at all. Whatever techniques ultimately evolve, the ability to (re)produce genius on demand will follow automatically from the decipherment of the genetic codes.

But even this level of ability may not define the limit of what genetic engineering may accomplish. The combinatorial possibilities of the human genome are, for practical purposes, infinite. All the humans who have ever lived have not begun to exhaust those possibilities. As understanding deepens, it may become possible not only to mimic genetic codes that have been notably successful in the past, but also to design new codes or select new combinations of known codes to raise mental abilities to levels not previously reached. Humans in their current form do not represent any sort of absolute upper bound.

240 Why, for example, would it be impossible to read and assimilate this book in a few hours, while also designing an airplane, carrying on a conversation, playing a game of chess, and composing a sonata? From the present human perspective, such a feat would seem miraculous. But natural human abilities would surely baffle and amaze any ape capable of contemplating them. Random mutation and recombination transformed ape intelligence into human intelligence over some tens of millennia. The next such leap may require little more than a century.

The creation of a new species is, of course, speculative. Improving this one by genetic selection and design is not. The machinery is already in motion. By the middle of the next century, a new generation will surpass its predecessor, not in the traditional realm of possessions or life-style, but in the more fundamental one of genetic endowment.

NOTES

1. For a contemporary account of von Neumann's genius, see Paul Samuelson, "A Revisionist View of von Neumann's Growth Model," in Dore et al. (eds.), *John von Neumann and Modern Economics,* Ch. 6, Oxford Univ. Press, 1989.

2. See Bouchard et al., "Sources of Human Psychological Differences: The Minnesota Study of Twins Reared Apart," *Science,* Vol. 250, p. 223, 12 Oct. 1990, for the most comprehensive such study and references to the prior literature.

3. Plomin & Neiderheiser, "Quantitative Genetics, Molecular Genetics, and Intelligence," *Intelligence,* Vol. 15, p. 369, Oct. 1991. The tests themselves are, of course, imperfect, but not nearly bad enough to explain away the predominance shown by genetic factors. Moreover, "[w]hatever else one may think of IQ tests, the traits they measure are those that are required to succeed in Western industrialized society." Bishop & Waldholz, *Genome,* Ch. 15, p. 317, Simon & Schuster, 1990.

4. "[T]he traditional view had been that 'nature' spelled destiny and 'nurture' freedom. . . ." Evelyn Keller. "Nature, Nurture, and the Human Genome Project," Ch. 13, p. 288, in Kevles and Hood (eds.), *The Code of Codes: Scientific and Social Issues in the Human Genome Project,* Harvard Univ. Press, 1992.

5. Clifford Grobstein, *A Double Image of the Double Helix: The Recombinant-DNA Debate,* Ch. 5, W.H. Freeman, 1978, describes the events leading up to the Cambridge moratorium.

6. *Economist,* 20–26 June 1992, p. 67.

7. Geneticists remained preoccupied with traditional hybrid studies, while chemists and biochemists explored and ultimately discovered the cellular basis of inheritance.

8. James Watson, *The Double Helix: A Personal Account of the Discovery of the Structure of DNA,* Atheneum, 1968, is an engrossing if not altogether uplifting chronicle of Watson and Crick's triumph. (This reader, for one, found himself cheering for Watson's rivals in the quest by midway through the saga.)

9. Richard Dawkins, *The Selfish Gene,* Ch. 3, p. 23, Oxford Univ. Press, 1989 ed.

10. National Research Council, *Mapping and Sequencing the Human Genome,* National Academy Press, 1988, surveys the objectives and approaches of the Human Genome Project. Christopher Wills, *Exons, Introns, and Talking Genes: The Science Behind the Human Genome Project,* Basic Books, 1991, is reasonably current and comprehensible to the scientifically literate nonspecialist. Stephen Hall,

242   "James Watson and the Search for Biology's 'Holy Grail,' " *Smithsonian,* Feb. 1990, p. 40, and Robert Kanigel, "The Genome Project," *New York Times Magazine,* Dec. 13, 1987, p. 44, describe the history and some of the personalities behind the project.

11. See *Science,* Vol. 237, p. 1411, 18 Sept. 1987, for differing cost estimates for the Human Genome Project.

12. Wills, *Exons, Introns, and Talking Genes,* Ch. 9, and Bishop & Waldholz, *Genome,* Chs. 1–9, describe the efforts to map the genes responsible for several hereditary diseases.

13. An older method of mapping that yielded useful but very-low-resolution chromosomal maps was cytogenetic banding. Staining chromosomes creates a characteristic pattern of ten to twenty light and dark bands that can be observed using an ordinary microscope. Genes can then be identified with particular bands. As each chromosome includes between 50 and 250 million pairs of nucleotides, a map that divides each chromosome into only ten to twenty segments has obvious limitations.

14. Deborah Erickson, "Hacking the Genome," *Scientific American,* Apr. 1992, p. 128, at p. 130.

15. Stephen Hall, *Mapping the Next Millennium: The Discovery of New Geographies,* Ch. 9, p. 186, Random House, 1992 (quoting Victor McKusick).

16. See, for example, Stephens et al., "Mapping the Human Genome: Current Status," *Science,* Vol. 250, p. 237, 12 Oct. 1990, which includes a wall chart with schematic maps of the chromosomes. *Science* annually publishes a genome issue (in October or November) that updates progress in mapping and sequencing efforts.

17. Erickson, "Hacking the Genome," *Scientific American,* Apr. 1992, p. 128.

18. Each exon is an uninterrupted "open reading frame," that is, a nucleotide sequence without a stop codon (nucleotide triplet that terminates protein synthesis). Known, conserved sequences always flank introns within the gene; these sequences identify the points for the RNA splicing to form messenger RNA.

19. Wills, *Exons, Introns, and Talking Genes,* Ch. 5, p. 92.

20. Frederic Richards, "The Folding Protein Problem," *Scientific American,* Jan. 1991, p. 54, and *Scientific American,* Apr. 1990, p. 24, discuss the difficulty of predicting protein structures and evolving neural network techniques for solving the problem.

21. Wills, *Exons, Introns, and Talking Genes,* Ch. 5, p. 91.

22. Bishop & Waldholz, *Genome,* Chs. 5–9, 11, and 12, describes how the genetic origins of disease are traced.

23. Wills, *Exons, Introns, and Talking Genes,* Ch. 9. Researchers have also traced the genetic sources of Li-Fraumeni syndrome, an inherited condition characterized by susceptibility to multiple forms of cancer (Malkin et al., "Germ Line p53 Mutations in a Familial Syndrome of Breast Cancer, Sarcomas, and Other Neoplasms," *Science,* Vol. 250, p. 1233, 30 Nov. 1990), muscular dystrophy, and some forms of artherosclerosis.

24. Wills, *Exons, Introns, and Talking Genes,* Ch. 13, p. 293.

25. Plomin & Neiderheiser, "Quantitative Genetics, Molecular Genetics, and Intelligence," *Intelligence,* Vol. 15, p. 369, at p. 380, Oct. 1991.

26. "It seems more a question of *when* rather than *whether* molecular genetic techniques will be applied to the study of intelligence." Plomin & Neiderheiser, "Quantitative Genetics, Molecular Genetics, and Intelligence," *Intelligence,* Vol. 15, p. 369, at p. 382, Oct. 1991. With this book already in the compositors' hands, scientists discovered the first learning gene, the gene for a calcium-calmodulin dependent protein kinase found in the hippocampus and neocortex. Silva et al., "Impaired Spatial Learning in α-Calcium-Calmodulin Kinase II Mutant Mice," *Science,* Vol. 257, p. 206, 10 July 1992. Mutant mice lacking that gene solve a maze normally the first time, but then forget their prior solution when confronted with the same maze again.

27. The National Research Council's report contains but a single reference to the genetic basis of intelligence: "Encoded in the DNA sequence are fundamental determinants of those mental capacities—learning, language, memory—essential to human culture." *Mapping and Sequencing the Human Genome,* Ch. 2, p. 12. Discussion of ethical issues concerning genetic engineering directed toward improving the human species is deferred until Chapter 13.

28. Holding & Monk, "Diagnosis of Beta-Thalassaemia by DNA Amplification in Single Blastomeres from Mouse Preimplantation Embryos," *Lancet,* 1989, p. 532. With this book already in galleys, British doctors announced the birth of a healthy baby girl who had been screened for cystic fibrosis as an eight-celled embryo before implantation. *Wall Street Journal,* Sept. 24, 1992, p. B5. This rapid advance from laboratory to clinical genetic screening of pre-implantation embryos, combined with the first attempts to correlate genetic variations with IQ (see *Science,* Vol. 257, July 10, 1992, reporting on a study begun by Robert Plomin at Pennsylvania State University), suggests that the genetic selection for intelligence forecast in the text could begin in crude form as early as the first decade of the next century.

29. Bishop & Waldholz, *Genome,* Ch. 15, p. 318, reports a Swedish study showing that people who metabolize tranquilizers poorly tend to make decisions more easily. It is simply a matter of time before such correlations are traced to their genetic sources.

30. See the discussion of the "technological imperative" in Chapter 13.

Chapter Nine

WETWARE ENGINEERING

For all their importance, genes are not the final word in human intelligence. They influence but do not completely define how the brain develops and how well it functions. This suggests an alternative path to mental enhancement: direct intervention in the biology of thinking. The understanding needed to support such intervention may not be far distant.

THE ORGAN OF THOUGHT

Attempting to describe intelligence in biological terms is itself a recent development. Philosophers and psychologists dominated the field through the nineteenth and early twentieth centuries. Limited to *a priori* reasoning and a few gross observations, they commonly posited some ineffable Cartesian mindstuff to explain thought, emotion, and the many other manifestations of consciousness. Only in recent decades have most investigators begun to analyze thinking as a biological process in the brain.

The brain is, ironically enough, the least understood organ in the body. High school biology texts describe in some detail how the heart pumps blood and the kidneys filter it. But the same texts treat the brain, the only organ in which humans represent a clear advance over other mammals, as a gray box that produces thought, in all its variation and splendor, by completely mysterious processes. And with some reason. Despite dramatic advances, thinking remains one of the half-dozen or so most pressing scientific puzzles still to be solved as the twentieth century ends.

The structure of the brain provides some clues to its function. One nerve cell (neuron) may receive input from and provide output to hundreds or thousands of others. (The Appendix describes the neurons and their connections—synapses—in more detail.) One electrochemical signal may thus spread through millions of cells after just a few relays. This suggests that the brain functions as a distributed network, without the kind of centralized processor found at the core of computers. The ability of the brain to function despite the routine death of many thousands of nerve cells each year after the age of forty points in the same direction. If particular abilities or memories resided in individual cells, the death of those cells would produce a sudden and specific loss of function, rather than the gradual and general degradation of thought processes that actually occurs. The speed with which the brain performs many routine tasks confirms that its power lies in its densely networked architecture. People are able, for example, to identify a familiar object in less than a second. Even the simplest pattern recognition tasks require many thousands of individual steps. The neurons and synapses operate too slowly to explain the brain's performance by any sequential process of searching for a match through a lengthy list of known objects (in the manner of mechanical punched-card readers or electronic database systems). The brain must employ some sort of parallel searching method, performing thousands of steps simultaneously.

Dr. Wilder Penfield's experimental work with epileptics revealed something about the nature and quality of the memories stored by the brain.[1] Penfield knew from electroencephalograph (EEG) recordings that seizures represent violent electrical episodes in the brain. He thought he could find the source of those episodes by stimulating the surface of epileptics' brains with mild electrical current while they were conscious. His efforts failed, but they produced some extraordinary effects. In certain areas of the brain, his probing would start a cascade of signals through connected neurons that would evoke intense and minutely detailed memories of forgotten incidents or impressions from his patient's past. Probing the same point again

246 produced the same recollection, while probing elsewhere produced another or none at all.

Anatomical studies of the brain show that evolution had gradually cobbled it together from pieces that worked in earlier species, rather than starting a new design for each new species. "Nature is not an intelligent engineer. It cannot dismantle the existing configuration and start from scratch with a preferred design or preferred materials."[2] The human brain stem, which controls many motor functions and such involuntary functions as respiration and circulation, differs relatively little from those of reptiles and birds. The limbic system (which largely governs emotional response) and olfactory lobe (processing of smells) are little changed from those of primitive mammals. Each of these systems has a characteristic cellular structure and pattern of connections, presumably adapted to performing the task(s) for which it is responsible.

The principal "innovation" in the human brain is its vastly enlarged cortex. This is the thin layer of cells that overlies the entire human brain and is responsible for most higher mental functions. The observable effects of surgeries and head injuries establish that the cortex has functional divisions, as damage to particular portions of the brain consistently produces fairly precise kinds of mental deficits. Destruction of Broca's area (in the left frontal lobe), for example, impedes verbal expression, although verbal understanding is not affected. (That is, the patient can act on verbal instructions, but cannot respond verbally.) Conversely, the loss of Wernicke's area (in the left temporal lobe) affects verbal comprehension rather than expression.[3] The structure of the brain thus suggests not one kind of thinking, but several different kinds, with specific anatomical adaptations designed for each.

But the most important clue to the biological origin of intelligence was the discovery that the brain is "plastic" (i.e., it changes over time).[4] Unlike most other organs in the body, a newborn infant's brain is not finished or fully functional. It has more neurons than an adult's, but weighs only one fifth as much because those neurons have not yet connected with each other. Each neuron rapidly extends its transmitting fiber (axon) from the cell body toward its final destination. The mechanisms by which the axon reaches the correct location are not yet known, but they are almost flawless.[5] Axons from the retina, for example, unerringly grow to the visual processing center (a relatively small target), bypassing other portions of the brain en route. Upon arrival, the axon branches and forms synapses with the dendrites (receptor regions) of other neurons. Relatively few of these synapses survive. Most axon branches and many complete neurons atrophy and die almost immediately.[6] The initial development process (sometimes called epigenesis) is thus one of proliferation followed by selection. It permanently fixes the general structure of the brain, but not the details of the "wiring." Synapses continue to form and disappear throughout life. One well-known manifestation of this continued plasticity is the process of recovery from a stroke or head injury. The death of the brain cells initially deprives the patient of motor function in the affected limbs. Although the dead area of the brain does not regenerate, patients often recover much of that function as other portions of the brain rewire themselves to perform the same tasks. (Researchers have replicated this result experimentally by surgically removing the minute portion of a monkey's brain responsible for controlling its thumb. The animal gradually recovers control over the thumb through the use of surrounding brain tissue.) Even in extreme cases, where surgeons have removed the entire left hemisphere of the brain, patients have gradually recovered some level of verbal skills.[7]

The individual's genetic endowment could not completely control this wiring process. Identical twins have identical genes, but their brains, although similar, differ in detail, differences that increase in more intelligent species and are largest in human twins.[8] The brain has tens of billions of neurons, with trillions of synapses between them. A few thousand genes relating to the central nervous system simply could not specify these connections in detail. Scientists therefore needed some other explanation for the brain's wiring.

LEARNING

That wiring, as it turns out, is at least partly the product of experience. The process begins during the brain's initial development. The axons and synapses that get used are those that survive the selection process. The visual cortex, for example, ordinarily organizes itself into equal alternating bands (ocular dominance bands), each one receiving input from only the left or the right eye.[9] In laboratory animals with one eyelid sewn shut at birth, the bands associated with that eye would narrow and the bands associated with the other would widen. In animals reared completely in darkness, the visual cortex never fully develops.[10] The axons remain immature and fail to connect with the neurons that carry visual signals elsewhere in the cortex.[11] The brain thus responds to neural activity by growing and losing connections, much as if a computer could add new transistors in response to the demands of its programming.

The same process continues, if less quickly, in mature animals. Canadian psychologist Donald Hebb, an early investigator of the mechanisms of memory, noticed that his children's pet rats consistently outperformed animals raised in the laboratory in complex learning tasks.[12] Later investigators tested this observation by housing some rats together in a large cage with changing toys and comparing them to rats raised alone in bare cages. The "enriched-environment" rats excel in learning mazes and performing other tasks that bear no direct relationship to the mental stimulation they had previously received.[13] Their brains bear direct evidence of their greater abilities. The cortexes of the enriched-environment rats are heavier than those of the controls, with more dendrites and more synapses. Stimulation thus manifests itself in the wiring of the brain, which in turn improves the brain's ability to learn.

Researchers have substantially replicated this experiment in monkeys.[14] Confirming similar effects in people is difficult without controls or microscopic examination of brain tissue, but intelligence researchers have achieved some suggestive results. After several years of extra creative problem-solving sessions, adolescents test slightly higher in fluid intelligence (general ability, unrelated to the command of any body of knowledge), even though the test questions bear no resemblance to the problems on which they practiced.[15] This suggests some overall tuning of the brain's thinking ability through use.

Only since the 1970s have researchers begun to trace the cellular origins of these effects. They were guided in their search by Hebb's theory that brains could store a memory as a set of connection strengths in its network of cells. The right pattern of inputs (the signals received from the retina on seeing a baseball, for example) would work through these connections to stimulate a certain pattern of neurons, which the brain would have learned to interpret as "baseball." Learning would then consist of changes in the strength of the synapses (and perhaps the creation of new synapses) in response to new patterns of inputs.

Long-term potentiation (LTP) fits Hebb's model almost exactly. Closely timed nerve impulses trigger a sequence of biochemical events that strengthen existing synapses (i.e., they respond more strongly to future impulses) and may also initiate the formation of new ones. (The Appendix describes some of the cellular mechanisms involved.) Researchers have detected LTP in the hippocampus, a small structure on the inner surface of the cortex that is involved in memory formation, and in several portions of the cortex.[16] Chemical interference with LTP processes impedes animals' ability to learn new tasks, confirming their role in memory formation.[17] LTP may itself be memory, or (more likely) it may be an initial record that the brain later transcribes for permanent storage.[18] In either event, it is a promising first step in the search for the cellular mechanisms of learning.

Much remains to be learned. There is not even the beginning of a theory to explain the mental processes that allow the reader to comprehend this book or the author to write it, or why either decided to undertake the task. But further progress is all but assured by the rapid advances occurring in the field. As recently as the 1970s, the biology of learning and memory had not even arrived on the scientific agenda; it was a "nontopic."[19] President Bush has declared the 1990s the decade of the brain, recognizing a tide that was already in full flood without any official sanction. This is due in part to a process of elimination: the lungs and the kidneys no longer hold many surprises. But improving tools for this research are also making a difference. As of mid-1991, molecular geneticists had mapped more than three hundred genes that are active in the central nervous system[20] and had cloned the genes responsible for synthesizing several receptors and ion channel proteins.[21] Neural nets (discussed in Chapter 10) allow researchers to simulate and test some theories of thought on computers.[22] Microscopic electrical probes and improved imaging techniques provide ever-higher-resolution pictures of basic perception, learning, and memory processes.[23] The rapidly rising stature of the neurosciences and the increasing promise of the research have begun to attract substantial funding and top-quality scientists. The annual indexes of the leading scientific and medical journals reveal an exponentially expanding body of work on the brain. In the meantime, some new directions in intelligence testing are yielding clues to the factors that affect the brain's performance.

BIOLOGICAL YARDSTICKS

The heated controversy over possible racial and cultural biases in IQ testing spurred research into other methods for assessing raw mental ability. That work has revealed certain biological indicia of intelligence that may improve the understanding of thinking processes and suggest ways to enhance those processes.

Standard IQ tests (called psychometric testing) measure performance on batteries of different kinds of problems. The assumption is that superior performance reflects superior ability, which is certainly true on the average. But cultural biases in the tests and differing levels of verbal skills, knowledge, motivation, and experience with certain kinds of problems can distort individual results; hence the search for tests less influenced by background.

Speed (or chronometric) tests are one promising approach.[24] These are based on tasks so simple that everyone is capable of perfect performance. (An example is determining whether the letter A appears before the letter B in a series of letters on a screen.) The subject practices the task for a few minutes to become familiar with it and with the apparatus, quickly reaching a performance plateau both in speed and accuracy. The simplicity of the task plus the practice time virtually excludes any advantage due to skill or knowledge. The test consists of measuring the subject's speed in performing the task many times in succession. Interestingly, no correction for accuracy is needed; those who perform faster are also more accurate. Statistical analyses show that this speed correlates very closely with results from the best psychometric tests. Advocates of chronometric testing have a theory to explain this correlation. People have very limited short-term memory (about seven random digits in sequence without rehearsal, for example). People who process information faster assimilate more and are better able to use it "on the fly," without loss of accuracy or the need for time-wasting and error-prone repetition. Performance on chronometric tests may in part be reflecting differences in nerve-conduction velocity (NCV), the speed with which a neuron in the brain propagates an impulse. NCV varies among individuals, and that variance correlates with intelligence.[25]

Another measure based directly on brain function is the average evoked potential (AEP).[26] The theory here is that smart brains propagate signals more clearly and consistently (or with less "noise" and errors) than dull brains. Analysis of the subjects' electroencephalograms (EEGs) can measure this difference. A sensory stimulus (a picture or sound, for example) briefly perturbs the subject's resting EEG as the brain processes it. This produces a spiky wave pattern called the evoked potential. Repetition of the stimulus should produce the same pattern if the subject's brain cells transmit clearly and reliably. Averaging the evoked potentials over several trials would therefore simply reinforce the initial pattern. But a noisy or error-prone brain produces a slightly different signal each time. These signals cancel to some extent, producing a flatter and less complex AEP. Quantifying the amplitude and complexity of the AEP produces a measure that correlates exceptionally well with standard IQ tests.[27]

Still another biological measure of intelligence is energy consumption in the brain.[28] Sophisticated radiographic techniques permit researchers to measure how much glucose the brain metabolizes while thinking. Studies have shown that bright people use less energy than their duller peers to perform the same tasks, a difference that widens as the tasks become more difficult. This may mean that they have smaller and therefore more efficient neural networks for learning and memory, or that their individual nerve cells function more efficiently. Recent advances in brain imaging may facilitate the study of these differences.

PRESCRIPTION FOR INTELLIGENCE

Any or all of these discoveries (and others)[29] may lead to better (i.e., less culturally influenced) measures of intelligence. But the potential for *measuring* intelligence is surely small change compared to the

252   potential for *enhancing* it. Flat and simple AEPs may be regarded as just confirmatory evidence of low intelligence, or as a symptom of a treatable disease called stupidity. Slow or noisy nerve transmissions and excessive cellular energy usage are biological conditions, like low blood sugar or dwarfism. As researchers uncover their underlying causes and modes of action, medical treatments will follow as surely as they have for every previously explained disease and condition, most of which once seemed just as mysterious and inevitable as low intelligence does now.

The basic neurobiology of learning presents even greater (although probably more distant) prospects. Whatever the precise role of LTP, learning and memory clearly arise from neurochemical and structural changes in brain cells induced by neural activity. These natural processes are susceptible to artificial re-creation and manipulation. Researchers have already identified a handful of naturally occurring neurotransmitters involved in memory formation or consolidation, although some of the processes remain mysterious.[30] Artificially increasing the activity of acetylcholine, one of these transmitters, improves the performance of monkeys on some memory tests.[31] Another of these chemicals (vasopressin) similarly improves the test performance of people over fifty.[32] Researchers have also been able to mimic some processes of synapse formation in the laboratory. Administering kainic acid (a chemical analog of the neurotransmitter glutamate) to rats initiates intense neural activity, which causes rapid proliferation and development of synapses in their hippocampus.[33] Another possible approach is to rejuvenate the brain with nerve growth factor (NGF). NGF is abundant during fetal and neonatal brain development, but declines rapidly thereafter. Direct administration of NGF stimulates nerve growth in adults, including individuals suffering from atrophying diseases of the brain such as Alzheimer's. It also enables scientists to culture brain cells *in vitro* by causing mature neurons to divide. This opens the possibility of modifying and implanting brain tissue to counteract the effects of aging or to enhance selected abilities. Both NGF injection and fetal-brain-tissue grafts have proved effective in restoring learning and memory function in aging rats.[34]

Admittedly, these are isolated effects with little current clinical utility. What they demonstrate, however, is the feasibility of intervening constructively in the biological processes of learning and memory. Doctors will initially use this ability to treat discrete defects, producing a brain capable of functioning at closer to normal levels. But the same techniques will make it possible to improve mental performance generally as understanding of the thinking process grows.

Which means will prove effective in enhancing brain power remains in the realm of speculation. Genius could prove to be nothing more than an optimal neurochemical balance, in which event drugs would almost certainly effect profound improvements. Or there may not be one optimal balance: different drugs may enhance initial learning, memory consolidation, creative problem-solving, etc. If, as seems increasingly likely, the wiring itself plays a central role, doctors may be able to intervene during the crucial formative period of the brain by activating key genes or regulating the levels of certain neuroactive chemicals to optimize development. Or it may prove feasible to restore youthful plasticity to portions of the mature brain for retraining or performing certain tasks. Young children, for example, learn a new language effortlessly, while adults must strain and study. Brilliance in mathematics and musical composition also tend to be qualities of youth, not experience. More generally, chemical or electrical stimulation treatments of adults may serve as mental steroids, inducing the entire brain (or certain portions of it or certain kinds of neurons within it) to "bulk up" with more synapses for better performance.

How far such enhancement may proceed is also a matter of speculation, but there is no reason to believe that the potential is small. Natural mental abilities extend over a very wide range. A few gifted individuals in the population exhibit intellectual prowess far greater than the norm. Their mental abilities are no less a function of biology than the athletic abilities of professional basketball players. Their brains simply function better. Even at the opposite end of the scale, so-called idiots savant sometimes display the kinds of superhuman memory, numerical, and musical ability depicted in *Rain Man*.[35] Tracing these abilities to their neuronal origins is a difficult task, but one that is likely to be largely accomplished within the next generation. And naturally occurring human abilities represent no absolute

254   limit. Intervention may raise human performance to levels never observed in nature, as it has with lower animals. Just as human muscles now seem a poor substitute for machines, future generations will likely consider twentieth-century brains to have been shockingly feeble instruments of thought.

NOTES

1. Robert Berman, "Electrical Brain Stimulation Used to Study Mechanisms and Models of Memory," Ch. 10, p. 409, in Martinez & Kesner (eds.), *Learning and Memory: A Biological View,* Academic Press, 1991, describes Penfield's work.
2. Churchland & Sejnowski, *The Computational Brain,* Ch. 1, p. 7, MIT Press, 1992.
3. Patricia Churchland, *Neurophilosophy: Toward a Unified Science of the Mind-Brain,* Ch. 4, pp. 159–68, MIT Press, 1986.
4. Churchland & Sejnowski, *Computational Brain,* Ch. 5, discusses several aspects of the brain's plasticity.
5. Aoki & Siekevitz, "Plasticity in Brain Development," *Scientific American,* Dec. 1988, p. 56, discusses some possible mechanisms of postnatal brain development.
6. Jean-Pierre Changeux, *Neuronal Man: The Biology of Mind,* Ch. 7, pp. 212–19, Pantheon, 1985, describes the postnatal process of neural growth and subsequent regression. Dendrites follow a similar sequence, growing a dense covering of spines, most of which disappear when no axon connects to them.
7. Churchland, *Neurophilosophy,* Ch. 5, pp. 188–89.
8. Changeux, *Neuronal Man,* Ch. 7, pp. 206–12.
9. Changeux, *Neuronal Man,* Ch. 7, pp. 234–35. Churchland & Sejnowski, *Computational Brain,* Ch. 5, pp. 309–15, and Ronald Kalil, "Synapse Formation in the Developing Brain," *Scientific American,* Dec. 1989, p. 76, describe the stimulation-dependent formation of ocular dominance bands in the developing brain.
10. Black & Greenough, "Developmental Approaches to the Memory Process," Ch. 2, p. 70, in Martinez & Kesner (eds.), *Learning and Memory.*
11. Kalil, "Synapse Formation in the Developing Brain," *Scientific American,* Dec. 1989, p. 76.
12. Donegan & Thompson, "The Search for the Engram," Ch. 1, p. 19, in Martinez & Kesner (eds.), *Learning and Memory.*
13. Black & Greenough, "Developmental Approaches to the Memory Process," Ch. 2, pp. 72–73, in Martinez & Kesner (eds.), *Learning and Memory.*
14. Donegan & Thompson, "The Search for the Engram," Ch. 1, p. 21, in Martinez & Kesner (eds.), *Learning and Memory.*
15. Lazar Stankov, "Kvashchev's Experiment: Can We Boost Intelligence?" *Intelligence,* Vol. 10, p. 209, July 1986.

256   16. Soumireu-Mourat & Roman, "Long-Term Potentiation and Learning and Memory," Ch. 20, p. 320, in Baudry & Davis (eds.), *Long-Term Potentiation: A Debate of Current Issues,* MIT Press, 1991.

17. Churchland & Sejnowski, *Computational Brain,* Ch. 5, p. 259; Roberta Brinton, "Biochemical Correlates of Learning and Memory," Ch. 5, p. 214, in Martinez & Kesner (eds.), *Learning and Memory;* George Johnson, *In the Palaces of Memory,* Part 1, pp. 54–55 and 81–82, Knopf, 1991.

18. There is evidence that memories stored during the day are somehow processed and consolidated during sleep. See Jonathan Winson, "The Meaning of Dreams," *Scientific American,* Nov. 1990, p. 86. The experimental evidence, however, suggests that memories stored in the hippocampus are consolidated in the cortex only after two weeks or more.

19. Johnson, *In the Palaces of Memory,* Part 1, p. 40, quoting Gary Lynch.

20. Plomin & Neiderheiser, "Quantitative Genetics, Molecular Genetics, and Intelligence," *Intelligence,* Vol. 15, p. 381, Oct. 1991.

21. See *Nature,* Vol. 342, p. 620, 7 Dec. 1989. Scientists have also pinpointed the gene responsible for one of the proteins involved in LTP. Silva et al., "Impaired Spatial Learning in α-Calcium-Calmodulin Kinase II Mutant Mice," *Science,* Vol. 257, p. 206, 10 July 1992.

22. Churchland & Sejnowski, *Computational Brain,* describes researchers' efforts to understand aspects of brain activity through the use of neural net models. Johnson, *In the Palaces of Memory,* pp. 95–108, describes development of a neural net that simulates the olfactory lobe, a primitive portion of the cortex.

23. The appendix to Churchland & Sejnowski, *Computational Brain,* surveys techniques for extracting information on the brain's biological functions. Positron emission tomography (PET) provides three-dimensional images of blood flow in the brain. Churchland, *Neurophilosophy,* Ch. 5, pp. 218–21, shows PET images during a number of different mental activities. The weakness of PET scans is their low resolution, which permit only gross mapping of brain function. Belliveau et al., "Functional Mapping of the Human Visual Cortex by Magnetic Resonance Imaging," *Science,* Vol. 254, p. 716, 1 Nov. 1991, reports on higher-resolution images obtainable using MRI. Another emerging technology is autoradiographic imaging, which shows the distribution of particular kinds of neurons in the brain. See Brinton, "Biochemical Correlates of Learning and Memory," Ch. 5, p. 203, in Martinez & Kesner (eds.), *Learning and Memory.* In animal experiments, microscopic electrical probes measure activity at the cellular level.

24. Arthur Jensen, "Speed of Information Processing and Population Differences," Ch. 4 in Irvine & Berry (eds.), *Human Abilities in Cultural Context,* Cambridge Univ. Press, 1988, describes chronometric testing. For an extended dialogue on the merits (and demerits) of chronometric testing, see McGue et al., "Information Processing Abilities in Twins Reared Apart," *Intelligence,* Vol. 8, July-Sept. 1984, and the responses and rejoinders in subsequent issues.

25. Philip Vernon, "Studying Intelligence the Hard Way," *Intelligence,* Vol. 15, p. 389, Oct.–Dec. 1991.

26. H.J. Eysenck, "The Biological Basis of Intelligence," Ch. 3 in Irvine & Berry (eds.), *Human Abilities in Cultural Context*, describes work on AEP.

27. Eysenck, "The Biological Basis of Intelligence," Ch. 3, pp. 97–99, in Irvine & Berry (eds.), *Human Abilities in Cultural Context*, reports correlations between AEP measures and IQ as measured by the Wechsler test of 0.83, which is actually higher than the correlation between scores on different psychometric IQ tests. On the causes of some failures to replicate such results using AEP, see Eysenck, pp. 93–94, and Vernon, "Studying Intelligence the Hard Way," *Intelligence*, Vol. 15, p. 389, Oct.–Dec. 1991.

28. Haier et al., "Cortical Glucose Metabolic Rate Correlates of Abstract Reasoning and Attention Studies with Positron Emission Tomography," *Intelligence*, Vol. 12, p. 199, Apr.–June 1988, describes the use of glucose consumption as a measure of the brain's efficiency in thinking. Vernon, "Studying Intelligence the Hard Way," *Intelligence*, Vol. 15, p. 389, Oct.–Dec. 1991, surveys the literature.

29. Christopher Wills, *Exons, Introns, and Talking Genes: The Science Behind the Human Genome Project*, Ch. 15, p. 318, Basic Books, 1991, reports one other curious biological correlation with mental ability. Poor hydroxylators, people whose nervous systems do not metabolize tranquilizers well, score well above average in tests of alertness, efficiency, and ease of decision-making. If future studies confirm this correlation, it may serve as a paradigm for medical approaches to enhancing mental ability. No more than one or two enzymes (and one or two genes) are likely to be involved in this condition, making its origin fairly easy to pinpoint. Investigators may then devise medications, gene therapy, or other techniques to replicate it.

30. In addition to the role of glutamate in LTP (discussed in the Appendix), see Martinez, Schulteis & Weinberger, "How to Increase and Decrease the Strength of Memory Traces: The Effects of Drugs and Hormones," Ch. 4 in Martinez & Kesner (eds.), *Learning and Memory* (vasopressin and epinephrine); and Brinton, "Biochemical Correlates of Learning and Memory," Ch. 5, p. 203, in Martinez & Kesner (eds.), *Learning and Memory* (noradrenaline). Typically, the role of a transmitter is demonstrated by inducing a shortage of it in laboratory animals. If the animals remain able to function, but fail to learn new tasks, and the deficiency is cured by injection of the transmitter, it is identified as having a role in memory formation or consolidation.

31. Mishkin & Appenzeller, "The Anatomy of Memory," *Scientific American*, June 1987, p. 80. C. A. Barnes, "Memory Changes with Age: Neurobiological Correlates," Ch. 6, pp. 282–83, in Martinez & Kesner (eds.), *Learning and Memory*, reports similar results with rats.

32. Feldman & Quenzer, *Fundamentals of Neuropsychopharmacology*, Ch. 10, pp. 304–5, Sinauer Associates, 1984. Administration of neuroactive chemicals has unpredictable and potentially serious side effects. It has therefore generally been limited to clinical, as opposed to research, applications in humans. Patricia Goldman-Rakic, "Working Memory and the Mind," *Scientific American*, Sept. 1992, p. 110, at pp. 116–17, reports the rejuvenation of memory function in aging monkeys by injection of dopamine and norepinephrine.

258   33. Petit & Markus, "The Cellular Basis of Learning and Memory: The Anatomical Sequel to Neuronal Use," pp. 87–124, in Milgram, MacLeod, & Petit (eds.), *Neuroplasticity, Learning, and Memory,* Alan R. Liss, 1986.

34. Barnes, "Memory Changes with Age: Neurobiological Correlates," Ch. 6, pp. 284–85, in Martinez & Kesner (eds.), *Learning and Memory.*

35. See Donald Treffert, *Extraordinary People: Understanding "Idiot Savants,"* Harper & Row, 1989. Research is proceeding into the source of the great disparity between savants' paucity of general intellectual ability and their unique talents. Treffert suggests that it is caused by severe abnormality in the brain's left hemisphere, resulting in right-hemispheric dominance, perhaps coupled with the hypertrophic proliferation of certain neurons relating to nonassociative memory. The evidence in support of this hypothesis, however, is slight.

Chapter Ten

CRYSTALLINE INTELLIGENCE

The popular reaction to the arrival of the digital computer included more than the usual Luddite undercurrent of anxiety. Intelligence is, after all, one of the few enclaves in which people continue to excel their machines. "We have long been accustomed to machinery which easily outperforms us in physical ways. . . . But to be able to think— that has been a very human prerogative."[1] Time had reconciled people to seemingly animate machines, but anthropomorphic ones remained threatening. The threat, however, evoked a comforting response: machines cannot *think,* they merely perform functions programmed by humans. Thus, the principal weakness of the computer became, psychologically at least, a positive attribute, and anxiety gradually lessened.

That comforting (or disheartening) perception continues to hold sway today. But it is becoming a bit tattered about the edges.

CAN MACHINES THINK?[2]

The *de facto* chess champion of the world in the year 2000 will be a computer. In late 1988, Deep Thought, a chess computer from Carnegie-Mellon University, tied for first place in a tournament with a strong international field, earning enough rating points in the process to qualify as an International Master. A few months later,

260 however, Gary Kasparov, the reigning world champion and one of the strongest players in history, "crushed" the computer in an exhibition. A more powerful version of Deep Thought will probably make its debut while this book is in press.[3] Hardware advances will allow it to examine positions one thousand times as fast as its predecessor. This added speed will provide the computer a formidable, and perhaps insurmountable, advantage over any human opponent. People have to rely on general strategic principles to forecast outcomes more than a few moves in advance. Deep Thought, on the other hand, will simply be able to examine all the possibilities up to fifteen or more moves ahead. As the first twenty or so moves following the opening effectively decide most games between top players, exhaustive analysis to that depth is likely to prove decisive. Even if it does not, the next generation of hardware, or the next, surely will, as human players have no means for improving at a comparable rate (if at all).

Skeptics will argue with some justice that this proves nothing. Chess is uniquely suited to mastery by mere machines. It involves a small number of variables completely constrained by formal rules. It has a single, well-defined objective. It requires no knowledge of the remainder of the universe. The number of possible positions and moves is finite (although large). In real life, the "rules" are unknown and constantly changing, the pertinent variables are very numerous and also changing, the objectives are not precisely definable, and people must gather information from their environments, supplement it with their own knowledge and assumptions, and act on it, despite ambiguity, uncertainty, and competing considerations. Even in such mundane tasks as driving, understanding conversation, or recognizing friends, people do not apply a series of "if . . . then" rules or any comparable logical scheme; the mind simply performs these tasks automatically and with the guidance provided by experience. In the language of epistemology, syntax (formal structure) entirely defines computers, and semantics (meaning) can never arise from syntax alone. Computers represent meaningless symbols with doubly meaningless electronic impulses; only human minds think, assigning significance to the symbols they invent. Playing chess, according to this argument, is mere symbol processing; it does not require real intelligence (an assertion that would surprise millions of patzers worldwide).

But this line of attack simply raises the issue; it does not decide it. Indeed, acceptance of these arguments would make it difficult to explain human intelligence.[4] Thought arises from complex electro-chemical impulses in the brain. Presumably, artificial intelligence skeptics would not contend that the coordinated passage of calcium ions through a synaptic membrane has greater intrinsic meaning than that of electrons through a transistor. The differences between inanimate circuit elements and neurons hardly seem fundamental enough to preclude the possibility of machine intelligence. Declaring the human mind free from computerlike rules does not make it so: the brain may be applying rules across large domains of intelligent behavior, even though people do not perceive their own thought patterns in that manner. Driving, for example, begins largely as the conscious application of a number of rules supplied by a driving instructor, parents, policemen, etc. That an experienced driver conforms to these rules automatically does not establish that they have disappeared from the process. And however the brain actually works, sufficiently flexible, sophisticated, and detailed rules may be able to *simulate* the process accurately enough for a machine applying those rules to exhibit intelligent behavior. Whether machines would ever think *in the same way* as people is an issue of only philosophical interest.[5] For most purposes, a machine that behaved intelligently while acting in some challenging and relatively broad domain would be deemed intelligent, however it accomplished the feat and whatever its motivation for doing so.[6]

EXPERT SYSTEMS

Medicine is not so easily trivialized as chess. It involves imprecise information obtained from the real world and cause-and-effect relationships that are less than completely predictable, at least with present knowledge. Physicians study and practice a specialty for years before approaching any degree of mastery.

Nevertheless, computers have achieved some notable successes in the field. MYCIN was an early example. It diagnosed bacterial infections of the blood about as well as newly minted internists. ONCO-CIN was a successor system designed for prescribing chemotherapy

262   protocols for cancer patients. The narrowness of these systems, however, proved a liability; they ascribed every symptom to a bacterial infection or cancer, because they had no knowledge of other possible causes. QMR (for Quick Medical Reference), a more recent system, contains information about 577 diseases spread over a fairly broad spectrum.[7] It represents each disease by a "frame" listing symptoms and signs, along with figures indicating how likely the specified disease is to cause each symptom, and how likely a patient suffering from each symptom is to have the disease. Each frame also provides information concerning secondary medical problems sometimes associated with the disease. QMR will either offer diagnoses based on symptoms and test results or simply list all diseases (or sets of diseases) consistent with a specified set of symptoms. Still another medical program, CADUCEUS, has been shown to diagnose many illnesses in the field of internal medicine better than most physicians.[8]

These are examples of expert (or knowledge-based) systems, programs designed to emulate the decision making of an expert in some narrow field.[9] Their designers intensively interview experts in an effort to translate their problem-solving approach(es) into a series of formal rules, sometimes hundreds or even thousands in number, then refine and test them in actual cases. The user, typically a general practitioner who needs a specialist's expertise in the field, accesses the system and provides initial data. The system applies its rules. If more than one result is consistent with the data provided, the system asks for additional information to distinguish among the alternatives or proposes tests to obtain such information. Once it reaches a conclusion, the system may also recommend a course of action. It can explain the basis for its conclusions by displaying the rules applied.

Speed is an endemic problem for expert systems. Extending their range or increasing their precision requires the addition of rules, which slows system response. This is never desirable, and it may be fatal when the system must respond in real time, as in medicine or meteorology: the perfect diagnosis or forecast is useless after the patient dies or the tornado strikes. Speeding up the hardware is the direct attack on this problem; the rise in the utility of expert systems has exactly paralleled the increasing power of microprocessors and the expansion of semiconductor memories. Hardware advances will continue to improve the performance of expert systems,[10] just as it does in chess-playing machines. But faster processing alone would never produce a robust and wide-ranging expert system. "[M]ost hard problems have search trees that grow exponentially. Even a million-fold increase in computing power will not change the fact that most problems cannot be solved by brute force but only through the judicious application of knowledge to limit the search."[11]

Expert system designers seek to circumvent this problem through heuristic reasoning. The most familiar form of reasoning is algorithmic. For example: All men are mortal; Socrates was a man; therefore, Socrates was mortal. With algorithmic reasoning, sufficient rules and facts lead to a definite conclusion; insufficient rules or facts lead to no conclusion at all. Heuristic reasoning, on the other hand, is a process of probabilistic inference. "If A, then B is more likely than if not A" would be a heuristic rule. A more complex example would be "if A is X, then B is likely to be approximately Y." With purely heuristic reasoning, no conclusion is unique or certain; it merely becomes more or less probable with the application of further rules and information.

But what heuristics lack in precision they make up in utility. First, they may constrain or at least order the possibilities to be examined.[12] If, for example, a heuristic rule in MYCIN and ONCOCIN strongly suggests one diagnosis, the program skips intervening steps to inquire about a symptom or test that would, by itself, exclude other possibilities. Only if further analysis disproves this possibility must the system return to examine less likely alternatives. This approach speeds solution and reduces processing demands. Second, a likely, approximate, or satisfactory solution reached in a short time may be preferable to the correct, exact, or optimal solution computed much later. In these situations, application of a few appropriate heuristics may end the analysis; the result may be probable enough or close enough to act upon without further investigation.

Faster and cheaper hardware and better-designed heuristics have pushed knowledge-based systems from scientific and experimental into purely commercial applications. One notably successful example has been Digital Equipment Corporation's XCON, which configures VAX machines to satisfy customers' needs, performing the repetitive work of hundreds of specialized technicians with substantially greater accuracy.[13] Thousands of expert systems of varying sophistication are

264 in routine use. They screen credit histories and loan applications, juggle airline load factors, diagnose faults in dams, and control complex manufacturing processes. They offer the potential of mass-produced, and therefore inexpensive, expertise. "Many of the skills that make tax accountants highly paid professionals—to pick a job more or less at random—may tomorrow be available shrink-wrapped on the shelves of the local software emporium."[14]

This impressive range of applications precludes the possibility of classifying expert systems with chess-playing machines, as computational curiosities of no real significance. Nevertheless, these systems represent the merest beginning of artificial intelligence. Designers and experts must spoon-feed rules and data to them. QMR, for example, was the product of ten years of collaboration between computer scientists and physicians. That problem does not disappear after initial development: MYCIN's knowledge base is now out of date because it proved too expensive to maintain. Expert systems' dependence on formal rules defined and explicitly programmed by humans keeps them narrow and somewhat fragile. One system used by banks to process car loans, for example, recommended lending money to a nineteen-year-old based on his twenty-year employment history. It had no rule telling it to cross-check those data for consistency. Advances on several fronts promise to remove or at least minimize such weaknesses.

NATURAL LANGUAGE

Computers' stubborn failure to comprehend human language has been a daunting barrier to more capable machines from the advent of digital computing to the present.

The solution as originally conceived was quite simple. "[A]ll the computer needed was to store a few rules of grammar and the meaning of a lot of words, and it could perform as a natural language processing system."[15] The main impediment was thought to be the difficulty of storing and searching a large dictionary fast enough for practical use, tasks that intervening hardware advances have rendered trivial. Nevertheless, computer scientists and linguistics researchers have struggled with the problem of natural language for more than four decades, with limited practical success.[16]

In one sense, the failure lies as much with people as with the machines that try to understand them. Ambiguity and complexity abound in even the simplest writing.[17] Sentence structure and organization vary greatly, with rules of grammar and syntax often honored in the breach. Pronouns and antecedents may be separated by a sentence or more and may be linked only by context. Words have different meanings and can even be different parts of speech. "Bank," for example, may refer to the boundary of a river or to a financial institution. "Light" may be a noun, verb, or adjective. Words and phrases have common metaphorical usages along with their literal meanings. "Dark days" may refer to overcast weather, but more likely to sad or threatening times. A word or phrase may fit into a sentence in alternative ways. "Stacie will marry a good cook" may mean that Stacie likes to eat or that her fiancé cooks well. Elaborate parsing programs and context checkers can often resolve such ambiguities, but only with a fearsome expenditure of computing resources.

This difficulty poses a mystery, because people understand language easily, even though few could hope to parse a sentence. A principal reason is the vast knowledge base that the reader brings to bear. Consider the two sentences "The cereal is ready to eat" and "The tiger is ready to eat." The first is written loosely—it should read "The cereal is ready to be eaten." But even a child has no difficulty ascribing the correct meaning to each sentence, because cereals do not eat and tigers are not often eaten. People apply their knowledge of the world automatically, rarely aware that they are doing so. The five-word sentence "Time flies like an arrow" is so direct that one must strain to think of any meaning other than the obvious one. But the computer would quickly generate three alternatives:[18]

1. The reader is commanded to time flies in the same manner as arrows are timed;
2. The reader is commanded to time only those flies that are similar to an arrow; and
3. Time flies (a species of fly) have an affection for arrows.

The reader never considers these possibilities because they make no sense in the real world. Writers do not bother to tell people that horses are animals and that automobiles are not, but that both may be used for transportation; that only people speak; that it is dark

266 outside at night; that causes precede effects—in short, the information that people acquire naturally during childhood. Such knowledge forms a substrate on which readers build. Without it, the automatic connections that are essential to understanding are lacking. The ability to read thus depends on the knowledge that could be acquired from reading.

The obvious (if arduous) way to cut this Gordian knot is to feed that mass of mundane knowledge from childhood to computers. This is the objective of the CYC project, headed by artificial intelligence pioneer Douglas Lenat at the industry-sponsored Microelectronics and Computer Consortium.[19] The project is working its way through a one-volume encyclopedia, encoding not what writers included in the encyclopedia, but what they felt comfortable in omitting because they assumed their readers would already possess it. Software engineers organize this information into frames consisting of slots. Most of the frames represent real-world "things": furniture, horses, the state of Texas. The slots define aspects of the subject of the frame. Slots in the furniture frame, for example, would state that furniture is tangible, made by and owned by people, and found in buildings, and includes chairs, tables, and sofas. Many slot entries are themselves frames, further expanding the knowledge available. A predicate calculus language (and, or, not, for every, etc.) states relationships that the frames cannot express. CYC also includes a few dozen "inference engines," dealing with temporality, causation, spatial relationships, and the like, that both extend and maintain the consistency of the system. (Knowing, for example, that a chair is a kind of furniture and that people make furniture, CYC would know that people make chairs. Or, knowing that X is the parent of Y, CYC would know that Y is the child of X and is younger than X. CYC also draws its own inferences from apparent consistencies in the data, then tests future data against them, and vice versa.)

CYC is the largest single artificial intelligence project undertaken to date. It began in 1985 and had consumed about five hundred programmer years to organize and encode about 1.5 million facts through 1991.[20] Sometime in 1995, when CYC contains about ten million facts, Lenat projects that it will be able to read and incorporate information directly, with checking and occasional assistance by its creators. In that event, it could begin to expand and diversify, subject only to the very elastic limits of hardware capacity. This would give

CYC access to the vast store of knowledge in print, making it a valuable adjunct across a broad range of artificial intelligence applications. It could, for example, supplement the deep but narrow knowledge bases of expert systems with a shallower but much broader knowledge of the world, making them less error-prone and perhaps enabling related systems to work together. Harnessed to massively parallel supercomputers, CYC could also begin to interact with people and more specialized computer systems in real time.[21]

More fundamentally, it could begin to convert computers from servile symbol processors into independent thinkers, that is, systems capable of recognizing and subsequently applying new results and concepts derived during problem-solving, modifying themselves in the process if necessary. Such learning programs have long existed, but they have always been restricted to narrow and formal domains like chess. One such program rediscovered Archimedes' principle (a solid floating in water displaces a mass equal to its own) and Ohm's law (voltage equals current multiplied by resistance) from collections of data concerning floating bodies and electrical circuits. EURISKO, not so coincidentally developed by Lenat before he began the CYC project, was a conspicuously successful example of this breed. It employed a small number of very high level concepts to investigate and reach conclusions in such diverse areas as war games and set theory.[22] Part of EURISKO's programming enabled it to derive new heuristics, add them to its program, and apply them to the domain under investigation, as well as to evaluate and modify existing heuristics. Such systems have some characteristics of intelligence: they solve problems with rules not explicitly supplied by others and not precisely predictable from their initial programming. But their tiny knowledge bases restrict them to artificial worlds in which meaning flows directly from structure, and even there their successes tend to be limited. EURISKO was no exception in this regard. After promising starts, it would regularly begin generating "uninteresting" (i.e., not very useful) results, a pattern that, oddly enough, EURISKO itself detected and tried to correct.[23] The problem is too little grist for the mill: not enough information to suggest analogies, make connections, and test and extend theories out into the real world. A basic substrate of knowledge, plus the ability to acquire more through a natural language interface, could vastly extend computers' range of competence.

SENSORY INPUT[24]

Machines detect sounds too faint for people to hear, resolve images of objects too small or distant for people to see, and identify vapors not concentrated enough for people to smell. Nevertheless, robots have difficulty crossing a room without serious mishap.

One reason is sensory overload. People do not see or hear everything indiscriminately. A listener, for example, focuses on one conversation in a crowded room.[25] This focus allows the necessary "signal processing" to occur simultaneously. By contrast, imagine attempting to follow several nearby conversations. The sounds could be heard, but the meaning would be lost. This is the problem machines confront in gathering information from the environment. A television camera permits the computer to "see" an array of pixels[26] sufficient to recreate an image faithfully and with more than adequate detail. The computer, however, lacks the judgment needed to disregard most of the data and process only those that are immediately pertinent (that is, to focus), which forces it to attempt to process all the data in real time. Despite exponentially rising processing speeds, this has not yet proved feasible in surroundings that change frequently or unpredictably. As a result, computers have generally been able to sense and act on information from the environment only in highly constrained circumstances, such as searching for a color-coded disk on an assembly line or monitoring and adjusting temperature and pressure in automated process control.

An important aspect of this problem is the weakness of conventional computers in recognizing patterns. People identify familiar objects with much less than perfect or complete information. A chair with clothes draped over it is readily recognizable without conscious thought. But this pattern recognition carries important information. The chair is known to have certain characteristics. It is not, for example, dangerously hot, nor will it get up and move. A person can safely disregard it until a seat is desired. A conventional computer cannot afford this luxury. It may identify the chair/clothing as a discrete object and, if so programmed, define its edges and compare it to known objects. It will find no match. This means that the object could be a person, a large pet, or a fork lift. The computer is thus forced to monitor it constantly, multiplying processing demands, particularly in a dynamic environment.[27] Sound presents very similar problems. The sound patterns of voices differ greatly from those of traffic noise or background music; indeed, each voice produces a discernibly different pattern. People effortlessly classify the kinds of sounds they hear and pay attention only to those that matter, but conventional computers do not easily distinguish these differences.

Continuing hardware improvements will ameliorate many of these problems. Increasingly parallel architectures may allow separate processors to concentrate on different sound sources or portions of the visual field, with integration of the important elements occurring at a higher level. In the meantime, however, qualitatively different kinds of computers are likely to begin assuming many of these tasks.

NEURAL NETS[28]

By accepted measures of computing power, machines should already surpass brains. Circuits on chips switch in billionths of a second, while nerve synapses require thousandths. Electronic signals propagate many thousands of times faster than electrochemical nerve impulses. One optical fiber may carry ten billion bits of data per second, more than ten times the capacity of the entire *corpus callosum* (the fifty million nerve fibers connecting the two hemispheres of the brain).[29] Optical data storage is potentially infinite, with the equivalent of hundreds of encyclopedias accessible on line, within seconds.

The brain's strength clearly lies in the realm of organization. For all the intervening advances in the technology of computers, their fundamental structure has not changed since John von Neumann's vacuum-tube-based Institute for Advanced Study machine, completed in 1950. The central processing unit consists of on-off switches and gates, arranged in complex combinations to form logic circuits. Processing instructions (the program) and data are separately loaded into memory or storage, whether magnetic, optical, or semiconductor. The processor sequentially follows instructions in the program, fetching data as needed using an address list. The program may alter the data, but not vice versa. This structure performs discrete algorithmic steps and processes symbols faster than can easily be described (or even imagined), but it is less well suited to other purposes.

As the preceding chapter discussed, the brain's structure differs

270   greatly. It is organized three-dimensionally and densely interconnected, with each neuron in the cortex forming synapses with hundreds or thousands of others. This permits massively parallel
processing, accomplishing in just a few dozen cycle times tasks that
require millions of serial steps. New synapses form and existing ones
change strength over time as part of the learning process.

This structure is the inspiration for neural nets. A neural net is
simply an array of amplifiers, usually in two or more "layers," densely
interconnected to form a network. Each connection has a variable
resistor, which allows its strength to be adjusted, and a threshold that
determines when the amplifier will fire.[30] Each output voltage may be
normal or inverted, so that one amplifier may either excite or inhibit
the amplifiers to which it connects.

Neural nets do not have programming in the traditional sense of
a precise list of instructions. Rather, they have training rules for
adjusting the thresholds and connection strengths of the amplifiers.
Consider, for example, a network for reading printed characters.
During training, it could easily mistake an "H" for an "M." The
"trainer" (whether a subsystem of the machine itself or a human)
would "clamp" the system, insisting on a correct identification. The
system would then use its training rules to fiddle with connection
strengths and thresholds until it arrived at the desired answer. It
could, for example, strengthen the inhibitory connection between a
node that senses the presence of a horizontal line and the "M"
output while lowering the threshold for an "H" output, "pushing"
itself toward the "H" response. But one beauty of the system is that
its designer need not be able to anticipate what training adjustments
the system will make to itself, or even know what it has done after the
fact. Indeed, two identical systems could arrive at different sets of
weights and thresholds, each of them effective in performing the same
task. If the training rules and examples are suitable, the system's
self-adjustments will converge on a set of weights and thresholds that
will work in practice.

Like conventional hardware, neural nets may be configured to
perform many different roles. When serving as a processor, the programmer may fix the strength of the connections and supply data in
the form of external voltage inputs. Each node sums the excitatory
and inhibitory signals it receives and sends out its own signal to other

nodes. The signals ripple throughout the net.[31] The process is massively parallel and dynamic. A node that is initially receiving a net positive voltage may flip to a net negative voltage as a result of later feedback. After a few iterations, the net stabilizes, and the stable state can then be read as the answer. In many configurations and for many kinds of problems, however, more than one stable state exists. In, for example, an optimization problem (e.g., cutting assorted shapes out of sheet glass with minimum waste), the neural net does not always arrive at the best solution, but it does arrive at a good solution very quickly.[32] It is thus, in effect, inherently heuristic.

Neural net memories also have interesting properties. Conventional computer memories (whether magnetic disk, optical disk, or DRAM) store data by address. When a program calls for data, it specifies a track on the disk (for example), which the hardware reads and returns. People remember content, not addresses. To conform to human mental process, and to make it possible to search for unknown information, conventional computers maintain indexes of the addresses of data based on content, then cross-reference those addresses to find entries that satisfy some combination of criteria. This is a fragile approach. Assume, for example, that a conventional computer database contains information about several people, including a female, brown-haired, free-lance writer living in Los Angeles. If queried about a female, brown-haired journalist living in Los Angeles, the conventional computer will dutifully report the absence of matches.[33] Neural nets access memory more like people, by the content of the memory; not as an address, but as a set of attributes. This allows retrieval of data from incomplete or inaccurate input. In the previous example, the match on three of the criteria (possibly reinforced by the similarity on the fourth) would "land" the query close enough to the attributes of the existing record to produce a positive response (just as a sloppily written H may be close enough to be identified as such after training).[34] The neural net would therefore return the presumptively correct name, along with an accurate record that would reveal the discrepancy. In this, neural nets more closely resemble the memories of people (fallible, but functional) than of computers (uselessly exact).

The same is true in the area of pattern recognition. People recognize a familiar face instantly and without conscious effort. For con-

272   ventional computers, the same task is an arduous process of edge definition and comparison, which may be defeated altogether by a change in angle or lighting or hairstyle. Neural nets, on the other hand, are able to store a composite image of a face from several differing views of it.[35] This ability allows neural nets to generalize, recognizing not only the same person under different conditions, but also various forms of a common type (cups, for example) from having been trained on a small sampling.[36] A commercially available neural net chip scans account numbers from checks at store checkout counters, despite overwriting by customers and variable lighting conditions.[37] The Gulf War demonstrated neural nets' pattern recognition capabilities in dramatic fashion: smart weapons, trained with reconnaissance photographs, navigated across hundreds of miles, often striking with incredible accuracy.

This ability to learn by example lends itself to many artificial intelligence applications. NETTALK, for example, learns pronunciation.[38] It begins with a set of phonemes (sounds), a training vocabulary of one thousand words, and a learning algorithm. NETTALK reads each word, assigning phonemes to each letter based on that letter and the three before it and after it. Initially, the sound is just a baby's babble. But after each attempt, the learning algorithm adjusts the weights of connections to achieve a better "fit" with the pronunciation supplied to it, and something comprehensible soon begins to emerge. In the process, the system effectively learns some "rules," although they are never expressed as such. It learns, for example, that "gh" sounds like "f" in the letter combination "ough" and that "ei" is "ee" after "c" but "ay" if before "gh." The machine can essentially master a training vocabulary and achieve about 80 percent accuracy in pronouncing new words, all in less time than would be possible with a rule-based system and with a fraction of the memory that would be needed to store the pronunciations of a complete vocabulary.[39] Note that the choice of data affects the "programming." Given a different text for use as examples, or even the same text in a different order, NETTALK arrives at slightly different pronunciation, just as children from different surroundings develop identifiable accents and speech patterns. The process closely parallels the interdependence between experience and learning characteristic of human intelligence.

Since NETTALK, investigators have begun to apply this learning ability to real-life tasks. A neural net trained on data from 356 suspected heart attack cases recently outperformed emergency room physicians in diagnosing heart attacks in patients admitted with chest pains.[40] The system not only diagnosed more of the heart attacks that had occurred, it diagnosed fewer that had not (false positives). This is particularly impressive given the proclivity of rule-based expert systems to ascribe everything to the illness for which they are trained. As the cost of neural net technology declines, it will surely spread to a wider range of activities.

None of this suggests that neural nets will soon supplant conventional computers generally or in the field of artificial intelligence. Such a conclusion would, first, be premature. While some of their capabilities offer hope of surmounting barriers that have previously frustrated progress in artificial intelligence, neural nets remain largely in the province of research and development. Few have yet been successfully scaled up to solve problems amid the complexities of the real world.[41] Researchers will need another decade or more to delineate neural nets' strengths and weaknesses.

More fundamentally, neural nets are more likely to supplement than to supplant existing technology. They appear ill suited to the high-speed, repetitive logical operations, floating-point operations, and other symbolic processing at which conventional computers excel. The technologies thus complement each other. Artificial intelligence systems may include both neural net and conventional subsystems, each performing the tasks to which it is better adapted. Recurring to the illustration of chess, skilled players play standard openings from memory, then analyze the middle game at a conceptual or heuristic level and the end game move by move, exhaustively. The same general division is apparent in many activities. An artificial intelligence could perform routine tasks on the basis of memory alone, much as people perform subconsciously or by habit. Neural nets could be used for real-time interaction with the environment, where their strengths in recognizing patterns, learning by example, associative memory, and reaching satisfactory solutions quickly would be most useful. Conventional computer components armed with an intelligent database like CYC would digest knowledge in printed

274 form, perform precise calculations and logical operations, confirm the neural net's conjectures, take instructions and report results, and generally manage the system. This combination of capabilities will supply artificial intelligence researchers with far more diverse tools than they have enjoyed in the past.

The momentum on several fronts promises to propel machines from their existing beachheads into ever larger areas currently reserved to human intelligence. The first of these will likely be the physical sciences and engineering, with their extensive and fairly well defined bodies of knowledge. From there, artificial intelligence will extend into less tractable fields such as the life sciences, business applications, and economics. None of this will seem to occur suddenly, but the progression will be rapid. Within a generation, machine intelligence will be making significant, independent contributions in several fields.[42]

The breakthrough will come when computer experts in crucial aspects of computer science excel their human counterparts, even slightly, enabling them to enhance their own capabilities. Thereafter, the cycle becomes self-reinforcing, as smarter machines design still smarter machines.[43] Once begun, that process has no foreseeable limits.

NOTES

1. Roger Penrose, *The Emperor's New Mind: Concerning Computers, Minds, and the Laws of Physics,* p. 3, Oxford Univ. Press, 1989.
2. The best discussion of the theoretical feasibility of artificial intelligence is John Casti, *Paradigms Lost: Images of Man in the Mirror of Science,* Ch. 5, William Morrow, 1989. Many of the skeptics are philosophers, who tend to argue from *a priori* conceptions of the mind and the nature of intelligence. In this respect, the computer scientists, who urge the building of systems to *see* whether they exhibit intelligent behavior, clearly have the better of the argument.
3. Hau et al , "A Grandmaster Chess Machine," *Scientific American,* Oct. 1990, p. 44. The April 1990 issue of *Artificial Intelligence* is a collection of papers on chess-playing programs.
4. An example of these difficulties is the argument against the possibility of machine intelligence based on Gödel's incompleteness theorem, which states in substance that no formal system can be both complete (capable of proving all true propositions) and consistent (free from contradiction). If computers can only embody formal systems and cannot cope with self-contradiction, they will be unable to arrive at many self-evident truths. But whatever constraints Gödel's theorem imposes apply equally to the human mind, which nevertheless manages to exhibit intelligence. The explanation may be that both the brain and appropriately designed computers are capable of changing rules in response to conditions, in which case Gödel's theorem does not apply. The best nontechnical presentation of the incompleteness theorem is Douglas Hofstadter, *Gödel, Escher, Bach: An Eternal Golden Braid,* Basic Books, 1979, which also discusses many of the fundamental issues underlying artificial intelligence, albeit in a somewhat whimsical format.
5. The issue is often cast as whether a machine would ever achieve consciousness, self-awareness, or intentionality, as opposed to merely simulating certain aspects of thinking. Popular treatments include George Johnson, *Machinery of the Mind,* Ch. 13, Tempus, 1986, and "Artificial Intelligence: A Debate," in *Scientific American,* Jan. 1990, p. 25. Penrose, *The Emperor's New Mind,* addresses the same topic at length, but is only for the mathematically intrepid. The issue has no discernible practical significance. A machine lacking consciousness could still display (or simulate) any level of intelligence (as Penrose acknowledges, p. 407).
6. The logical possibility of intelligent machines does not, of course, prove that

276 human minds are capable of designing them. "[T]he interesting issue is not whether machines can be made smarter [than humans] but if humans are smart enough to pull it off. A raccoon obviously can't make a machine as smart as a raccoon." Johnson, *Machinery of the Mind,* p. xi, quoting Patrick Winston, director of MIT's artificial intelligence laboratory. This is part of the reason for concentrating on systems that are expert in system design. If these excel their creators by ever so little, they begin a self-reinforcing cycle that circumvents human limitations on the process.

7. Rennels & Shortliffe, "Advanced Computing for Medicine," *Scientific American,* Oct. 1987, p. 154, describes QMR and some of its predecessors.

8. Harry Pople, "CADUCEUS: An Experimental Expert System for Medical Diagnosis," Ch. 5, in Winston & Prendergast (eds.), *The AI Business: The Commercial Uses of Artificial Intelligence,* MIT Press, 1984; Raymond Kurzweil, *The Age of Intelligent Machines,* Ch. 8, p. 296, MIT Press, 1990.

9. Kurzweil, *Age of Intelligent Machines,* Ch. 8, outlines the technology of expert systems.

10. See Kurzweil, *Age of Intelligent Machines,* Chs. 7 and 8. The current generation of expert systems implemented on serial computers typically process no more than one hundred inferences per second. Planned applications will require thousands of inferences per second, which will demand parallel-processing architectures. Kurzweil, p. 301.

11. Douglas Lenat, "Computer Software for Intelligent Systems," *Scientific American,* Sept. 1984, p. 204. Lenat describes the heuristic methodologies referred to in the text. The difficulty of exponentially expanding decision trees overwhelming any level of processing power is pervasive in artificial intelligence applications and is sometimes referred to as the combinatorial explosion. A chess computer proceeding by brute force, for example, must consider perhaps thirty-five first moves, and thirty-five responses to each of those moves, and so on. Thus, exhaustive analysis to a depth of five moves requires consideration of nearly three quadrillion possibilities.

12. People apply heuristics more or less automatically. Recurring to the chess analogy, skilled players consider only a tiny fraction of the possible moves. They give no consideration to moves that are either harmful or pointless. They consider "unthematic" moves (those that are inconsistent with the overall strategy of the position) only briefly to determine if they would yield a material gain or some other tactical advantage. This leaves very few first moves to investigate deeply. They will similarly consider only a few responses to each possibility, only a few second moves, and so on. The player may also be able to "prune" some decision trees by evaluating the position reached without explicitly considering further moves.

13. See Arnold Kraft, "XCON: An Expert Configuration System at Digital Equipment Corporation," Ch. 3, in Winston & Prendergast (eds.), *The AI Business;* Kurzweil, *Age of Intelligent Machines,* Ch. 8, p. 292.

14. *Economist,* 14–20 Mar. 1992, "Survey of Artificial Intelligence," p. 6.

15. Daniel Schutzer, *Artificial Intelligence: An Applications-Oriented Approach,* Ch. 4, p. 147, Van Nostrand Reinhold, 1987.

16. Some of the difficulties and history of efforts to enable computers to understand natural language are described in Aleksander & Burnett, *Thinking Machines: The Search for Artificial Intelligence*, Ch. 5, Oxford Univ. Press, 1987; M. Mitchell Waldrop, *Man-Made Minds: The Promise of Artificial Intelligence*, Ch. 5, Walker, 1987; Kurzweil, *Age of Intelligent Machines*, Ch. 8, pp. 304–12; and Johnson, *Machinery of the Mind*, Chs. 5 and 6.

17. The ambiguities of natural language are discussed in greater detail in Terry Winograd, "Computer Software for Working with Language," *Scientific American*, Sept. 1984, p. 130, from which several examples in the text are taken.

18. Kurzweil, *Age of Intelligent Machines*, Ch. 8, p. 304.

19. Lenat & Guha, *Building Large Knowledge-Based Systems: Representation and Inference in the Cyc Project*, Addison-Wesley, 1989, describes the CYC project early in its evolution. *Scientific American*, Dec. 1991, pp. 132–34, provides a brief update.

20. *Scientific American*, Dec. 1991, pp. 132–34.

21. See *Scientific American*, July 1992, p. 32.

22. Examples include the concept "consider extreme cases." When considering the function "divisors" and applying this concept, a predecessor of EURISKO "discovered" the attribute "primeness" and concluded that each whole number is the product of a unique set of prime numbers, a nontrivial theorem of mathematics. Lenat describes EURISKO in "EURISKO: A Program That Learns New Heuristics and Domain Concepts," *Artificial Intelligence*, Vol. 21, p. 61, 1983.

23. In the course of evaluating its own heuristics, EURISKO concluded that those having EURISKO itself as their creator were generally less useful than those created by Lenat. It therefore generated a new rule that would have eliminated all EURISKO generated heuristics, effectively negating its own meta-heuristic abilities. This heuristic, however, promptly selected itself for elimination, thereby preserving the program's other creations. This episode may not suggest that human intelligence is soon to become superfluous, but it does illustrate how far programs like EURISKO depart from traditional computing functions.

24. Kurzweil, *Age of Intelligent Machines*, Ch. 7; Aleksander & Burnett, *Thinking Machines*, Chs. 7 and 8; and Waldrop, *Man Made Minds*, Ch. 4, describe the problems and technology of machine vision.

25. Sight involves the same sort of mental focus. Amateur photographers regularly experience disappointment because the camera lacks the mind's selectivity. The mind's eye "sees" only the flower, deer, or hawk out of an entire scene. The camera captures the complete visual field, and the effect is lost.

26. A pixel is a single, digitally defined element (a dot) in a matrix that depicts a scene.

27. Kurzweil, *Age of Intelligent Machines*, Ch. 7, pp. 224–27, describes the computational demands of common approaches to pattern recognition by machines.

28. The literature on neural nets tends to be sparse and forbidding, and the treatment in the text is necessarily summary. Churchland & Sejnowski, *The Computational Brain*, Ch. 3, MIT Press, 1992, and Aleksander & Morton, *An Introduc-*

278   *tion to Neural Computing,* Chapman & Hall, 1990, provide reasonably accessible introductions. W.F. Allman, "Neural Nets, Computers That Think the Way We Do," *Technology Review,* May/June 1987, pp. 59–65, and Tank & Hopfield, "Collective Computation in Neuronlike Circuits," *Scientific American,* Dec. 1987, p. 104, describe particular nets and applications.

29. Thomas Simpson, "The New Pythagoreans III: The Scientists of the Mind," p. 142, at p. 161, n. 24, in *The Great Ideas Today 1991,* Britannica.

30. The variable strength of the connections between amplifiers makes neural nets inherently analog, rather than digital like von Neumann computers. Digital components often simulate analog signals in neural nets (as they do in, for example, communications), because digital semiconductor technology is so much more advanced. See Aleksander & Morton, *Introduction to Neural Computing,* Chs. 4 and 10.

31. This rippling effect creates detectable external electrical fields similar to the brain waves measured by the electroencephalograph. Whether this similarity is significant or coincidental is not yet known.

32. See, for example, Churchland & Sejnowski, *Computational Brain,* Ch. 3, pp. 82–92. In practice, the system may be optimized by combining the output from the first "cycle" through the net with the original data input and feeding it back into the net. See Aleksander & Burnett, *Thinking Machines,* pp. 172–74. For other methods of preventing the net from stabilizing in a nonoptimal state, see Aleksander & Morton, *Introduction to Neural Computing,* Ch. 7.

33. Note that a conventional database manager equipped with CYC or its equivalent would also be able to solve the problem posed in the text. A frame in the system would link the closely related occupations of "journalist" and "free-lance writer" and report the match. Thus, many of the problems of artificial intelligence admit of both hardware and software solutions.

34. See Tank & Hopfield, "Collective Computation in Neuronlike Circuits," *Scientific American,* Dec. 1987, p. 104, for a description of the computational energy by which neural nets store information.

35. Churchland & Sejnowski, *Computational Brain,* Ch. 3, pp. 89–96, and Aleksander & Burnett, *Thinking Machines,* Chs. 9 and 10, describe the processes by which a neural net learns to recognize a face or pattern.

36. *Economist,* 14–20 Mar. 1992, "Survey of Artificial Intelligence," p. 18.

37. *Scientific American,* Aug. 1992, p. 119, describes the neural net check reader.

38. Matthew Zeidenberg, *Neural Network Models in Artificial Intelligence,* Ch. 5, pp. 172–76, Ellis Horwood, 1990, describes NETTALK.

39. Zeidenberg, *Neural Network Models in Artificial Intelligence,* Ch. 5, p. 174, estimates that NETTALK used eighty thousand bits of memory, compared to two million bits for a memorized dictionary of twenty thousand words.

40. *Wall Street Journal,* Dec. 2, 1991, p. A7C.

41. See Churchland & Sejnowski, *Computational Brain,* Ch. 3, pp. 125–30, on the problems of scaling up neural nets.

42. "The 1990s will, in my estimation, witness the emergence of a . . . generation

of ubiquitous intelligent machines that work intimately with their human creators."
Kurzweil, *Age of Intelligent Machines,* Ch. 6, p. 213. This estimate may appear a
bit sanguine, given the history of disappointment in the field. But as a pioneer and
still a leader in the field of pattern recognition, Kurzweil's opinion deserves some
weight.

43.

"Why *can't* I patent myself?"

From *The Wall Street Journal,* May 19, 1989, p. A15; reprinted by permission of Cartoon
Features Syndicate.

Chapter Eleven

LIFE EXTENSION

The days of our years are threescore years and ten;
And if by reason of strength they be fourscore years,
Yet is their strength labour and sorrow;
For it is soon cut off, and we fly away.[1]

Thus it has remained from Biblical times to the present. People lucky enough to survive the other hazards of life have aged and died at the same rate throughout history. Genesis to the contrary notwithstanding, there is no evidence of people elsewhere or elsewhen who have enjoyed greatly extended life spans. The people of Bulgaria, Soviet Georgia, and Abkhazia, widely reputed to have exceptionally long lives, in fact have a culture that venerates extreme old age, predictably leading to exaggeration. Most people die before reaching eighty, and those who live past ninety often regret having done so. Medicine allows many more people to live out full life spans, but it has done nothing to extend the life span itself.[2]

Until now. Laboratories scattered around the world already house animals of various species that have lived half again as long as their natural life spans. Based on the present pace of progress, children born in the next decade should be among the first to enjoy significantly lengthened lives.

This chapter begins by outlining the theories and results that underlie this progress. As with the many previous diseases and conditions conquered by scientific medicine, knowledge of the pathology at a fundamental level leads ineluctably to techniques for intervening in the process. (The principal difference is that past medical break-throughs—vaccines and antibiotics, for example—focused on the life and death of invading organisms, while longevity research addresses the human life cycle itself.) The chapter concludes by describing the research programs that are pushing these results up the evolutionary ladder toward a populace eager to postpone the burdens of aging.

THE EVOLUTION OF AGING[3]

If it were not so familiar, the very fact of aging would be surprising. Evolution selects for fitness. Carriers of alleles (genetic variations) that cause or permit early death (physical weakness or susceptibility to disease, for example) produce fewer children on the average in each generation. Within a few hundred years, this "selection pressure" eliminates the deleterious allele from the gene pool altogether, leaving only "fitter" forms of the gene. How, then, could a process as obviously pernicious as aging develop and persist over the course of thousands of generations?

The solution to this mystery lies in Thomas Hobbes's apt description of life in the state of nature: nasty, brutish, and short (with the emphasis on short), under the continual fear and danger of sudden death.[4] "Wild animals almost never die of old age: starvation, disease, or predators catch up with them long before they become really senile. Until recently this was true of man, too."[5] Comparatively few people lived past thirty, fewer still past fifty. They preserved the species by mating and producing as many offspring as they could as early as they could, certainly beginning in their teens, a practice that remained almost universal until the modern era.[6] Now imagine that half the population carries an allele that leads to some aspect of aging (loss of immunity, for example) in people over fifty. (Random muta-tions in the germ line caused by environmental and cellular processes would occasionally produce such genes, even if they were not origi-nally present.)[7] More of them would die each year after fifty, and they would therefore be underrepresented in that age group. But, by then, evolution would have become relatively indifferent to their fates. They

282   would already have passed their gene on to enough children to keep it from disappearing, and the entire fifty-and-over age cohort would have been so diminished by earlier disease and accidents as to have little further effect on the gene pool. The selection pressure could therefore be too weak to eliminate such aging genes (sometimes called "gerontogenes") from the population.

In some instances, evolution may even select *for* a gerontogene. An allele could, for example, increase vigor and strength during youth while causing slight but cumulative cellular damage that would shorten the maximum life span. The person carrying such a variation would be more likely to survive the rigors of nature long enough to reproduce. The added strength could also enhance the chances of attracting, finding, or winning a mate.[8] The greater likelihood of leaving offspring would easily outweigh the slight evolutionary disadvantage of aging and death. Youth will be served, even by natural selection and even at the expense of shortening the life span. Over hundreds of generations, the chromosomes thus become garbage cans, collecting an assortment of genes with harmful effects that appear only in old age. Aging is the combination of these effects.

The humble roundworm provides a striking example of this trade-off between youthful reproductive fitness and long-term survival, which is dauntingly called antagonistic pleiotropy. A single mutant recessive gene extends the worm's life span by 60 to 110 percent, but reduces its fertility by 75 percent.[9] Evolution obviously selects against this mutation (whatever the wishes of the worm) because the selection pressure favoring fertility among the many young worms outweighs that favoring longer life among the few older worms.

Proof of this process is not limited to such laboratory oddities. Life-span differences throughout the animal kingdom clearly reflect these evolutionary pressures. Some species are naturally better protected against predation and other causes of death than their fellow animals. The shells of adult turtles, for example, render them nearly invulnerable. As a result, predators thin their population much less quickly with advancing age. The force of natural selection therefore remains strong for many more years after the onset of reproduction and produces defenses or cures for conditions that would otherwise kill or debilitate aging turtles. Thus, turtles should have longer life spans than their relatives without shells. The facts decisively confirm this prediction: large turtles live up to seventy years, compared to twenty years for large reptiles without a shell. Bats, with their ability to evade predators by flying, enjoy a similar advantage over other small mammals, with a similar result. Their average maximum life span is twenty-one years, compared to nine years for earthbound rodents of comparable size. The long life spans of whales, elephants, gorillas, giraffes, and other large mammals, which have few predators as adults, provide further confirmation.

The same evolutionary dynamic operates within a single species, as nature has conveniently demonstrated on an island near the Georgia coast. The opossums that live there are, to all outward appearances, identical to the mainland opossums from which they descended. But the island has fewer natural or unnatural (i.e., vehicular) predators. As a result, these opossums have multiplied through many generations with a lower risk of early death. With selection pressure maintained through more years, they have evolved maximum life spans more than half again as long as their mainland brethren.[10]

Evolution thus explains why people age. It does not explain how they age. Efforts to alter the process will require detailed knowledge of the physiology of aging. That research is already underway.

THE AGING BODY

Doctors know what happens to people as they age.[11] The heart pumps less blood. Effective lung capacity declines, as does the efficiency of oxygen transport into the bloodstream. Metabolism slows. The body becomes more susceptible to disease. Blood vessels, muscles, and connective tissues lose strength and flexibility. Motor function deteriorates. The output of various hormones decreases. Cell division slows. Protein synthesis declines. Neurons die, and learning, memory, and other mental functions deteriorate. Waste products accumulate in many cells. Chromosomal damage afflicts an ever larger number of cells. These conditions are ultimately fatal, even if no acute disease or condition intervenes. The challenge of aging research lies not in elaborating these manifestations, but in deciding which are symptoms and which, if any, are causes.[12] Theories have proliferated, with a clear favorite yet to emerge.

284   One view is that aging is a predetermined developmental process, like growth or puberty, programmed into the neuroendocrine glands, which regulate such bodily processes as growth and maturation, metabolism, homeostasis, reproduction and sexuality, and immune response. With age, the output of many of these glands declines and the hormonal tone of the body deteriorates. One potential source of a neuroendocrine aging program is DHEA, a hormone produced by the adrenal gland that inhibits the metabolism of glucose. DHEA output falls sharply with age. Compensating for the loss of DHEA and related hormones by injection has delayed or reversed the onset of several aging symptoms in laboratory animals (although without extending the maximum life span).[13] On the other hand, some tissues age and die more rapidly because of the action of hormones.[14] Hormone damage, for example, contributes to the death of some brain cells. Under the neuroendocrine theory, aging is some combination of direct and indirect effects of programmed changes in hormonal levels.

Another "program" theory of aging focuses on the deterioration of the immune system with age. This deterioration causes the characteristic susceptibility of the elderly to disease.[15] The thymus gland, which is principally responsible for the development and regulation of the immune system, shrinks rapidly after the age of twenty-five, almost disappearing by the age of fifty. Aging immune system cells produce less interleukin-2, a key factor in the growth of thymus-derived lymph cells (T-lymphocytes).[16] Those cells decline in number and in their ability to respond to foreign proteins. This improves the survival chances not only of disease organisms, but also of cancerous, mutated, or otherwise defective cells and proteins produced by the body itself. One branch of the immune system theory holds that aging results from the body's declining response to such foreign and aberrant cells and by-products.[17]

An even more important contributor, according to this theory, is increasing autoimmunity.[18] Autoimmunity is the immune system's misidentification of a naturally occurring protein as foreign.[19] This defective recognition of "self" results from a change in either the target cells or the immune system itself. Cells of the immune system then proceed to attack the body's own tissues as if they were invading pathogens, much as they may reject an implanted organ. The results are predictably harmful. Multiple sclerosis is one of the best-known and most serious of the autoimmune diseases. Some forms of arthritis result from autoimmune attacks on connective tissues in the joints. Other examples include some forms of anemia and diabetes. Autoimmunity may not, however, be confined to such acute, discrete, and readily diagnosable conditions. Autoantibody levels increase with age, suggesting that aging itself may result, at least in part, from more diffuse, low-grade autoimmune responses to key proteins in the body.

Like much of biology, aging research has concentrated more attention on the molecular level in recent years. An important starting point is the Hayflick limit, named after its discoverer, Leonard Hayflick. Cells extracted from the body and placed in a nutrient solution will continue to live, grow, and divide. Hayflick discovered that such a colony of cells has a finite and predictable life history in culture. It divides only a certain number of times. As it approaches that limit, division slows, then stops, and the cells die. The cells even have a "memory"—if part of a colony of cells is frozen, then later thawed and allowed to continue dividing, it will ultimately divide the same number of times as the portion of the colony that was not frozen.

The Hayflick limit suggests that the body's cycle of growth, aging, and death could be preprogrammed in each cell, rather than through the neuroendocrine system. Several observations tend to support some connection between cellular and bodily aging. Cells extracted from older animals stop dividing and die sooner. In addition, the maximum life span of a species correlates strongly with the number of times that its cells will divide in culture.[20] Cells in transplanted organs function at a level fixed by the age of the donor, not that of the recipient, suggesting a cellular rather than bodily program of genetic regulation. Both protein synthesis and messenger RNA levels decline in older animals of all higher species.[21] How these changes in genetic expression are governed and whether they can be controlled are current research topics.

Despite such tantalizing suggestions, the Hayflick limit by itself will not explain the limits on life spans. A cell divides much more slowly in the body than in a petri dish. As a result, cells in an organism undergo many fewer divisions than can be induced in culture before the Hayflick limit is reached.[22] Cells extracted from eighty- to ninety-year-old people will still divide about twenty times in culture (about

286 40 percent of the total Hayflick limit for human fetal cells).[23] Thus, mechanisms other than the finite life spans of individual cells must contribute to aging.

Another cellular explanation for aging is free radical damage. A free radical is an atom or molecule with an unpaired electron in its outer shell. This free electron makes these agents highly reactive. Free radicals are always present in the body, formed by natural and man-made radiation and by natural biological processes. For example, the basic cellular energy production process sometimes fails to complete its cycle and produces an oxygen ion called the superoxide radical. Superoxide may then react with hydrogen to form hydrogen peroxide, which may, in turn, split into two hydroxyl radicals.

Such free radicals attack and chemically alter cellular structures, including cell membranes, mitochondria, chromosomes, and enzymes, with effects that are not always biologically reversible.[24] Free radical damage has been implicated in a number of diseases and conditions, including some forms of arthritis, emphysema, and cataracts. To prevent such damage, the body produces "scavenger" enzymes that rapidly eliminate most free radicals. Molecular biologists have identified different scavengers for superoxide, hydroxyl, and other radicals. A separate series of enzymes repairs much of the damage caused by free radicals that the scavengers miss.[25] But these systems cannot prevent free radical damage from accumulating with age. In its simplest form, the free radical theory holds that aging is not some elaborate hormonal or cellular program, but simply this accumulation of random damage.[26] When the damage becomes too extensive, the body dies. Every hour wounds, the last one kills.

Several observations support the theory. Species with high metabolic rates generally have short lives, and free radicals are a by-product of metabolism. Species with higher levels of free radical scavengers in their tissues tend to have longer life spans. Special laboratory animals with low scavenger levels age faster than otherwise identical strains with higher levels.[27] In all species, the output of scavenger enzymes declines with age. Together, these facts suggest that free radicals have a role in the process.

This is just a sampling of the theories advanced to explain aging.[28] Each of the theories successfully explains some aspects of aging, but none of them commands universal assent. The theories are not mutually exclusive. Part of a neuroendocrine aging program, for example, could suppress production of free radical scavengers or reduce immune system response. Or free radicals may cause mutations that initiate autoimmune responses. None of these theories standing alone seems likely to explain all manifestations of aging.[29]

More research will thus be needed to forge the accumulating evidence and theories into a comprehensive synthesis. But the lack of complete knowledge is not delaying work on the next step—prevention.

EXTENDING THE LIFE SPAN[30]

The funding devoted to research on postponing old age (less than $100 million annually in the United States, compared to $2 billion of research on cancer and $1.2 billion on AIDS,[31] which afflicts less than one million people) seems surprisingly meager at first.[32] The explanation, of course, is that such research seemed obviously futile until recently. Tangible results have begun to prove otherwise, evoking a rising tide of interest in the field. Scientists have proved methods for extending the life spans of various animals by 50 percent or more in the laboratory. The present challenge is to explain these results in fundamental biological terms and to extend them progressively to higher species and ultimately, of course, to people.

UNDERNUTRITION. The most widely proved method for extending life spans is undernutrition, also known variously as food, dietary, energy, or caloric restriction.[33] Laboratory rats restricted to a diet having only 60 percent of the calories consumed by freely feeding rats of the same species live 50 to 60 percent longer. (Dietary supplements assure that the animals receive adequate vitamins, minerals, proteins, and other nutrients. Undernutrition lengthens lives; malnutrition shortens them.) The effect is greatest if the diet is restricted immediately after weaning, but a gradual transition to undernutrition beginning in middle age also lengthens the life span.

Dietary restriction clearly slows the aging process itself. Underfed rats that are chronologically elderly are biologically middle-aged: they are friskier, more sexually active, and smarter than their freely feeding

288   siblings. The composition of the diet apparently matters little. Rats given restricted diets high in fats, proteins, or carbohydrates respond very similarly, always provided that the diet includes the essential nutrients.

Researchers have duplicated these results many times with different strains of rats and with mice, fish, caterpillars, spiders, fruit flies, and protozoa. The connection between dietary restriction and longevity has proved easier to demonstrate than to explain, not because there are too few effects and theories, but because there are too many. DNA repair mechanisms deteriorate less with age in underfed rats.[34] The genes that produce free radical scavengers remain more active longer.[35] Undernutrition lessens the shrinkage of the thymus and improves immune response in mature animals while reducing the incidence of autoimmune responses.[36] It also slows the rate of cell division in rapidly replicating cell populations,[37] suggesting that it could postpone the effect of the Hayflick limit. The blood glucose level is lower in underfed than in fully fed animals. Glucose metabolism produces free radicals, and glucose in the blood has been associated with the harmful cross-linking of proteins and nucleic acids.[38] Dietary restriction enhances protein synthesis and levels of messenger RNA in several tissue groups. Although undernutrition apparently does not affect the overall metabolic rate,[39] some (but not all) studies have suggested that calorically restricted animals have a lower mean body temperature.[40] As noted below, cold-blooded animals live longer with a lower body temperature. Which (if any) of these manifestations contribute to the extension of life spans is the subject of ongoing investigation.

The obvious question is whether dietary restriction would have the same longevity effect on people as it has on rats, which would produce a human life span of some 130 years. Most gerontologists have refused to acknowledge this likelihood publicly, despite the increasingly imposing body of animal data. This insistence on absolute proof is a curious attitude for the medical research community to adopt toward such results. If a food additive increases the incidence of cancer in rats or mice (even if only in massive doses and not in other species), toxicologists do not hesitate to conclude that it would have the same effect on people. The FDA and EPA have banned many otherwise useful drugs, food additives, and pesticides on the basis of much weaker evidence. Gerontologists have offered little reason for applying a different standard to the undernutrition results.[41] Their reticence may derive from a central tenet of medical practice, that the physician should do no harm. This produces a sort of professional risk aversion, in which unknown but possible ill effects of a dietary restriction regime weigh more heavily than the potential positive effects. A less charitable explanation is pervasive paternalism—the obvious appeal of long life would induce hasty and ill-informed life-style choices by millions, many of whom would mismanage undernutrition into malnutrition, with its attendant ill effects. Other experts apparently fear the social consequences of increased longevity and therefore do not wish to publicize the possibility of life extension.

Whatever the motivations, public awareness of dietary restriction research and its potential in humans is certain to grow in the next few years. One epidemiological study has already suggested a link between undereating and the human life span. Okinawan Japanese consume about 20 percent fewer calories than the average Japanese, and about twenty times as many Okinawans as Japanese live to be one hundred, even though the Japanese live longer than the people of any other advanced nation. This is far from proof positive that undernutrition lengthens people's lives. As noted below, Okinawans exhibit a genetic difference that may explain some or all of their longevity. No Okinawan has lived to 120, suggesting that any stretching of their maximum life span has been limited. Nevertheless, the nexus between slightly restricted food intake and living longer is suggestive and will certainly receive further study.

The central thrust of ongoing undernutrition research is to push laboratory results up the evolutionary chain.[42] Researchers at the University of Wisconsin began an undernutrition test with rhesus and squirrel monkeys in 1987. The early indications are encouraging. Preliminary results suggesting the extent of any life span extension should be reported in 1993. If these results are positive, human experimentation (both controlled and freestyle) will surely follow, with the first meaningful results appearing perhaps a decade later. But even successful undernutrition would not likely be more than an interim step in extending the human life span. The required reduction of 40 to 50 percent in food intake throughout adulthood is a fairly

290 severe regimen with some known side effects.[43] The unwillingness of many people to stay on modest weight-loss diets even temporarily suggests that undernutrition would lose favor as soon as any alternative existed, and perhaps even before.[44] In the longer term, the focus will therefore be on uncovering the physiological mechanisms by which undernutrition works, in order to substitute medical intervention for self-denial. Despite the remaining uncertainties, the likelihood that undernutrition research will produce some life extension method appears quite high.

SELECTION FOR LONGEVITY. The genes responsible for causing or permitting aging have persisted through countless generations because animals reproduce before aging takes its toll. The selection pressure against those genes is therefore slight. But scientists can force longevity to evolve in the laboratory simply by postponing reproduction through a number of generations, thereby enhancing the genetic advantage of the longest-lived animals in each generation. "Direct artificial selection is not necessary. In effect, natural selection in the laboratory does the 'work.' "[45]

This has already been accomplished with fruit flies. Researchers simply discard all eggs laid by young flies, restricting the gene pool to the offspring of older flies. Life spans lengthen by up to 50 percent, with significant extension regularly appearing after only ten generations of selection.[46] The physiology of the longer-lived flies differs materially from that of the controls. They are more resistant to starvation and to some other forms of environmental stress. They are less fertile when young and more fertile when old. This experimentally confirms the existence of antagonistic pleiotropy: the artificially imposed delay in reproduction selects for pleiotropic genes that confer long life at the expense of early fertility, as with the roundworm mutant noted earlier. Evolution in nature would, of course, strike the opposite balance. Preliminary studies indicate that the longer-lived flies and the controls differ in a number of genes.

A strategy for extending these results to human aging within a few decades is already in place.[47] The first step is to develop long-lived strains of one or more rodent species by artificially postponing reproduction. The process is the same as with fruit flies; the longer life spans of rodents simply drag it out. This work is underway and should yield long-lived laboratory strains within six to eight years. In the meantime, scientists are searching for other long-lived strains, like the Georgia island opossums, from protected natural environments.

With such naturally or unnaturally selected species in hand, the focus will shift to finding the sources of their longevity. Physiological keys to aging (probably including a number that are already being investigated) can be isolated by a direct comparison of long-lived and normal strains. This effort has begun with fruit flies. Unlike underfed animals, however, these long-lived strains will differ genetically from the controls. This will bring the rapidly developing tools of molecular genetics to bear on longevity research. Scientists will be able to trace particular traits that appear to lengthen the life spans of the selected strains to their genetic origins. People share most of their genes with chimpanzees and even with mice, which assures the relevance of animal studies to human aging. Laboratory selection thus offers a fairly direct and reliable route to discovery of the genetic sources of aging.

The final step will be intervention. This may also be physiological (by drug therapies or implants, for example) or genetic (by activating or inserting genes to replicate the effects of those found in the long-lived strains). Successful intervention in the original experimental species will be extended progressively through higher mammals and lower primates to people.

Without trivializing the remaining difficulties, the success of this strategy is reasonably predictable. It is straightforward and simple in design. It requires no speculative or conceptual breakthroughs. The theory behind it has strong empirical support. Under that theory, "there is no biochemical necessity to aging."[48] The only barriers to longer life are practical, and those will be overcome.

OTHER APPROACHES. Undernutrition and laboratory selection are merely the most general approaches to slowing the aging process. Research continues in several other promising directions.

Zoologists had long known that reptiles live longer in cooler climates. Researchers have now replicated and extended this result under controlled conditions, doubling the life span of certain annual fish by cooling their water.[49] Fruit flies also survive longer in a cooler environment. Achieving the same result in mammals presents an

292 obvious difficulty. The hypothalamus closely regulates body temperature; cooling the environment merely raises the metabolism, likely causing faster aging. Some but not all of the mechanisms that govern this thermal set point are understood. The known methods for manipulating it cause harmful side effects. If scientists were able to circumvent this difficulty, however, the potential for life extension would be significant.[50]

Molecular geneticists have many clues to pursue even before long-lived animal strains are bred. The Human Genome Project will have mapped human chromosomes by the mid-1990s. Aging researchers will focus particular attention on the major histocompatibility complex (MHC), a collection of related genes on chromosome 6. The MHC is central to the development and regulation of the immune system and is an important determinant of autoimmunity.[51] It also directly or indirectly governs the rate of DNA repair,[52] as well as levels of at least two free radical scavengers. Variation in the MHC produces life span differences of more than 20 percent in different mouse strains.[53] Genetic studies of the long-lived Okinawan Japanese suggest some involvement of the MHC in human aging as well.[54]

Once researchers understand the genetic components of aging, they will begin to intervene in the process, using gene therapy techniques being developed for cancer treatment. Direct genetic intervention is a much less certain method for lengthening life spans than the laboratory selection process described above, but it has one distinct advantage. Selection through a number of generations brings genetic variations that naturally occur in the population to the fore. But some genes that would favor long life may never have existed or may have disappeared completely. Genetic engineering is not limited to naturally occurring genes. Animal tests are already in progress.[55]

Research into the physiology of aging also continues apace. This work complements the genetic research, both by targeting the genes that may be relevant to the process and by explaining the effect of genes already identified. Cancer cells are of particular interest to those pursuing a cellular aging program because they defy the Hayflick limit by continuing to grow and divide indefinitely both in the body and in culture. (It would be ironic if cancer, one of the few remaining killers, held the key to understanding an even more dreadful one, old age.) Adding certain substances to the culture medium also stretches the Hayflick limit, appreciably increasing the number of divisions that occur before death of the cell.[56]

Free radical damage may be slowed or prevented by enhancing or substituting for natural safeguards. One approach currently being pursued is to clone multiple copies of the genes responsible for producing scavenger enzymes into fruit fly chromosomes to determine the effect of overexpression of those genes on life span.[57] An alternative is to supplement the diet with antioxidants, such as selenium, Vitamin E, Vitamin C, and BHT. Experiments with rodents have produced mixed results.[58] An obscure bacterium, *Micrococcus radiodurans,* may aid research into the prevention and repair of chromosomal and other free radical damage. It thrives in the water of nuclear power plant cooling towers, where radiation levels would quickly kill other species. The bacterium has adapted by developing highly active and efficient DNA-repair and free-radical-scavenging mechanisms. Replicating or simulating those processes in human cells could retard age-related damage.

How any of these approaches will contribute to the final synthesis cannot now be projected. But some working understanding of aging is all but certain within a few decades. Like the biology of thinking, the aging process is complex, but not magical. It is susceptible to human comprehension and therefore alteration. U.C. Irvine professor Michael Rose, a pioneer in the evolutionary biology of aging and a leading researcher in the aging field, expresses unqualified confidence in the outcome: "[A]ging can now be regarded as a problem that is well on its way toward a scientific solution. . . . [T]he problem of postponing aging will become a soluble one."[59] A virtually infinite consumer demand will call forth gene therapies, drugs, implants, and other products and techniques to retard or counteract aging, with profound effects on society.

THE METHUSELAH SOCIETY[60]

The effects of longer life lie largely in the realm of speculation. A few predictions can, however, be made with some confidence.

First, and somewhat paradoxically, longer lives should not unduly expand the population. The population growth rate depends almost

294 entirely on fertility. If each couple has an average of 2.1 children, whenever they have them and however long they live, the population is stable in the long term. Fertility in developed nations has declined to near, and in some instances below, this replacement level. This has obviously been a matter of taste, not necessity: very few couples have as many children as biology or financial considerations would allow. Affluence, on the average, decreases the desire for large families, and added longevity will, if anything, reinforce this dynamic (see below). The same considerations may not apply in subsistence economies, assuming that the technology of life extension would be made available there before they emerged from poverty. On the other hand, life extension would have less impact in nations where famine and infectious disease are more common causes of death than old age.

Another seeming paradox is that allowing people to live longer should afford society some respite from the problems threatened by an aging populace. Medical costs in the United States are rising alarmingly, largely because of the ever graying population that results from eliminating premature death without postponing old age. Most serious diseases in advanced nations are essentially symptoms of aging—they primarily afflict the elderly, exploiting some age-related breakdown in their bodies. Yet, the United States spends billions of dollars for research and hundreds of billions of dollars annually treating those diseases, thousands of times what is spent on longevity research. Treating the symptoms rather than the underlying cause seems a nonsensical waste of resources. The other disproportionate users of medical services are young children, with their regular round of illnesses and minor mishaps. But life extension will expand these population segments little if at all: tampering with the maturation process of children and adolescents is unlikely, and few people would choose to extend their decrepitude. Retarding the aging process will stretch the healthy years of young adulthood, middle age, and early old age, thus reducing the demand for medical services.

Stretching productive years will also lighten the burden caused by the increasing portion of the population in retirement. With the retirement of the Baby Boomers and the reduced birthrate after 1970, projections indicate that less than two payroll taxpayers will be supporting each Social Security beneficiary by 2035, compared to sixteen in 1950 and three presently. Trends are similar in other developed nations; indeed, Japan's population is aging even faster than that of the United States.[61] Absent an unexpected rise in the birth rate, the shift to an older population will be permanent. These demographics will severely strain the Social Security system. The trust fund is illusory, the surplus fictive. The burden of supporting retirees and other beneficiaries has always fallen and will continue to fall entirely on their taxpaying contemporaries. A payroll tax of 20 percent or more would be needed to meet legislated benefit levels if current projections prove to be accurate.[62] Even if the economy did not collapse from such a burden, the political strains would be severe. Life extension will reverse the current trend by disproportionately expanding the working-age segment of the population.[63] This will not occur in time to forestall the budgetary problems entirely, but it could ameliorate those problems from the middle of the next century onward. For the intergenerational harmony of society, it cannot begin too soon.

Extending the human life span may thus address threatening demographic trends better than the cosmetics commonly applied by politicians. Ultimately, though, longevity will have its largest impact on the quality of life. Aging is the most awful affliction imaginable. Everyone suffers from it, it debilitates both the mind and the body, and it is always fatal. The brevity of life restricts human potential as severely as any other single cause.

> [A] person's allotted span of life is simply too short to permit a satisfying exploration of the world's outer wonders and the realms of inner experience. We are cut off in the midst of our pleasures, separated too soon from our loved ones, shelved at the mere beginning of our understanding.[64]

The hardships caused by such dreaded conditions as heart disease, cancer, and AIDS pale by comparison. People endure the onset of old age with comparatively little complaint simply because they have no choice. But postponing the inevitable will soon be possible. Although no amount of time may ever be enough, more will surely be better.

1. Psalms 90:10 (King James version).
2. Leonard Hayflick, "Prospects for Increasing Human Longevity," Ch. 2, 29, in Johnston (ed.), *Perspectives on Aging: Exploding the Myths,* Ballinger, 1981.
3. Michael Rose, *Evolutionary Biology of Aging,* Chs. 1–4, Oxford Univ. Press, 1991, describes the evolution of aging. Except as otherwise noted, it is the source for the following discussion in the text.
4. *Leviathan,* Part 1, Ch. 13.
5. Richard Dawkins, *The Selfish Gene,* Ch. 7, p. 112, Oxford Univ. Press, 1989 ed.
6. Juliet's betrothal to Paris at the age of thirteen was in no sense unusual for pre-Renaissance Europe. Japanese traditions during the same era arranged for strangers to copulate with any girl who reached her late teens without mating. Nicholas Bornoff, *Pink Samurai: Love, Marriage and Sex in Contemporary Japan,* Ch. 7, pp. 124–26, Pocket Books, 1991.
7. In reality, humans would have inherited many if not most of the mechanisms of aging from species lower in the evolutionary chain.
8. Dawkins, *Selfish Gene,* Ch. 9.
9. Tedesco et al., "Cloning a Gene for Life Extension in *Caenorhabditis elegans,*" p. 3, in Finch & Johnson (eds.), *Molecular Biology of Aging,* Wiley-Liss, 1989.
10. Virginia Morell, "A New Bestiary for Aging Research," *Science,* Vol. 250, p. 622, 2 Nov. 1990, describes the long-lived opossum strain.
11. Alex Comfort, *The Biology of Senescence,* Elsevier, 3d ed., 1979, is a reasonably accessible survey of the biology of aging.
12. A correlation between two phenomena, X and Y, does not indicate whether Y is a cause or a consequence of X (or they are both a result of Z). Fire engines and police cars are commonly observed at fires, but neither is a cause of fires or of each other. Thus, changes observed to occur with aging may be causes or symptoms of aging, or symptoms of other, unidentified causes.
13. See J. Meites, "Neuroendocrine Biomarkers of Aging in the Rat," *Experimental Gerontology,* 1988, p. 349 (reproductive decline, increased tumors, and decrease in growth hormone secretion due to decline in norepinephrine and dopamine secretion caused by deterioration of the hypothalamus; temporarily reversed by drugs stimulating hypothalamic activity).
14. See Everitt & Meites, "Aging and Anti-aging Effects of Hormones," *Journal of Gerontology,* Nov. 1989, p. B139.

15. Henry Claman, "The Biology of the Immune Response," in *Journal of American Medical Association*, Nov. 27, 1987, Vol. 258, p. 2834, provides an excellent overview of the human immune system. Richard Miller, "The Cell Biology of Aging: Immunological Models," *Journal of Gerontology*, 1989, Vol. 44, p. B4, and Makinodan et al., "Cellular, Biochemical, and Molecular Basis of T-Cell Senescence," *Archives of Pathology and Laboratory Medicine*, Oct. 1987, p. 910, summarize the effects of aging on immune functions.

16. Ann Gibbons, "Gerontology Research Comes of Age," *Science*, Vol. 250, p. 622, 2 Nov. 1990.

17. Even if the decline in immune system response is shown to be a symptom rather than a cause of aging, it will require attention in any effort to extend the human life span. A maximum life span of 140 years in people whose immune systems had essentially failed by age ninety would be largely theoretical.

18. Roy Walford, *The Immunologic Theory of Aging*, Williams & Wilkins, 1969, is an early statement of this theory.

19. Irun Cohen, "The Self, the World and Autoimmunity," *Scientific American*, Apr. 1988, p. 52, explains several aspects of autoimmune diseases.

20. Rose, *Evolutionary Biology of Aging*, pp. 129–32 and Fig. 7.3.

21. See, for example, Danner & Holbrook, "Alterations in Gene Expression with Aging," in Schneider & Rowe (eds.), *Handbook of the Biology of Aging*, Ch. 6, 3d ed., Academic Press, 1990.

22. Gerald Feinberg, *Solid Clues: Quantum Physics, Molecular Biology, and the Future of Science*, Ch. 4, p. 129, Simon & Schuster, 1985.

23. Rose, *Evolutionary Biology of Aging*, Ch. 7, p. 134.

24. Free radical biology is surveyed briefly in Janet Glover, "Free Radical Biology: A Paradox in Cancer Research," *J. Nat'l Cancer Inst.*, 1990, p. 902. Sun & Sun, "Dietary Antioxidants, Membrane Lipids, and Aging," in Armbrecht et al. (eds.), *Nutritional Intervention in the Aging Process*, Springer-Verlag, 1984, Ch. 9, describes the reactions of free radicals with the compounds that form cell membranes. The body itself uses the reactivity of free radicals as part of its immune system. White blood cells, for example, employ free radicals to destroy some pathogens. There is also evidence that free radicals mediate the action of tumor necrosis factor on malignancies. See Glover, "Free Radical Biology."

25. Davies et al., "Repair Systems in Oxidative Stress," p. 123, in Finch & Johnson (eds.), *Molecular Biology of Aging*, reviews the cellular mechanisms for repairing free radical damage.

26. Denham Harman, "The Aging Process," *Proc. Nat'l Acad. Sci.*, Nov. 1981, Vol. 78, p. 7124, summarizes the free radical theory of aging. Articles pertinent to the subject are collected in Armstrong et al. (eds.), *Free Radicals in Molecular Biology, Aging, and Disease*, Raven Press, 1984.

27. Mackay et al., "Genetic and Molecular Analysis of Antioxidant Enzymes in *Drosophila* etc.," p. 157, in Finch & Johnson (eds.), *Molecular Biology of Aging*.

28. Two other theories of aging have also been widely discussed. The DNA repair deficit theory posits that minor DNA damage accumulates over time, an accumulation that accelerates in later years. The theory that this deterioration is a central

298   cause of aging was supported by a widely reported correlation between the maximum life span of a species and its rate of DNA repair. See, for example, Christian de Duve, _A Guided Tour of the Living Cell,_ Vol. 2, Ch. 17, p. 333, Scientific American Books, 1984. Subsequent studies have raised serious questions about the strength and significance of this correlation. See Hanawalt et al., "DNA Repair in Differentiating Cells in Relation to Aging," in Finch & Johnson (eds.), _Molecular Biology of Aging,_ p. 45. Deterioration of the function of particular tissues because of cumulative DNA damage remains a distinct possibility and is being actively investigated.

    Another widely investigated phenomenon of aging is collagen cross-linking. The connective tissues of the body consist primarily of collagen. Studies clearly show that this collagen becomes less flexible with age due to cross-linking between fibers. Whether this change contributes to the important declines in function associated with old age is not clear.

29. See C.B. Olson, "A Review of How and Why We Age: A Defense of Multifactorial Aging," _Mechanisms of Ageing and Dev.,_ Nov. 1987, p. 1.

30. Richard Cutler, "Life-Span Extension," Chapter 3 in McGaugh & Kiesler, _Aging: Biology and Behavior,_ Academic Press, 1981, surveys the theories and prospects of extending the life span. Research has, however, advanced considerably in the intervening years. _FDA Consumer,_ Oct. 1988, p. 20, surveys some aging theories and the status of ongoing research.

31. _Wall Street Journal,_ Apr. 22, 1992, p. A9.

32. Gerontology researchers naturally express the view that their field is chronically underfunded. See, for example, Rose, _Evolutionary Biology of Aging,_ Ch. 8, p. 176.

33. Weindruch & Walford, _The Retardation of Aging and Disease by Dietary Restriction,_ Charles C. Thomas, 1988, surveys the extensive literature on dietary restriction longevity studies. It is the basis for the ensuing discussion in the text except as otherwise noted.

34. Weraarchakul et al., "The Effect of Aging and Dietary Restriction on DNA Repair," _Experimental Cell Research,_ Mar. 1989, p. 197. Earlier studies are surveyed in Weindruch & Walford, _Retardation of Aging and Disease by Dietary Restriction,_ Ch. 5, pp. 270–72.

35. Rao et al., "Effect of Dietary Restriction on the Age-Dependent Changes in the Expression of Antioxidant Enzymes in Rat Liver," _Journal of Nutrition,_ June 1990, p. 602 (higher expression of free radical scavengers in dietary-restricted rats, apparently because of change in messenger RNA levels); Yu et al., "Mechanism of Food Restriction: Protection of Cellular Homeostasis," _Proceedings of the Society for Experimental Biology & Medicine Proceedings,_ Jan. 1990, p. 13 (protection of cellular membranes). Weindruch & Walford, _Retardation of Aging and Disease by Dietary Restriction,_ Ch. 5, pp. 256–60, surveys earlier studies.

36. See, for example, Fernandes et al., "Modulation of Gene Expression in Autoimmune Disease and Aging by Food Restriction and Dietary Lipids," _Proc. Soc. Exp. Biol. Med.,_ Jan. 1990, p. 16 (rats); Ogura et al., "Undernutrition Without Malnutrition Restricts the Numbers and Proportions of Ly-1 B Lymphocytes in

Autoimmune Mice," *Proc. Soc. Exp. Biol. Med.,* Jan. 1990, p. 6; Weindruch & Walford, *Retardation of Aging and Disease by Dietary Restriction,* Ch. 5, pp. 282–85.

37. Ogura et al., "Decrease by Chronic Energy Intake Restriction of Cellular Proliferation in the Intestinal Epithelium and Lymphoid Organs in Autoimmune-prone Mice," *Proceedings of the National Academy of Science,* Aug. 1989, Vol. 86, p. 5918.

38. Cerami et al., "Glucose and Aging," *Scientific American,* May 1987, p. 90.

39. See, for example, Edward Masoro, "Dietary Restriction and Metabolism and Disease," in Armbrecht et al. (eds.), *Nutritional Intervention in the Aging Process,* Ch. 6.

40. Duffy et al., "Effect of Chronic Caloric Restrictions on Physiological Variables Related to Energy Metabolism in the Male Fischer 344 Rat," *Mechanisms of Ageing and Development,* May 1989, p. 117 (average body temperature significantly lower in dietary restricted rats); Cheney et al., "The Effect of Dietary Restriction of Varying Duration on Survival, Tumor Patterns, Immune Function, and Body Temperature in B10C3F1 Female Mice," *J. Gerontology,* July 1983, p. 420. But see Volicer et al., "Effect of Dietary Restriction and Stress on Body Temperature in Rats," *Journal of Gerontology,* 1984, Vol. 39, p. 178, finding no significant effect of undernutrition on average body temperature.

41. The evolutionary reasons for undernutrition to extend the life span are more compelling with short-lived species. A rat has a reproductive life span of only about two years. A female rat (like other mammals) will not reproduce if her body fat is too low, as would occur during a food shortage. Rats that responded to a food shortage (that is, naturally occurring undernutrition) with an extended life span would therefore enjoy a distinct evolutionary advantage. See R. Holliday, "Food, Reproduction and Longevity: Is the Extended Lifespan of Calorie-Restricted Animals an Evolutionary Adaptation?" *Bioessays,* Apr. 1989, p. 125. The same consideration would apply far less strongly to species with lengthy reproductive spans. But, of course, medical researchers routinely overlook even greater differences between species in extrapolating the effects of food additives, drugs, and pesticides from animals to people.

42. *New York Times,* Apr. 17, 1990, Sec. C., p. 1, surveys recent dietary restriction studies.

43. Undernutrition prior to adulthood stunts growth and otherwise delays or alters development. Women too low in fat content are infertile. Dietary-restricted laboratory animals have proved susceptible to cold stress. See Weindruch & Walford, *Retardation of Aging and Disease by Dietary Restriction,* Ch. 6, pp. 323–26.

44. "Any method [for increasing] human longevity is unacceptable if it affects, even minimally, the enjoyment of life." Hayflick, "Prospects for Increasing Longevity," in Johnston (ed.), *Perspectives on Aging,* Ch. 2, p. 40.

45. Rose, *Evolutionary Biology of Aging,* Ch. 7, p. 179.

46. Rose et al., "Genetics of Longer-Lived *Drosophila,*" in Finch & Johnson (eds.), *Molecular Biology of Aging,* p. 19.

300   47. Rose, *Evolutionary Biology of Aging,* Ch. 8, describes the strategy for achieving longevity through selection.

48. Rose et al., "Genetics of Longer-Lived *Drosophila,*" in Finch & Johnson (eds.), *Molecular Biology of Aging,* pp. 20–21. To similar effect is Rose, *Evolutionary Biology of Aging,* Ch. 8, p. 185.

49. Roy Walford, *Maximum Life Span,* Ch. 6, W.W. Norton, 1983, describes the experiment with annual fish. The temperature-reduced fish showed less collagen cross-linking than those maintained in warmer waters, indicating that the fundamental aging processes were slowed.

50. Rosenberg et al., "The Kinetics and Thermodynamics of Death in Multicellular Organisms," *Mechanisms of Ageing and Development,* Oct.–Nov. 1973, p. 275.

51. Faustman et al., "Linkage of Faulty Major Histocompatibility Complex Class I to Autoimmune Diabetes," *Science,* Vol. 254, p. 1756, 20 Dec. 1991.

52. Walford et al., "The Main Histocompatibility Complex, DNA Repair Capacity, and Aging," in Segre & Smith (eds.), *Immunological Aspects of Aging,* p. 235, Marcel Dekker, 1981.

53. Roy Walford, "The Major Histocompatibility Complex and Aging in Mammals," in Finch & Johnson (eds.), *Molecular Biology of Aging,* p. 31.

54. Okinawan nonagenarians and centenarians display a high level of expression of MHC region genes associated with immune response and a low level of expression of genes associated with autoimmunity. Takata et al., "Influence of Major Histocompatibility Complex Region Genes on Human Longevity," *Lancet,* 10 October 1987, p. 824. This correlation may, however, reflect a lower incidence of death at earlier ages because of superior immunity to disease, rather than any extension of the maximum life span.

55. See, for example, Rose, *Evolutionary Biology of Aging,* Ch. 8, p. 178; and Walford, "The Major Histocompatibility Complex and Aging in Mammals," in Finch & Johnson (eds.), *Molecular Biology of Aging,* p. 31 (splicing MHC region genes from long-lived deer mouse into shorter-lived ordinary mouse).

56. Feinberg, *Solid Clues,* Ch. 4, p. 129.

57. See, e.g., Mackay et al., "Genetic and Molecular Analysis of Antioxidant Enzymes in Drosophila etc.," in Finch & Johnson (eds.), *Molecular Biology of Aging,* p. 157.

58. Rose, *Evolutionary Biology of Aging,* Ch. 7, pp. 154–55.

59. Rose, *Evolutionary Biology of Aging,* pp. vii, ix.

60. This discussion assumes, in accordance with the stated goals of longevity researchers, that the life span would be increased primarily by extending the middle years, not by prolonging survival of the elderly. Discussion of several social and ethical issues relating to life extension is reserved for Chapter 13.

61. Nearly one quarter of Japan's population is expected to be over the age of sixty-five by 2020, a significantly higher percentage than in either the United States or Germany. See Bill Emmott, *The Sun Also Sets: The Limits to Japan's Economic Power,* Ch. 4, Simon & Schuster, 1989.

62. See Strauss & Howe, *Generations: The History of America's Future 1584 to*

2069, pp. 402, 517, William Morrow, 1991 (citing sources projecting a 30 percent payroll tax to support legislated benefit levels). The demographic trends in Germany and Japan portend increases even greater than in the United States. See *Economist,* 20–26 June 1992, p. 20, citing OECD estimates.
63. Laurence Kotlikoff, "Some Economic Implications of Life-Span Extension," Ch. 5, p. 114, in McGaugh & Kiesler (eds.), *Aging: Biology and Behavior.*
64. Walford, *Maximum Life Span,* xi.

Chapter Twelve

KNOWLEDGE FROM AFAR

Those who cannot foresee the future are condemned to live it. People had to endure generations of poverty and hardship because they could not anticipate such discoveries as fertilizers, antibiotics, vaccines, electricity, steel, plastics, automobiles, airplanes, telephones, and computers. A preview of the nineteenth century would have averted or mitigated the rigors of early industrialism, environmental damage, and other unforeseen consequences of progress. Foresight could have exposed the fallacies of a thousand social experiments without using people as test subjects and avoided the mammoth twentieth-century blights of fascism and communism. And how many of the momentous and vexing scientific questions of the nineteenth century remain unanswered today?

People must continue to grope their way through a shrouded future, unless perchance that future is some other planet's past. Hence the search for extraterrestrial intelligence (SETI).

ARE WE ALONE?

SETI obviously differs from the other areas discussed in this part, because it may be doomed to failure before it even begins. Whether intelligent extraterrestrials exist has been much debated among astronomers and biologists, with no consensus in sight. (The Appendix provides a more detailed treatment of that debate.)

The argument in favor of their existence begins (and essentially ends) with the vast number of possibilities. The Milky Way contains approximately 400 billion stars. One of those, the Sun, has nine planets with several dozen natural satellites. Current theories suggest that planets often form around stars.[1] Wobbles in the paths of some nearby stars, disks of gas and dust visible around a few stars, and other astronomical observations tend to confirm this hypothesis.[2] Within this solar system, Earth is obviously suitable for life, Venus and Mars appear to have been near misses, and some of the moons of Saturn and Jupiter present farfetched possibilities. Bacteria appeared very soon after the Earth cooled, suggesting that life is not improbable given the correct conditions, even though scientists have searched in vain for the mechanism.[3] Intelligence would then evolve automatically, because it would enhance the chances of survival in any mobile animal. In a galaxy with billions and billions of planets (to quote one of SETI's best-known advocates), how could Earth be the only one on which intelligent life has evolved?

Skeptics are at no loss for an answer to that question.[4] The center of the Milky Way contains a large portion of its stars, but radiation levels there are almost surely too high for life to evolve. Stars that are much hotter than the Sun burn out too quickly, while those that are much cooler provide too little energy to support life. First-generation stars lack the heavy elements needed for organic compounds. Binary star systems, which are very common, may not produce planets or retain them in stable, life-sustaining orbits. Planets that are either too close or too distant from even a suitable star will lack water in its liquid state, widely assumed to be essential for life. The narrowness of this habitable zone excludes most planets from consideration.[5] Planets within that zone must be large enough to develop and retain an atmosphere. A planet that does not spin, or that spins on an axis that points toward its star, would have permanent torrid and frigid zones over most of its surface. Planets without a large moon would have no tides, which figured prominently in life's emergence from the oceans on Earth. Thus, the number of planets suitable for the evolution of advanced life could be small, even vanishingly so. The fortunate circumstances enjoyed by Earth do not prove the contrary, as generalizations cannot be drawn from a single example.

Skeptics particularly attack the assumption that intelligence is likely to evolve once life appears. The evolutionary path between the first

304   single-celled organisms and people passed through countless species of increasing complexity. The creation of a new species (unlike the incremental improvement of an existing species) is a puzzling and comparatively rare event that almost certainly requires a coincidence of biological and environmental factors (the opening of an ecological niche as a mutation fitting that niche appears, for example). Too constant an environment would create too few niches; overly frequent or radical changes would prevent a new and complex organism from becoming established. Intelligence would provide little or no evolutionary advantage at many of these branches, and a large brain imposes biological costs on an organism. On this line of reasoning, the appearance of a thinking species at the tip of an evolutionary branch seems incredibly unlikely. Earth's history supports this view. Life appeared very quickly, but animals with even a modicum of intelligence did not emerge for billions of years. The reptiles that ruled the planet for tens of millions of years (ample time for intelligence to have evolved) remained decidedly stupid. The immediate ancestors of man made their debut only within the last few hundred thousand years. This long delay suggests that intelligence would be anything but routine even on life-bearing planets.

Evolutionary biologists have formed a virtual consensus in support of this argument.[6] Nevertheless, it is hardly compelling. The evolution of multicellular organisms may have been delayed on Earth compared to typical life-bearing planets. Earth may have been too steady, gentle, and salubrious to force the earlier or more frequent appearance of intelligent life. Or simple bad luck may have retarded the "normal" evolutionary progress: some fossil evidence suggests that higher intelligence began to evolve much earlier in Earth's history, only to be squelched by the mass extinction that marked the end of the Cretaceous Period. Human intelligence is admittedly puzzling from an evolutionary perspective, but no more so than eyes, mammalian ears, various adaptations of cetaceans, and many other widely distributed attributes.[7] In short, generalizing on the experience of one planet is no more reliable for SETI skeptics than it is for SETI advocates.

The other argument commonly raised against the existence of extraterrestrial intelligence is the so-called Fermi question: "Where are they?"[8] The Milky Way is about 100,000 light-years across. At a fairly modest speed of three hundred kilometers per second (a speed reached by accelerating steadily at one G for eight and a half hours), one expansionist civilization beginning at the very edge could colonize the entire galaxy within 100 million years. If, as SETI advocates contend, thousands or millions of technological civilizations have existed in the galaxy for at least ten billion years, one or more of them would surely have settled on every habitable planet. That obviously has not happened on Earth, nor does the fragmentary evidence from radio astronomy suggest a galaxy swarming with colonies and space-ships. Hence, the premise that technological civilization is a common occurrence in the galaxy must be false: Earth must be either unique or very nearly so in producing intelligent life.

The fragile link in this argument is the assumed feasibility of interstellar travel.[9] The reasons for believing that beings would almost never leave their home systems are fairly persuasive.[10] Suitable stars would not often be located nearer than ten light-years. At one tenth of the speed of light, an unattainable velocity using any current human technology, the transit time would be one hundred years. This negates any analogy to the Polynesians or other bold colonizers from Earth history, none of whom embarked with the expectation of spending a lifetime en route. The energy expenditure to accelerate a colonizing vessel to that speed, even assuming technologies that are 100 percent efficient, would be hundreds of times the current annual energy usage on Earth.[11] (Above one tenth of the speed of light, relativistic effects would raise the energy requirements even more sharply.) This assumes that it is possible to determine whether an uninhabited planet orbiting another star is habitable. If not, a civilization intent on colonization would be required (1) to send robot ships to investigate, with a time delay of not less than 110 years (one hundred years for the trip plus ten for a signal to return) and an energy investment nearly equal to that required for the voyage itself, or (2) to prepare colonizing voyages for the prospect of two or even three interstellar crossings. However advanced the technology of the home planet, this implies a fantastic commitment of resources to a project with no prospect of a return. It would seem that nothing less than the impending demise of the home planet would justify such a journey. If that conclusion is correct, it answers the Fermi question.

The arguments for and against the existence of other intelligent

306 beings thus amount to little more than dueling guesses, an assessment not belied but confirmed by the vigor with which the opposing camps espouse those arguments. ("[N]othing is so firmly believed as what we least know.")[12] But the means are now at hand to move the question from the realm of speculation to that of experiment.

FOOTPRINTS ON THE COSMOS

Although any life on other planets would be noteworthy, only technological civilizations offer the prospect of enlarging human knowledge. This is a happy coincidence, because technology leaves tracks. Some of these, like the use of metals or synthetic fertilizers, may not occur in all civilizations, or may be apparent only on the planet's surface. But others seem likely to be both universal and detectable over interstellar distances.

Radio waves are the most promising of these footprints. (For these purposes, "radio" refers to a very broad range of the electromagnetic spectrum, including, for example, commercial radio and television, microwave, radar, and satellite transmission frequencies.) People discovered radio very shortly after the industrial era began, and it remains the principal means of broadcast communication because of its inherent efficiency. Radio waves transmit information to many receivers over great distances almost instantaneously with little energy expenditure or capital investment. They are essentially the only means of communication with aircraft or spacecraft.[13] Thus, any technologically advanced civilization would be unlikely to forgo their use, whatever additional means of communication it had devised. And the senders of these signals specifically intend them to be detectable very far away. They may therefore serve to mark planets that are homes to intelligent life even over interstellar distances.

The tools for this search are already available in the form of radio telescopes. (A radio telescope is simply an antenna writ large, with precise tuning, aiming, and focusing mechanisms to bring in weak signals.) In principle, searchers could simply scan the entire sky to detect any (or every) radio transmitter in the galaxy. In practice, this would be an undertaking of nightmarish proportions. The universe is full of natural radio sources, including stars, pulsars, quasars, black holes, and other galaxies. These are, of course, grist for the radio astronomer's mill. For SETI, they are static (or "noise"). As on Earth, picking the signal out of the static means increasing the gain of the antenna, that is, narrowing its directional focus and frequency range (and, in the case of SETI, lengthening the observational period). But each of these measures multiplies the number of observations needed for complete spatial and frequency coverage. (The Appendix discusses the trade-offs in more detail.) Their compound effect precludes even the possibility of a comprehensive search, which would consume all the radio telescopes on Earth for centuries to come.

SETI researchers address this difficulty by devising selective search strategies, each predicated on some hypothesis about how extraterrestrial intelligence is most likely to be detected. One approach is to limit the search to certain "magic" frequencies. The rationale for this strategy is that advanced civilizations would actively attempt to signal their presence to others and, toward that end, would transmit beacons on frequencies selected for their universal significance. The Megachannel Extraterrestrial Assay (META) conducted by Paul Horowitz at Harvard is the most ambitious example of this strategy undertaken to date. This project uses advanced receiver technology (purchased with a donation from Steven Spielberg out of his *ET* proceeds) to scan the entire sky on 8.4 million narrow-frequency channels clustered tightly around the natural emission frequency of hydrogen, which any civilization that had advanced to radio astronomy would know.[14] Other searches have covered other frequencies or a broader band at lower sensitivity or searched only selected portions of the sky.

META and other SETI searches to date have covered only a minuscule fraction of 1 percent of the complete search space.[15] These searches have resulted in a few exciting false alarms and a number of anomalous and still unexplained signals, but nothing approaching proof that intelligent life exists elsewhere. These negative results are too fragmentary to establish anything.[16] SETI advocates naturally urge a much greater commitment of resources and time. The NASA SETI project (which began, after many delays, in October 1992) is a start in this direction.[17] One portion of that project will survey the entire sky with relatively low sensitivity, while the other targets 773

308 sunlike stars located within eighty light-years of Earth with narrower search channels. Each prong of the search covers a total frequency range thousands of times broader than the META project. The NASA project is entirely automated, with specially designed chips scanning the data as it is received and recording any anomalous readings for more detailed analysis and, if appropriate, further observation. The project is expected to continue for about ten years, during which time it will have explored many times the possibilities of all previous SETI efforts combined, but still only a tiny fraction of the total search space. Searches can thus be expected to continue for many decades.

The unavoidable weakness of such strategies is that they require the accurate prediction of alien behavior. There is no shortage of possible "magic frequencies." An alien civilization could choose its broadcast frequency for the lowest level of background noise, or the least atmospheric absorption, or ease of high-power transmission, or some other criterion that no human has guessed. The NASA search seeks to avoid this difficulty by covering a broader frequency range, but the sensitivity of that search still assumes that an alien civilization has built and maintained a powerful space beacon to signal its presence to other civilizations. The motivation for such an effort is plausible, but hardly compelling, and the resource commitment would be formidable. Outside a radius of fifty light-years, aliens would have almost no means of knowing that intelligent life has evolved on Earth. They would therefore reach Earth only with an omnidirectional beacon, which, if designed to cover an appreciable portion of the galaxy, would consume enormous amounts of power for a very long time.[18] Even if initiated, the undertaking could fall prey to boredom within a few hundred years, the merest blink on a cosmic time scale. Current SETI strategies could thus easily miss advanced civilizations of the greatest practical interest. As just the most obvious illustration, Earth itself does not operate a space beacon. The NASA search would therefore miss an exact twin of Earth orbiting Alpha Centauri, just four light-years away.

Given the demonstrated difficulty of understanding even human conduct, strategies based on accurate predictions of alien behavior inspire slight confidence. This suggests another search strategy, defined instead by the potential to benefit from the discovery of an alien civilization.

SETI projects, past and present, reflect their proponents' relatively pure scientific motivations. The question they seek to answer is whether intelligent life exists elsewhere in the universe. Even limiting the search to technological civilizations within the Milky Way is a grudging concession to intractable practical considerations; if new search technology could detect extraterrestrial pond scum from half-way across the universe, the proposed strategies would expand accordingly. As long as investigators frame the question in this way, SETI will reside comfortably in the pantheon of Big Science, where answers are always decades and many billions of dollars in the future. (The discovery of life on one other planet would not, of course, end SETI projects. On the contrary, it would confirm the value of further searching.) But the potential tangible payoff from SETI—the possibility of tapping another civilization's collective intellectual achievements—can be explored much faster and at a fraction of the expense.

The Milky Way is a flat disk approximately 100,000 light-years in diameter. The Sun is on one of the spiral arms radiating out from the center of that disk, about 35,000 light-years from the center. A star located only a few hundred light-years distant is thus in the immediate neighborhood, galactically speaking. For practical purposes, however, intelligent beings on a planet orbiting such a star could as well be in another galaxy across the universe. Life here would be unknown to them, as Marconi's first transmissions would have traveled only a fraction of the distance between the planets (even if such a weak signal were detectable at such a range). If a search detected these beings, Earth could promptly build a directional antenna to beam a strong signal at them. Their first response could not arrive before the twenty-sixth century.[19] The people receiving that response would have no more (and probably much less) in common with those who initiated the dialogue than people of the present have with those from the Middle Ages. Very few questions or issues last more than a few generations, and people of one century rarely know enough even to ask the questions that will occupy those of the next. Social concerns like pollution, overpopulation, and drug use had barely broached the public consciousness as recently as the nineteenth century. Genetic engineering, medically enhanced brains, and the like will add a new

310 dimension to change, as people will soon begin to change not only culturally but also biologically. It is almost impossible to conceive of a meaningful conversation in which at least one of the parties metamorphoses completely in the time it takes to communicate. (Such mundane considerations have not noticeably deterred SETI enthusiasts. They beamed the first message intended for aliens in the direction of a star cluster located 25,000 light-years from the Sun. The 50,000-year round-trip signal time would about equal the duration of man on Earth to date.)

This one consideration defines the initial search: investigate only those stars located within thirty light-years of the Sun.[20] Within that radius, aliens could be aware of life on Earth from the reception of radar or television signal leakage. If so, they may already have directed a signal beacon toward Earth or may at least be observing Earth for signs of deliberate communication. Most important, their messages would, when received, be based on information concerning this civilization that would be no more than sixty years old. Some useful communication may be possible with delays of less than two generations between message and response.[21]

This restriction also simplifies the search considerably. Only about fifty reasonably promising stars lie within the sphere thirty light-years in radius centered on the Sun.[22] With so few targets, a meticulous search is quite feasible. Radio astronomers could devote hundreds of hours to observing each star, covering the entire spectrum with the narrowest possible search channels and the tightest possible focus. This approach eliminates the need to guess a magic frequency and greatly increases the sensitivity of the search. Readily feasible technology would detect not only beacons, but also reasonably strong signal leakage (comparable to a television carrier wave, satellite communications, or military radar) from planets located this close to Earth. This strategy thus offers the prospect of finding alien civilizations that, like Earth, are not expending vast resources to announce their presence to the galaxy at large.

The proximity of these stars also brings other search options into play. Astronomers using space-based telescopes may be able to directly observe planets within a few dozen light-years. This may allow spectral analyses of their atmospheres. Molecular oxygen would be a telltale sign that at least plant life had evolved, because it is too reactive to persist without being replenished by biological processes

like photosynthesis.[23] Infrared photographs of Earth suggest another
possibility: waste heat from industry, power generation, transportation, and other technology creates visible hot spots around cities. A
more highly developed technology could produce an even brighter
and more distinctive infrared signature, which infrared sensors in
space may be able to detect around nearby stars.[24]

Neighboring stars thus offer both the best chance of detecting
other intelligent beings and the only possibility of exploiting their
intelligence and accumulated knowledge.[25] Limited in this manner, a
fairly exhaustive search could be completed within a decade. A negative result would say little about the existence of other life in the
galaxy, but it would establish that future progress on this planet will
receive no external assistance.[26] A positive result, on the other hand,
would open the prospect of interstellar dialogue.

ET: PHONE EARTH

Detection should not be confused with communication. The long
journey across space would weaken and distort any leaked alien signal
beyond any hope of recovering the content, a fact that should exor-
cise the recurring nightmare that *Three Stooges* broadcasts will shape
aliens' first impressions of Earth. Detection would therefore be followed by signaling with narrowly focused beams sent by more powerful versions of the antennas used to communicate with *Voyager*.

The decision to talk as well as listen would surely provoke a debate
on Earth, with opponents arguing that the aliens could choose to
interfere or even attack if man's presence became known. But the
principal purpose of finding some other civilization is the chance of
communicating with it. Popular science fiction to the contrary notwithstanding, the incremental risk of revealing man's existence would
be exceedingly slight. A civilization sufficiently advanced and powerful to project force across interstellar distances (no small undertaking)
would also likely be capable of detecting Earth's signal leakage and
would, therefore, be aware of life on Earth long before a purposeful
beacon arrived. Such a civilization would, in any event, have little to
gain from exploiting a planet as comparatively backward as this one,
which is barely able to mount a peaceful assault on its own satellite.

Even a strong and deliberate alien signal would be meaningless until scientists and cryptographers deciphered its coding and translated the language. The probable lack of commonality between the cultures would complicate these tasks. On the other hand, an alien seeking to communicate with another civilization would surely make the signal as easy to decipher as possible. Universal physical constants, abstract mathematical concepts, and a video dictionary would provide an initial basis for communication, which would lay the foundation for learning the alien language.[27]

The useful portion of any such communications would almost certainly be scientific and technological. SETI advocates' frequent suggestions that alien intelligence may provide the keys to eliminating violence, preventing nuclear or biological warfare, protecting the environment, and avoiding overpopulation reflect more enthusiasm and faith than thought. The causes of such problems are embedded in human evolution and history. Alien civilizations may have faced very different problems or addressed even similar problems in ways that have no applicability on Earth. Nor would alien culture (in whatever form it could take) be likely to find an appreciative audience here. Mere differences in historical development create deep cultural divisions. When Japan and the West met for the first time in the late sixteenth and early seventeenth centuries, for example, each marveled at the uncivilized barbarity of the other. The Japanese found the music, art, food, religion, language, and cultural mores of the Dutch and Portuguese either incomprehensible or intensely distasteful, and the Western explorers regarded the Japanese as subhuman. The far more fundamental and less malleable differences of biology and evolutionary history would surely leave aliens and humans little if any common aesthetic ground. Thus, contrary to oft-repeated suggestions, Bach or Mozart may be less than ideal content for the first interstellar messages.

Science and technology are inherently less provincial.[28] Every imaginable civilization would have certain needs in common, such as food, energy, materials with various properties, transportation, and communication. The elements, forces, and physical laws that provide the ultimate framework for addressing those needs are the same everywhere. And aliens would almost certainly formulate their scientific knowledge numerically and mathematically.[29] This commonality of means, ends, and "language" seems likely to provide a basis for useful communication. Of course, if alien intelligence or technology were far more advanced, much of the information received would initially be incomprehensible, but investigators would simply record and store it for later decipherment. The task would be analogous to archaeology, an exploration of the remnants of some future civilization, with scientists and engineers serving as the principal explorers.

The technologies that aliens may have mastered are diverse beyond imagination. Possibilities in traditional fields include matter-antimatter reactors, ion propulsion, and nanoscale engineering.[30] In basic science, aliens may long since have unified gravity with the other forces of nature and discovered gravitons and the "missing" quarks and bosons. Aliens may also have answered scientific questions or solved technological problems that humans will not ask or confront for generations. But the greatest potential lies in the new realms of progress. A more advanced civilization would almost certainly have developed artificial intelligence in one or more forms. (Indeed, it would not be surprising for the first alien communicant with Earth to be nonliving, given the numbing boredom of monitoring radio astronomy data for signs of an artificial signal.) Genetic or life span information may not be useful because of fundamental differences in aliens' biology (although some degree of convergence is not impossible), but their technology or approach could nevertheless be adaptable. What aliens would almost surely offer would be another form of living intelligence, naturally occurring or enhanced, with different and probably greater strengths than the human intellect. Whether through long-distance communication or replication of that intelligence on Earth, that discovery would radically alter both the scope of human abilities and the nature of the human experience.

None of this is certain or even probable. The nearby planets may be altogether lifeless or inhabited only by bacteria. But this would be a poor excuse for not looking. "The probability of success is difficult to estimate; but if we never search, the chance of success is zero."[31] The potential rewards are simply too great to ignore.

1. Astronomers believe that each star begins as a spinning gas cloud. Gravity draws in the top and bottom of the cloud, but the spinning motion holds gas located near the "equator" against the gravitational force. The planets then coalesce from this material.

2. See Bruce Campbell, "A Place to Live: Looking for Extrasolar Planets," Ch. 3, p. 97, in Bova & Preiss (eds.), *First Contact: The Search for Extraterrestrial Intelligence,* NAL Books, 1990; and Stephen Maran, "Stalking the Extrasolar Planet," *Natural History,* May 1989, p. 70. One of the stars showing indications of surrounding planets is Epsilon Eridani, a K-class star (slightly cooler than the sun) only eleven light-years distant.

3. Laboratory simulations of the prebiotic environment on Earth have produced amino acids and (with more difficulty) nucleic acids. The presence of organic chemicals on comets and other planets further suggests that the chemical precursors of life are quite commonplace. The step from such chemicals to primitive metabolism or replication is, however, long and uncertain. See Richard Dickerson, "Chemical Evolution and the Origin of Life," *Scientific American,* Sept. 1978, p. 70, and John Casti, *Paradigms Lost: Images of Man in the Mirror of Science,* Ch. 2, William Morrow, 1989.

4. Rood & Trefil, *Are We Alone? The Possibility of Extraterrestrial Civilizations,* Chs. 1–8, Charles Scribner's Sons, 1981, presents the skeptics' argument in some detail.

5. Kasting et al., "How Climate Evolved on the Terrestrial Planets," *Scientific American,* Feb. 1988, p. 90, describes the role of distance from the sun in defining a planet's climate and the concept of the continuously habitable zone surrounding a star.

6. See Dale Russell, "Speculations on the Evolution of Intelligence in Multicellular Organisms," in Billingham (ed.), *Life in the Universe,* MIT Press, 1981, p. 259; Ernst Mayr, "The Probability of Extraterrestrial Intelligent Life," in Regis (ed.), *Extraterrestrials: Science and Alien Intelligence,* Cambridge Univ. Press, 1985, p. 23.

7. See Francis Hitching, *The Neck of the Giraffe: Darwin, Evolution, and the New Biology,* Ch. 4, Ticknor & Fields, 1982.

8. The Nobel-prize-winning physicist Enrico Fermi is said to have posed this

question while working on the Manhattan Project. See Finney & Jones (eds.), *Interstellar Migration and the Human Experience*, pp. 298–300, Univ. of Cal. Press, 1985. The Fermi question is addressed from various perspectives in Hart & Zuckerman (eds.), *Extraterrestrials: Where Are They?* Pergamon Press, 1982, and Rood & Trefil, *Are We Alone?* Chs. 12–14. A later refinement of the same argument is that technologically advanced cultures would have launched self-replicating robots (sometimes called von Neumann machines) to explore other worlds and report back. See Frank Tipler, "Extraterrestrial Intelligent Beings Do Not Exist," *Quarterly Journal of the Royal Astronomical Society*, Vol. 21, pp. 267–81, 1980. Most of the arguments against interstellar travel would apply equally to this variation.

9. Interestingly, many SETI advocates address the Fermi question on grounds other than the enormous difficulties inherent in interstellar travel, apparently because they favor programs directed toward developing the capability of long-distance space travel and do not wish to question its feasibility.

10. "[S]pace travel, even in the most distant future, will be confined completely to our own planetary system, and a similar conclusion will hold for any other civilization, no matter how advanced it may be." Sebastian von Hoerner, "The General Limits of Space Travel," Ch. 37, at p. 204, in Donald Goldsmith (ed.), *The Quest for Extraterrestrial Life: A Book of Readings*, Univ. Science Books, 1980.

11. See, for example, Gregg Easterbrook, "Are We Alone: The Search for Extraterrestrial Life," *Atlantic Monthly*, Aug. 1988, p. 25. This lengthy feature article surveys many of the issues concerning the possibility of extraterrestrial life. Casti, *Paradigms Lost*, p. 391, estimates that the amount of energy required to send a single passenger to a nearby star would equal that consumed by the United States for several hundred years.

12. Montaigne, *Essays*, Book 1, Ch. 31.

13. Streams of charged particles could theoretically substitute for radio waves, but magnetic and electric fields would cause greater interference. Moreover, the energy expenditure to accelerate particles to relativistic speeds is very high compared to that of sending photons.

14. Horowitz & Alschuler, "The Harvard SETI Search," Ch. 6, p. 202, in Bova & Preiss (eds.), *First Contact*, describes the history of the META search. META's division of the narrow-frequency range surrounding the natural emission of hydrogen into 8.4 million separate channels in order to pick up a *beacon*, that is, a signal specifically designed to traverse interstellar distances, suggests the magnitude of the total task. META has since searched the band surrounding the natural emission frequency of the hydroxyl radical, which would also be known to any technically advanced society.

15. Joseph Baugher, *On Civilized Stars: The Search for Intelligent Life in Outer Space*, Ch. 5 and Table 5.2, Prentice-Hall, 1985, and *Los Angeles Times*, July 13, 1990, Section E, p. 1, describe a number of the SETI projects to date. See also Bova & Preiss (eds.), *First Contact*, Chs. 5–7.

16. "Absence of evidence is not evidence of absence" is the common litany of

316   SETI advocates. It is, of course, false. A continuing absence of evidence that extraterrestrial intelligence exists after fairly comprehensive searching would be persuasive, albeit not conclusive, evidence of its absence. At present, the distortion is probably harmless, because of the tiny fraction of possibilities investigated to date. In one respect, the position of SETI advocates is distinctly preferable to that of their detractors. Believers in extraterrestrial intelligence will most assuredly not be proved wrong within their lifetimes.

17. Jill Tarter, "Planned Observational Strategy for NASA's First Systematic Search for Extraterrestrial Intelligence," Ch. 20, p. 314, in Finney and Jones (eds.), *Interstellar Migration and the Human Experience,* and Michael Papagiannis, "The Hunt Is On: SETI in Action," Ch. 5, p. 181, in Bova & Preiss (eds.), *First Contact,* describe the NASA SETI project. Vigorous Congressional opposition (including one Golden Fleece award from Senator Proxmire) delayed the beginning of that project for several years after the technology became available, reflecting the failure of elected officials to recognize the shift in the nature of progress. On the political history of SETI, see Linda Billings, "From the Observatory to Capitol Hill," Ch. 7, p. 223, in Bova & Preiss (eds.), *First Contact.*

18. Baugher, *On Civilized Stars,* Ch. 5, p. 221, estimates that a galaxy-wide omnidirectional beacon would consume on the order of one thousand times the total power production of Earth.

19. A few SETI advocates have sought to circumvent the practical import of the unavoidable delays in receiving extraterrestrial information by hypothesizing that advanced planets may constantly broadcast the *Encyclopedia Galactica* in all directions. Such omnidirectional interstellar communication would entail vast resource expenditures with only an uncertain prospect of conferring a benefit on another unknown race, and none at all of receiving anything in return for the effort. Positing such massive interstellar altruism crosses the line that separates scientific conjecture from religious faith.

20. Although any outer boundary line is somewhat arbitrary, thirty light-years is within the correct range. Restricting the search to less than twenty light-years would be somewhat myopic; utilitarian justifications for extending it beyond sixty light-years are farfetched. The search effort required is quite sensitive to the outer limit selected. Doubling the search radius increases the volume of space to be searched eightfold.

21. Advanced aliens may be able to minimize the effect of the delay by projecting the general course of development in a less advanced culture and formulating their message accordingly.

22. Ronald Bracewell, *The Galactic Club: Intelligent Life in Outer Space,* Ch. 6, W.H. Freeman, 1975.

23. Papagiannis, "The Hunt Is On," p. 184, in Bova & Preiss (eds.), *First Contact.*

24. For an extreme possibility of an extraterrestrial infrared source, see Freeman Dyson, "Search for Artificial Stellar Sources of Infrared Radiation," Ch. 22, p. 108, in Goldsmith (ed.), *Quest for Extraterrestrial Life,* suggesting that an advanced

civilization could build a partial shield around its star (by dismantling a spare planet) to capture more of its radiated energy.

25. SETI advocates have never urged an intensive search limited to nearby stars, probably because it would divert resources from more general searches and risk the loss of public support for SETI generally if the limited search produced no results. SETI skeptics, on the other hand, regard any search as a waste of time and money. Although (or perhaps because) it will please neither side in the debate, the search strategy outlined in the text is almost certain to be pursued: it is too simple and too potentially important not to be.

26. Note that a search limited to a radius of thirty light-years is very likely to produce a negative result. Optimistic estimates of the prevalence of life in the galaxy would make the average distance between technological civilizations some hundreds of light-years.

27. In "Answer, Please Answer," a short story by Ben Bova, reprinted in Bova & Preiss (eds.), *First Contact*, p. 262, aliens used the table of atomic weights to provide a decoding key. Many such universal physical constants can be imagined.

28. For a contrary argument, see Nicholas Rescher, "Extraterrestrial Science," in Regis (ed.), *Extraterrestrials, Science and Alien Intelligence*, p. 83. Science and technology emerge as extensions of a species' unaided observations. Thus, people developed telescopes and microscopes to extend their natural power of sight. Aliens with different senses and in a different environment would have produced different technologies and would, as a consequence, have formulated their science differently. The immutability of natural law, however, would appear to force some convergence even between technologies with totally disparate origins. Humans, for example, neither see nor hear radio waves, but stars and other extraterrestrial objects emit them; hence, radio astronomy. The science and technology of particle physics seem profoundly alien to all but a few practitioners. It is the subject more than the observer that dictates the forms of advanced science.

29. Rescher's suggestion to the contrary is, with respect, bizarre.

30. On the potential of nanoscale engineering (devices on the order of billionths of a meter in size), see K. Eric Drexler, *Engines of Creation: Challenges and Choices of the Last Technological Revolution*, Doubleday, 1986. Notwithstanding Drexler's unrestrained enthusiasm, the self-replicating nanoscale robots that he hypothesizes lie centuries in the future on Earth, even assuming they are possible. (Drexler's bleak assessment of the prospects for significant gains on other fronts, implicit in the title of his book, accords with that set forth in Chapter 4.)

31. Cocconi & Morrison, "Searching for Interstellar Communications," reprinted in Goldsmith (ed.), *Quest for Extraterrestrial Life*, Ch. 20, p. 102.

Chapter Thirteen

ISSUES WITHOUT ANSWERS

In predicting the future, everyone has amateur standing. Time will certainly disprove some of the preceding forecasts. But progress of the *kind* projected in this part is inevitable. Science will begin delivering the power to extend and circumvent the limits of human abilities within the lifetimes of today's children.

This watershed event is generating a notable lack of controversy. What passes for public discussion of the issues it raises is typical Luddite fare. Several commentators have, for example, fretted that insurance companies could require genetic screening and charge higher premiums to those diagnosed as having a predisposition for some disease or condition. Of course they will, and should, just as they charge higher premiums to policyholders with high cholesterol or a history of heart disease. Those in newly created low-genetic-risk categories will benefit, those in the high-risk categories will suffer, just as candle makers suffered from the invention of electric light. Progress always creates winners and losers, but the gains exceed the losses, as they will here. Bad genes already place people at risk. The only difference is that those people will *know* of their risk and be able to take precautions.

Issues like insurance rates hold center stage not by their significance, but by their familiarity. Critics and commentators can fit them into the familiar framework of nineteenth- and twentieth-century progress: science and technology advance, shoving some people aside in the process. Pity the victims. But the new kind of progress brings a new paradigm. People are becoming the subjects rather than the instruments of change. The coming round of progress will alter what people are rather than just what they do or how they live. This raises issues of an altogether different order, and efforts to force them into the old mold offer only confusion.

The eerie silence on these issues is due in part to a lack of candor among those few who savvy the drums. The longer-term implications of the breakthroughs in molecular genetics, the neurosciences, artificial intelligence, and the like can hardly be lost on the participants, but they are rarely mentioned in public. Not that researchers keep their results secret: they report them dutifully and proudly, but only to each other, in a language and form that is all but impenetrable to the nonspecialist. Titles like "Diagnosis of Beta-Thalassaemia by DNA Amplification in Single Blastomeres from Mouse Preimplantation Embryos" do not exactly trumpet the imminent ability to select the traits of offspring after *in vitro* fertilization. The only implication thought fit for public consumption is the prospect of treating or avoiding some rare disease or condition. But the ability to select *against* one trait implies the ability to select *for* another, and advances in the neurosciences promise much more than a cure for Alzheimer's. When obscurity and evasion will not serve,[1] participants sometimes resort to the preemptive denial of reality. Listen to Leroy Hood, a respected leader in biotechnology, talking about the future of human genetic engineering:

> [I]t's important to make a distinction between the two kinds of genetic engineering. When we correct the mistakes in the book of life [i.e., defective chromosomes], the corrections will only be done in the cells that carry out that particular function you're interested in. . . . This is . . . in distinction to rewriting the book of life in sex cells, or the germ cells that create new individuals. If we rewrite anything there, then you pass those traits on to your children and you've permanently altered the gene pool of humanity, and that is a ban that I can't imagine being lifted again into the indefinite future. In man, we will not do sex cell genetic engineering.[2]

To the extent that such statements are to be taken seriously, they display naiveté (or cynicism) of a very high order. Who is supposed to enforce such a ban, and how? The technology is the same, whether applied to the liver, the brain, a germ cell, or a zygote. People will not long remain ignorant of the possibilities. The exploitation of those possibilities by even a few will trigger a cascade, just as anabolic steroid use ran rampant among athletes before the recent crackdown. People accept limitations on human abilities because everyone else labors under similar limitations and because they have no choice. The knowledge or even suspicion that others were artificially enhancing their intellects would surely and quickly undermine that acceptance. Many parents may, on principle, prefer a world of natural conception. Far fewer would continue to participate in the genetic lottery, potentially saddling their children with irremediable disadvantages, in order to vindicate that principle. And how many people will remain satisfied with a normal life span if daily confronted by seemingly ageless neighbors?[3] The use of such knowledge thus quickly becomes self-reinforcing. "[I]t only takes one in 1,000 or 10,000 . . . to start a trend."[4]

The same dynamic would operate internationally. The knowledge and technology will be available worldwide. Any nation that enhanced the abilities of its people would gain an incalculable economic and possibly strategic advantage over any rivals that chose not to, and, conversely, would find itself at a substantial disadvantage if one of its rivals became the successful pioneer. Apart from economic considerations, it is impossible even to imagine the Japanese or the Germans, as only two of the most obvious examples, voluntarily accepting genetic or intellectual inferiority. The instability of such a situation is evident. Any nation that suspected its rivals of overtly pursuing or covertly allowing genetic enhancement would be forced (with the greatest reluctance) to follow the same route, possibly on an accelerated basis, and the perception would soon become the reality. Similar considerations dictate the same result (probably with less controversy) with respect to chemical enhancement of brain function, increasing longevity, and exploitation of artificial intelligence.

Opponents of these kinds of progress would thus face the heavy burden of achieving and maintaining a worldwide consensus in opposition to forestall a process that, once begun, will feed on its own momentum. Their arguments are not up to the task.

The initial appeal of just maintaining the status quo is undeniable. "[T]here is a tendency for people to fear the unknown, to resist change, to preserve comfortable preconceptions, to resent new circumstances not of their own making."[5] The mere mention of such topics as human genetic engineering often evokes a reaction of unmitigated dread.[6] Malevolent aliens, machines run amok, and man-made monsters have been recurrent plots among mankind's nightmares. But tangible reality tends to quell such fears. Interstellar distances would present a formidable deterrent to any would-be galactic Napoleon, no matter how advanced. Whatever their intellectual prowess, computers remain helplessly dependent on people for energy, maintenance, and other physical needs. And the crude genetic selection of dogs, horses, cattle, and other domestic animals by generations of breeders has produced hundreds of distinct breeds, none of them monstrous.

Critics therefore tend to rely on moral rather than utilitarian grounds. Past advances have altered only the trappings of humanity; those of the future attack its very essence. DNA ultimately defines the species. Changing it changes man. The prospect of people late in the next century regarding their ancestors as so many Cro-Magnons is understandably and profoundly unnerving. Other developments discussed here fare little better from this perspective. Intellect is the unique and defining trait of the species, even taxonomically *(sapiens)*. Enhancing the brain alters that trait directly, artificial intelligence transfers it to mere machines, and the discovery of intelligent aliens would share it with other beings. Critics can easily discern the evil lurking in such enterprises.

Not surprisingly,[7] the Catholic Church (speaking in its role as "an expert in humanity"[8]) has been among the more vocal of these critics. The Church flatly condemns "[c]ertain attempts to influence chromosomic or genetic inheritance [that] are not therapeutic but are aimed at producing human beings selected according to . . . predetermined qualities" as inconsistent with human dignity.

> [A] human person . . . cannot be desired or conceived as the product of an intervention of medical or biological techniques; that would be equivalent to reducing him to an object of scientific technology. No one may subject the coming of a child into the world to conditions

of technical efficiency which are to be evaluated according to standards of control and dominion.[9]

The World Council of Churches sounds similar themes (albeit in more muted tones), cautioning against the "transformation of procreation into a laboratory science and of offspring into products with interchangeable parts to be selected at will" and against the reductionist "view of humanity as an object to be manipulated."[10]

Such themes have also found secular expression. Joseph Weizenbaum created Eliza, an early foray into artificial intelligence that simulated conversation. Workers in Weizenbaum's office, well aware of the programming tricks that he had used, began treating Eliza as a confidante, seeking her advice, depending upon her. Some journals began to discuss the possibility of creating versions of Eliza to serve as computerized psychotherapists. Weizenbaum reacted with revulsion, condemning as "obscene" the possibility of allowing a computer to perform any task in which a person may exhibit wisdom, understanding, respect, judgment, or other uniquely human attributes.[11] Weizenbaum's antipathy extended beyond artificial intelligence to instrumental reason and technological inevitability in all its forms. He applauded those biologists engaged in urging their colleagues to cease all recombinant DNA research. Indeed, he was appalled that they needed to justify their position, so obvious to him was the need to "exempt life itself from the madness of treating everything as an object."[12]

But the advocates of continued progress need not yield critics the moral high ground. Self-awareness distinguishes man from both machines and lower forms of life. Western thought, including its Judeo-Christian threads, has enshrined the need to "know thyself" as a central imperative of humanness from ancient Greece to the present. Adam and Eve pursued knowledge, including self-knowledge, even in defiance of God. The Human Genome Project is perhaps the ultimate manifestation of this drive, with research into intelligence, life span, and the uniqueness of terrestrial life not far behind. These are not perversions or betrayals of humanity, but the supreme expression of one of its central drives. Investigating the bases of uniquely human qualities and using that knowledge to mold and enhance those qualities is, from this perspective, merely the natural culmination of the very attributes that critics of such research exalt. The sanctity of man and his mental gifts thus may be thought to justify, not condemn, to compel, not prohibit, invasion of the innermost sanctum. The selfless ends further dignify the effort. The benefits of the knowledge will accrue almost entirely to those not yet living. Conferring advantages on future generations follows in a long and noble tradition.

Such advantages, and particularly their selective availability, are the worst nightmares of committed social engineers, who see them not as progress, but as threats to equality.[13] Like every innovation through history, the availability of genetic selection, mental enhancement, and longer life will initially be limited. The privileged few will use their preferred access to these technologies to perpetuate the advantages already accruing to wealth, assuring themselves or their children of superior talents as well as better opportunities. But the advantage will be temporary. Pioneering these advances is inherently expensive; applying them will not be. Market forces will make the perfected techniques routine, cheap, and ever more widely accessible as more practitioners learn them. More to the point, parents stubbornly refuse to view themselves as conscripts in a crusade against privilege in its every protean form. To the contrary, most wish to afford their children every possible advantage, fair or not. Impugning that desire as "ghoulish"[14] will not cause it to vanish.

Reasonable minds may differ on such issues, which will, by itself, decide the outcome for practical purposes. Those who see no legitimate objection to using the techniques will face few practical impediments in doing so. This will begin the cascade, and the ayes will have it.

Nor will coercion substitute for persuasion. Even majority opposition to the use of such technologies could be difficult to muster after knowledge of the possibilities begins to percolate. Witness how greatly just a few years of living with the Human Genome Project have changed the terms in which science writers discuss the potential for human genetic engineering. 1985: "It is important to point out that genetic engineering does *not* seek to address complex multi-gene traits in complex multicellular organisms. The thought [of using] the technology to create a superman of great strength or intelligence (or whatever) is out of the question."[15] 1990: "[S]hould therapy be applied simply to improve one's offspring, not only to prevent an

324   inherited disease?"[16] Familiarity transforms the unthinkable into the conjectural, en route via controversial toward acceptable.[17]

Even if enacted, mere law would not long restrain those who are able from acquiring the benefits of the new technologies. Billions of dollars of criminal enforcement and educational efforts have failed to suppress recreational drug use by millions of otherwise law-abiding Americans, despite general agreement about those drugs' health hazards and lack of any redeeming value. More immediately to the point is the burgeoning black market in anabolic steroids and, more recently, human growth hormone, an early product of genetic engineering prescribed to treat some forms of dwarfism. Many youths, most but not all from the inner cities, perceive the combination of size and athletic skills as their passport to success, and neither laws, nor expense, nor health risks will prevent them from acting on that perception. The notion of a 100 percent effective ban on technology that promises to make people (or their children) smarter or longer-lived can only be deemed fanciful. The advantages that would accrue to those flouting such a ban would generate irresistible pressure for change.

A preemptive strike against funding the research has no better prospect of succeeding than an *ex post facto* ban on using its results. The sums required, a few tens of billions of dollars over the next twenty to thirty years, sound substantial, but are actually piddling compared to the totals spent on research and development in the United States alone. The government will continue to contribute, intentionally or otherwise, because research ostensibly directed to one purpose often advances another. Basic medical and biological research would virtually halt if the genes and the brain were excluded from investigation. Artificial intelligence is one of the cutting edges of computer technology, a commercial sector that the United States is not likely to abandon. Every radio telescope is a listening post for extraterrestrial intelligence, whether dedicated to that search or not. And private money will increasingly flow into these fields as the profit potential becomes apparent and the returns available in other fields diminish. Commercial research and development already accounts for many of the advances in artificial intelligence and genetic engineering.[18] In short, progress will continue. The level of public support will influence when and how, not whether, developments will unfold.

Moreover, the United States cannot end the race by refusing to run. Attempts to control innovation would not long succeed in a politically divided world. Any country that successfully suppressed these advances domestically would soon find itself isolated and inferior, like Tokugawa Japan in the nineteenth century and with the same outcome. "Bottles will continue to be uncorked, the genies can never be put back, and the polities [and individuals] that take the uncorking in stride will prosper at the expense of those that try to prevent it."[19] Even Robert Wright of the *New Republic,* no fan of this future, acknowledges that "there is a very large problem with following the Luddite plan: the United States can't, in the real world, do it alone."[20]

The availability of the knowledge will thus dictate its widespread use. The question is not whether mere mortals should exercise these powers, but who will do so and to what ends.

This raises the question of regulation. The social engineers, frustrated in their desire to outlaw progress, will certainly wish to regulate it into riskless and egalitarian submission, and they are not likely to harbor many doubts about the need for such regulation or their qualifications for undertaking it.[21] They will find a receptive audience in Washington. Whether their competence and integrity would match their aspirations is open to serious question —the spectacle presented by government has been less than inspiring in recent decades. More often than not, regulation has simply raised the cost of new products and services (particularly in medicine), accentuating rather than ameliorating the advantages of wealth. Even when government is not overtly hostile to innovation, its involvement can scarcely be other than detrimental to the rate of progress. "In all well-ordered societies, political authority is dedicated to stability, security, and the status quo. It is thus singularly ill-qualified to direct or channel activity intended to produce instability, insecurity, and change."[22] With Asia and Europe so ready to fill any vacuum, any meaningful form of regulation would serve more to shift technological leadership from one nation to another than to alter its course.

More fundamentally, control by the government hardly assures constructive and benign use of such technologies. As Louis Brandeis observed, "The greatest dangers to liberty lurk in insidious encroachment by men of zeal, well-meaning but without understanding."[23]

326 Hitler's final solution was only a lunatic vision until it became official policy. The central government in Aldous Huxley's *Brave New World* controlled the machinery of eugenics for what its enlightened planners and most of its citizens considered justifiable and beneficent ends. Individual decision-making risks isolated folly and abuse, as irresponsible people use the power of these new technologies for silly and immoral purposes. But subjecting those decisions to the will of regulators would intrude deeply into intensely personal matters, vesting authority without responsibility or any assurance of competence and consolidating thousands of tiny, divergent, and therefore comparatively harmless rivulets into one potentially menacing flood. "The destructive capacity of the individual, however vicious, is small; of the state, however well-intentioned, almost limitless."[24] Dispersing the power rather than concentrating it offers not only the best hope of the social diversity, experimentation, and ferment that promote progress, but also the best protection against the well-meant tyranny of Utopians and would-be saviors.[25]

Discussions of prospective developments in technology often end with their authors' visions of life in the future. Such visions seem to be about equally divided between the inspirational and the apocalyptic. They are rarely equivocal. They even less rarely resemble events as they later unfold. With caution borne of that history, this conclusion will hew to the less ambitious aim of sorting out a few of the issues and possibilities that these kinds of progress raise.

First, in the interests of internal coherence, the apparent tension between Parts I and II of this book must be addressed. Sudden advances in the ability to learn and invent seemingly should contribute to material prosperity, as should the greater accumulations of physical capital made possible by longer productive lives. But I doubt that they will. The slowdown in material progress is due not to any lack of human ingenuity in devising new technologies, but to absolute or effective limits on the tangible benefits that any technology can deliver. Enhanced mental powers may quicken the pace with which we approach such limits, but they will not alter the limits themselves.[26] Longer life spans would certainly make larger capital accumulations possible. But people could easily save more money if they wished to. It is the motivation, not the ability, that is lacking.

Neither longer lives nor enhanced abilities are likely to supply that motivation. On the contrary, a rapid expansion of intellectual powers may further attenuate the desire to seek material gain; first-rate intellects rarely lust after riches. Genetically or chemically enhanced intellects (or ordinary intellects aided by artificial or alien intelligence) could, of course, perform the same tasks faster than their unaided predecessors. But the result would be increased output only if the time saved were devoted to labor rather than leisure. Again, it is the desire, not the ability, to work harder that is in question. Thus, the advances discussed in this part may not have much effect on the slowing of material gains. (Even if they did, the resumption of material progress might go almost unnoticed in the changes wrought in people themselves.)

Fear of unknown consequences from new technology is never far from the surface of discussions about the future, and nightmare scenarios are easy enough to concoct. But experience has tended to belie similar concerns in the past. The safety record of nuclear power plants through their multicentury collective operating history, for example, has done little to justify the fearful predictions of their opponents. The issue that dominated political debates over recombinant DNA research during the 1970s was the potential for accidental release of dangerous artificial organisms into the environment. The experience of nearly two decades has stamped paid to those concerns in the minds of everyone to whom opposition to change is not a religious faith.[27] Technologies often exceed expectations so greatly as to negate the original basis for concern. Joseph Weizenbaum, for example, assumed that computerized speech recognition would be used primarily for government surveillance, because only the government could afford the supercomputers that the software would require. Speech recognition technology will, as it turns out, appear on desktop machines within this decade, with no more sinister purpose than that of decreasing secretarial employment. Expanding knowledge of genetics will similarly remove at least some objectionable side effects of genetic screening (such as increased abortions and higher insurance rates). Finer gene maps will refine the diagnosis of inherited defects, and genetic cures will become the common response.

But progress will not resolve every issue it raises. For at least a generation, people with enhanced abilities will coexist in society with

328 others who lack them. The techniques for creating those abilities will initially have only limited availability, and many people will choose for themselves or their children not to opt for enhancement. A discrete category of learning-advantaged children will emerge. Will the then existing teachers be capable of instructing them beyond some low level? Can such children be integrated with others? As the enhanced portion of the population increases, will they lose respect for and patience with those who possess only natural abilities? Or will superior intelligence itself defeat any such tendency? Will children or adults without the benefits of enhancement lose the motivation to excel because of the apparent inequality of the competition? Even those rare and happy accidents of the genetic lottery, a da Vinci, Maxwell, or Schweitzer, might not have achieved greatness if marked from childhood as genetically inferior. (Here again, advances in genetic interpretation may moot the issue by allowing naturally created geniuses to be identified at an early age.)

In time, however, the knowledge and expertise will become sufficiently widespread to permit general use. The issues will then become social and political: is a society consisting entirely of gifted individuals viable, and, if not, must talents be rationed, with a permanent, intellectually inferior underclass relegated to performance of the most menial tasks? Technology may, however, provide machines (or genetically enhanced animals?) to perform the bulk of such tasks. The resolution may also be economic: an abundance of intellectual talent may reduce the high price it currently commands in the market, while the value placed on the willingness to perform menial work may rise. Enough people may respond to such market incentives to supply the need. Some may even prefer work without mental challenge in order to reserve their intellectual energies for avocational pursuits. A *Brave New World* thus does not appear to be the inevitable consequence of enhancement.

If chemical and genetic enhancement and the products of artificial intelligence become universally available, will the result be a loss of human diversity? The natural process of meiosis and sexual reproduction constantly reshuffles the genetic deck, yielding almost infinite chromosomal variation. Environment adds more diversity. Ignorance concerning genetic coding may also contribute. Each person's assessment of his innate abilities and limitations is necessarily vague, uncertain, and subjective, leaving more degrees of freedom in the choice of pursuits and goals than would more precise and definite knowledge. Genetic and chemical alteration could produce a degree of homogenization. Parents could choose from a comparatively narrow library of known positive attributes in "designing" their children. Each child (and later adult) would know his genetic makeup, and that knowledge would surely guide subsequent decisions. People could begin to employ drugs or medical procedures to target a single "ideal" neurochemical balance, eliminating in the process variations that contribute to individuality. At another level, artificial intelligences may become the leading authorities on many subjects on which opinions now differ sharply. The pronouncements of such authorities may suppress many of the disagreements that currently add both to diversity and, in J.S. Mill's words, to "the clearer perception and livelier impression of truth, produced by its collision with error."[28]

But none of these consequences is inevitable. Genetic libraries may expand to include not only a wide range of naturally occurring sequences, but also some that do not currently exist. Medical enhancement may similarly broaden rather than narrow the potential range of brain function. Artificial experts may simply add further voices and perspectives to public debate. New technologies thus may either expand or contract the range of human diversity and experience, depending on how we manage them.

Although the discussion has focused on the initial appearance of new technologies, none of the anticipated developments will be once for all. As in every earlier field of progress, advancing knowledge will produce continuing improvements. Indeed, progress in a field may be self-reinforcing (an artificial intelligence designing a more powerful artificial intelligence, for example), or may accelerate progress in another field (an artificial intelligence assisting in genetic interpretation). The same kind of cycle has existed in the realm of material progress. Progress in energy, for example, spawned progress in transportation and manufacturing, which, in turn, further improved the efficiency of energy production and utilization. That dynamic is nearly exhausted. Does intelligence have similar inherent limits, where further knowledge or ability yields no meaningful increment in understanding? Will the coming cycle of human progress reach an effective end, to be supplanted by still another form of progress, the shape of which cannot even be glimpsed?

Such questions could be multiplied endlessly. Satisfying answers

330   cannot. The exact shape of the advances to come will, of course, affect their impact. The approach of those advances will therefore improve the quality of prognostication, but only slightly. The changes at hand are fundamental and unprecedented. They alter not external factors, but the very frame of reference for decision-making. Asking a chimpanzee what it would do with the power of speech is not likely to elicit a correct or even an interesting response. We are not qualified to decide for the vastly more talented and knowledgeable people of the future how they should use their abilities or to predict what their decisions will be. Even superior generations of the future may admire the endeavors of the lesser beings that planted the seeds of their enhanced abilities. The presumption to dictate how those abilities should be used would likely be received with less charity.

Those people will, in any event, need to fend for themselves. The present provides ample challenges without anticipating those of the future. Many will regard the slowdown in material progress as the deprivation of a birthright. Demagogues will fan and exploit resentment, finding or creating devils (both foreign and domestic) to blame for the inability of technology and the market to deliver ever increasing bounties. The temptation to fight over slices of a fixed pie will grow. Elections will be won and notoriety earned by playing variations on these themes.

But the opportunities, if anything, exceed the challenges. The new realms of progress should more than compensate for the loss of the old. The traditional fields have been heavily worked; theirs is the comfort of familiarity, not the excitement of the unknown. Human abilities offer an even richer medium of expression, a more varied palette, than the external world that has occupied us throughout history.

Such prospects may frighten. They should also inspire.

NOTES

1. See Robert Wright, "Achilles' Helix," *New Republic,* July 9, 1990, p. 21, discussing James Watson's unwillingness to address the larger implications of the Human Genome Project.
2. WGBH-TV Boston, *Nova:* "Decoding the Book of Life," transcript pages 12–13, Oct. 31, 1989. Professor Hood's views have since changed. He now believes it quite possible that parents will employ "homemade eugenics" to produce more intelligent babies, although he hedges a bit by asserting that their ability to do so will not arrive "soon." Kevles & Hood, "Reflections," Ch. 14, pp. 319–20, in Kevles & Hood (eds.), *The Code of Codes: Scientific and Social Issues in the Human Genome Project,* Harvard Univ. Press, 1992. What qualifies as "soon," when the anticipated event is the remaking of the human species?
3. "[T]he temptation to try to lengthen our life spans will be overwhelming. . . . Faced with such a prospect, ethical qualms about tampering with the essence of humanity will surely be swept aside. Few people will want to serve as controls, condemned to a life of threescore and ten when everyone around them is living sevenscore." Christopher Wills, *Exons, Introns, and Talking Genes: The Science Behind the Human Genome Project,* Ch. 14, p. 310, Basic Books, 1991.
4. Wright, "Achilles' Helix," *New Republic,* July 9, 1990, at p. 28.
5. G.J.V. Nossal, *Reshaping Life: Key Issues in Genetic Engineering,* Ch. 10, p. 119, Oxford Univ. Press, 1985.
6. "[L]ittle rejoicing is likely when the ability to design children genetically is attained." Herman Kahn, *World Economic Development: 1979 and Beyond,* Ch. 3, p. 153, Westview Press, 1979.
7. The Church's steadfast opposition to progress did not end with its condemnation of heliocentrism as heresy. In the mid-nineteenth century, Pope Pius IX branded as error the proposition that "the Roman Pontiff can, and ought to, be reconciled and come to terms with progress . . . and with modern civilization." Quoted in J.B. Bury, *The Idea of Progress: An Inquiry into Its Origin and Growth,* Ch. 17, p. 323, Macmillan, 2d ed., 1932.
8. Joseph Cardinal Ratzinger, *Instruction on Respect for Human Life in Its Origin and on the Dignity of Procreation,* p. 1. Cardinal Ratzinger is a noted Catholic theologian and frequent Church spokesman on procreative issues. (Cardinal Ratzinger is strongly identified with the "conservative" wing of the Catholic Church.

332 Whether contrary views concerning the issues of interest here are prevalent within the Church cannot be readily determined; prelates have not been encouraged to express dissenting opinions publicly in recent years. Pope John Paul II approved the Instruction.) The discussion in the text is limited to the secular aspects of the Instruction. Some positions are ultimately justified by the light of revelation, a basis that leaves those not favored with divine inspiration out of the discussion.

9. Instruction, II.4.

10. World Council of Churches, *Manipulating Life: Ethical Issues in Genetic Engineering,* pp. 7–8, 1982.

11. Joseph Weizenbaum, *Computer Power and Human Reason: From Judgment to Calculation,* Ch. 10, p. 268, W.H. Freeman, 1976. See also Weizenbaum, Ch. 8, p. 227: "Since we do not now have any ways of making computers wise, we ought not now to give computers tasks that demand wisdom."

12. Weizenbaum, *Computer Power and Human Reason,* Ch. 10, p. 260. Weizenbaum was writing during the period surrounding the Asilomar Conference on Recombinant DNA Molecules, a period punctuated by one complete moratorium and several competing sets of restrictions on experimentation in genetic engineering. See Clifford Grobstein, *A Double Image of the Double Helix: The Recombinant DNA Debate,* W.H. Freeman, 1979.

13. Political rectitude may even require concern about "the ominous implications of inherited talent for social equality" when the inheritance is *natural,* particularly in light of the awful prospect that smart men and women may seek to pair off and have smart children. See Mickey Kaus, "The End of Equality," *New Republic,* June 22, 1992, p. 21.

14. Wright, "Achilles' Helix," *New Republic,* July 9, 1990, p. 21.

15. Nossal, *Reshaping Life,* Ch. 6, pp. 73–74 (emphasis original).

16. Inder Verma, "Gene Therapy," *Scientific American,* Nov. 1990, p. 68.

17. Robert Shapiro, *The Human Blueprint: The Race to Unlock the Secrets of Our Genetic Script,* Ch. 19, St. Martin's Press, 1991, quotes the views of various observers on germ line engineering.

18. Kevles & Hood, "Reflections," Ch. 14, p. 312, in Kevles & Hood (eds.), *Code of Codes.*

19. Rosenberg & Ezell, *How the West Grew Rich: The Economic Transformation of the Industrial World,* Ch. 8, pp. 265–66, Basic Books, 1986.

20. Wright, "Achilles' Helix," *New Republic,* July 9, 1990, at p. 29.

21. "It is when left to the free market that the fruits of genome research are most assuredly rotten." Wright, "Achilles' Helix," *New Republic,* July 9, 1990, at p. 27.

22. Rosenberg & Ezell, *How the West Grew Rich,* p. 265.

23. *Olmstead* v. *United States,* 277 U.S. 438, 479 (1928).

24. Paul Johnson, *Modern Times: The World from the Twenties to the Nineties,* Ch. 1, p. 14, HarperCollins, rev'd ed., 1991. "There are many who would assuage their fears about the future of the genome project by having governments interfere with it. . . . If nothing else, the history of the twentieth century ought to have taught us that individuals can sometimes behave badly, but they can never behave as badly,

or as destructively, as governments can." Ruth Cowan, "Genetic Technology and Reproductive Choice: An Ethics for Autonomy," Ch. 12, pp. 262–63, in Kevles & Hood (eds.), *Code of Codes.*

25. See, for example, Friedrich Hayek, *The Constitution of Liberty,* Chs. 2, 3, 11, and 14, Univ. of Chicago Press, 1960, and the introduction to Henry Simons, *Economic Policy for a Free Society,* Univ. of Chicago Press, 1948.

26. "In a race toward the limits set by natural law, the finish line is predictable even if the path and the pace of the runners are not. . . . [T]he unchanging laws of nature draw the line between what is physically possible and what is not. . . ." K. Eric Drexler, *Engines of Creation,* Ch. 3, p. 41, Doubleday, 1986. "[T]he key force for increasing benefits to mankind derives not from an increase in human genius but from . . . accessible and objective instruments." Breit & Culbertson, *Science and Ceremony: The Institutional Economics of C.E. Ayres,* Ch. 1, p. 23, Univ. of Texas Austin Press, 1976.

27. See Bernard Davis, "Fear of Progress in Biology," Ch. 8, pp. 184–86, in Almond, Chodorow & Pearce (eds.), *Progress and Its Discontents,* Univ. of California Press, 1982.

28. *On Liberty,* Ch. 2.

APPENDIX

THE ECONOMICS OF PROGRESS

COMPETITIVE INNOVATION

Economics textbooks devote little space to the forces that disrupt their elegant equilibrium models. For readers not allergic to graphs, the following provides a fast day tour of the topic, tracing one cycle of innovation, beginning from a perfectly competitive equilibrium.[1]

Each firm incurs an array of costs, both fixed and variable. Fixed costs per unit of production (FC) decline over a wide range. Variable costs per unit increase as production approaches capacity because of the need for overtime, the use of inferior suppliers, and the diminishing quality of available labor. At some volume, this causes total costs per unit to increase, as shown in the following graph:

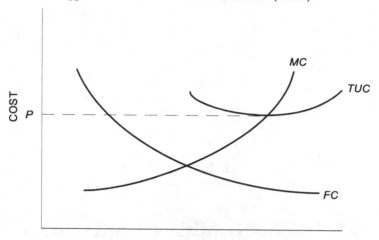

The marginal cost curve (MC) represents the incremental cost to produce one additional unit. It intersects total unit costs (TUC) at the minimum cost designated (arbitrarily for the moment) P; once an additional unit costs more to make than the average, the average begins rising.

In an idealized, perfectly competitive market, many firms exist, all with identical or very similar cost curves, and other fungible firms may enter or leave the market at any time. This produces the first graph seen in (and frequently the only one remembered from) elementary economics.

App. 2 MARKET SUPPLY AND DEMAND

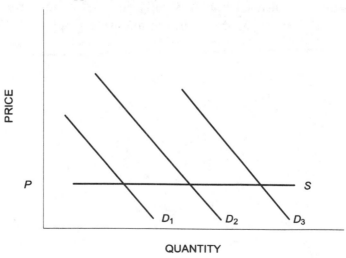

The supply curve is essentially horizontal throughout the relevant range because, together, these firms can increase their output indefinitely (for practical purposes) at their minimum total cost per unit. Whatever the demand curve D_X, the market clearing price at equilibrium will remain the same, P. At any lower price, demand exceeds supply, and the shortage produces a price increase; at any higher price, supply exceeds demand, and the surplus produces a price decrease. Only consumers whose demand (expressed in money) equals or exceeds P will buy. Only those suppliers whose costs of production are equal to or lower than P will continue producing and selling in the market. The pricing mechanism thus automatically causes the optimal quantity of each good to be produced by the most efficient firms and sold to the consumers to whom the goods are of greatest value.

Impressive as this effortless allocation of production and consumption is, it is perhaps the least important contribution of the free market to economic progress. Equilibrium "is like a single frame of a movie: taken alone, it misses all the action, and it is the action that . . . holds the promise of economic advance."[2] Innovation disrupts this equilibrium, at least temporarily.

The cost-lowering innovation has a straightforward and calculable effect. Assume in the graph below that a firm implements new technology that lowers its total unit cost from TUC_1 to TUC_2.

App. 3 COST-LOWERING INNOVATION

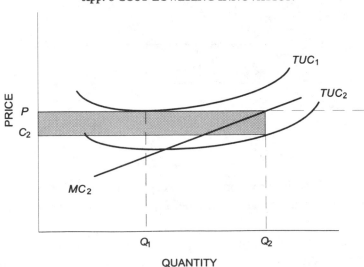

338 The market price will remain unaffected at P, because other firms cannot (by hypothesis) produce at lower cost. The innovating firm will increase its sales from Q_1 to Q_2, where the marginal cost (MC_2) of producing an additional unit just equals P. It will earn an economic profit of P less C_2 (the firm's total unit cost at Q_2) multiplied by Q_2, depicted by the shaded area on the graph.

The effect of a product-improving innovation is similar. With competitors temporarily unable to supply the improvement, the innovating firm has a differentiated product, with a demand curve influenced by but not the same as that faced by its competitors. The firm can therefore behave as a quasi-monopolist, charging a price determined by the intersection of its (unchanged) marginal cost curve and the higher demand curve.[3]

In each case, the result is higher volume and higher profits for the innovator, lower volume and lower profits for its competitors. This pressures the competitors to match the original innovation. When enough succeed in lowering their costs, a new industry supply curve (S_2) results.

App. 4 GAIN FROM COST-LOWERING INNOVATION

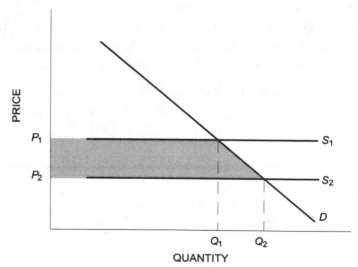

The result is a higher volume of sales (Q_2) at a lower price (P_2). The shaded trapezoid represents the net increase in social utility from the innovation.

When competitors match a product improvement, the original innovator must return to the competitive market price. The industry supply curve is the same as before the innovation, but the added feature or improved performance provides more value to some consumers, raising the demand curve.

App. 5 GAIN FROM PRODUCT-IMPROVING INNOVATION

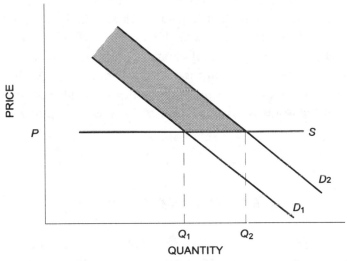

The result is higher volume (Q_2) at the original price, with an increase in the consumer surplus depicted by the shaded area on Figure App. 5.

A high-wage economy encourages such innovation, as the following graph illustrates:[4]

App. 6 EFFECT OF LABOR-SAVING TECHNOLOGY

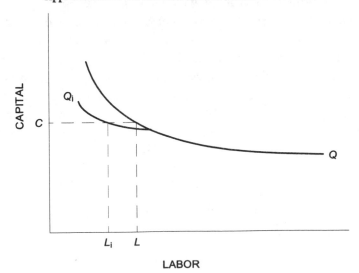

340 Q is an equal output curve, or isoquant, for an industry, with each point representing one combination of capital and labor to achieve a given level of output. The lower portion of the curve represents the use of much cheap labor and little machinery, typical in under-developed economies. The other end of the curve represents advanced economies, with highly paid workers, amply supplied with capital equipment. Q_i represents the isoquant after a labor-saving innovation: for a given level of capital C, the required quantity of labor for the same level of output declines from L to L_i. As the graph suggests, however, such an innovation may not shift the low-wage portion of the isoquant, that is, labor may be too cheap to be worth saving.

FACTOR ANALYSIS

Economists have labored mightily to quantify the sources of growth. The most detailed of these efforts have been so-called factor analyses, which apply sophisticated statistical methods to segregate the individual contributions of various production factors to output. Despite some fairly heroic assumptions, these studies are typically able to account for only about half of the observed growth. The residual is ascribed, largely for want of an alternative, to "advances in knowledge,"[5] the principal factor for which no direct accounting is possible. Given this provenance, too great a reliance on the apparently precise quantitative results is unwarranted. Nevertheless, the studies do tend to support the overriding importance of innovation, market expansion, and capital accumulation. The following table shows some of the results from a factor analysis of the U.S. economy from 1948 to 1973.[6]

Factor	Factor Contribution (% per year)	As Percentage of Total
Average annual income growth per employed person	2.16	100
Education of work force	0.40	19
Capital	0.50	23
Economies of scale	0.32	15
Advances in knowledge	1.09	50

The study included the contributions of a dozen other factors, but these four accounted for the entire increase in national income during the twenty-five-year period. The first two reflect the accumulation of intangible and tangible capital, the next is a direct result of market expansion, and the last reflects gains from innovation. Factor analyses of other economies over different periods show only minor deviation from this pattern.[7] The economic statistics thus tend to confirm the leading roles of these forces.

GENETIC ENGINEERING

The following sections explain some of the molecular genetics and genetic engineering techniques that are coming to bear on the problem of deciphering and then altering the human genome. For deeper and more comprehensive treatments, the reader should consult the sources referenced in the notes.[8]

DNA IN NATURE

The routine role of DNA in the cell is in protein manufacture. When a gene is active, the DNA segment "unzips" itself into two strands, one of which serves as a template for the formation of a ribonucleic acid (RNA) molecule. RNA is a single-stranded version of DNA,

342 except that uracil (U) substitutes for thymine. This first form of RNA, called nuclear RNA, then shortens itself, removing noncoding portions of the sequence.[9] This shortened RNA, called messenger RNA (mRNA), leaves the nucleus and attaches to a ribosome (itself composed largely of RNA). There it finds transfer RNA (tRNA), which has three nucleotides plus an amino acid. Each possible nucleotide "triplet" corresponds to only one amino acid. GAC, for example, always has aspartic acid attached.[10] Transfer RNA molecules link in sequence to each triplet on the mRNA. This brings together the amino acids, which bond to form a growing chain. When all the mRNA sites have been filled, the chain is a completed protein. At each stage from DNA to tRNA, complementary base pairing maintains the original coding sequence.

The structure of DNA also provides a ready explanation for the process of cell division (mitosis).[11] The DNA molecule unzips down its whole length, breaking the weak hydrogen bonds in the middle of the staircase and producing two complementary nucleotide strands. Free nucleotides bind to the resulting "half step" sites on each strand. An enzyme (DNA polymerase) forms bonds between the sugars along the sides. Each newly forming strand matches the preexisting strand exactly, courtesy of complementary base pairing. The result is DNA replication, two copies of the original chromosome, for use in two daughter cells. By this process, each cell in the body (except sperm or egg cells) receives the same genetic complement. The same genes are thus present in a liver cell and a brain cell, but different subsets of those genes are active (i.e., producing protein).

The role of DNA in sexual reproduction is slightly more complex. During meiosis, both chromosomes in the pair replicate, simultaneously and in close proximity. During replication, each chromosome exchanges nucleotide segments with the other member of the pair, producing four composite chromosomes.[12] The cell then divides twice, creating four separate gametes, each with twenty-three composite chromosomes.

The discussion in Chapter 8 outlined the mapping process in seven steps. The following describes some methods by which researchers are able to accomplish those steps.

1. PICKING ONE CHROMOSOME.   Biological means have proved the best for this task. Fusing a human cell with a mouse cancer cell creates an immortal, hybrid cell with a surfeit of chromosomes. As the cell divides, the extras begin to be lost. By random chance, some cell lines end up with just one human chromosome among many mouse chromosomes. Chemical differences make human and mouse chromosomes fairly easy to separate. The hybrid cell line thus becomes a specialized factory, producing copies of one chromosome.[13]

2. SEPARATING THE DNA FROM THE PROTEIN AND WATER PACKING.   The DNA molecule is badly tangled, and enzymes naturally present in the cell will begin to digest it as soon as its protective packaging is removed. The only solution to date is to wash the chromosomes in fairly harsh detergents, which inevitably breaks up the DNA. Fortunately, the next step would have done this anyway.

3. BREAKING THE DNA INTO SEGMENTS.   A complete chromosomal DNA molecule (50 to 250 million base pairs) is too long to process, either chemically or biologically. Researchers must therefore fragment it, but in such a way that they can reconstruct the original order. Biology again provides the solution, in the form of restriction endonucleases. These are enzymes, each one derived from a bacterium, that cut the DNA chain at a precisely defined point. Over one hundred have been isolated. *Eco*RI is one example.[14] *Eco*RI binds to one nucleotide sequence, G-A-A-T-T-C, and breaks the phosphodiester bond between G and A. Statistically, this sequence should occur about once every 4,096 (4^6) bases. *Eco*RI would break a typical DNA molecule into about twenty thousand pieces, leaving an impossible jigsaw puzzle. Researchers therefore do not permit the

344 reaction to run to completion. The *Eco*RI cleaves each molecule at some but not all G-A-A-T-T-C sites, creating a collection of overlapping fragments. The process may be repeated with a different restriction enzyme, creating more and different overlapping fragments. The overlaps enable researchers to identify adjacent fragments, at least in principle.[15]

4. CLONING THE SEGMENTS. Mapping or sequencing requires millions of identical fragments. Single-celled organisms become the fragment factories. When *Eco*RI cuts a segment out of DNA, it leaves a single strand of A-A-T-T at one end and T-T-A-A at the other.[16] Treating a plasmid (a simple ring DNA molecule) with *Eco*RI cleaves the molecule in the same way, leaving an open ring with a single strand of A-A-T-T on one side of the break and T-T-A-A on the other. Adding the DNA fragments to the plasmids along with DNA ligand, another enzyme, causes the complementary single strands to bond, forming a new and larger plasmid ring. The net effect is to splice a foreign gene into a plasmid. Incubation of these recombinant plasmids with bacteria in a solution that increases the permeability of the bacterial cell membrane introduces some of the plasmids into the bacteria, where they begin replicating. Researchers can then harvest the cells and treat them with the same restriction enzyme to yield the desired fragments.

Bacterial plasmids suffer one severe limitation: inserting DNA fragments more than about ten kilobases (ten thousand nucleotide base pairs) in length causes them to become unstable and break down.[17] Longer sequences mean fewer fragments per chromosome and fewer overlaps to be identified. The best solution discovered to date has been the introduction of artificially constructed chromosomes into yeast.[18] The researcher first breaks yeast plasmid clones into three segments, two needed for the DNA to function inside the yeast cell and a third that is separated and discarded. The two useful segments are then attached (ligated) to the large DNA fragment to be cloned, creating a composite chromosome called a yeast artificial chromosome (YAC). Introduced into yeast cells, these replicate along with the natural chromosomes. Researchers have used this technique to reproduce segments of up to five hundred kilobases in length, a tenfold increase over other methods. This capability allows staged mapping, using YACs to map chromosomes, and plasmids to map YACs.

5. LOCATING NUCLEOTIDE SEQUENCES ON THE SEGMENTS.

The researcher first splits the strands of the fragments to be mapped, creating single-stranded nucleotide sequences, then subjects them to a probe, which is a short, known sequence of nucleotides, labeled with fluorescent or radioactive atoms. Several different probes with different labels may be used. The probe strands will "hybridize" (bond) only to complementary sequences of nucleotides that appear on the fragments. Each fragment thus acquires a pattern of labels.[19]

6. FIXING THE POSITIONS OF FRAGMENTS ON THE CHROMOSOME.

Before the physical mapping methods described above had become feasible, medical researchers had begun to locate specific genes on the chromosomes using markers called restriction fragment length polymorphisms (RFLPs), so named because they are sequence differences (polymorphisms) that cause the length of fragments produced by a given restriction endonuclease to vary. A polymorphism may, for example, create or eliminate restriction sites, or it may lengthen or shorten the segment between restriction sites. The pattern of fragment sizes becomes a sort of genetic fingerprint, identifying which allele (one form of a polymorphic gene or sequence) the chromosome has. A gene located in close proximity to such a marker is very likely to be inherited together with that marker. This linkage is weaker if the gene and marker are located farther apart[20] and altogether lacking between genes and markers on different chromosomes. Detailed studies of inheritance patterns in large families have allowed geneticists to ascertain the relative positions of many genes (especially those that cause hereditary diseases) on each chromosome.[21] When one of those genes or the RFLP associated with it shows up in a segment, it allows the mapper to fix the segment on the chromosome and begin building segments around it (rather like finding the piece with the eye in a jigsaw puzzle of a cat).

7. IDENTIFYING ADJACENT SEGMENTS.

Each segment carries a pattern of markers, indicated by fluorescent or radioactive probes. Portions of those patterns may match when two segments overlap. Researchers can confirm such overlaps with sequence information.

Sequencing is even more daunting than mapping because it involves billions of individual nucleotides instead of tens of thousands of genes. In principle, however, the process is straightforward. The sequencer breaks cloned segments (from, for example, YACs or plasmids) into fragments a few hundred nucleotides in length, clones them, and divides the clone sample into four solutions. Each solution contains A, C, G, and T, plus a low concentration of a chemical analogue of one of these nucleotides (G, for example) and a naturally occurring enzyme (DNA polymerase) that initiates DNA synthesis from one end of the sequence. The analogue is a chain terminator; polymerase will add it to the growing chain, but the next link will not attach to it. Synthesis therefore stops whenever, by chance, a G analogue is incorporated instead of a G. After the reaction is completed, the solution contains only DNA chains that end in the G analogue.[22]

The sequencer now has four solutions containing DNA chains, with each solution containing only chains that end in one nucleotide. Among the four solutions can be found chains of every length from one nucleotide (if an analogue was incorporated immediately) up to the entire original fragment (if no analogue was incorporated). The sequencer then places these solutions at the beginning of four parallel tracks of a gel film and puts the film in an electric field that pulls the DNA in one direction. The smallest chains migrate the fastest. When the film is removed from the field and developed, the one-link chain will therefore be at one end. If it is in the track with the G analogue solution, the first nucleotide in the sequence is a G. If the chain that moved the next farthest is in the T analogue track, the next nucleotide is a T, and so on. The researcher can simply read the sequence directly from the gel film. The process has become sufficiently routine to be automated.[23] It remains relatively slow because the fragments longer than a few hundred nucleotides cannot be read. Potentially faster alternatives are being explored.

Biotechnology, even in its nascence, has accomplished some note-worthy scientific and commercial feats. For the current discussion, the progression in the range and sophistication of the available techniques is more significant than the resulting processes and products.

At its most fundamental level, all genetic engineering consists of replication and placement. Despite the many continuing challenges, scientists have effectively solved the problem of replication. They are able to clone DNA sequences in any length from a few thousand base pairs in length (in bacteria), to hundreds of thousands (in yeast), to complete human chromosomes (in hybrid myelomas, or hybridomas).[24]

The problems associated with placing the completed sequences have proved more daunting. In some commercial applications, genetic engineers have learned to insert genes by physical means. Commonly used methods include micropipettes, to inject DNA into large cells without rigid walls; electroporation, in which precise electrical currents open pores in the target cell walls, admitting the DNA molecules; and gene guns, which literally shoot DNA-coated pellets less than one micron in diameter into the cell.[25] Physical methods avoid the genetic baggage inevitably carried by biological vectors (discussed below). But they are unpredictable: successful gene implantations may occur in no more a few percent of the target cells. Such uncertainty is tolerable in a laboratory setting or where the objective is to obtain a few genetically altered cells for cloning, but not in clinical or eugenic applications. Physical methods may nevertheless have some potential for human genetic engineering. Researchers have induced sperm cells to absorb foreign DNA by incubation and to carry it into the egg during fertilization. The crudest form of intervention would be substitution of an entire cellular nucleus for the nucleus in the zygote, effectively cloning the individual from whom the transplanted nucleus was obtained. Researchers have accomplished complete nuclear transplantation with lower mammals, although the success rate has been low.

The most widely successful placement methods to date have used biological vectors, organisms that naturally carry DNA into foreign

348   cells as part of their life cycles. The bacterial plasmids described above are an example. Viruses are also commonly used as vectors. A virus is little more than an RNA molecule wrapped in a protein coating; it uses the machinery of the cell it infects to supply its needs. Of particular interest for genetic engineering applications are so-called retroviruses. A retrovirus uses reverse transcriptase to produce a DNA molecule from its RNA strand, then splices that DNA into the cellular DNA, to be replicated during ordinary cellular processes. This life cycle is anything but beneficial to the host organism in nature, but it makes the retrovirus a naturally perfect vector. Researchers can splice a sequence into RNA in essentially the same manner as into a plasmid DNA ring. The retrovirus can then infect the target cell, and natural cellular processes accomplish the needed splicing and replication. Another advantage of viruses as vectors is their natural specificity. Many viruses infect only particular kinds of cells in particular species. This specificity allows the targeting of genes in plants, animals, or the environment, where life is more complicated than in a petri dish in the laboratory.

The retrovirus, however, is not interested in replacing any of the target cells' DNA, only in placing its own. True genetic design will require the ability to alter a specific DNA sequence or replace it with an analogous one. Methods of achieving such homologous recombination are still crude. One approach involves formation of a composite DNA segment with three genes: the desired sequence, a gene that confers resistance to a specific antibiotic, and a gene that makes the cell sensitive to an antiviral compound. Inserted into mouse embryo cells by electroporation, this composite DNA may (1) fail to be incorporated, (2) be incorporated, but in the wrong location, or (3) replace the target gene. Treating the cells with the antibiotic and the antiviral compound kills the cells in categories (1) and (2). The antiviral susceptibility gene, however, is designed to fall off when the foreign DNA replaces the target gene. Thus, those cells survive. By injecting these cells into mouse embryos, creating compound animals called mosaics, and crossing the mosaics, scientists can produce some offspring with only the foreign DNA copy of the target gene.[26]

Neither this nor any other existing technique is far enough advanced for direct genetic intervention in the reproductive process. But the rate of advance in the field is breathtaking. Refining the techniques enough for eugenic use is only a matter of time.

WETWARE

The following supplies some background for Chapter 9 to readers unfamiliar with the neurosciences. The descriptions of neurons and the overall organization of the brain reflect relatively mature and stable bodies of knowledge. Synapses and long-term potentiation, on the other hand, are fast-moving targets, with new discoveries announced each month. Scholarly books and journals are the only sources of up-to-date information, as the popular media have not yet recognized the significance of the developments now occurring.

NERVE CELLS

The principal cell types of the central nervous system are neurons and neuroglia. Neuroglia (or glial cells), which outnumber neurons roughly ten to one, carry no nerve impulses, but serve important ancillary functions. Some form a fine three-dimensional weblike structure to supply support. Mobile microglia scavenge dead cells and other waste products. Other glial cells wrap themselves around the long axons of vertebrate neurons, improving nerve signal transmission more than a hundredfold.[27] Neuroglia are an integral part of the blood-brain barrier, forming a dense network around blood vessels in the brain that selectively filters components from the extracellular fluid before they encounter the neurons. Glial cells also perform key cellular metabolic functions, in effect nourishing the neurons with certain needed metabolites.

Neurons initiate and carry nerve impulses. Informed estimates of the number of neurons in the brain generally range between 10 and 100 billion. (The breadth of that range suggests the relative ignorance that prevails concerning man's most important organ.) Neurons are of several types, but all consist of three basic parts: dendrites, the central cell body (sometimes called the soma), and the axon. Dendrites are the receptors of the neuron. They are fine (on the order of one hundredth of the diameter of a human hair) and densely branched, with microscopic spines projecting from the branches. The soma contains the nucleus and is the site of most ordinary cellular functions. The axon is the transmitter of the neuron. It is long,

350   extending from a few millimeters in the cortex up to a meter or more for sensory or motor neurons in the spinal column. Most axons are branched, although not as densely as the dendrites. Each branch terminates in one or (more commonly) a number of bulbs, which are, in turn, "connected" across a junction called a synapse to the dendrites of other neurons.

The neuron at rest maintains an ionic imbalance with its surroundings. Inside the neuron are negatively charged organic ions that are too large to pass through the cell membrane. The fluid surrounding the neurons contains potassium (K^+), sodium (Na^+), calcium (Ca^{++}), and chlorine (Cl^-) ions. At rest, only potassium can pass through the membrane of the neuron. The negative ions inside the neuron attract the potassium ions from the surrounding fluid across the membrane, while the sodium and calcium ions remain concentrated outside the cell. The increase in potassium inside the neuron creates a steepening concentration gradient across the membrane. This difference in concentration creates a tendency (similar in principle to osmotic pressure) for the potassium ions to diffuse out of the neuron. The process reaches equilibrium when this concentration gradient balances the effect of the electrical gradient (caused by the organic anions inside the neuron). This leaves the interior of the neuron with a negative charge relative to its surroundings, a potential difference on the order of seventy millivolts. This charge, acting across the thin neuron membrane, strongly attracts the positive ions outside the cell. The equilibrium of the neuron is thus a dynamic tension between electrical and chemical forces, awaiting only a trigger to initiate vigorous activity.

The trigger is a stimulus to the dendrites. The cell membrane is pierced by selective inlets, called single channels, that admit one kind of ion (e.g., Na^+ or Ca^{++}). A molecular gate on the inside of the membrane opens and closes each channel. At rest, the electrical potential difference across the membrane closes the gate, maintaining the ionic imbalance described above. The proper chemical or electrical stimulus temporarily opens the gate, allowing ions to pass through, driven by both the concentration and the electrical potential gradients. This influx of positively charged ions is itself an electrical stimulus which opens other single channels in the vicinity. The result is a localized decrease in the electrical potential difference across the cell membrane. A sufficient aggregate stimulus to the dendrites causes the current at the base of the axon to exceed a threshold. The membrane of the axon is densely populated with sodium channels. Each sodium channel on the axon consists of a macromolecular protein having a strong dipole moment that penetrates the axon membrane. The changing electrical potential across the membrane acts on the dipole, causing the protein to change shape, temporarily opening the channel to sodium ions. The resulting influx of sodium ions abruptly shifts the local electrical potential from about -70 millivolts to $+55$ millivolts, which opens neighboring sodium channels, and so on. This electrical signal propagates at more than one hundred meters per second in a sheathed axon.

One aspect of this process should be emphasized. The magnitude of the ion flux through the membranes of the dendrites depends on the number and intensity of stimuli received by the dendrites, as well as the density of ion channels in the vicinity of the stimuli. Dendrites also receive inhibitory stimuli that hyperpolarize the membrane (i.e., increase the negative charge inside the neuron) by admitting chlorine ions, tending to cancel the excitatory (depolarizing) stimuli that decrease the negative charge. Stimuli thus combine in the dendrites, which transmit an electrical potential shift of varying magnitude to the cell body. The axon does not exhibit this variable or graded potential. If the "signal" from the dendrites exceeds the threshold (about ten millivolts), by however much or little, the axon pulses. The electrical potential shift in the axon does not vary with the size of the stimulus from the dendrites. Each neuron thus integrates inputs continuously to arrive at discrete "yes or no" outputs.

After firing, the neuron must restore its ionic imbalance. The positive charge inside the neuron destroys the equilibrium between the electrical and chemical forces on the potassium ions, causing them to exit the cell. Each neuron has on the order of one million ion pumps in its membrane, which selectively eliminate sodium ions from the neuron, to be replaced by potassium ions from the surrounding fluid.[28] This restoration requires on the order of one millisecond (the refractory period), during which the axon cannot pulse.

The individual neuron is thus a fairly simple mechanism that receives stimuli as inputs and produces a single output. The more interesting but more complicated subject is the nature of the inputs and output.[29]

The synapse is the junction between a terminal bulb of an axon (the presynaptic membrane) and a dendrite (the postsynaptic membrane). Arrival of the nerve impulse at the presynaptic membrane opens channels that allow the passage of calcium ions into the axon bulb. These calcium ions trigger release of neurotransmitter molecules into the synaptic cleft.[30] Neurotransmitters are generally small, ionic, water-soluble molecules.[31] The axon terminal bulbs produce these and store them in vesicles and diffused in the cytoplasm. These molecules diffuse across the narrow gap between the axon bulb and the dendrite. The molecules attach to receptors on the dendrite. Receptors are macromolecular protein structures that penetrate the postsynaptic membrane. Binding of a neurotransmitter changes the conformation of the structure such that sodium or other selected ions can pass through into the dendrite, which begins the neural firing sequence described above. Given their nature and complexity, these processes are quite rapid, with depolarization of the postsynaptic membrane beginning on the order of one millisecond after the arrival of the nerve impulse at the axon bulb. Cell structures in the axon transport calcium ions away from the bulb, stopping the release of neurotransmitter into the junction. Neurotransmitter molecules remaining in the synapse are absorbed by the axon and surrounding glial cells or are destroyed by enzymes, thus restoring the synapse for the next impulse.

A number of complications intrude on this picture. Neurotransmitters may be either excitatory or inhibitory. The dendrites of a single neuron may receive signals from hundreds or thousands of axons. The cancellation and summation of inhibitory and excitatory impulses at the base of the axon determines whether the neuron fires. Receptors also appear on the terminal bulbs of axons. Some of these presynaptic receptors may form a "serial" synapse with the terminal bulb of another axon; one axon may inhibit another axon, which in turn may inhibit or excite the dendrite to which it is connected. One signal may thus block the action of another. Other presynaptic receptors are not associated with a particular terminal bulb of another axon. Rather, such receptors respond to some neurochemical (which may or may not be the one released by the axon on which the receptor is located), modulating in some way the signal of the axon on which they are located. Neurons also produce neuropeptides. These are larger molecules (commonly containing dozens of amino acid links) that may act as cotransmitters or as neuromodulators, enhancing or diminishing the effect of other chemical or electrical stimuli on the neuron membrane. For reasons that are not yet known, they are sometimes released in areas distant from any synapse.

NEUROANATOMY

The brain consists of several well-defined anatomical structures. The medulla oblongata, located at the top of the spinal cord, controls many involuntary functions (including heart action and respiration). At the base of the skull is the cerebellum, which mediates motor coordination. The thalamus, consisting of two egg-shaped structures in the center of the brain, integrates the major sensory signals and forwards them to the cortex. The midbrain, a small structure located between the cerebellum and the thalamus, is a connection and relay area for certain cranial nerves. All of these structures constitute perhaps one seventh of the brain's mass. The remainder, overlying the whole, is the cerebrum. It is divided, both anatomically and functionally, into right and left hemispheres,[32] which are connected by a nerve bundle called the *corpus callosum*. The cerebrum is the locus for most higher mental functions.

The principal distinguishing feature of the human cerebrum is its greatly enlarged cortex.[33] The cortex is a relatively thin layer of cells that overlies the entire cerebrum. It is stratified over its entire surface into six layers (or laminae), distinguishable under the microscope by the predominance of certain characteristic cells. This organization is functional, with each layer dominated by one kind of neuron and connected to one or two other portions of the central nervous system. The cortex is also organized horizontally.[34] Sensory nerves

354 "map" to particular regions of the cortex. Within that region, the brain preserves relative position (e.g., the area that registers sensation from the middle fingertip is located between the areas corresponding to the index and ring fingertips). The relative importance of different sensory inputs is reflected in the sizes of the cortical regions devoted to them. The visual cortex is by far the largest. This topographic mapping can be quite detailed. In the visual cortex, for example, thin alternating vertical bands (ocular dominance bands) receive input exclusively from the right or left eye.

Researchers have also localized the areas of the brain in which some higher mental processes occur. The traditional approach has been to study mental deficits in patients with localized brain damage caused by surgery or trauma and in laboratory animals in which particular sections of the brain have been lesioned. More recently, sophisticated radiography has enabled neurobiologists to correlate heightened levels of cellular activity in discrete areas of the brain with particular mental tasks. It is known, for example, that the frontal lobes are active during performance of cognitive tasks. The left temporal lobe processes verbal stimuli, the right temporal lobe responds to music. The limbic system, a primitive part of the brain similar in humans and lower animals, produces various emotional responses.[35] Even such gross conclusions as can be reached from this evidence are far from neat. Completely different areas of the brain are active in the processes of hearing words, seeing words, generating words, and speaking words. Memory is similarly not localized to a single area of the brain.[36] Short-term and long-term memory are apparently different neurological processes. The structures used in memory formation are not the same as those responsible for memory storage and retrieval. The temporal cortex accomplishes visual recognition of an object, but the parietal cortex is responsible for spatial relations. This seemingly haphazard arrangement of mental functions in the brain reflects evolutionary accretion rather than any top-down design. New species retained functional processing centers already possessed by lower species, occasionally adding capabilities as new brain regions appeared.

LONG-TERM POTENTIATION[37]

The hot topic *du jour* in memory research is long-term potentiation (LTP). Hebb had hypothesized in the 1940s that repetitive stimulation of the connection between two neurons could strengthen that connection, so that a later signal would produce a stronger response. LTP, first demonstrated in 1973, confirmed that hypothesis. Researchers sent closely timed pulses into the hippocampus of anesthetized rabbits, then measured the resulting output signal. The output from later signal volleys was stronger, and sometimes more than twice as strong, as that from the first volley. Repetitive signals had strengthened at least some synapses in the hippocampus. The effect can persist for long periods in conditioned animals. Chemicals that interfere with LTP also interfere with learning, suggesting that it is a crucial link in the chain.

Intervening research has elaborated LTP at the cellular level. Indeed, that research has provided a superabundance of mechanisms to explain the effect. LTP has been shown to cause the axon to release more neurotransmitter in response to a single signal, thus heightening the effect in the dendrite.[38] But it also produces extensive changes in the dendrite. Researchers have studied one class of glutamate receptors, called N-methyl-d-aspartate or NMDA receptors, in particular detail.[39] This receptor is activated only by two closely timed signals across the synapse. The first triggers other receptors, producing an electrical signal that removes a magnesium atom that normally blocks the NMDA receptor. The next signal then causes the receptor to open a nearby calcium channel. The NMDA initiated mechanism is particularly interesting to scientists because it requires two closely timed signals, which conforms not only to Hebb's original prediction, but also to the observations of LTP in the laboratory. This fit is too good to be coincidental. Calcium entering the cell may start any one of several chemical cascades that change proteins inside the cell membrane, making the dendrite more sensitive to future signals.[40] These include the creation of new receptors, new ion channels, and complete new synapses, all of which have been observed within minutes after LTP and as a result of learning in animals.[41] Researchers in the field also assume that LTP activates selected genes in the cell

356 body to consolidate long-term memory, although the exact mechanisms for doing so have not yet been uncovered.[42] Researchers have also identified several mechanisms by which signals can decrease synaptic sensitivity.[43] The role of these mechanisms has not been determined, although it seems plausible that they relate in some way to forgetting and to brain plasticity generally.

It bears repeating that LTP will not likely provide the full cellular explanation for learning and memory. Despite its name, LTP has never been shown to persist long enough to explain the multidecade memories of which the brain is capable, nor have scientists yet demonstrated LTP in all the cell types and regions of the brain involved in memory. LTP occurs at the cellular level; memory and other thought processes surely involve at least networks of cells. LTP has generated such excitement in part because it is the first biological process worked out in some detail that has the properties needed for memory. In general, however, the first step in unraveling scientific mysteries proves in retrospect to have been the hardest and most time-consuming. The pace of discovery will likely quicken as memory research continues.

THE SEARCH FOR EXTRATERRESTRIAL INTELLIGENCE

Despite (or perhaps because of) the lack of useful data, scientists have speculated at length about the likelihood that extraterrestrial intelligence exists. The following outlines the "results" of that discussion and the scope of the challenge confronting those who have begun to listen rather than talk.

THE DRAKE EQUATION

SETI pioneer Frank Drake first set out a formula for estimating the number of technological civilizations in the galaxy in 1961. It has since gained almost universal acceptance. The Drake equation is as follows:[44]

$$N = Sf_pnf_ef_lf_if_tf_s$$

where

N = the number of technological civilizations in the galaxy;
S = the number of stars in the galaxy;
f_p = the fraction of stars with planets;
n = the average number of planets orbiting such stars;
f_e = the fraction of planets ecologically suitable for life;
f_l = the fraction of those planets on which life develops;
f_i = the fraction of those planets on which intelligence develops;
f_t = the fraction of those planets on which technology develops;
and
f_s = the fraction of those planets on which technological civilization survives to communicate with Earth.

SETI advocates and skeptics generally agree that the Milky Way has about 400 billion stars and that one tenth or more of those probably have planets. That ends the area of agreement. SETI advocates extrapolate from the Solar System to estimate that one planet in ten would be suitable for life. Skeptics, noting the happy coincidence of circumstances that make life possible on Earth and denying that extrapolation from Earth's experience is valid,[45] place the figure nearer one in a thousand. According to SETI advocates, the rapid appearance of life on Earth establishes that it is nearly automatic given the right conditions. To skeptics, the lack of any plausible mechanism to explain the emergence of metabolism and replication, despite much effort devoted to searching for one, marks the event as an incredible fluke. Advocates and skeptics swap positions on the evolution of intelligence, with advocates relying on the obvious evolutionary advantage that intelligence should confer, while skeptics argue that the long-delayed appearance of intelligence on Earth establishes its improbability. Given intelligent life, the appearance of technology seems quite likely to SETI advocates, but not to skeptics who have never seen porpoises making tools. On the likelihood of survival, skeptics have filled the literature with descriptions of the ways in which technology may destroy the conditions essential to life.[46] Of the civilizations that avoid rapid self-destruction, comparatively few

358 may now (relativistically) be in their technological phase, the others being pretechnological or the victims of irreversible and uncontrollable stellar or planetary changes or other natural forces. Some SETI advocates (particularly those who are active in environmental protection and disarmament movements) depart from their generally optimistic attitudes and concur that technology poses a grave threat to life. Others, including Drake himself, regard inclusion of any factor for extinction of an advanced society as very if not unduly conservative.[47]

Such arguments lead SETI advocates to estimates that range into the millions of technological civilizations in the galaxy, and skeptics to an estimate of one. Both camps are obviously just guessing, and their guesses are just as obviously influenced by their respective desired outcomes. The only solution is to look.

THE COSMIC HAYSTACK

Three variables define the scope of any search for extraterrestrial radio waves: the area of space searched, the range of frequencies covered, and the sensitivity of the search (i.e., the minimum signal strength that would be detected). The technology of radio telescopes forces trade-offs among these variables. The telescope arrives at a signal strength essentially by integrating the area under the curve that describes the energy it receives. Natural sources produce noise at each frequency and from every point in the sky. The larger the telescope's field of view and the broader the frequency channel it searches, the more noise an extraterrestrial signal would have to overcome.[48] The narrowest search area and channel thus produces the most sensitive search, but at the expense of coverage. The META search, for example, had extremely narrow and therefore sensitive 0.05-hertz channels. Unfortunately, about two trillion of these channels would be needed to cover the plausible frequency search space,[49] a number that makes the eight-million-channel spectrum analyzer developed for the NASA search seem rather inadequate. Observation time imposes similar trade-offs. Because background noise is random, it tends to cancel itself over time, making the steady signal easier to detect.[50] But extending the time devoted to each observation reduces the area of space or the range of frequencies that can be searched.

Every search thus begins with the decision as to which search dimensions to emphasize and which to sacrifice. Magic frequency searches sacrifice frequency range. Whole-sky searches usually sacrifice both sensitivity and frequency range. The NASA search will compromise a bit on each dimension, with broader channels but much wider frequency coverage than the META search. The search strategy advocated in the text would radically reduce the area of the sky covered (by targeting each nearby star as narrowly as possible) to achieve the maximum sensitivity and signal coverage. This is an extreme version of the targeted portion of the NASA search, which will probably not achieve enough sensitivity to detect signal leakage.

NOTES

1. Kamien & Schwartz, *Market Structure and Innovation*, Ch. 2, pp. 36–41, Cambridge Univ. Press, 1982, analyzes the return to innovation in an oligopoly. The differences are immaterial for the present purposes.

2. Rosenberg & Ezell, *How the West Grew Rich: The Economic Transformation of the Industrial World*, Ch. 5, p. 144, Basic Books, 1986.

3. Note that the innovation enhances consumer welfare even before competitors duplicate it, despite the innovator's quasi-monopoly pricing. Each consumer would have the choice of purchasing the original product at the original price or the improved product at a premium price. For those consumers whose demand for the improvement exceeds the premium, the innovation represents a clear gain, while other consumers are unaffected. For more formal treatments, see Cheung, "Property Rights and Invention," *Research in Law & Economics*, Vol. 8, p. 5, at p. 10, 1986; Usher, "The Welfare Economics of Invention," *Economica*, Vol. 31, p. 278, at pp. 279–87; and Kamien & Schwartz, *Market Structure and Innovation*, Ch. 2, p. 41.

4. Graph App. 6 is after Harvey Leibenstein, "Technical Progress, the Production Function, and Development," Ch. 11 in W.W. Rostow (ed.), *The Economics of Take-off into Sustained Growth*, Macmillan, 1963.

5. See Edward Denison, *Accounting for United States Economic Growth 1929–1969*, p. 131, Brookings Inst., 1974.

6. The data in Table App. 7 are from Edward Denison, *Trends in American Economic Growth, 1929–1982*, Table 8-3, Brookings Inst., 1985. More recent data begin to reflect the limits to progress described in Chapters 3 through 6.

7. Jorgenson et al., *Productivity and U.S. Economic Growth*, Harvard Univ. Press, 1987, applies slightly different categories and methods to arrive at a higher contribution for physical capital and a lower contribution for intangible capital than Denison. The differences are not critical to the current discussion. For tabulated summaries of several factor analyses of the postwar economies of the United States and Western Europe, see Edward Wolff, "Comment," in Kendrick (ed.), *International Comparisons of Productivity and Causes of the Slowdown*, p. 47, Ballinger, 1984.

8. Horace Judson, "A History of the Science and Technology Behind Gene Mapping and Sequencing," Ch. 2 in Kevles & Hood (eds.), *The Code of Codes:*

Scientific and Social Issues in the Human Genome Project, Harvard Univ. Press, 1992, and G.J.V. Nossal, *Reshaping Life: Key Issues in Genetic Engineering,* Chs. 2 and 3, Cambridge Univ. Press, 1985, provide excellent introductions to molecular genetics and genetic engineering for the lay reader.

9. Even within a gene, long stretches of DNA do not code for protein. These stretches, called introns, may serve some regulatory function, or they may be evolutionary detritus. The coding portions of the genes are called exons. The RNA splicing process described in the text thus eliminates the portions of the sequence corresponding to the introns.

10. With four different nucleotides, there are 4^3 or sixty-four possible sequences of three nucleotides. Human proteins include a total of twenty amino acids. Thus, two or more nucleotide triplets code for most of the amino acids. Three of the sixty-four possible triplets are stop codons, which terminate the transcription process. Christian de Duve, *A Guided Tour of the Living Cell,* Vol. 2, Ch. 15, p. 259, Scientific American Books, 1984, describes the protein synthesis process.

11. De Duve, *A Guided Tour of the Living Cell,* Vol. 2, Ch. 19, describes mitosis and meiosis.

12. Richard Dawkins, *The Selfish Gene,* Ch. 3, pp. 27–29, Oxford Univ. Press, 1989 ed., provides a lucid description of the crossing-over process.

13. See Christopher Wills, *Exons, Introns, and Talking Genes: The Science Behind the Human Genome Project,* Ch. 6, pp. 122–26, Basic Books, 1991, which also discusses physical separation means.

14. Restriction endonucleases are too large and complex to have had their compositions and structures determined chemically, although progress is proceeding with X-ray diffraction studies. Molecular geneticists follow a precise naming convention to avoid confusion. *Eco*RI is the first (I) restriction endonuclease (R) isolated from the *E. coli (Eco)* bacterium.

15. Wills, *Exons, Introns, and Talking Genes,* Ch. 6, pp. 127–29.

16. Note that the restriction site is palindromic, that is, one strand of the DNA read in reverse is the same as the other strand (G-A-A-T-T-C and C-T-T-A-A-G). The sequence G-A-A-T-T-T, for example, is not a restriction site because the enzyme would not bind to the opposite strand (C-T-T-A-A-A).

17. Wills, *Exons, Introns, and Talking Genes,* Ch. 6, p. 131.

18. Burke, Carle & Olson, "Cloning of Large Segments of Exogenous DNA into Yeast by Means of Artificial Chromosome Vectors," *Science,* Vol. 236, p. 806, 15 May 1987, describes the technique for producing yeast artificial chromosomes.

19. Wills, *Exons, Introns, and Talking Genes,* Ch. 6, pp. 134–43, describes several variations on the theme outlined in the text.

20. As explained above, the single chromosome in each gamete is a composite formed from the pair found in other cells by genetic exchange, a process of cutting and splicing pieces of each chromosome. The likelihood of a cut occurring between two genes on a single chromosome depends on the distance between them. Therefore, the incidence of genetic traits being inherited together translates into a measure of proximity between the responsible genes. Two genes separated by one

million nucleotide pairs have about a 99 percent probability of being inherited together, on the average.

21. White & Lalouel, "Chromosome Mapping with DNA Markers," *Scientific American,* Feb. 1988, p. 40; Wills, *Exons, Introns, and Talking Genes,* Ch. 9; and Bishop & Waldholz, *Genome,* Chs. 2–4, Simon & Schuster, 1990, describe genetic linkage mapping.

22. The Nobel laureate Frederick Sanger developed the sequencing method outlined in the text, which is the most widely used. Sequencing can also be accomplished with a chemical that breaks the DNA chain at a specific nucleotide, but only infrequently. This reaction yields a collection of fragments that end in the same nucleotide, which can be ordered by gel electrophoresis, as in the Sanger method. Wills, *Exons, Introns, and Talking Genes,* Ch. 2, describes both methods and some possible alternatives.

23. Akiyoshi Wada, "Automated High-Speed DNA Sequencing," *Nature,* Vol. 325, p. 771, 26 Feb. 1987, describes Japanese efforts to automate sample processing. The goal of those efforts, sequencing at a cost of 10 cents per base pair, has not yet been approached. Wills, *Exons, Introns, and Talking Genes,* Ch. 7, describes automation of parts of the Sanger technique by Leroy Hood's biotechnology research group at Cal Tech.

24. Myeloma cells, like other cancer cells, are immortal; they will multiply indefinitely in proper conditions. This trait, deadly in nature, is harnessed in the laboratory by fusing the genetic content of another cell into a myeloma cell. The added chromosomes replicate along with those originally in the myeloma cell, creating many exact copies.

25. Gasser & Fraley, "Transgenic Crops," *Scientific American,* June 1992, p. 62, describes physical methods for introducing foreign genes.

26. Mansour, Thomas & Capecchi, "Disruption of the Proto-oncogene int-2 etc.," *Nature,* Vol. 336, p. 348, 24 Nov. 1988, describes the homologous recombination process.

27. A deterioration of the sheath that glial cells form around vertebrate axons (called myelin) produces multiple sclerosis.

28. The restoration process is not fully understood, and the discussion in the text oversimplifies what is known. For a more detailed account, see Feldman & Quenzer, *Fundamentals of Neuropsychopharmacology,* Ch. 4, Sinauer Assocs., 1984.

29. H.F. Bradford, *Chemical Neurobiology: An Introduction to Neurochemistry,* W.H. Freeman, 1986, is an exceptionally clear textbook treatment of the neurochemistry of the synapse. Roberta Brinton, "Biochemical Correlates of Learning and Memory," Ch. 5 in Martinez & Kesner (eds.), *Learning and Memory: A Biological View,* Academic Press, 2d ed., 1991, provides a close and relatively current look at the cellular processes.

30. The axon bulb includes internal vesicles (pockets) that contain a few thousand molecules of neurotransmitter. The influx of calcium causes the membrane surrounding a vesicle to fuse with the presynaptic membrane, with the vesicle voiding its contents into the synaptic gulf. There is also evidence that neurotransmitter

molecules diffuse directly from the cytoplasm through pores in the presynaptic membrane.

31. Feldman & Quenzer, *Fundamentals of Neuropsychopharmacology*, provides a systematic discussion of the different classes of neuroactive chemicals.

32. Primarily for ease of reference, each hemisphere is divided into five lobes. These are, from front to back, the frontal, precentral, parietal, and occipital, with the temporal lobe lying under the first three and in front of the occipital.

33. For some quantitative comparisons of the size of the human cortex with those of lower mammals, see Jean-Pierre Changeux, *Neuronal Man: The Biology of Mind*, Ch. 2, p. 45, Pantheon Books, 1985.

34. Changeux, *Neuronal Man*, Ch. 2, pp. 58–65, and Patricia Churchland, *Neurophilosophy: Toward a Unified Science of the Mind-Brain*, Ch. 3, pp. 119–31, MIT Press, 1986, describe topographic mapping in the cortex.

35. For an arresting description of emotional responses not correlated with any real emotion, caused by damage to the limbic system, see Churchland, *Neurophilosophy*, Ch. 5, pp. 222–23.

36. Mishkin & Appenzeller, "The Anatomy of Memory," *Scientific American*, June 1987, p. 80 (lesion studies in monkeys).

37. Long-term potentiation is described in Kandel & Hawkins, "The Biological Basis of Learning and Individuality," *Scientific American*, Sept. 1992, p. 78; Baudry & Davis (eds.), *Long Term Potentiation;* Timothy Teyler, "Memory: Electrophysiological Analogs," Ch. 7 in Martinez & Kesner (eds.), *Learning and Memory;* and Yadin Dudai, *The Neurobiology of Memory: Concepts, Findings, Trends*, Ch. 6, Oxford Univ. Press, 1989.

38. Mary Kennedy, "Synaptic Memory Molecules," *Nature*, Vol. 335, p. 770, 27 Oct. 1988. See also George Johnson, *In the Palaces of Memory*, Part 1, p. 69, Knopf, 1991; Malinow et al., "Persistent Protein Kinase Activity Underlying Long Term Potentiation," *Nature*, Vol. 335, p. 820, 27 Oct. 1988; and Carol Ezzell, "Memories Might Be Made of This," *Science News*, Vol. 139, p. 328, May 25, 1991.

39. The most lucid and accessible description of the Hebbian behavior of NMDA receptors is Churchland & Sejnowski, *The Computational Brain*, Ch. 5, pp. 260–64, MIT Press, 1992.

40. See Daniel Alkon, "Memory Storage and Neural Systems," *Scientific American*, July 1989, p. 42; Teyler, "Memory: Electrophysiological Analogs," Ch. 7 in Martinez & Kesner (eds.), *Learning and Memory;* Johnson, *In the Palaces of Memory*, Part 1, pp. 40–55 and 74–77. Genetic research confirmed the role of calcium in memory just as this book went to press. Scientists created a mutant strain of mice lacking the gene for a calcium-calmodulin-dependent protein kinase. These mice could solve a maze as fast as their normal siblings, but could not then remember the solution. Silva et al., "Impaired Spatial Learning in α-Calcium-Calmodulin Kinase II Mutant Mice," *Science*, Vol. 257, p. 206, 10 July 1992.

41. Johnson, *In the Palaces of Memory*, Part 1, pp. 37–40, and Alkon, "Memory Storage and Neural Systems," *Scientific American*, July 1989, p. 42.

364 42. Brinton, "Biochemical Correlates of Learning and Memory," Ch. 5, pp. 231–35, in Martinez & Kesner (eds.), *Learning and Memory;* Johnson, *In the Palaces of Memory,* Part 1, pp. 74–77.

43. See *Nature,* Vol. 347, p. 16, 6 Sept. 1990; Churchland & Sejnowski, *Computational Brain,* Ch. 5, pp. 290–95; and Stanton & Sejnowski, "Associative Long-Term Depression in the Hippocampus Induced by Hebbian Covariance," *Nature,* Vol. 339, p. 215, May 18, 1989, for possible mechanisms of long-term depression.

44. The Drake equation has been stated with many variations. This version simplifies somewhat by considering the galaxy as fixed at a point in time. In reality, of course, new stars are constantly being created and old ones extinguished. The analysis is not significantly affected. The text generally follows Thomas McDonough, *The Search for Extraterrestrial Intelligence: Listening for Life in the Cosmos,* Ch. 7, John Wiley & Sons, 1987, with minor definitional changes and some different values assigned. Joseph Baugher, *On Civilized Stars: The Search for Intelligent Life in Outer Space,* Chs. 2 and 3, Prentice-Hall, 1985, contains a more detailed treatment of the variables. John Casti, *Paradigms Lost: Images of Man in the Mirror of Science,* Ch. 6, William Morrow, 1989, discusses the Drake Equation, along with extrinsic arguments for and against the existence of extraterrestrial intelligence.

45. Planets with life suggest to their inhabitants that life appears and evolves routinely. Planets without life have no inhabitants to pose the question. The sample of all those planets where the question is asked is thus severely skewed. This is one variant of the weak anthropic principle.

46. See, for example, Baugher, *On Civilized Stars,* Ch. 3, pp. 119–29, which discusses nuclear war, overpopulation, exhaustion of resources, pollution, and genetic deterioration as possible near-term causes of the end of human life.

47. Frank Drake, "The Drake Equation: A Reappraisal," Ch. 3, p. 115, in Bova & Preiss (eds.), *First Contact: The Search for Extraterrestrial Intelligence,* NAL Books, 1990. Technological civilizations' likelihood of survival is the most wildly and unavoidably speculative of all the variables in the Drake equation. Indeed, statistical analysis has suggested that more of the dispersion in the estimates of the number of civilizations in the galaxy arises from this variable than from all others combined. See Casti, *Paradigms Lost,* pp. 365–66.

48. See Jill Tarter, "Planned Observational Strategy for NASA's First Systematic Search for Extraterrestrial Intelligence," Ch. 20, pp. 323–24, in Finney and Jones (eds.), *Interstellar Migration and the Human Experience,* Univ. of California Press, 1985.

49. Space is relatively "quiet" in the microwave range of frequencies from one to about one hundred gigahertz. Earth's satellite communications generally occur between one and ten gigahertz because of interference from the atmosphere at higher frequencies. See Michael Klein, "Where and What Can We See?" Ch. 4, p. 143, in Bova & Preiss (eds.), *First Contact.*

50. See Rood & Trefil, *Are We Alone? The Possibility of Extraterrestrial Civilizations,* Ch. 9, p. 142, Charles Scribner's Sons, 1981.

INDEX

About the Author

C. OWEN PAEPKE, a scholar, lawyer, former research chemist, and unabashed generalist, is a graduate of Stanford University and the University of Chicago Law School. He lives in Phoenix, Arizona, where he is an attorney specializing in antitrust and intellectual property.

ABOUT THE TYPE

This book was set in Galliard, a typeface designed by Matthew Carter for the Mergenthaler Linotype Company in 1978. Galliard is based on the sixteenth-century typefaces of Robert Granjon, which give it classic lines yet interject a contemporary look.